A Guide to Careers
in Physical Anthropology

A Guide to Careers
in Physical Anthropology

EDITED BY ALAN S. RYAN

BERGIN & GARVEY
Westport, Connecticut • London

Library of Congress Cataloging-in-Publication Data

A guide to careers in physical anthropology / edited by Alan S. Ryan.
    p. cm.
  Includes bibliographical references and index.
  ISBN 0–89789–693–9 (alk. paper)
  1. Physical anthropology—Vocational guidance.   I. Ryan, Alan S., 1950–
  GN62.G85   2002
  599.9′023—dc21   2001037651

British Library Cataloguing in Publication Data is available.

Library of Congress Catalog Card Number: 2001037651
ISBN: 0–89789–693–9

First published in 2002

Bergin & Garvey, 88 Post Road West, Westport, CT 06881
An imprint of Greenwood Publishing Group, Inc.
www.greenwood.com

Printed in the United States of America

The paper used in this book complies with the
Permanent Paper Standard issued by the National
Information Standards Organization (Z39.48–1984).

10 9 8 7 6 5 4 3 2 1

Contents

Introduction

Alan S. Ryan

The field of physical or biological anthropology is intrinsically interesting and compelling. Students are drawn to the discipline because it sheds light on fundamental questions of interest to everyone. Answers to questions such as What makes us human?, How do we differ from other animals and from one another?, How did we evolve?, and What is the relationship between human biology and culture? provide clues to our understanding of human nature and the evolutionary history of our species since its origins.

Interest in physical anthropology has benefited greatly from increased attention from the media, from popular books, and from television series such as *NOVA, National Geographic,* and *Discovery.* In the media, the physical anthropologist is often portrayed as a pith-helmeted adventurer, tracking chimpanzees through the forest or discovering bones of our million-year-old ancestors. Although some physical anthropologists truly study chimpanzees and the fossils of human ancestors, many others consider different fascinating subjects. The diversity of topics investigated by physical anthropologists seems endless. Research interests include human and primate origins, primate societies, growth and development, genetics, osteology, human reproduction, forensic science, and nutrition, to name a few.

What pulls these different subjects together is that they share interest in the same subject—human beings. Physical anthropology is a sub-field of anthropology. Other sub-fields include cultural anthropology, anthropological archaeology, and linguistic anthropology. As a whole, anthropology has a wider scope than its sub-fields and encompasses almost everything pertaining to humans. In fact, the traditional textbook definition of anthropology is "the study of humans." What makes anthropology different from other subjects that study human beings and human behavior, such as history, geography, political science, philosophy, sociology, economics, and psychology, is that anthropology considers both biology and culture. Culture is learned behavior. Culture includes the social and economic systems, customs, religion, and other behaviors that are acquired through the process of learning. The joint emphasis on both culture and biology is central to anthropology and vital to our understanding of the human condition. The biocultural perspective of anthropology establishes its strength as a science: it is holistic, in that it takes into consideration all aspects of human life. Another important strength of the discipline is that it is temporally unbounded—it considers humans today and in the remote past.

Physical anthropology focuses on biological evolution of humans and their ancestors, the relationship of humans to other organisms, and patterns of biological variation within and among human populations. Physical anthropology is sometimes referred to by another name—biological anthropology. There are several specialties of physical anthropology including primate studies (primatology), paleoanthropology, and human variation, which will be further described in Chapter 1. Because of its broad scope, physical anthropology has borrowed principles from evolutionary biology, comparative anatomy, genetics, medicine, paleontology, zoology, geology, and demography. The knowledge and skills needed for one specialization, such as primatology, may differ greatly from those needed to study another specialization. There is, however, agreement over what basic principles should be taught in physical anthropology coursework. Thus, students acquiring an undergraduate or graduate degree in physical anthropology not only learn the fundamentals of the discipline but also obtain additional training according to their specialization and requirements of the departmental program.

The subject of this book is careers in physical anthropology. Most physical anthropology graduate students have traditionally aspired to a career as a college or university faculty member in an anthropology department. Until the early 1970s, such a career was a reasonable expectation. However, during the last decade there has been increased interest in alternative careers. This is largely due to the fact that in the mid-1970s the number of new Ph.D.s in physical anthropology that were produced exceeded the job market for positions in U.S. anthropology departments. Formal recognition of this crisis was made in 1982 when the American Association of Physical Anthropologists (AAPA) established an *ad hoc* committee to study and act upon the problem. In 1985, the *ad hoc* committee was elevated to the status of a standing committee (Career Development) and in 1990, the AAPA gave the committee funds to produce a brochure devoted to describing non-academic careers for physical anthropologists. The brochure was distributed to every anthropology department in the United States. Subsequently, the

Career Development Committee has presented a series of symposia at the annual meeting of the AAPA that consider the nature of the academic job market and ways to help graduate students prepare for and find satisfying alternative positions. Because physical anthropology has a strong biocultural emphasis and its subject matter is enormously diversified, today's students of physical anthropology have a wealth of potential nontraditional career opportunities.

Although academic opportunities have declined, there has been continued growth in the discipline. The popularity of physical anthropology is evident from the growing number of physical anthropologists who are contributing to scientific programs of the AAPA and the establishment of new scientific organizations (e.g., The American Society of Primatologists, the Paleopathology Association, the Paleoanthropology Society, the Human Biology Association, and the American Association of Anthropological Genetics). In addition to the official journal of the AAPA, *The American Journal of Physical Anthropology*, new journals devoted to different aspects of physical anthropology have appeared. These include the *Journal of Human Evolution*, the *Annals of Human Biology*, the *American Journal of Primatology*, the *American Journal of Human Biology*, and *Evolutionary Anthropology*.

The emergence of nontraditional opportunities in physical anthropology appears primarily in biomedical research. Biomedical interests overlap with those of physical anthropology. Biomedical scientists focus on issues concerning public health, growth and development, nutrition, aging, disease, pathology, epidemiology, genetics, and forensic science. The theoretical bases of evolution, human adaptation, biological human variation and their relationship to cultural factors are particularly relevant to biomedical applications. A growing number of physical anthropologists are bringing these orientations to full-time research careers in private industry and schools of medicine and public health.

Nonacademic careers for physical anthropologists have some common characteristics. One is a strong emphasis on applied research, which considers the application of anthropological principles to contemporary issues. Another is the need of applicants for nonacademic jobs to acquire additional skills and/or course work not traditionally part of graduate training in physical anthropology. A third is that entry into such careers often occurs using employment-seeking techniques that are not typically taught by faculty members in anthropology departments.

Pursuing career opportunities within and outside the academy requires thoughtful planning and training. To be competitive, appropriately trained physical anthropologists must market themselves aggressively as uniquely qualified for a variety of careers. To be successfully trained, physical anthropologists need to know what their colleagues are doing in a variety of settings and how the skills, knowledge, and perspectives they bring to their positions as physical anthropologists are essential to their job responsibilities and company needs.

This book has been written in response to the need of providing students with a reference they can use when contemplating a career in physical anthropology within and outside academia. It describes several career paths that physical anthropologists have chosen and how anthropological theory, methods, and training have been useful for job acquisition, daily responsibilities, and career development. This guide can also help professors and anthropology departments adapt their course work and training programs to the needs of students headed toward a variety of nontraditional careers in physical anthropology.

The contributors of this volume were asked to describe their present careers and how their knowledge of physical anthropology provided the tools necessary to be successful at their jobs. Authors describe the training (courses, post-doctoral positions, etc.) that was acquired to make them competitive for the positions that they currently hold. A description of accomplishments (research, teaching, consulting, managing, etc.) is also provided so that readers understand the role that physical anthropology plays in different work environments. Many authors offer students advice on what courses and/or training are necessary to compete for positions within and outside the academy. Lastly, authors describe not only the attributes of their job but also its challenges and problems.

The book begins with an overview of physical anthropology. Alan S. Ryan describes the specialties of physical anthropology and some recent developments, both positive and negative, which have impacted the field. In the next five chapters, traditional academic careers within an anthropology department are described. Curtis W. Wienker considers career preparation of a physical anthropologist seeking a teaching position at a university with a graduate program. What is expected of a newly hired assistant professor is also outlined in detail. Weinker's description of the university tenure/retention system is an important guide for all graduate students aspiring to academic employment.

Philip L. Stein draws on his thirty-five years of experience to describe what it is like to teach and work at a community college where teaching, rather than research, is the primary focus. Stein offers an insider's view of how to compete for a position at a community college. As Douglas H. Ubelaker demonstrates, museums offer exciting opportunities to conduct research in physical anthropology. Serving as a curator in the Smithsonian Institution's National Museum of Natural History, Department of Anthropology, Ubelaker is involved in skeletal biology research, forensic science (in collaboration with the FBI), and is active in museum activities such as lectures, exhibition work, and collections.

Andrew Kramer describes the challenges he faces as a university professor and field paleoanthropologist. Finding a fossil hominid is a thrilling experience. However, it is far more difficult than it appears. Many students may be unaware of the incredible amount of planning and hard work that must be accomplished before discoveries are possible. Kramer sheds light on what is required to assemble and manage an international team of professionals for a fossil-hunting expedition.

Many students are fascinated by the behavior of our closest living relatives. The spectacular images of primates swinging on branches through the forest are exciting to watch. A career as a primatologist in an anthropology department is often perceived as adventurous and exciting. However, as Kevin D. Hunt describes, there is more to primatology than watching primates. The day-to-day experience of working in the field can be daunting, physically challenging, and sometimes disappointing. It takes special skills and talents to persevere in the environments where primates live. Hunt provides insight into what a student can expect when contemplating a career as a primatologist in an anthropology department.

Participating in post-doctoral training before acquiring a position in either an academic or in a nontraditional setting is common in the life sciences and is becoming more common in physical anthropology. Anne C. Stone describes what a "post-doc" does, how to become one, and whether post-doctoral research is an attractive feature to potential employers. Additionally, Evelyn J. Bowers-Bienkowski considers her graduate and post-doctoral experience as a member of the Philadelphia Cleft Palate and Facial Reconstruction Team in the Philadelphia Children's Hospital. She shows how her training in physical anthropology directly contributed to research in an applied biomedical setting.

The remaining chapters in the book consider alternative careers in physical anthropology. One option for physical anthropology Ph.D.s who aspire to an academic career is teaching and/or research in a university department other than anthropology. Although teaching anatomy at a university seems like a break with tradition, many of the founding fathers of physical anthropologists served as anatomists. Today, many physical anthropology Ph.D.s are finding faculty positions in departments of anatomy. Mark F. Teaford describes his training and responsibilities as an anatomist in the Department of Cell Biology and Anatomy at Johns Hopkins University School of Medicine.

Because physical anthropologists often have acquired expertise in human biology research and quantitative methods, they can effectively contribute to biomedical research conducted in schools of medicine, nursing, and public health. Stephen T. McGarvey and Gary D. James comment on physical anthropologists working within medical or public health schools that have adapted their research to fit the interests and funding opportunities available in health-related disciplines. As shown by Bert B. Little, with the appropriate skills and background, physical anthropologists are effective at teaching genetics in medical schools and conducting genetic counseling in obstetrical and maternal-fetal medicine units.

Some physical anthropologists have established impressive research programs in university departments other than anthropology. Presently, Reynaldo Martorell is the Robert W. Woodruff Professor of International Nutrition and Chair of the Department of International Health at Emory University. Martorell describes his accomplishments and the training required for opportunities in public health in general and in international health in particular.

Robert M. Malina used his training in physical anthropology and interests in youth sports, physical activity, and sports science to take on the position as Director of the Institute of Youth Sports in the Department of Kinesiology at Michigan State University. There is considerable overlap between physical anthropology and the physical activity sciences. However, students interested in physical activity science need to appreciate the basic sciences involved in the study of physical activity, motor development, and performance.

Opportunities for employment for physical anthropologists are also found in dozens of different government and private organizations. Ralph M. Garruto describes the training and responsibilities needed for a position as an NIH scientist. Employment opportunities in biomedicine or public health at a federal institution are an untapped resource for physical anthropologists. Garruto provides useful recommendations to take advantage of these opportunities, keeping in mind that prerequisite training may require wet laboratory experience as well as field research skills.

Alan S. Ryan, who has worked in a pharmaceutical company for twenty years, highlights the importance of human biology research in nutritional product development, marketing, and professional services. Although Ryan's graduate training was traditional in many respects, his post-doctoral experience made it possible for him to break with tradition and find a research position in private industry. He is able to maintain ties with his professional colleagues by conducting and publishing research relevant to both physical anthropology and to his company.

Other physical anthropologists have shown their entrepreneurial leadership. For example, Marilyn R. London has established a rewarding and exciting career as a private consultant. Kate Wong, with an undergraduate degree in physical anthropology and zoology, is a journalist at *Scientific American*. And, Moses S. Schanfield supervises a genetics-testing laboratory for civil and criminal cases, including paternity suits and criminal investigations of rapes and murders.

The future of physical anthropology appears to be healthy, given its broad scope and biocultural orientation. Undoubtedly, the kinds of careers available for physical anthropologists will continue to grow. Today's students in physical anthropology have a wealth of traditional and nontraditional professional career options. Pursuing these opportunities is not only a matter of adequate training but also career flexibility, imagination, and an open mind. The diversity of careers that are described in this book represents just the starting point of the possibilities that will become available in future decades.

I am deeply grateful to Dr. Curtis W. Wienker, who encouraged me to serve as the editor for this book. I would like to thank my colleagues who have contributed to making this book a reality. All are sincerely concerned with the future of the discipline and with career opportunities available to their students. Jane Garry, editor for anthropology at Greenwood Press, was enthusiastic about this project from the outset. I thank her for her support and professionalism. Finally, I dedicate this book to my wife and best friend, Trina, who has helped make my career as a physical anthropologist in private industry rewarding and worthwhile.

Chapter 1

The Meaning of Physical Anthropology

Alan S. Ryan

Physical anthropology is the science that considers humans as biological organisms in terms of both their evolutionary history and biological variation. It is a subfield of anthropology that also includes cultural anthropology, archaeology, and linguistic anthropology. Physical anthropology is sometimes referred to by another name—biological anthropology.

At the beginning of the twentieth century, the field was first known as physical anthropology because the focus was on the physical variation of modern and fossil humans and nonhuman primates. Much of the early research was based on descriptions of physical variation with little or no theoretical background. In the 1950s, with the development of genetics and evolutionary science, research in physical anthropology became more focused on biological and genetic processes. As a result, the term "biological anthropology" became popular to emphasize the new focus on biological processes within a genetic and evolutionary framework. Tod   rms are often used interchangeably.

The field o   ndamental questions abou   concerned with what hum   e or similar? How are h   The second question is   derived from the discovery a   ssil human and nonhuman primates provides insight into their origins and evolutionary history. The third question is concerned with biological variation among modern humans. How are humans alike or dissimilar from each other? Are there patterns of biological variation? Can the processes of evolution explain such variation? And, finally, the fourth question considers the relationship between human biology and culture. How do culture and biology interact? How have cultural changes during the course of evolution shaped our biology?

Today, physical anthropologists study a variety of topics, including the origins and evolution of primates (including humans), behavior of living primates, and human biology, which itself includes adaptation, variation, human demography, forensic anthropology, paleopathology, growth and development, life history, and genetics. One of the most important features of anthropology—and physical anthropology is no exception—is the consideration of the interaction between culture and biology. This *biocultural approach* distinguishes anthropology from other disciplines that study humans (e.g., sociology, economics, anatomy, and biochemistry). The biocultural approach is an important strength of anthropology as a science because it is *holistic,* meaning that all aspects of the human condition, both cultural and biological, are taken into consideration. An additional strength of physical anthropology is that it considers humans today and in the distant past, even before humans as we know them now were living.

PHYSICAL ANTHROPOLOGY—AN EVOLUTIONARY SCIENCE

Physical anthropology is a science that is founded on evolutionary principles. Evolution is simply defined as genetic change over time. The relative frequencies of genes change over time because of four evolutionary forces or mechanisms. Natural selection is one of these evolutionary forces. The others include mutation, genetic drift, and gene flow. Coursework in physical anthropology provides numerous examples of how evolution works in the past and present. It is important to realize that evolution is a documented fact. Living organisms have changed in the past and continue to change. Organisms that have lived in the past are often referred to as fossils; these are no longer living today. Living organisms, including humans, have shown changes in their anatomy which reflect their evolutionary history. For example, today humans have larger brains and smaller teeth than they did 2 million years ago. Some anatomical features, such as brain size, gradually changed over millions of years; others have changed over shorter intervals of time. For example, human teeth are smaller today than they were only 5,000 years ago.

The principles of modern evolutionary theory have withstood years of scrutiny and scientific challenges. Evolution is called a "theory." This has caused a great deal of misunderstanding of what evolution means and what a theory implies. What is the definition of a theory? In the physical sciences, "a theory is a set of hypotheses that have been tested repeatedly and that have not been rejected" (Relethford, 1997:15). Evolutionary theory fits nicely into this definition. However, because a theory is a set of hypotheses, the term "hypothesis" must also be defined. A hypothesis is simply a testable explanation of observable facts. Although evolution can be explained by many hypotheses, each must be testable. A possibility must exist that a hypothesis can be rejected. For example, one can argue, based on the fossil record and our knowledge of evolution, that humans existed at the same time as dinosaurs. To confirm this hypothesis, all that is needed is conclusive evidence of fossil humans and dinosaurs sharing the same habitat at the same time. However, the possibility also exists that the hypothesis can be rejected. After years of looking for human remains associated with dinosaurs, we have found no evidence to support their association, and the hypothesis can be unquestionably rejected. Thus, science is based on hypotheses that are derived from accumulated evidence, observation, experimentation, and repeated testing.

THE DEVELOPMENT OF EVOLUTIONARY THOUGHT

Charles Darwin (1809–1882) is credited as the "father of evolutionary thought." However, he developed his theory of evolution based on the ideas of earlier scholars. In fact, Darwin's model was not the first evolutionary theory. It was, however, the one that has withstood the test of time.

For centuries before Darwin's seminal work on evolution, the concept of biological change was not universally accepted in Western society. Many scholars believed that a supernatural force created earth and all its living creatures in their present form; species did not change over time. The science of biology (or natural history) was based primarily on descriptions and classifications of living organisms. Carolus Linnaeus (1707–1778), a Swedish naturalist, compiled the first formal classification, or taxonomy, of all known living creatures. Living organisms were placed into categories representing their genus and species. A species is defined as a group of populations whose members can interbreed and produce fertile offspring. A genus is a group of similar species, sharing many of the same adaptations. Modern humans are known by the name *Homo sapiens*—the first word represents their genus, and the second is their species. In addition to genus and species, Linneaus' classification organized living creatures into broader categories of family, order, class, phylum, and kingdom. The assignment of animals into different categories is based on similarity of traits. For example, animals with mammary glands, such as humans, cows, horses, dogs, and cats, were placed into the class *mammalia,* that is, they are mammals. Linnaeus' taxonomy helped clarify relationships between different organisms, especially those that seem to possess similar traits. For example, although bats have wings like birds, they are classified as mammals because they have mammary glands.

Linnaeus and other natural historians did not consider the reasons for similarities or differences between living creatures. The living world was perceived to be static and immutable. However, this view began to change in the eighteenth and nineteenth centuries when fossils were discovered and described. Many of the fossil remains were of creatures that did not fit neatly into Linnaeus' classification system. For example, excavations uncovered the fossil remains of unusual creatures no longer living, such as dinosaurs and woolly mammoths. Other excavations produced fossils of creatures that resembled modern animals but were anatomically different. Fossil horses were smaller than modern horses and had five toes instead of a single hoof. It was impossible to reject the fact that in the past there existed horses that were similar in many ways to modern horses but also different as well. Discoveries of fossils began to alter the view that the world and its creatures had never changed. The concept of change was finally incorporated into treatises on natural history that attempted to explain the origins of life. However, different hypotheses were developed that described how the change took place.

Georges Cuvier (1769–1832), a French anatomist, recognized that many animals preserved as fossils no longer existed, that is, they became extinct. Cuvier, a professor of natural history at the Collège de France, discovered the remains of elephants, an assortment of fossil reptiles as big as whales, mammoths with long tusks, and other animals that did not resemble any living species. Cuvier wondered how extinct species could be succeeded over time by modern forms. The prevalent view of the earth's age did not allow enough time for a process of gradual change, and to argue that change took place would have cast doubt on his faith in a special creation. Thus, to explain the extinctions, Cuvier postulated a hypothesis called *catastrophism*. The hypothesis involved a series of catastrophes in the planet's past, during which time many animals were destroyed. Following these catastrophes, creatures from unaffected areas moved in and replaced the extinct forms. Thus, changes over time in the fossil record were explained as a sequence of catastrophes followed by population replacement.

Charles Lyell (1797–1875) provided a more convincing theory of change than that formulated by Cuvier. Lyell rejected catastrophism and argued that the uniformitarian principles developed by Compte de Buffon applied to the organic as well as the inorganic world. Uniformitarianism, introduced by de Buffon, implied that if natural forces such as wind, flowing water, frost, volcanic activity, and faulting now effect the earth's surface, then it is reasonable to conclude that such forces also operated in a similar, or *uniform*, fashion in the past. The concept of uniformitarianism demonstrated that the earth was much older than previously thought. Various layers of different kinds of sediments (river gravel, sands, limestone), one layer beneath another, indicated that the layers have been laid down over long periods of time.

Jean-Baptiste Lamarck (1744–1829), a French scientist, provided the first theory that explained organic change. He developed a hypothesis in which evolution occurred through a natural process of living organisms adjusting to their environment. He recognized that animals are finely adapted to their environments and that their relationship with their surroundings was dynamic. Environmental change would lead to biological change and adaptation. Lamarck suggested that an organism could change anatomically during its lifetime and pass on the changes to its offspring. He argued that during daily life, animals recognized certain needs and that these needs generated forces within their body that stimulated the development and growth of organs. The hypothesis of evolution through *acquired characteristics* meant that a giraffe has a long neck because its neck grows longer during life through constant reaching for food in trees. The giraffe's longer neck would be passed on to its offspring. However, the hypothesis of evolution through acquired characteristics did not stand up to scrutiny. It was easy to reject this hypothesis knowing that if a person loses his leg in an accident, his offspring would be born with two legs.

The contributions of Cuvier, Lyell, and Lamarck set the stage for the ideas developed by Charles Darwin. Combining information from different fields, such as biology, geology, and economics, Darwin revolutionized our understanding of the living world by his theory of evolution by natural selection.

During a five-year journey as a naturalist, aboard the scientific survey ship the HMS *Beagle*, Darwin formulated several basic ideas about biological variation in living species. One of the most important parts of his voyage was the time he spent on the Galapagos Islands. Darwin noticed that several species differed slightly from island to island, even though the islands were only fifty to sixty miles apart. Most striking were the anatomical differences he noticed among finches. On one island they had strong, thick beaks for cracking nuts and seeds; on another island, they had smaller beaks for catching insects, and on another their beak was long and thin for feeding on flowers and fruit. Each species of finches had adapted in a manner that made them better able to survive in their own specific environment.

Darwin's experiences as a naturalist convinced him that individuals within species varied considerably from place to place and that species were not fixed, rigid entities as described by other biologists of his time. Birds who had to crush hard shells to extract the softer fruit had strong beaks well designed for this purpose. Creatures in cold regions often had fur for protection. Thus, organisms were well adapted to specific environments. Darwin came to the conclusion that the environment acted to change organisms over time. Every species arose through the same evolutionary process. This process determines why organisms look and act the way they do. The physiology, morphology, and behavior of species changed through time. New species were formed by the transformation of existing species.

In 1859, Darwin published his work *On the Origins of Species by Means of Natural Selection*. He was encouraged to publish his treatise after seeing the work of Alfred Russel Wallace (1823–1913) who, working independently, came to similar conclusions.

Both Darwin and Wallace realized that a kind of natural selection was at work but did not know exactly how it happened. An understanding of the means by which natural selection operated arose from the ideas of Thomas Malthus (1766–1834). Malthus showed that the reproductive potential of humans far exceeded the natural resources that were available to support it. Malthus argued that the size of human populations is limited by food, poverty, and ultimately death. Malthus' principles also applied to other living organisms. In most species, more individuals are born than can possibly survive. Thus, many organisms die before they can reach maturity and reproduce. If all the offspring lived to reach reproductive age, populations would grow too large for their environments to support them. For example, some frogs produce hundreds of eggs. If every frog lived long enough to reproduce and produce another hundred eggs, it would not take long for the planet to be smothered in frogs. Thus, some eggs become diseased and die, predators eat others, and many frogs die before they can reproduce.

To Darwin, the ideas of Malthus provided the information needed to address the issue of adaptation and evolution. Not all individuals within a species survive and live to reproduce. Although some failure to reproduce may be random, most is probably related to specific characteristics of an individual. If an individual has characteristics that affect his survival and reproduction, these traits will be passed on to the next generation. For example, if there are two frogs within the same species, one with a short tongue and another with a long tongue, in an environment that requires reaching across long branches to capture insects undetected, it seems likely that the frog with the longer tongue is more likely to feed itself and survive to reproduce. If a longer tongue is an inherited characteristic, then the trait will be passed on to the next generation. Thus, individuals in a population show a great deal of variation; those that survive have specific characteristics that are better adapted to their environment. Successive generations of individuals within a species will either maintain or improve their adaptation to an environment by gradual changes in every generation, depending on whether the environment remains the same or changes. Species that cannot adapt to meet the demands of a changing environment will eventually die out.

In many ways, Darwin's ideas were not new. Animal and plant breeders used the principles of adaptation and variation within species for centuries. Artificial selection and careful breeding have resulted in many traits that are seen in domesticated plants and animals. Cattle body size and composition, milk production in cows, fruit and vegetable yield, and the behavioral and structural characteristics of domestic dogs and cats have been modified through controlled breeding and artificial selection. Darwin, however, noted that, in nature, it was the environment that selected individuals that were best adapted to survive and later reproduce.

In describing variation and environmental factors that were responsible for evolutionary change, Darwin could not address questions concerning the origin of variation. Because natural selection operates on existing variation within species, where did the variation originate? Natural selection can only act on existing variation; it does not create new variation. Other important questions that were not addressed by Darwin included, How are traits inherited? What is the mechanism responsible for their inheritance? Natural selection implies that certain traits are selected for and passed on to the next generation. Darwin also did not explain how new anatomical structures arose through time.

Answers to these questions were provided through developments in biology, genetics, embryology, physiology, and comparative anatomy. Contributions from these fields have been brought together to establish the modern synthesis of evolutionary thought. It is now known that biological evolution involves changes in the genetic composition of populations. The relative frequency of genes changes over time as a result of natural selection, mutation, genetic drift, and gene flow. Individuals with genetic characteristics that improve their relative survival or chance of reproduction pass on their genetic material to the next generation. The origin of variation within a population is due to genetic mutation.

Modern evolutionary theory will continue to be refined and changed as new scientific information supports, clarifies, or rejects previous ideas. That is the nature of science. Because science is an ongoing process, the fundamentals of evolutionary theory have been refined over the years as more knowledge became available. The principles of evolution allow us to understand the diversity of life, and to appreciate why people and other living creatures are the way they are. This knowledge can help us answer many fundamental questions that confront us each day. Some of these questions include, Why do some people have darker or lighter skin color than others? Why do we have large appetites for sweets, fat, and salt? Why are we better long-distance walkers and runners than mountain climbers? Why do we sweat when it is hot and shiver when it is cold? Why do only women nurse their infants? These questions and many others that deal with human variation, evolutionary processes, and adaptation are considered in detail in physical anthropology course work and research.

THE DEVELOPMENT OF PHYSICAL ANTHROPOLOGY

To a large extent, the founding fathers of physical anthropology were involved in human diversity research. At the turn of the eighteenth century, one of the basic questions facing the pre-Darwinian scholar was whether different human populations that were encountered around the world were derived from the same ancestral stock (Adam and Eve) or were created separately. The monogenists favored the first view and the polygenists the second.

Johann Friedrich Blumenbach (1752–1840), professor of anatomy at the University of Göttingen, Germany, is often given the title the "father of physical anthropology" (Brace and Montagu, 1977). Blumenbach was an outspoken monogenist. However, he was best known for his scheme of racial classification referred to as the "five-race theory of anthropology" in which humans were placed into five varieties: Caucasoid, Mongoloid, American Indian, Ethiopian, and Malayan (Stanton, 1960). As a pre-Darwinian scientist, he was not influenced by evolutionary concepts. However, he argued that human variation was not large, fixed, or static (Wolpoff and Caspari, 1997). Blumenbach attempted to explain human differences, such as variation in skeletal features, hair and skin color, and tooth size, as the result of adaptive responses to the environment. Unfortunately, Blumenbach's racial classification had a much larger influence on anthropological thought than his view that population diversity was related to environmental factors.

In the first half of the twentieth century in the United States, the discipline of physical anthropology was "largely disconnected and individualistic" comprised of anthropologists who were physicians, specializing in anatomy or physiology (Hrdlička, 1919:28–29). Aleš Hrdlička noted that physical anthropology began in 1830 with Samuel G. Morton, a physician who was appointed professor of anatomy at the University of Pennsylvania (Hrdlička, 1919:32). In his book *Crania Americana* (Morton, 1839), Morton used cranial measurements of Native Americans recovered from mounds in the Ohio Valley to construct typological categories or "racial types." He was convinced that different races exhibited different head shapes. The strength of Morton's claims was primarily based on his carefully constructed measurement techniques which were viewed as objective and scientific (Stanton, 1960; Wolpoff and Caspari, 1997).

Morton's subsequent work on ancient Egyptians in his *Crania Aegyptiaca* (Morton, 1844) was important in the context of the view held in his time that the date of creation was approximately 6,000 years ago. Based on accounts of Egyptian history as documented in hieroglyphic writings, Morton established that modern humans flourished at the time of creation. Moreover, Morton's description of two populations (Native Americans and Egyptians), in two continents, with no evidence of convergence, supported the views of the polygenists of the day, those that favored a "multiple-center-of-creation" interpretation (Brace and Montagu, 1977). Although Morton's work, a scholarly comparison of crania, earned him widespread recognition as the successor of Blumenbach, he is most remembered for his polygenist views. Polygenism as a respected explanation for human variation was dealt a fatal blow with the publication of Darwin's work. The process of natural selection implied gradual changes over a relatively unlimited time. Typological thinking was replaced with a population approach that took into consideration human variability as determined by the interaction between the environment and genetic systems.

During the 1840s and before Darwin's publication of the *Origin of Species*, the first conclusive evidence that humans lived in a prehistoric period was reported. Boucher de Perthes, an amateur archeologist from Abbéville, France, described quantities of shaped flints that he discovered in the gravel pits by the Somme River. These flints, prepared by humans, were associated with extinct animals. However, scholars of the time, including Cuvier, immediately denounced Boucher's claims without much consideration.

Two representatives of a stage of human evolution earlier than that of modern humans were also found. In 1848, a fossil human skull was discovered on the Rock of Gibraltar. The Gibraltar skull was sent to England, and in 1862 it was described by Hugh Falconer, a paleontologist, "as a case of a very low type of humanity—very low and savage, and of extreme antiquity— but still man, and not a halfway step between man and monkey" (Falconer, 1868:561). Unfortunately, the Gibraltar skull attracted little attention until the turn of the century.

In August 1856, miners at a quarry in the Neander valley were working in a cave where they came across some old bones. They were given to Carl Fuhlrott, a teacher interested in geology and paleontology. Recognizing their importance Fuhlrott contacted Hermann Schaaffhausen, professor of anatomy at the University of Bonn. Schaaffhausen and Fuhlrott described the materials and presented their interpretations at meetings of scientific societies. They felt that the Neanderthal fossils represented an ancient form of humanity, evidence for a former stage in human evolution. To many, however, the Neanderthal remains were regarded as pathological but still a member of modern humanity.

During the late 1800s, skeletal remains of more than a dozen fossil humans were discovered in Europe. And beginning in 1890 with Eugene Dubois' discovery in Java of *Homo erectus* (*Pithecanthropus erectus*) and Raymond Dart's description of *Australopithcus africanus* from South Africa in 1924, the evidence for the antiquity of man was accumulating at an unprecedented rate. By the twentieth century, one could no longer deny the existence of human fossils, but debates about where they fit into the evolutionary history of humankind continue until today.

Although the study of anthropology in the United States extends back to early colonial times (Hodgen, 1964; Stanton, 1960), it was not until the end of the nineteenth century that anthropology was regarded as a profession rather than an avocation (Spencer, 1981). By the time of First World War, anthropology became an important component of the academic community (Spencer, 1981). Much of the professional anthropology prior to that time was being conducted in museums and in a few research-oriented institutions such as the Bureau of American Ethnology (Spencer, 1981).

The growth of academic anthropology in the United States has been largely attributed to Franz Boas (1858–1942) who came to physical anthropology from ethnology (Stocking, 1968). Boas established a program at Columbia University in the 1900s with a link to the American Museum of Natural History (Spencer, 1981). He was interested in biological processes, growth, and in environmental factors that influence growth. He was less interested in racial classification, but rather in understanding the forces that shaped human variation. Boas argued against the stability of many biological features. His studies on head form, a feature that was commonly used to distinguish races, indicated that it changed significantly over a short period of time. Boas reported that head form of the first American-born generation of Italian immigrants that settled in the United States was significantly different from that of their parents. The heads of children of relatively longer-headed people developed broader heads, and vice versa. Not only was the change in head form rapid, but it was also accompanied by a convergence to a similar head shape. Boas attributed these changes to environmental factors. Boas demonstrated that a feature that was often used to characterize a static "racial type" was in fact *plastic*, one that could be modified within one generation.

Boas' scientific contributions also included his seminal research on human growth and development. He was the first to initiate a longitudinal growth study and point out that some individuals are throughout their lifetimes more physically mature than others. He introduced the concepts of physiological and developmental age, and the phase "tempo of growth" to describe how fast the processes of childhood growth occur. Boas published three of the most important papers in the field of growth and development (Ulijaszek et al., 1998). In these articles, he described height curves from longitudinal individual data, classifying the curves by age at peak height velocity or age at menarche. Boas provided individual growth curves from different populations, laying the foundation for growth reference data used by future scientists to study population differences.

The first autonomous program in academic anthropology was established at Harvard in 1887 (Spencer, 1981). Harvard was responsible for producing the first Ph.D. in physical anthropology. Few other physical anthropology Ph.D.s were produced until Earnest A. Hooton arrived at Harvard in 1913. Hooton developed a program that produced an unequaled number of doctorates in physical anthropology, many of whom became leaders in the field after the Second World War. In fact, the direction of the field was determined almost exclusively by students that Hooton trained during his thirty-year tenure (Spencer, 1981).

Aleš Hrdlička founded the *American Journal of Physical Anthropology* in 1918. This was an important event because the journal defined the discipline as legitimate and independent from physiology and medical science. Hrdlička was trained in Paris at the École d'Anthropologie founded by Paul

Broca. Hrdlička campaigned for an establishment of an American Institute of Physical Anthropology similar to "Broca's Anthropological Institute" (Spencer, 1981). However, it took another eighteen years before the American Association of Physical Anthropologists held its inaugural meeting in Charlottesville, Virginia, with over eighty members present, the majority of whom were anatomists (Spencer, 1981).

As the result of the "baby boom" and access to a university education through the GI Bill, there was an unprecedented growth of higher education during the 1950s and 1960s. Several academic departments, including Arizona, Berkeley, Chicago, Columbia, UCLA, Michigan, Pennsylvania, and Wisconsin, began to expand their graduate programs to include physical anthropology (Spencer, 1981). Programs in these departments were led by either former students of Hooton or by a student of a Hooton student. For an excellent description of the history of American physical anthropology see Spencer (1982, 1997).

The growth of physical anthropology is in many ways related to the development of the modern evolutionary synthesis. Following the rediscovery of the principles of Mendelian genetics in 1900, the mechanisms involved in the transmission of characters became known. In the 1930s, a group of mathematical geneticists that included J.B.S. Haldane, R. A. Fisher, and Sewell Wright developed the quantitative basis for the modern evolutionary synthesis and showed how Mendelian genetics could be used to explain evolutionary change in a population. The major principles of the synthesis were described in three separate volumes by the geneticist Dobzhansky (1937), the ornithologist Ernst Mayr (1942), and the paleontologist George Gaylord Simpson (1944). When the work of Wright, Fisher and Haldane was combined with Darwin's theory of natural selection, and with the seminal writings of Dobzhansky, Mayr, and Simpson, a powerful, scientific explanation of organic evolution emerged. With the development of the modern evolutionary synthesis, the stage was set for one of the most important discoveries in the history of science, the discovery of the exact structure and mode of action of the basic genetic material. In 1953, James D. Watson, Francis H. C. Crick, and Maurice M. Wilkins described the structure for deoxyribonucleic acid, or DNA. Now we know how DNA stores information, how this information relates to Mendelian genetics, and why there are new genetic variations. We also know about the genetic nature of inheritance and that evolutionary processes must involve changes in the genetic composition of populations.

The 1950s and 1960s ushered in the "new physical anthropology" in which static typological and descriptive methods were replaced with an evolutionary, adaptive, and dynamic approach (Washburn, 1951). The focus was on real populations instead of "racial types." There was also more emphasis on explanation, that is, showing how evolutionary processes shaped human diversity.

Today scores of universities and colleges in the United States have a doctoral program in anthropology, and offer a program in physical anthropology. Despite the growth of the field, with many more students showing interest in the discipline, because of the shrinking number of opportunities in academic institutions, future programs may consider placing a greater emphasis on the biomedical sciences and/or creating links with other disciplines.

SUBFIELDS OF PHYSICAL ANTHROPOLOGY

There are three traditionally defined subfields of physical anthropology: primatology, paleoanthropology, and human variation.

Primatology

Primatology is concerned with defining the place of humans in relation to other primates (a group that includes prosimians, monkeys, apes, and humans). Primatologists study the anatomy, social behavior, and evolution of nonhuman primates, past and present. Closely related species tend to be similar in morphology and behavior. Comparisons with nonhuman primates shed light on what it is to be human. If we can understand how evolution has shaped the behavior of animals so much like humans, we will have a greater appreciation of the ways that evolution affected the behavior of our ancestors and perhaps explain why we behave the way we do today.

The subfield of primatology has benefited greatly from the pioneering work of Jane Goodall, Birute Galdikas, and Dian Fossey (Morell, 1993). Because of their insight and painstaking commitment to the study of primates, the behavior of chimpanzees (Goodall, 1986), gorillas (Fossey, 1983), and orangutans (Galdikas, 1985) is much better known to the scientific community and general public than it was twenty-five years ago. These scientists also serve as role models for many students interested in primate behavior; many have followed in their footsteps and became primatologists.

The future of primatology is uncertain, however. Several species of nonhuman primates are facing extinction. During the last two decades, our planet has experienced significant erosion that has depleted the extent and quality of the habitats in which nonhuman primates live. Humans have caused most of the erosion. Unfortunately, much of the erosion has taken place in the tropical rain forests. Only recently have public officials begun to listen to the pleas by primatologists and others to take immediate action and address this serious situation.

Paleoanthropology

Paleoanthropology is the study of the fossil evidence for human and nonhuman primate evolution. Paleoanthropologists are involved with determining who our ancestors were, where they lived, how they lived, and why they evolved or went extinct. In the field or in the laboratory, paleoanthropologists use a multidisciplinary approach, working with archaeologists, geologists, and other scientists to reconstruct the behavior and culture of our past.

A series of spectacular fossil discoveries have increased interest in the field. Some of the most prominent discoveries include "Lucy" and the "first family" (Johanson et al., 1982; Johanson, 1976); KMN-ER 1470 (Leakey, 1973); Olduvai Hominid 62 (Johanson et al., 1987); the "Black Skull" (Walker et al., 1986); the Laetoli footprints (Leakey and Hay, 1979); the partial skeleton of *Homo erectus* from Kenya (Brown et al., 1985); *Ardipithecus ramidus* dated to around 4.4 million years ago (White et al., 1994, 1995); *Australopithecus anamensis* dated at 4.2 million years ago (Leakey et al., 1998); the proposed earliest hominid remains dating to 6 million years ago (Balter, 2001); a 2.5 million-year-old hominid, *Australopithecus garhi* (de Heinzelin et al., 1999), associated with the earliest stone tools used to butcher large mammal carcasses; and the first evidence for the ancestor to Neanderthals and modern humans in Europe (Bermudez de Castro et al., 1997).

Despite the many new discoveries and additional data they provide, there is little consensus as to how these materials should be interpreted. The proposed number of early human species and their suggested phylogenetic relationships continue to be hotly disputed. Over the years, many phylogenetic scenarios have been suggested, each offering a different way of looking at our evolutionary history. The debates have not been limited to the earliest humans, but also to more modern populations. The evolutionary fate of the Neanderthal populations of Western Europe and the Middle East dating from 100,000 to 40,000 years ago is at least as controversial. The incredible discovery of a mitochondrial DNA segment from the arm of a Neanderthal has sparked considerable disagreement as to whether the Neanderthals should be considered a different species that did not contribute genetically to populations that evolved into modern humans (Wolpoff, 1998; Tattersall, 1998). The combination of spectacular fossil discoveries and continued debate as to how to interpret the evidence of our evolutionary past will ensure that paleoanthropology continues to be a popular and intriguing field of study.

Human Variation

The study of human variation considers how and why human populations differ genetically from each other. Physical anthropologists who study human variation have a wide range of interests, including human adaptation, genetics, growth and development, demography, health, epidemiology, nutrition, life history, and disease.

Human beings differ from one another in a variety of ways. Intrinsic to the study of human variation is the recognition of human differences, that is, the study of what is often considered "race." Until the 1950s much of physical anthropology was devoted to racial description and classification. Because the concept of race was, and still is, so ingrained in society, physical anthropologists have examined this issue in terms of evolutionary processes rather than racial classifications defined by society. Physical anthropologists have determined that race is merely a descriptive concept; it explains nothing about human biological variation and the evolutionary forces that shaped the differences we see among living people and populations (Brown and Armelagos, 2001).

The field of human variation has grown considerably during the last two decades. Because of its relevance to issues encountered in contemporary society, research in biological variation interfaces with biology, medicine, public health, genetics, and epidemiology. Today the study of human variation represents one of the largest areas of research within physical anthropology (Wienker, 1997), and several specialties have emerged. There is a greater understanding of human adaptation to a variety of environments (e.g., high altitude, heat, and cold). Research in human adaptation has grown to include studies on the detrimental effects caused by urbanization and environmental pollution (Schell, 1991; Schell et al., 1993).

Physical anthropologists interested in human variation are also involved in the Human Genome Diversity Project (HGDP) (Weiss et al., 1992). The HGDP is assembling a DNA data bank from different populations around the world, especially groups that are threatened with "genetic" extinction. However, this project has been the subject of much publicity and controversy (Marks, 1995). Undoubtedly, this project will continue to grow in an effort to document the extent of human genetic diversity.

Research in human variation has also provided a better understanding of factors affecting growth and development in the United States and elsewhere (Eveleth and Tanner, 1990; Ryan and Roche, 1990). Growth and development research not only considers variation in infant and childhood growth but also factors influencing the aging process (Crews and Gurruto, 1994). The results of these studies are relevant to the interests of many scientists other than anthropologists, especially those involved in public health and medicine.

NEWLY EMERGING SPECIALTIES AND TECHNOLOGICAL INNOVATIONS

Over the last decade, several new specialties have emerged. These include human adaptation to infectious and noninfectious diseases (Stinson et al., 2000), human and nonhuman social organization and sociobiology (Fuentes, 2000), dental anthropology (Jernvall and Jung, 2000), and taphonomy (Behrensmeyer, 1984). Other new teaching and research interests include forensic anthropology, biomedical, and molecular anthropology. Notably, studies of molecular biology have considered patterns of human migration (Cann, 2001), the evolution of our ancestors (Mountain, 1998), the strengths and weaknesses of different genetic models used to infer genealogical relationships (Stumpf and Goldstein, 2001), the evolution of non-human primates (Ruvolo, 1994), and adaptation at high altitude in modern humans (Torroni et al., 1994).

Forensic anthropology has direct application to law enforcement and the criminal justice system. Physical anthropologists engaged in this specialty (such as Ubelaker and Schanfield in this volume) demonstrate how research using techniques in forensic anthropology have helped solve crimes. Forensic anthropology has benefited from new technological innovations in computing and superimposition (Janssens et al., 1978), DNA identification (Holland et al., 1993), and data collections procedures (Moore-Jansen et al., 1994). In fact, recent survey data have shown that forensic anthropology is the most rapidly growing specialty of physical anthropology in terms of popularity (Wienker, 1995). The popularity of forensic anthropology is reflected by frequent stories in the lay press and in recent popular books (Maples and Browning, 1994; Rhine, 1998).

Emerging as a specialty that has wide appeal and job potential is biomedical anthropology. Biomedical anthropology has an applied approach that is relevant to researchers working in biology, medicine, public health, and epidemiology. As shown in this book and in a variety of publications, physical anthropologists are actively engaged in studying cardiovascular disease (Gerber and Halberstein, 1999), cancer (Micozzi, 1990), metabolic diseases (Yannicelli and Ryan, 1995), transmission of infectious disease (Sattenspiel, 2000), iron-deficiency anemia (Ryan, 1997), and physical activity and fitness (Malina, 2001), to name a few. In fact, in 1976, two physical anthropologists were awarded the Nobel Prize for medicine. Blumberg was recognized for his research on the Australian antigen (Au) and its relationship to hepatitis (Blumberg and Hesser, 1975) and Gajdusek (1977) for his work on the origins of the neurological disease kuru.

These newly emerging areas of study and the well-recognized contributions that physical anthropologists have made bear witness to the fact that the scientific community and general public have a greater understanding and awareness of the discipline. These developments speak well for the future of physical anthropology, but there are still many challenges that need to be addressed.

CHALLENGES

One of the challenges facing the field of physical anthropology in particular and of science in general is the growing popularity of teaching *creationism* and the effect that it may have on public education. *Creationism*, misnamed as creation science, is not a science at all. Creationism is based on the belief that species are created as separate and immutable entities. It is a modern version of traditional beliefs based on the Book of Genesis. It is not a scientific theory and cannot be tested or refuted. Rather, creationism is simply a statement of religious beliefs that for support uses passages from the Bible. It cannot rival scientific explanations for the origins of organic life that employ testable hypothesis.

Although many people who may have little understanding of evolutionary principles feel that the theory of evolution threatens fundamental religious belief, the modern theory of evolution does not in any way negate the existence of God. It only describes the mechanisms by which species are created and change over time. There is little doubt that the beauty of nature and all the creatures within it are truly inspirational.

CONCLUSION

Physical anthropology deals with issues that everyone thinks about and cares about—our origins and our evolutionary history. Physical anthropology attracts public and scientific attention not only because it considers human origins but also human differences as well. One of the major contributions of physical anthropology is the understanding that it no longer makes sense to explain human variation in terms of socially defined racial categories. Instead, clines and distributions of characteristics associated with evolutionary processes have greater scientific validity and meaning.

As a science, physical anthropology has certain requirements and attributes. Hypotheses are formulated to explain observable facts. To be a hypothesis, it must be testable and verifiable. A theory is a set of hypotheses that have been tested and have withstood scientific scrutiny. The main theoretical basis of physical anthropology is the theory of evolution. Physical anthropology is concerned not only with human biology but also with culture. Humans are not solely biological entities. Humans interact with their culture. This biocultural perspective represents one of the unique strengths of the discipline: it is holistic, in that it takes into consideration all aspects of the human condition.

The field of physical anthropology has grown dramatically during the last two decades. The discipline has branched out to include a multitude of research opportunities and interests. Several career paths that physical anthropologists have taken are described in this book. Its growing popularity indicates that the discipline will continue to expand and diversify. Undoubtedly, the values and strengths that physical anthropologists bring to the workplace, whether in the academy or elsewhere, demonstrate its relevance to issues faced by everyone.

REFERENCES

Balter, M. 2001. "Scientists Spar over Claims of Earliest Human Ancestor." *Science* (291):1460–1461.

Behrensmeyer, A. K. 1984. "Taphonomy and the Fossil Record." *American Scientist* (72):558–567.

Bermudez de Castro, J. M., J. L. Arsuaga, E. Carbonell, A. Rosas, I. Martinez, and M. Mosquera. 1997. "A Hominid from the Lower Pleistocene of Atapuerca Spain: Possible Ancestor to Neanderthals and Modern Humans." *Science* (276):1392–1395.

Blumberg, B. S., and J. E. Hesser. 1975. "Anthropology and Infectious Disease." In A. Damon, ed. *Physiological Anthropology*. New York: Oxford University Press, pp. 260–294.

Brace, C. L., and A. Montagu. 1977. *Human Evolution: An Introduction to Biological Anthropology*, 2nd ed. New York: Macmillan Publishing Co., Inc.

Brown, F. H., J. M. Harris, R.E.F. Leakey, and A. R. Walker. 1985. "Early *Homo erectus* Skeleton from West Lake Turkana, Kenya." *Nature* (316):788–792.

Brown, R. A., and G. J. Armelagos. 2001. "Apportionment of Racial Diversity." *Evolutionary Anthropology* (10):34–40.

Cann, R. L. 2001. "Genetic Clues to Dispersal in Human Populations: Retracing the Past from the Present." *Science* (291):1742–1748.

Crews, D. E., and R. M. Garruto, eds. 1994. *Biological Anthropology and Aging: Perspectives on Human Variation Over the Life Span*. New York: Oxford University Press.

de Heinzelin, J., J. D. Clark, T. White, W. Hart, P. Renne, G. Wolde-Gabriel, Y. Beyene, and E. Vrba. 1999. "Environment and Behavior of 2.5 Million-year-old Bouri Hominids." *Science* (284):625–629.

Dobzhansky, T. 1937. *Genetics and the Origin of Species*. New York: Columbia University Press.

Eveleth, P. B., and J. M. Tanner, eds. 1990. *Worldwide Variation in Human Growth*. Cambridge, England: Cambridge University Press.

Falconer, H. 1868. *Paleontological Notes and Memoirs*. London: Robert Hardwicke.

Fossey, D. 1983. *Gorillas in the Mist*. Boston: Houghton Mifflin.

Fuentes, A. 2000. "Hylobatid Communities: Changing Views on Pair Bonding and Social Organization in Hominoids." *Yearbook of Physical Anthropology* (43):33–60.

Gajdusek, D. C. 1977. "Unconventional Viruses and the Origin and Disappearance of Kuru." *Science* (197):943–960.

Galdikas, B.M.F. 1985. "Subadult Male Orangutan Sociality and Reproductive Behavior at Tanjung Puting." *American Journal of Primatology* (8):87–99.

Gerber, L. M., and R. A. Halberstein. 1999. *Blood Pressure: Genetic and Environmental Influences*. Human Biology, Special Issue, Volume 71, Number 1. Detroit, MI: Wayne State University Press.

Goodall, J. L. 1986. *Chimpanzees of Gombe*. Cambridge, MA: Harvard University Press.

Hodgen, M. T. 1964. *Early Anthropology in the Sixteenth and Seventeenth Centuries*. Philadelphia: University of Pennsylvania Press.

Holland, M. M., D. L. Fisher, L. G. Mitchel, W. C. Rodriguez, J. J. Canik, and C. R. Merril. 1993. "Mitochondrial DNA Sequence Analysis of Skeletal Remains from the Vietnam War." *Journal of Forensic Sciences* (38):542–553.

Hrdlička, A. 1919. *Physical Anthropology: Its Scope and Aims; Its History and Present Status in the United States*. Philadelphia: Wistar Institute of Anatomy and Biology.

Janssens, P. A., C. R. Hansch, and L. L. Voorhamme. 1978. "Identity Determination by Superimposition with Anthropological Cranium Adjustment." *Ossa* (5):109–122.

Jernvall, J., and H.-S. Jung. 2000. "Genotype, Phenotype, and Developmental Biology of Molar Tooth Characteristics." *Yearbook of Physical Anthropology* (43):171–190.

Johanson, D. C. 1976. "Ethiopia yields first 'family' of early man." *National Geographic* (150):790–811.

Johanson, D. C., C. O. Lovejoy, W. H. Kimbel, T. D. White, S. C. Ward, M. E. Bush, B. M. Latimer, and Y. Coppens. 1982. "Morphology of the Pliocene Partial Hominid Skeleton (A.L. 288-1) from Hadar Formation, Ethiopia." *American Journal of Physical Anthropology* (57): 403–452.

Johanson, D. C., F. T. Maseao, G. G. Eck, T. D. White, R. C. Walter, W. H. Kimbel, B. Asfaw, P. Monega, P. Ndessokia, and G. Suwa. 1987. "New Partial Skeleton of *Homo habilis* from Olduvai Gorge, Tanzania." *Nature* (327): 205–209.

Leakey, M. D., and R. L. Hay. 1979. "Pliocene Footprints in Laetolil Beds at Laetoli, Northern Tanzania." *Nature* (248):317–323.

Leakey, M. G., C. S. Feibel, I. McDougall, C. Ward, and A. Walker. 1998. "New Specimens and Confirmation of an Early Age for *Australopithecus anamensis*." *Nature* (393): 62–66.

Leakey, R.E.F. 1973. "Evidence for an Advanced Plio-Pleistocene Hominid from East Rudolph, Kenya." *Nature* (242): 447–450.

Malina, R. M. 2001. "Physical Activity and Fitness: Pathways from Childhood to Adulthood." *American Journal of Human Biology* (13): 162–172.

Maples, W. R., and M. Browning. 1994. *Dead Men Do Tell Tales*. New York: Doubleday.

Marks, J. 1995. "The Human Genome Diversity Project: Good *for* If Not Good *as* Anthropology?" *Anthropology Newsletter* (36): 4:72.

Mayr, E. 1942. *Systematics and the Origin of Species*. New York: Columbia University Press.

Micozzi, M. S. 1990. "Applications of Anthropometry to Epidemiologic Studies of Nutrition and Cancer." *American Journal of Human Biology* (2): 727–739.

Moore-Jansen, P. M., S. D. Ousley, and R. L. Jantz. 1994. "Data Collection Procedures for Forensic Skeletal Material." *Report of Investigations* No. 48, Department of Anthropology, Knoxville: University of Tennessee.

Morell, V. 1993. "Called 'Trimates,' Three Bold Women Shaped Their Field." *Science* (261): 1798–1802.

Morton, S. G. 1839. *Crania Americana*. Philadelphia.

———. 1844. *Crania Aegyptiaca*, Philadelphia.

Mountain, J. L. 1998. "Molecular Evolution and Modern Human Origins." *Evolutionary Anthropology* (7): 21–37.

Relethford, J. H. 1997. *The Human Species, An Introduction to Biological Anthropology*, 3rd edition. Mountain View, CA: Mayfield Publishing Co.

Rhine, S. 1998. *Bone Voyage: A Journey in Forensic Anthropology*. Albuquerque: University of New Mexico.

Ruvolo, M. 1994. "Molecular Evolutionary Processes and Conflicting Gene Trees: The Hominoid Case." *American Journal of Physical Anthropology* (94): 89–114.

Ryan, A. S. 1997. "Iron-Deficiency Anemia in Infant Development: Implications for Growth, Cognitive Development, Resistance to Infection, and Iron Supplementation." *Yearbook of Physical Anthropology* (40): 25–62.

Ryan, A. S., and A. F. Roche, eds. 1990. "Growth of Mexican-American Children: Data from the Hispanic Health and Nutrition Examination Survey (1982–1984)." *American Journal of Clinical Nutrition* (Supplement to Volume 51).

Sattenspiel, L. 2000. "Tropical Environments, Human Activities, and Transmission of Infectious Diseases." *Yearbook of Physical Anthropology* (43): 3–32.

Schell, L. M. 1991. "Effects of Pollutants on Human Prenatal and Postnatal Growth: Noise, Lead, Polychlorobiphenyl Compounds and Toxic Wastes." *Yearbook of Physical Anthropology* (34): 157–188.

Schell, L. M., M. Smith, and A. Bilsborough, eds. 1993. *Urban Ecology and Health in the Third World*. New York: Cambridge University.

Simpson, G. G. 1944. *Tempo and Mode in Evolution*. New York: Columbia University Press.

Spencer, F. 1981. "The Rise of Academic Physical Anthropology in the United States (1880–1980): A Historical Overview." *American Journal of Physical Anthropology* (56): 353–364.

———, ed. 1982. *A History of American Physical Anthropology, 1930–1980*. New York: Academic Press.

———, ed. 1997. *History of Physical Anthropology: An Encyclopedia*. 2 volumes. New York/London: Garland/Taylor & Francis.

Stanton, W. 1960. *The Leopard's Spots: Scientific Attitudes toward Race in America 1815–59*. Chicago: University of Chicago Press.

Stinson, S., B. Bogin, R. Huss-Ashmore, and M. O'Rourke, eds. 2000. *Human Biology: An Evolutionary and Biocultural Approach*. New York: John Wiley & Sons.

Stocking, G. W., Jr. 1968. *Race, Culture, and Evolution: Essays in the History of Anthropology*. New York: The Free Press.

Stumpf, M.P.H., and D. B. Goldstein. 2001. "Genealogical and Evolutionary Inference with the Human Y Chromosome." *Science* (291): 1738–1742.

Tattersall, I. 1998. "Neandertal Genes: What Do They Mean?" *Evolutionary Anthropology* (6): 157–158.

———. 2000. "Paleoanthropology: The Last Half-Century." *Evolutionary Anthropology* (7): 2–16.

Torroni, A., J. A. Miller, L. G. Moore, S. Zamudio, J. Zhuang, T. Droma, and D. C. Wallace. 1994. "Mitochondrial DNA Analysis in Tibet: Implications for the Origin of the Tibetan Population and Its Adaptation to High Altitude." *American Journal of Physical Anthropology* (93): 189–200.

Ulijaszek, S. J., F. E. Johnston, and M. A. Preece, eds. 1998. *The Cambridge Encyclopedia of Human Growth and Development*. Cambridge, UK: Cambridge University Press.

Walker, A. R., R.E.F. Leakey, J. M. Harris, and F. H. Brown. 1986. "2.5 myr *Australopithecus boisei* from West of Lake Turkana, Kenya." *Nature* (322): 517–522.

Washburn, S. L. 1951. "The New Physical Anthropology." *Transactions of the New York Academy of Sciences,* Series II (13): 298–304.

Weiss, K. M., K. K. Kidd, and J. R. Kidd. 1992. "Human Genome Diversity Project." *Evolutionary Anthropology* (1): 80–82.

White, T. D., G. Suwa, and B. Asfaw. 1994. "*Australopithecus ramidus,* A New Species of Early Hominid from Aramis, Ethiopia." *Nature* (371): 306–312.

———. 1995. "Corrigendum: *Australopithecus ramidus,* A New Species of Early Hominid from Aramis, Ethiopia." *Nature* (375): 88.

Wienker, C. W. 1995. "Jack Daniel and the AAA Guide." *Connective Tissue* (11): 4–5.

———. 1997. "Biological Anthropology: The Current State of the Discipline." In N. T. Boaz and L. D. Wolfe, eds. *Biological Anthropology, The State of the Science.* Bend, OR: International Institute for Human Evolutionary Research.

Wolpoff, M. 1998. "Concocting a Divisive Theory." *Evolutionary Anthropology* (7): 1–3.

Wolpoff, M., and R. Caspari. 1997. *Race and Human Evolution.* New York: Simon & Schuster.

Yannicelli, S., and A. S. Ryan. 1995. "Improvements in Behaviour and Physical Manifestations in Previously Untreated Adults with Phenylketonuria Using a Phenylalanine-Restricted Diet: A National Survey." *Journal of Inherited Metabolic Disorders* (18): 131–134.

Chapter 2

Teaching Physical Anthropology in a University: The Traditional Career

Curtis W. Wienker

Writing about a career teaching physical anthropology at a university is rather akin to writing about what it is like to undergo a colonoscopy or to visit Seattle. It is simply impossible to do justice to the experience with oral or written descriptions. One must truly experience it to appreciate everything that it is, in all of its marvelous nuances. This essay makes a stab at a written description that will hopefully give the reader who is contemplating a career teaching physical anthropology in a university a flavor of what to expect and, to a degree, how one might prepare for it.

What follows is slanted toward an academic career as a faculty member teaching physical anthropology at a comprehensive university, one that offers undergraduate and graduate programs in anthropology. Where relevant, comments are made with regard to how life in a four-year, baccalaureate-granting college or university might be different. To a faculty member, a career in a public or private institution is very similar, regardless of whether one's university is large and comprehensive or smaller and without a graduate program. Typically, all things being equal, private universities have a bit more flexibility built into everything about them, because they are usually not fueled directly with taxpayers' money and therefore accountable to politicians and to the public itself. Faculty in universities without anthropology graduate programs may find themselves teaching more and doing less research than those in institutions with anthropology graduate programs.

THE AUTHOR'S PERSPECTIVE

My undergraduate and graduate degrees are in anthropology; for the M.A. and Ph.D. degrees, I focused on physical anthropology. I earned my doctorate from the University of Arizona in 1975, where I studied under the supervision of Frederick Hulse. Then, my interests in physical anthropology were with living human biological variation, cultural influences on that variation, and African-derived New World populations. Today those interests remain, but they have been augmented with forensic anthropology, biomedical anthropology, and a geographic interest in Cubans and Cuban Americans.

I have been at the University of South Florida (USF), which has a master's and doctoral program in applied anthropology, since 1972. I was hired ABD (All But Dissertation) and completed the Ph.D. degree while functioning as a full-time instructor. During my tenure at USF, the anthropology department took a prominent orientation toward the applications of anthropology. The university as a whole matured (it opened in 1960) into a comprehensive and large institution, emphasizing graduate education and research. Accordingly, its standards for tenure and promotion have become correspondingly more rigorous over the years.

I was promoted to the rank of professor after a dozen years as a tenured associate professor. One reason for the lengthy time as associate professor was that I had a protracted period of administrative service related to academic matters. That assignment began on a small level and evolved into a full-time position.

My first administrative service was within the anthropology department; after a few years I moved into college-level academic administration. I then returned to regular faculty status for several years, but with a significant and less-than-typical service assignment related to intercollegiate athletics. A few years ago I accepted another full-time assignment in academic administration, at the university level.

During the course of my teaching career, I have been responsible for courses in basic anthropology, introductory biological anthropology, and a number of senior-level biological anthropology electives (research methods, human variation, paleoanthropology, primate biology, and forensic anthropology, for example) in the undergraduate program, as well as a physical anthropology core course in the master's program. I have supervised many master's theses, served on and chaired doctoral dissertation committees, and directed undergraduate honors thesis committees. Almost every semester I have supervised undergraduate students on some kind of independent study project. I have also taught our undergraduate anthropology honors seminar and an anthropology-related university honors program seminar.

For many years I have had a joint appointment in the department of pathology and laboratory medicine in USF's Medical School, and at one time a courtesy appointment in the department of criminology. I have been a member of or chaired countless departmental, college, and university committees throughout my career. I have also continued to be professionally active, even until now, in the arenas of biological and forensic anthropology, in terms of the activities of national scientific organizations and ongoing research related to physical anthropology.

BIOLOGICAL ANTHROPOLOGY IN THE ACADEMY

It is difficult to envision a profession that, if pursued effectively and successfully, yields the practitioner greater tangible and intangible rewards These are myriad and regular. However, that is getting ahead of the game—to consider the rewards of an academic career as a point of departure. Thus, they will be summarized at the end of this discussion, after a thorough review of what a faculty member teaching physical anthropology does professionally to realize those rewards.

Teaching, though, is just one of many activities the typical faculty member pursues. Today some aspects of the profession associated with teaching physical anthropology in a university are identical to what they were a generation ago. Others have changed somewhat in more recent years and still others are currently changing, as Cartmill (2000) has recently discussed.

This discussion focuses on a career teaching physical anthropology in an anthropology department of a university. Most of what follows is also generally applicable to biological anthropologists in academic units other than anthropology departments. Such positions are widespread among physical anthropologists. Some are housed in schools of medicine. Teaford's and McGarvey and James's contribution to this collection speak to such careers.

Physical anthropologists are also sometimes housed in joint academic departments (most typical of those is a department of sociology and anthropology, but there are many variations on the joint department model). That is frequently the case in smaller universities. Regardless, physical anthropologists in joint anthropology/some other discipline(s) departments usually teach physical anthropology, either exclusively or in addition to introductory anthropology and/or courses in another subdiscipline within anthropology.

Other physical anthropologists are scattered in academic units ranging from biology departments to schools of public health, in part because physical anthropologists have diverse kinds of scientific expertise. Physical anthropologists in such units are less likely to teach physical anthropology; however, these career tracks do not differ substantially from one in an anthropology department, in terms of one's professional activities and what is expected of one. Normally, physical anthropologists in such units teach subjects more akin to the disciplinary focus of the academic unit. In a biology department, for example, a physical anthropologist may teach evolution, genetics, and perhaps human biology. In a school of public health, that person might teach epidemiology and such topics as human disease or biocultural correlates of human disease.

CAREER PREPARATION

Physical anthropologists with appointments in anthropology or joint departments must have earned a Ph.D. in anthropology and almost invariably must have traditional expertise and interests. Wienker and Bennett (1992) delineate the many areas within biological anthropology and their relative popularity as of a decade ago. One's graduate training would best include some exposure to the major areas within physical anthropology and/or some substantial training in archaeology, for example. Most entry-level (typically assistant professorships) academic position vacancy announcements indicate desirable areas of teaching experience or expertise. Often more than one specialization is listed.

Vacancies in smaller institutions may call for applicants who can teach cultural and/or archaeological anthropology, especially for undergraduate audiences. If the position is as "*the*" biological anthropologist in an anthropology department, often applicants are asked to teach courses in the different major content areas within the field: osteology, paleoanthropology, primatology, and human biology/variation. Only in larger anthropology departments do vacancies typically carry a single area of emphasis (osteology/forensic anthropology, for example) in biological anthropology.

Today, because of the competitive academic marketplace, almost all entry-level university faculty positions require that the Ph.D. be earned prior to the onset of employment; most require the Ph.D. at the time of application. ABD applicants may be entertained. However, it is extraordinarily difficult to complete a dissertation while working full time as an academic (typically· faculty members spend much in excess of forty working hours a week, if they are to develop professionally, and achieve tenure and promotion). An ABD person who accepts full-time academic employment as a faculty member may well find that after two years on the job without completing the Ph.D., a terminal clause is part of the employment contract, should the doctorate not be earned by a specified date.

Research experience beyond one's dissertation work is a definite asset in preparing for a career teaching biological anthropology in a college or university. That is because, in addition to teaching, one is almost invariably expected to continue an active research program. This usually involves the supervision of students who also participate in the research, and may include supervising them in their own research programs. Thus, the more experience one has in research as a graduate student, the better one is prepared for the research expectations that come with an academic position. The same is true for teaching experience. Indeed, many academic vacancy announcements call for documented teaching experience and the demonstration of one's research productivity (reprints of publications, for example).

The traditional background of young Ph.D. biological anthropologists has typically not included a stint as a post-doctoral fellow following receipt of the doctoral degree. However, such a career course is probably becoming more common, as other contributors to this volume indicate. A post-doc could substantially enhance one's competitiveness in securing a tenure-track position in an academic department, anthropology or otherwise. In particular, tenure-track entry positions in biology departments usually call for some post-doctoral experience. The post-doc, usually a two-year position, gives the fledgling professional transitional experience in teaching and the supervision of graduate student research while permitting one to participate in research that often leads to publication. The post-doc experience only enhances the competitiveness of one's application portfolio with respect to competing for an entry-level faculty position in academia. Stone's contribution to this collection provides a more detailed overview of physical anthropology post-docs.

These qualities, teaching experience and publication, are highly valued by academic search committees. Demonstrable experience in teaching and publication are generally the qualities that get one's application portfolio into the stack of potential interviewees and into the stack of finalists, the legendary "short-list." Only a small number of finalists are invited for personal interviews at the institution with the vacancy.

GETTING THAT TENURE-TRACK POSITION

Advice about how to secure an entry-level academic position nowadays has filled books, and is really beyond the scope of this discussion. Some good sources for advice include one's major professor, other departmental faculty members, former graduate students who have successfully secured such positions, and the Internet.

Most positions that involve teaching physical anthropology in universities are advertised in the American Anthropology Association's *Anthropology News*, published monthly from September through May. These vacancies are also available online at http://www.aaanet.org/position.htm. The AAPA's Career Development Committee maintains an electronic list, http://www.pajobs@lists.cas.usf.edu, of professional opportunities related to physical anthropology. However, most of these positions, although they are usually at universities, are not in anthropology or joint anthropology departments.

The *Chronicle of Higher Education* has a careers page on the Internet, http://chronicle.com/jobs/archive/advicearch.htm, with lots of very useful information for someone seeking an entry-level academic position as a faculty member at a university. The Web page of the American Association of Physical Anthropologists (AAPA), http://www.physanth.org, lists some academic position announcements for biological anthropologists and also has a careers link. The latter resource includes a link to advice regarding the academic job search, developed by Dr. Kerry Feldman, a biological anthropologist at Portland State University. The Volume 1, No. 3 issue (Fall, 2000) of *Physical Anthropology*, the official newsletter of the AAPA, is primarily devoted to career advice. It is accessible at http://www.physanth.org.

Typically, application portfolios call for letters of recommendation and often a statement of one's research interests and plans, and teaching philosophy. These documents are very important and should be as focused and explicit as can be, but not lengthy. The application letter should be the same, and give an indication of why in particular one is interested in that specific position. The composition of one's academic resume, the Curriculum Vitae or CV, is also important. It should not be padded in any way and should highlight in chronological order from the recent year backward in time, postsecondary education, publications, grants, papers presented at academic conferences, and the academic/scientific honors/scholarships one has received. A good idea would be to ask a faculty member to review candidly a draft of one's first CV and provide constructive feedback. A good source of information and links pertinent to CVs of anthropologists can be found at http://web.lwc.edu/staff/ddalton/CVScoop.htm.

It is critically important for the potential applicant to learn as much information as possible about the vacancy, prior to applying. If one's application portfolio is clearly not suited to the specific parameters of the position, the time, expense, and energy expended in applying are almost always wasted. Basic professional responsibilities associated with the vacancy are generally discernible from the position announcement. Additional details regarding the position can be gleaned during the interview process. One needs a clear and explicit understanding of one's teaching assignments, especially the number and subject of the courses. Also pertinent is what, if any, teaching assistant help one will receive and the number of students that one can expect in a course. There is quite a difference in the amount of energy and time spent on, for example, a small graduate seminar and an introductory survey course taught in a large lecture hall.

Teaching assignments are a function of many things, including departmental and/or institutional policy and tradition, one's research assignment, class size, and the amount of student research supervision, and academic advising, if any, one is expected to do. Often, a new faculty member enjoys a reduced teaching load during the first year, to allow adjustment to the new university environment and to permit time to get a research agenda started. Also important is whether one is expected to teach a course that one has not taught before, one that will therefore involve a great deal of preparation on the part of the faculty member. New preparations are very time and energy consuming.

Finally, one should inquire as to the opportunities for summer teaching. Most faculty appointments do not include formal responsibilities during the summer (and no pay either!); for many faculty members, the ability to augment one's regular salary during the summer is highly desirable—after all, the rent is due, among other regular financial obligations.

A second vital piece of information to get before accepting a faculty position is the expectation with regard to research productivity; that must be played off against the teaching load and other professional obligations, in terms of one's work assignment. Faculty members with significant research assignments are usually expected, down the road, to be able to document the results and productivity of such work. It will not do the faculty member well to come up with reams of collected data and piles of statistical analyses. In academia, research productivity is measured by publications, presentations at academic conferences, and grants, for the most part.

A third very important topic to cover during the interview process is "start-up" costs. What does a new faculty member need to inaugurate a research agenda in terms of hard assets (e.g., computers, lab equipment and space, and expendable materials) and such other things as research assistants? Some universities might provide a new assistant professor with funds to support field or lab-based research during the first few summers at the institution and/or a research assistant to contribute time and expertise to the fledgling research program. Most institutions expect that soon into one's professional career, external grants will be secured to underwrite ongoing and future costs of research.

However, in smaller universities, funded, ongoing research on the part of a new assistant professor (the typical rank upon entry to academia) might not be as important, and therefore start-up costs might not be as significant a concern to a prospective candidate. Often, departments without graduate programs expect faculty to involve undergraduates in research of some sort.

If one is fortunate enough to be offered an assistant professorship, the contractual agreement between the faculty member and the university is very important. It specifies, among other things, the conditions upon which renewal of employment is contingent. Know, even informally, before you accept employment, what the future holds, to the extent that you can. Most contracts indicate that one's appointment is a specified time frame of less than twelve months, and contain language related to the conditions of renewal and how much notice of termination is given. Most regular faculty positions involve employment (and pay) for the three-quarters or two semesters of the regular academic year, beginning in the fall and ending in the late spring or early summer.

There are a number of important questions related to continuing employment. Assuming satisfactory performance, what kind of job security is involved? Is there a tenure system, and, if so, what are the conditions, expectations, and timetable involved? If not, is there provision for continuing employment? What are the specifics? Is there a faculty union, and, if so, what does that mean to a new assistant professor in terms of obligations and possible benefits?

Many universities today, especially public ones, have faculty unions. A discussion of the pros and cons is beyond the scope of this presentation, but knowing about one, if you are going to work in such a system, is important knowledge to have up-front.

Finally, at some point before signing a contract, it is wise to inquire about one or two other things, depending on one's situation. Many universities will pay some to all of the costs of moving. All one can do is ask, be laughed at, and told no. Second is to inquire, if it is relevant and important, about the employment possibilities for one's spouse or significant other. These, like most other possible conditions of employment, may be subject to negotiation before a contract is finally signed.

ENTERING THE PROFESSORATE

Today most universities have accountability mechanisms for academic matters. What this means to a faculty member is that you often formally state or negotiate with your chairperson, at the onset of the academic year, what your professional intentions are for the year—how much of your energy and time will be dedicated to teaching, research and service (more about these individually later). Then, typically at the conclusion of the academic year, one is evaluated on one's performance, often with the intentions as a benchmark.

Almost all faculty members at universities typically participate in some sort of annual evaluation exercise. The annual evaluation usually calls for a formal report of the faculty member's teaching, research, and service activities and accomplishments for the year; documentation of these may be required. Thus, keeping a list of activities and accomplishments as they occur, and documentation relevant to them, can only serve a faculty member well, in the long run. Typically the department chair and a committee of peers elected by the department's faculty evaluate a faculty member's performance in teaching, research, and service. The faculty member receives written notification of the results of the evaluation and may have the opportunity to respond to it. The evaluation may form the basis for salary raises for the upcoming academic year. This process is extremely important and should be taken very seriously.

For untenured faculty or those in a system of periodic contract renewal based on continuing satisfactory performance, the annual evaluation may include statements with regard to the faculty member's progress toward tenure or contract renewal and promotion. It is critical for a new assistant professor to understand this process upon institutional entry, if he or she is to benefit from it professionally. In particular, a working knowledge of institutional standards for tenure/renewal/retention and promotion is paramount entry-level knowledge for any new faculty member.

Tenure/renewal/retention is usually a function of teaching quality, research productivity, and, to a lesser extent, service. It is typically not enough to be effective and satisfactory. One must usually be at least a good teacher, and have demonstrated visibility as a researcher beyond one's institution and region to get promoted, to be granted tenure, or to have some kind of job security. Nowadays, one is also expected to be a collegial colleague to achieve tenure and promotion.

Research productivity is more important in comprehensive universities, and less so at institutions without graduate programs. For new faculty subject to strong research productivity as a criterion for promotion and job security, it is paramount to protect the time one sets aside for research. It is easy for such time to erode as one's energies are expended on service activities, for example.

Usually, universities sponsor a number of institutional programs to support new and especially beginning faculty members. These programs tend to be fully developed in comprehensive universities and less well developed, in some respects, in smaller institutions or those without graduate programs. For example, most universities have orientations for new faculty at the onset of the new academic year. In addition to exposing the participant to the tangible benefits of employment (health insurance, etc.), academically related information (such as the institution's grading scale, calendar, and attendance policy) is provided. Many institutions have mentoring programs in which a new faculty member is paired with an experienced one. The relationship between the two faculty members and the nature of the program itself is highly variable. Some programs are well structured and others less so.

Another institutional office common at universities today, one with activities geared toward new faculty members, is a center oriented toward quality pedagogy. Such centers, devoted to teaching enhancement, offer different kinds of programs, ranging from test composition to institutional technology resources available for the support of teaching. Also, many universities have internal research grant and/or professional travel programs targeted at helping new faculty get their research programs and professional organization activity up and running.

Today's university strives to make the new assistant professor's transition to the professorate a smooth one. Nevertheless, it is probably not possible to fully prepare oneself for a career teaching physical anthropology in a university. There is a lot more, in terms of expectations, than meets the eye. Moreover, there are many, many professional nuances that one acquires with experience.

One certainty is that technology has changed the professional activities of all physical anthropologists dramatically in the last decade or so. That is particularly true of the Internet. The future of the professorate will undoubtedly change, perhaps in ways that are not envisionable now, and perhaps in ways that are not all positive. Cartmill's (2000) brief essay touches upon some of the possible ways the Internet may impact our teaching and research, and it will probably impact service activities we undertake too. Teaching, research, and service comprise the typical institution's expectations of almost all faculty members, and these three parameters of professional activity are the usual responsibilities of all physical anthropologists who teach the subject in university settings.

TEACHING, RESEARCH, AND SERVICE

Teaching duties involve classroom experiences, the supervision of students on their research (and sometimes on their teaching), and a lot of "behind the scenes" kinds of activities. There is also more to conducting research than undertaking an investigation through to the successful completion of a written report. As well, there are several different kinds of service activities that one may well be expected to pursue. Faculty members, within that professional framework, enjoy enormous freedom and have considerable choice. However, associated with that freedom is a concomitant amount of responsibility involved in all of a faculty member's professional activity. And although these activities are considered separately in this discussion, often they feed back into one another. One often incorporates the results of a research project into one's courses. In that regard, the interface between teaching and research is not unlike the synergistic relationships between tool use, bipedalism, and cranial capacity in early hominids, a topic that we always cover in our basic physical anthropology courses.

Teaching

Teaching is a great challenge with equally great rewards. It is usually not possible to gain tenure by simply being an adequate teacher, regardless of how accomplished a researcher one might be. A generation ago, classroom teaching was simply lectures, readings, audiovisual supplements, and classroom discussion of what one was learning. Today there is a lot more to it than that.

Technology has drastically altered the classroom experience for the faculty members and students alike. Today's technology, with the seemingly unlimited resources of the World Wide Web and CD ROMs, gives faculty members the ability to engage students in the learning experience to a degree unimagined a generation ago. A generation ago, planning for a new semester's class was simple. One ordered the textbook and teacher's guide (which might well have contained very helpful "canned" essays, short answer objectives, and multiple-choice exam questions, as well as topics for classroom discussion) and composed the syllabus. Planning for and conducting a course today involves more preparation, in seeing that students experience a well-structured, meaningful learning experience, given the many technological tools related to biological anthropology that are available today.

Planning a course in physical anthropology, regardless of whether it is an introduction to the subject or a course focusing on one of the many topical areas within the discipline and regardless of whether it is undergraduate or graduate-level, is particularly labor-intensive because of the importance of giving students hands-on learning experiences. Indeed, at many universities, introductory physical anthropology has weekly lab sessions linked to the lecture topics. Also, exposure to fossil casts, human and nonhuman primate skeletal material, and the techniques of anthropometry, for example, are desirable parts of the learning experience in graduate and undergraduate physical anthropology courses. Thus, planning for and the conduct of such learning sessions involve extra planning, time, and energy. At some universities, anthropology departments employ student help, often in the form of teaching assistants (TAs), to help the faculty member. It is common practice, but by no means universal, that TAs are actually partly or fully responsible for the lab sessions, under the supervision of the faculty member.

There are not many recent published resources related to teaching physical anthropology. Durham's (1992) compendium of audiovisual resources is dated but still useful, especially for some basic, if not classic listings. Hoopes et al. (1999) is oriented toward Internet resources for students; it is very basic and focuses on each of the subfields of anthropology. Rice and McCurdy (2000) have some material relevant to physical anthropology.

Another significant aspect of teaching physical anthropology is supervising students on independent study efforts (a guided reading program or research project, sometimes involved with the faculty member's research program), including undergraduate theses (most often associated with an honors program internal or external to the department), master's thesis, and doctoral dissertations. These are almost invariably a one-on-one phenomena that require the regular and direct attention and supervision (and therefore energy and time) of the faculty member. As such, they are labor intensive because of the often unique nature of each project. Usually these projects are at the solicitation of the student, but an enterprising faculty member needing help with some aspect of his or her research program may initiate the activity.

It is best to have a clear, if not codified, understanding of what is expected of each participant in these "outside the classroom" educational endeavors. A well-supervised student independent study project (a thesis or otherwise) can on occasion yield the faculty member and student unexpected rewards (a professional conference presentation or even a publication). The opposite is also true: the lack of effective supervision may lead to a botched project, an unrealized opportunity, interpersonal animosity, and wasted time, energy, and effort.

Three other phenomena associated with teaching physical anthropology deserve comment. One is that, frequently, the physical anthropologist (especially in a smaller department) may be called on to teach introductory anthropology. That requires special planning, and one may profit considerably from seeking the advice of other anthropologists in the department who teach basic anthropology.

A second is team-teaching, which may well be more frequent and popular today than in the past. It requires additional planning and coordination, so as to make the academic experience a meaningful one for the students, simply because the physical anthropologist is working with one or more colleagues.

Third, and perhaps most important, is that being a good teacher has the very positive result of recruiting students for future courses. If the introduction to anthropology is well taught, you will find that some of the students who enjoyed that class register in the basic physical anthropology course, and so on. The net result is that being a good undergraduate teacher can yield the benefit of ultimately bringing talented and well-prepared students to pursue postgraduate study under your supervision. This scenario can result in the existence of an intellectual or scientific legacy, as it were.

Any number of details go into one's teaching, and although they are details, they are by no means trivial. Regular office hours are kept, and it is important to be available to students for any number of reasons, which may or may not relate to teaching itself. Another detail is maintaining accurate records regarding the evaluation of students. Seeing to the availability of assigned readings aside from textbooks requires time, regardless of how it is accomplished (preparation by a private photocopy enterprise or posting such readings to the Web using resources provided by the university's library, for example). Indeed the selection of specific readings requires thought, as well as time. The same is true of selecting textbooks, if they are used. The nuance of details associated with teaching physical anthropology are also characteristic of doing research.

Research

Often, a doctoral student's dissertation research is related to some aspect of his or her major professor's research program. A faculty member is typically expected to carry on an independent, and often self-supporting, research program. At comprehensive universities, a further expectation often is that graduate students are supported by and involved with this research. At baccalaureate-level institutions, the importance of a research program to a faculty member's tenurability and promotion varies. It is sometimes the case at such universities, that it is desirable, if not expected, for undergraduate students be involved in your research. There is a true synergy to involving students in research and teaching. The results of the research feed back into teaching, as they are disseminated to graduate and undergraduate students in the classroom and on a one-on-one basis, as described earlier in the teaching section. Research in comprehensive universities is usually the linchpin to tenure. It typically must be of sufficient quality, quantity, and visibility to bring credit to the institution and to withstand (if that is the word) the professional scrutiny of peers within and external to your university.

A research program typically has cohesion to it, a common scientific, geographic, temporal, or theoretical thread that integrates different research projects. However, the research program probably should not be so solidly cast in stone and direction so as to preclude major changes in orientation. In my own case, after a number of years, because our anthropology department implemented an applied graduate program, I intentionally began to focus some of my professional time and research on forensic anthropology. That aspect of my professional involvement continues today and is very enjoyable.

After twenty years of a purely domestic research agenda, the opportunity to conduct investigations in Havana with Cuban colleagues presented itself in the early 1990s, and I jumped at the chance. That experience unquestionably has been the most rewarding of my professional life, and among the most rewarding of my entire life.

The bottom line to a research program is productivity, which is typically measured by grants, publications, and conference presentations. Grants to support research are highly valued for a number of reasons. Publications are typically valued more than conference presentations.

Grants have several positive aspects. One is that many, if not most, grants have a portion of funds dedicated to institutional overhead, to defray the costs the institution incurs as a result of the grant. Usually a portion of grant overhead funds is returned to the department and then on to the grantee. These resources may be used with some discretion to support research-related activities, including travel to academic conferences. Another asset to obtaining a grant is that it may have funds to buy the faculty member out of teaching (funds to hire someone else to teach a course), permitting the extra time needed to conduct the investigation. Also, grant funds can provide one with a partial or even full salary during the summer, when many academics are not employed or paid. Often grant funds support research assistants and graduate students, who do important work, including data collection and analysis, during the investigation.

Publishing is highly valued by virtually all universities, including those with academic missions primarily involving teaching and education. That is because publishing gives the university, the department, and the faculty member visibility within the profession. The greater the visibility, the more value. Obviously, publishing in outlets that give one visibility around the world (internationally known journals or publishing companies) is more valued than outlets with regional visibility. Typically, publishing is the most important aspect of research with respect to tenure and promotion, in research-oriented universities. Usually promotion and tenure come with documented national, professional visibility and external reviews of tenure/promotion packages by nationally known colleagues with some expertise in the research area.

Publications that are sole-authored are valued more than those jointly authored, and it is much better to be the senior author than the second author. High value publications include books, monographs, and articles in peer-reviewed journals. The scope and visibility of the journal are important. However, because physical anthropology research touches upon many topics relevant to other disciplines (anatomy, biology, paleontology, ethology, genetics, etc.), it is not critical that the journals in which one publishes are anthropology journals. Much more important is the scientific reputation and visibility of the journal. Although a forensic anthropology research report could easily be published in the *American Journal of Physical Anthropology,* it might just as appropriately appear in, for example, the *Journal of Forensic Sciences,* or any of several osteology- or anatomy-oriented journals, without meaningful loss of value.

Although presentations at academic conference have some value in terms of research productivity, their real scientific importance and value are of a different kind. First, academic conference presentations of one's current research give the investigator an excellent opportunity to get immediate professional feedback from knowledgeable colleagues. Second is that such presentations allow the faculty member to form professional relationships (and friendships that may turn out to have professional benefits in the future) that may positively impact your future research agenda. Such relationships may lead to collaboration on a future research project of mutual interest between you and a colleague or colleagues from another university in the United States or overseas. Indeed, such relationships may also positively impact one's teaching and service too. Such professional networks, almost always formed at academic conferences, serve physical anthropologists well throughout their professional careers.

Therefore, it behooves the physical anthropologist to give polished professional presentations. Few things are more difficult at academic conferences than being part of an audience for a presentation that is ill prepared, rambling, and too long, given the time constraints of the scientific program. Such a presentation may actually negatively impact the opportunity to build professional networks.

A discussion of university-based physical anthropology research would be incomplete without touching on the institutional review process, liability, and collaboration. All universities have a process whereby research using human and other animal subjects undergoes review prior to the initiation of the work to determine the propriety of the research in all its aspects. It is important to learn the particulars of the institutional review process very early on, so that if it does pertain to one's research, adequate planning for it can be made.

Liability is another important issue related to a research program. One should learn institutional policy regarding what, if any, liability is involved with performing research, and particularly with involving students in research, especially in field settings.

For example, it may be that institutional liability coverage is pertinent to students that a faculty member supervises in research *if* students are enrolled in credit for the experience, but not otherwise, unless, perhaps, the students are paid and are then considered employees of the university. One can never be too careful in learning the ropes with respect to liability involving research. An ounce of prevention in this case is probably much more significant that a kilogram of cure.

Physical anthropologists, because the field is related to so many other sciences, such as medicine and genetics, to name just two, often collaborate with colleagues in the discipline and in other fields. Such research is rewarding in ways that individual investigations cannot be. My perception is that collaborative research is growing in prevalence, and perhaps popularity. It is important, going into such projects, that all parties have an explicit understanding of their role in the project and in project outcomes, such as authorship of publications.

Service

Although virtually all universities expect most faculty members to undertake some service activity, typically this is less important than teaching and research. Service activity usually does not involve nearly the expenditure of time and effort. I have found it beneficial to keep a running ledger of my service activities, including individual osteological consultations (identifying the bone a citizen finds in her garden, for instance), for reporting purposes during the course of the annual evaluation exercise. That is because some service activities tend to be ad hoc and escape one's memory before very long. Service activities fall into three categories: university, professional, and public.

All institutions expect faculty to be involved in some university service. Typically this involves serving on committees at the department, college, or university level having to do with some aspect of university life. Such aspects include undergraduate and graduate curricula, research, student advising, student activities, and many other matters related to university life. When such service entails membership on a committee beyond the anthropology department, it gives the faculty member an opportunity to interact with other faculty and staff. This interaction can lead to possible future professional activity. My joint appointment in USF's College of Medicine's department of pathology and laboratory medicine is a direct result of such university service.

University service activity, as is the case with my career, may eventually lead to administrative opportunities related to anthropology, or to the broader nature of the university. Many years ago I temporarily filled in as graduate program director in our anthropology department, when the incumbent took a sabbatical. A year later the role became vacant, and I accepted it as a regular part of my service assignment. I performed those duties for seven years.

Eventually the anthropology graduate directorship led to academically related service in the dean's office and broader administrative responsibilities. As a consequence, I enjoyed more university support of my professional travel as a physical anthropologist, and a summer salary to boot. Service in the dean's office ultimately led me to another administrative opportunity at the university level. Many academics would probably abhor administrative opportunities, but for me they have been rewarding personally and economically. However, had I not continued to be active in physical anthropology and in my home department while administrating, that service would not have been nearly as rewarding professionally.

Many institutions expect faculty also to be involved, even to a very small degree, with service to the profession or discipline. Such activities range from the obvious—editing a journal or serving the AAPA in some formal capacity, for example—to the less obvious, such as reviewing grant applications for the National Science Foundation or reviewing books or manuscripts for professional journals. Greater value is generally associated with the added national visibility that such service might bring to the faculty member's department and university.

Active involvement in the profession, especially via academic organizations such as the AAPA and many others, can lead to opportunities for collaborative work, work that may be important to one's professional development, if undertaken early in a career. My active participation in the annual meeting of the Physical Anthropology Section of the American Academy of Forensic Sciences and in the affairs of the AAPA has given me such opportunities.

Volunteering to serve on a committee of a professional association is one way to begin such service. Another is to organize a symposium or serve as a session moderator for part of the scientific agenda of an association's annual meeting. I have viewed such activity as a way to give back to physical anthropology—reciprocity to the discipline that has been so rewarding to me over the years.

Full engagement in the profession of physical anthropology as a faculty member teaching the subject involves significant research activity and some service activity. Full engagement, doing pretty much what one wants to in a field one loves, is a reward that is probably enjoyed much less frequently in professions outside the academy. Indeed there are many rewards to a career teaching physical anthropology in a university.

THE REWARDS

These rewards are plentiful and both tangible and intangible. Of course, they depend, to a great degree, on being a good teacher, a cooperative and cheerful colleague, an unselfish servant, and a productive researcher—year in and year out.

Perhaps the most tangible reward is job security, if one's professional accomplishments are commensurate with that honor, given institutional standards—tenure. Typically tenure is job security beyond what one would find in the private sector, in business and industry, for example. Tenured faculty members typically only lose their academic positions under the most extreme circumstances, such as gross professional or personal malfeasance, or an extraordinary economic calamity at the institution.

A second tangible benefit is a decent salary, with opportunities to supplement one's salary for the regular academic year with summer teaching. A third is that most regular faculty members have reasonably priced, if not gratis, health, dental, and life insurance for themselves and their families, as well as the opportunity to participate in solid investment programs. Another tangible fringe benefit is participation in a reasonable and secure pension program. Some universities provide tuition waivers for the faculty member's family. Most universities reimburse faculty members for travel to academic meetings; however, the parameters of that support vary widely (partial to full reimbursement, for example) and may require the faculty member to be on the scientific agenda or an officer of the organization sponsoring the meeting.

Most universities today have a sabbatical program of some sort. A sabbatical is usually a paid leave from teaching and service activity and may be either for an entire academic year or part of one. The sabbatical may be at partial or full pay. It typically permits a faculty member to focus on research productivity. At some universities, sabbaticals are automatically granted upon request, within particular, specific time constraints. At other institutions the program may be competitive. Regardless, sabbaticals are usually only infrequently taken, perhaps only every five to ten years or so.

Another tangible benefit that many faculty members enjoy is that there are staff people and often student employees in the department to provide help with the mundane day-to-day tasks of academic life, such as photocopying and errand running. Other less evident tangible benefits exist because of the nature of academic life.

Most anthropologists are rather laid back people and often faculty will find that professional dress standards in the classroom are not as formal as they once were. Another very positive asset in a faculty member's life is the ability, within certain limits and constraints (departmental needs and the nature of the student body), to set one's own daily schedule. An academic life is typically not an 8:00–5:00, Monday–Friday circadian rhythm; there is usually the luxury of "setting one's hours."

Despite the number and nature of the significant tangible benefits of an academic career, the intangible ones are perhaps the most rewarding. There is never a larger paycheck because of them, but in a certain sense they are priceless in that it is impossible to buy them. These are the rewards associated with contributing to the education and enlightenment of students, mostly young men and women, year after year. This occurs in the classroom, in your office, and also in your research—in the laboratory or in the field. With respect to the latter, it is palpable when an instructor is present as a student first obtains the results of an analysis of data, or discovers an unusual feature in a skeleton, for example.

Most rewarding is to hear from former students who have continued their training in biological anthropology because of your influence, or to encounter them at professional meetings, where they are beginning their professional lives as scholars and scientists. In that regard, having an intellectual legacy is perhaps the ultimate intangible benefit of an academic life teaching physical anthropology.

Indeed, the list of tangible benefits noted a bit earlier is a lot longer than the list of intangible ones I have listed. However, if one considers the intangible rewards in terms of the number of students whose lives have been touched during the course of a career teaching physical anthropology in a university, it is the intangible that are most numerous and of a quality nonexistent in tangible rewards. They are also largely nonexistent in professions outside of academia, because of the inherent nature of teaching—having students to learn from you.

An intangible benefit of a sort is that faculty members, college professors, are usually accorded a good deal of respect by the public-at-large and by one's neighbors and acquaintances in the community. People generally hold relatively high regard for those who have invested the many years of postgraduate effort that are required to earn a doctoral degree.

Given the many rewards to the traditional career of a physical anthropologist, it should not be surprising that there are some less than desirable aspects to it. However, they are not nearly as many as the rewards, nor are they as negative as shortcomings as the rewards are positive.

THE DOWNSIDE

For the most part, once a physical anthropologist has received tenure by a university, opportunities for a switch in career paths as well as for a move to another university are rare. The skills attendant to a successful academic career teaching physical anthropology are not usually readily marketable in the nonacademic sector, either private or public. Individuals with especially strong academic research portfolios in paleoanthropology or bioarchaeology may occasionally find such opportunities in museums (see Ubelaker's chapter for more detail about museum-based careers). Someone with good academic research experience related to biomedical anthropology may find an occasional opportunity in a medical school or a private or public health or disease-related research enterprise (see Garruto's and Martorell's contributions to this volume for details regarding such health/disease careers outside of the university setting). But such opportunities are about all that are currently available.

In other words, one downside is that upon receiving tenure, a faculty member is usually pretty well locked into his or her career track and university. The latter is in part the case because senior (associate and full professor) vacancies teaching physical anthropology are very infrequently advertised. When an anthropology department receives permission to replace a senior physical anthropologist, it is usually authorized to hire an assistant professor. That unbalanced replacement typically saves the university considerable salary money. For the same economic reason, new positions in an anthropology department are almost invariably advertised at the junior (assistant professor) level.

Other downsides are rather trivial, but they are part of one's career teaching physical anthropology—they come with the job. They include the occasional problem student and sometimes having to interact with a problem student's parents. Other shortcomings are the inevitable forms associated with being a faculty member and having to say no from time to time.

In some universities, especially larger and public ones, regardless of whether they offer a graduate program in anthropology, the amount of bureaucratically-related paperwork is at times a little overwhelming and a little much. Most of it has to do with accountability to the university and its external constituencies (including taxpayers). Here at USF if I were to move a piece of equipment from my office, where I might have used it for some time, to a storage area nearby, or to take it off campus for on-site research use, there are forms to be filled out and approved *a priori*. The approvals may merely be internal to the anthropology department or they may include additional layers of university administration. Each year I must file, again before the fact, a form reporting anticipated forensic anthropology consultation activity. I have found it best just to do what is expected accurately and in a timely fashion. That minimizes the likelihood of other hassles.

About the only other drawback to teaching physical anthropology in a university that comes to mind is that a good teacher, unselfish servant, and productive researcher has to learn to say no. If one does the job well, new opportunities and requests for involvement with some project, event, or cause regularly come forth. It is both unprofessional and embarrassing to accept an assignment or invitation to be involved with some kind of professional activity and to ultimately have to renege or do less than a good job on it. The best way to avoid such jeopardy is to say no and provide a thoughtful explanation why, in terms of one's current and anticipated responsibilities. I have also found it useful to be able to suggest someone else who might be interested in and willing to undertake such projects when I am unable to.

A cursory tally of the shortcomings and rewards yields a clear result: The positive aspects of a career teaching physical anthropology in a university overwhelm the very few negative aspects involved. That makes, in my mind, such a career highly desirable.

CONCLUSION

I have been blessed in my career, even before accepting the position at USF. I had the extreme good fortune to have a choice of academic positions when I entered the career marketplace late in 1971. Ken Bennett (1979) has shown that physical anthropology passed a sort of Rubicon in about 1975. Prior to then, there were more vacancies in higher education for those seeking a career teaching physical anthropology. Since then, the production of Ph.D. physical anthropologists has far exceeded the academic market's ability to absorb them, especially into anthropology departments.

What, then, does the future hold for students now in graduate school and those who come after them? The cohort of physical anthropologists hired by anthropology departments during the 1960s and 1970s are in the process of retiring and that will continue to take place for another decade or so. To the extent that anthropology departments are able to convince their universities that these physical anthropologists should be replaced with new physical anthropologists, the job market should not be as bad as it was perhaps ten years ago. Indeed the market may improve beyond its current status, which is not bad.

I would encourage any physical anthropology graduate student so-inclined to aspire to a career teaching the subject in a university. Every day is different; there is surely no rut in this career. It does, like most professions, require flexibility. Knowing what I know now, I would not have changed anything during my more than twenty-eight years here, to any significant degree. My entry-level blessing has followed me throughout the years. I would do it all over again, in a heartbeat.

However, teaching physical anthropology in a university is not the career for everyone. There are many other opportunities, for those who are not into teaching, or not very good at it. The other contributions to this collection introduce the curious reader to many, but not all, career opportunities for physical anthropologists.

REFERENCES

Bennett, K. A. 1979. "Trends and Developments in Physical Anthropology, 1978–79." *American Journal of Physical Anthropology* (51): 393–402.

Cartmill, M. 2000. "A View of the Science: Physical Anthropology at the Millennium." *American Journal of Physical Anthropology* (113): 145–149.

Durham, N. M. 1992. "Review of Audiovisual Materials for Use in Teaching Biological Anthropology." *Yearbook of Physical Anthropology* (36): 59–70.

Hoopes, J. W., J. Campbell, and M. Keene. 1999. *Mayfield's Quick View Guide to the Internet for Anthropology, 2ⁿᵈ ed.* Mountain View, CA: Mayfield.

Rice, P. C., and D. W. McCurdy, eds. 2000. *Strategies in Teaching Anthropology.* Upper Saddle River, NJ: Prentice-Hall.

Wienker, C. W., and K. A. Bennett. 1992. "Trends and Developments in Physical Anthropology, 1990–91." *American Journal of Physical Anthropology* (87): 383–393.

Chapter 3

Teaching Physical Anthropology in the Community College

Philip L. Stein

An essential part of the majority of careers presented in this volume is teaching or training. For many professional anthropologists, teaching is not simply a facet of our professional lives; teaching is the focus of our interest and one of our great joys. I have been teaching at the same community college for thirty-six years. Here I would like to present community college teaching as a career path for those seeking a lifetime experience within the realm of physical anthropology.

Community colleges, and other two-year colleges, are degree-granting institutions of higher learning that are associated with local communities. Some are very small with just a few hundred students; other have enrollments exceeding 30,000 students. Although more students tend to be from the local area than at a university, many community colleges, especially those with special programs, have a sizable number of out-of-state and international students. Few have on-campus housing.

Being local institutions, community colleges often serve as a stepping-stone between high school and the university for many students. They offer instruction at the freshman and sophomore level that parallels instruction at the four-year college and university and prepares students for transfer to the four-year institution in their junior year. In addition, community colleges provide extensive programs in remedial education and vocational or technical education.

There are 1,742 two-year degree-granting institutions in the United States, which account for about 43 percent of all degree-granting colleges and universities. Community and two-year colleges enrolled in 1996–1997, the latest year for which information is available, 5,563,327 students, or 38.7 percent of all students enrolled in degree-granting institutions of higher learning (U.S. Department of Education, 1998).

Community colleges are diverse institutions. Most are independent public colleges under the control of locally or state elected or appointed boards (95.5 percent of two-year colleges are public compared with 66 percent of four-year institutions) (U.S. Department of Education, 1998). Several colleges may be grouped together to form a community college district. Some two-year colleges are branches of a university that bring the first two years of college education closer to the students' homes.

Community college classes are small, and instructors are focused on teaching. Students have direct access to instructors and are not insulated from the professor by teaching assistants. Support services, such as tutoring and computer labs, are usually well developed.

COMMUNITY COLLEGE STUDENTS

What are community college students like? A community college class is not a class of eighteen- and nineteen-year-old full-time students who have completed college-prep programs at their high schools, although such students do enroll. A community college class contains a much greater diversity of students.

Many community college students are qualified to enter the university. However, they choose to begin their college career at their local community college because it is close to home and it is relatively inexpensive. For many students, the low fees reduce the total amount of needed student loans. Many students spend their first two years working part time saving money to pay the higher tuition and living costs at the university, which they can enter in their junior year. Community colleges are more flexible than many universities in that students can enroll part time; they may take classes in the day and evening, and often on weekends.

Many community colleges have agreements with nearby universities guaranteeing students university admission in their junior year. This is especially true in situations where universities have large numbers of freshman applicants and wish to focus more on upper division and graduate education. These students automatically transfer to the university if they maintain a set grade point average in the community college. At my college preadmitted university students are required to take a number of special honors courses which are limited to an enrollment of twenty-five students, all of whom have completed the first semester of freshman English. (Since many of the universities that our students transfer to accept physical anthropology for general education, physical anthropology is routinely offered as a honors class.)

Historically, students who complete their first two years of college work at a community college often maintain a higher junior/senior grade point average than those students who begin at the university as freshmen.

Others who qualify for freshman university admission may attend the university only to enter the community college after their first year. Some students may have found that they are too immature to succeed and are returning to the community college for a second chance. Some have difficulty working in the world of large impersonal lectures. Others need to work to support themselves and find greater scheduling flexibility and lower cost at the community college.

In addition to the more traditional college student, community college students include students who cannot afford to go to the university or must remain in their local communities because of family obligations; older people who have finished raising their families and now want a college education; people in the workforce who want a college degree and want to upgrade their skills; first-generation children of immigrants, the first in their families to go to college, who feel the need to remain with a supportive family; students with learning disabilities; and students who are unprepared for college work and need to upgrade skills, primarily in math and English.

Many students enroll in two-year programs with the ultimate goal of earning a two-year associate degree. Although few colleges actually offer an associate degree in anthropology, my college has developed a certificate of achievement for students who complete a series of four to five courses in anthropology.

Anthropology is involved to a limited degree in vocational or occupational training. Although there are few vocational programs leading to a degree in anthropology (a program in Archaeological Technician comes to mind), anthropology may be a required course for other programs. Examples at my college are cultural anthropology for nursing students and anthropological linguistics for the Interpreter for the Deaf Program.

You will find relatively few anthropology majors in a community college anthropology class. My college has a relatively large program, yet a survey done in the early 1990s revealed that about 0.3 percent of all students are declared anthropology majors and less than 4 percent of students enrolled in anthropology classes are majors.

TEACHING PHYSICAL ANTHROPOLOGY AT A COMMUNITY COLLEGE

What is it like teaching at a community college? Unlike the university, the emphasis at the community college is on teaching. Teaching loads, usually between twelve and fifteen hours a week, are high when compared with university standards. But there are few obligations beyond teaching other than office hours and, perhaps, some presence on campuswide committees. Classes tend to be small, and the instructor is involved with all aspects of teaching. There is time to meet and talk with students and to assist students on a one-on-one basis. However, there are usually no teaching assistants or readers.

Teaching has always taken a backseat to other issues in both the American Anthropological Association and the American Association of Physical Anthropologists. University faculty focus on research and publishing, and some, certainly not all, treat teaching as a necessary evil. News reports occasionally surface in campus newspapers about popular professors who perish because of their failure to publish and bring in grant funds.

Also, and I believe that this is all too often overlooked, the health of physical anthropology, including physical anthropology at research universities, depends on an educated public. Much of our subject matter excites the nonanthropological community, and there is a lot of misinformation out there. College and university administrators, who have a profound effect upon our employment, budgets, and position of our departments in the institution, are usually not anthropologists. An understanding of what anthropology is all about, most likely gained from a general education course, lets them know what we are about. This is especially critical when our campus administrators are faced with an ever-militant segment of our community opposed to the teaching of evolution in the classroom. Elementary and high school teachers of science need to understand evolutionary theory and to have an acquaintance with the anthropological subject matter for the same reason. We should agree with Conrad Kottak that "anthropology is valuable, that it has commitments, that teaching is a central part of our field, that anthropology has something to say to the public, and that we should be saying it to a wider audience" (Kottak, 1997:1).

FOUR-FIELDS ANTHROPOLOGY

The community college is the last bastion of four-fields anthropology. However, to many anthropologists, such as myself, this is highly desirable. Because of the number of classes that I teach, I find it intellectually satisfying to teach other courses besides physical anthropology and the physical anthropology lab. I also teach the anthropology of religion. Although I specialize in physical anthropology, I value the opportunity to explore other aspects of the field.

This four-field emphasis is certainly in opposition to what is happening in many four-year and graduate institutions where at most a physical anthropology student takes a single additional course in cultural anthropology and archaeology. In 1990–1991, members of the American Association of Physical Anthropologists were surveyed about their training. C. W. Wienker and K. A. Bennett write:

These results indicate without doubt that the traditional four-field or holistic anthropological approach toward training physical anthropology graduate students is no longer applicable. Cultural anthropology is thought to be of only marginal importance to our field. . . . It seems apparent that the great majority of physical anthropologists feel that graduate students in departments still demanding the holistic approach cannot be adequately prepared for a future professional career in physical anthropology unless these students further their education with postdoctoral research in more relevant areas. (Wienker and Bennett, 1992:388)

Yet community college teaching demands a generalized holistic training. As college enrollments increase during the next decade, will there be enough candidates for teaching positions with adequate training for two-year college teaching, that is, holistic training?

The subject matter in lower division anthropology tends to focus primarily on hominid evolution. A good idea of the subject matter can be gleaned by reviewing the tables of content of the major textbooks in the field. Subjects usually include Mendelian genetics, population genetics, evolutionary theory, human variation, primatology, and paleoanthropology.

What is missing? If we look at Wienker and Bennett's list of research interests among physical anthropologists, subjects that usually do not appear in community college courses include growth and development, dental anthropology, demography, population biology, paleodemography, dermatoglyphics, forensic anthropology, paleopathology, biomedical anthropology, epidemiology, nutrition, disease, aging, health and nutrition, human physiology, paleonutrition, and others (Wienker and Bennett, 1992:390). This can be a disappointment for a faculty member interested in these topics who is unable to teach them in a course or seminar.

THE POSITION OF PHYSICAL ANTHROPOLOGY IN THE CURRICULUM

The position of anthropology in the community college curriculum is often the result of history. Some institutions have no anthropology courses; others have large programs. The strength of an anthropology program depends heavily on the position and strength of anthropology at neighboring colleges and universities to which students transfer and how the discipline is placed in the general education package. Physical anthropology enrollments are highest in those institutions where physical anthropology provides an alternative to biology to meet the general education requirement in the natural sciences. In many community colleges, however, physical anthropology exists as an elective with very few sections, in combination with archaeology, or as a section of an general introduction to anthropology course.

The first anthropology course was introduced at my college in the late 1950s. It was a course in physical anthropology taught by a zoologist. Within a few years, the first instructor with a graduate degree in anthropology was hired, and the program was expanded. Today my college has five full-time anthropologists, and a few part-timers as well, teaching an extensive program of thirteen courses. However, this large of a program is unusual in a community college.

Many colleges teach a general introduction to anthropology course, or an introduction to physical anthropology and archaeology course. My college introduces each subfield as a separate offering. Besides physical anthropology, we also offer a physical anthropology laboratory and an introductory laboratory course in forensic anthropology.

Consistently high enrollments in physical anthropology at my college result from the fact that physical anthropology and the lab course fulfill the general education requirement in the biological sciences. The fact that the first physical anthropology course was introduced by a zoologist in the biology department, and the fact that a nearby major university also teaches physical anthropology as a biological science, places us in competition with biology for the general education science student. Physical anthropology is a very attractive alternative to general biology for students who have had little background in the sciences or math and who have had previous negative experiences in these areas.

GETTING A POSITION IN A COMMUNITY COLLEGE

An issue in many institutions is, Who teaches physical anthropology? In earlier times anthropology was taught by instructors without graduate degrees in anthropology, especially in those institutions that cannot field a full program of anthropology courses. Conrad Kottak notes that in the early 1960s "only ten out of fifty-six introductory courses in California's junior colleges were being taught by people with advanced degrees in anthropology" (Kottak, 1997:2).

The teaching of anthropology by unqualified instructors, however, is waning, and many states have enacted the minimum standard of a graduate degree for teaching specific subjects in the community college. However, some small institutions cannot afford to teach a complete program, only a few courses, and need people qualified to teach in more than one subject.

With the exception of those whose true interest is in teaching, I suspect that the vast majority of those in graduate school working on their master's degrees or doctorates in physical anthropology do not have community college teaching as their goal. Most are dreaming of a tenure-track position at a prestigious university backed-up with hundreds of thousands of dollars in grant funds and major research projects. The simple fact is that the number of qualified persons far exceeds the number of such positions.

People who have degrees in anthropology drift into community college teaching for a variety of reasons. Sometimes there is a post-M.A. letdown after which students rethink their commitment to continue on to the doctorate. You can teach at a community college with a master's degree. Sometimes it is family commitments and the need to earn a good salary. Tenure at a community college is usually earned in less time than at most research universities (four years at my college) and is usually based upon success in the classroom or, more often, a lack of negative evaluations. Salaries vary greatly, but are often comparable with those earned at a university.

How does one begin a community college career? Most often community college teaching begins with taking a part-time assignment teaching a single anthropology class in the evening at the nearby community college and discovering the thrill of teaching and realizing that you have talent.

Although there are no data on this, I suspect that a significant number of new full-time hires began their careers in part-time positions, often while they were still in graduate school. My first community college job was the result of seeing a card on the bulletin board of my graduate department less than four weeks before the start of the fall semester. A last-minute panic to find a qualified person to teach a class is a frequent happening—be prepared to jump. Getting that first part-time class is a matter of perseverance and a great deal of luck.

Because community colleges are associated with local communities, there is seldom a nationwide search for candidates when a tenure-track position opens. When that occurs, there is usually already a group of candidates available. These might include instructors teaching part time at the institution or nearby institutions and graduate students at nearby universities. Thus there is usually no real need to advertise nationally or at an annual meeting.

A good way to start is a letter to the personnel department. In some districts, applications are accepted only if a position is available; others maintain an application pool that accepts applicants at any time. When a position opens, a selection committee selects from the pool of applications that the committee wishes to consider.

It is also a good idea to send a letter of interest along with a Curriculum Vitae to the department at the college. When received, these letters are often placed into a file; sometimes they trigger a formal application form. If there is pool, a letter may trigger recognition when your application is read. In either case, if a position opens you may or may not receive a call.

You need to remember that there is seldom a department of anthropology because anthropology is often represented by one or two faculty members. Do not look for any logic to department or division organization—it's more a matter of history and politics than anything else. Anthropology is perhaps most often found associated with sociology or social sciences, but anthropology can be lumped together with the sciences. At my institution we are in a department with geography.

WHAT DO THOSE DOING THE HIRING LOOK FOR?

Because community college instructors teach at the lower division level, a master's is usually required. However, with the large number of Ph.D.s having difficulty finding positions, more and more applicants have doctorates. Whether a Ph.D. positions a candidate ahead of an M.A. applicant is a matter for debate. Although the Ph.D. carries a higher level of education and perhaps prestige, it is a research degree, and sometimes selection committees question the applicant's commitment to teaching. Your long list of research activities and publications may or may not impress those on the hiring committee. Activities related to teaching, however, will impress. This would include working on textbooks. If you have an opportunity to write an instructor's manual or workbook for a text, do it!

Generally speaking, teaching experience, including teaching assistantships and part-time teaching, is important. Some interviews include a teaching sample or the applicant is asked to teach a class session. Letters of recommendation attesting to your teaching skills will carry weight.

Flexibility in teaching subjects is important. Community college anthropologists are generalists. More often than not they are not hired for a particular specialty, although there may be exceptions to this in a large department. (For example, at my institution, with five full-time anthropologists, everyone teaches physical anthropology, our highest enrolling course. Yet at our last hire, we looked for someone capable of teaching archaeology.)

As mentioned previously, four-fields anthropology is still strongly endorsed at the community colleges. Although there is some degree of specialization in the larger departments, be prepared to be able to teach a wide range of classes. The ability to teach in other subjects may also be a plus in smaller colleges that simply do not have the enrollment to sustain a full-time anthropology position. However, without a graduate degree, how much you can teach in a minor or collateral field is usually quite restricted.

What happens in a community college that can support only a half-time anthropologist? The college either relies on part-time instructors or seeks someone with a second teaching field such as biology, geography, sociology, or psychology, and so forth. People going into community college teaching, especially at smaller institutions, would be better positioned if they have completed graduate level work in anthropology and a related field. The second field is one that is supported by a B.A. degree or extensive course work. For example, my B.A. in zoology has enabled me to teach an occasional course in biology.

Do people without graduate degrees teach anthropology in the community college? Not as frequently as they used to. Many states, including California, have adopted minimum requirements that demand a graduate degree in anthropology or archaeology. Yet districts can and do make exceptions for equivalencies. For example, a graduate degree in Native American studies, which includes a significant amount of course work in anthropology, would be given equivalency.

LEARNING MORE ABOUT COMMUNITY COLLEGE ANTHROPOLOGY

Compared with university faculty, community college faculty can be quite isolated. National and regional organizations are usually focused on research issues, not on teaching. Even though research requires a great deal of contact with colleagues working in your specialty, teaching does not. The programs of the annual meetings of the American Anthropology Association and the American Association of Physical Anthropologists attest to this fact.

About twenty years ago, a group of community college anthropologists banded together to form the Society for Anthropology in Community Colleges (SACC). Today SACC is a section of the American Anthropological Association (AAA). SACC sponsors an annual meeting where community college faculty and others are provided the opportunity to present papers on a variety of topics, attend workshops, and meet with colleagues from two-year colleges throughout the United States and Canada. A traditional feature of these meetings is a field trip to nearby sites of anthropological interest. SACC sponsors several sessions at the annual AAA meeting, including the traditional Five Fields Update where a scholar from each of the fields—physical, cultural, archaeology, linguistics, and applied—updates us on what is presently happening within each of the fields. SACC also publishes a biannual journal, *Teaching Anthropology: SACC Notes,* and maintains a Web site. SACC represents an important resource for those interested in teaching in the community college.[1]

NOTE

1. See the SACC Web page at http://www.ccanthro.org.

REFERENCES

Kottak, C. P. 1997. "The Transmission of Anthropological Culture Today." In C. P. Kottak, J. J. White, and R. H. Furlow, eds. *The Teaching of Anthropology: Problems, Issues, and Decisions.* Mountain View, CA: Mayfield.

U.S. Department of Education. 1998. National Center for Education Statistics, Integrated Postsecondary Education Data System (PEDS), "Fall Enrollment," "Staff," and "Completions" surveys. Table 170, prepared December 1998.

Wienker, C. W., and K. A. Bennett. 1992. "Trends and Developments in Physical Anthropology," *American Journal of Physical Anthropology* (87): 388.

Chapter 4

The Practice of Physical Anthropology in a Museum Environment

Douglas H. Ubelaker

Museums offer unique environments to facilitate work in physical anthropology. Although the public tends to think of museums as primarily exhibition and collections facilities, most are complex research and educational institutions that are involved in diverse academic activities. Museums certainly have important exhibition and collection functions. However, in addition, most serve as broad research and educational institutions, sponsor public lectures and courses, and provide many public-oriented services. Such a diverse mission offers abundant opportunities for physical anthropologists to do their work and disseminate their knowledge and research results.

Throughout my own professional career, I have worked in the Smithsonian Institution's National Museum of Natural History in Washington, DC. The Smithsonian consists of a network of some twenty museums and research institutes. Most are located on the Mall in Washington, but some are elsewhere, such as the Cooper-Hewitt National Design Museum in New York City and the Smithsonian Tropical Research Institute in Panama.

The National Museum of Natural History building was constructed in the early 1900s using congressional funding. From the beginning, the facility included a major anthropology department. Physical anthropology was added to the department with the hiring of Aleš Hrdlička (1869–1943). Hrdlička was an early pioneer in American physical anthropology, and he founded the American Association of Physical Anthropologists and its journal, the *American Journal of Physical Anthropology* (Stewart, 1940). Hrdlička worked tirelessly to build up collections and research in physical anthropology at the

Smithsonian and initiated a scholarly tradition that continues today. Hrdlička was succeeded by his long-term assistant T. D. Stewart (1901–1997) who also enjoyed a productive career. Through the work of Hrdlička, Stewart, J. Lawrence Angel (1915–1986), and others, physical anthropology has had a presence in the museum that extends back to the very foundations of both the museum and the discipline.

I was hired in the early 1970s for a position created by the retirement of T. D. Stewart. Apparently, a decision was made to hire a junior scholar rather than a more accomplished senior one. I had interacted with Stewart and others at the Smithsonian on various research projects and welcomed the opportunity to strengthen this relationship through employment. The Smithsonian was thoughtful enough to allow me to finish the Ph.D. degree at the University of Kansas before joining the curatorial staff. Although Stewart retired when I was hired, he continued to conduct research at the Smithsonian, and we interacted for many years.

Presently I hold the position of curator of physical anthropology on the anthropology staff. Three other colleagues also hold this position, with specialties in paleoanthropology, skeletal biology/forensic anthropology, and paleopathology. Together, we are largely charged with representing physical anthropology on museum issues. Structurally, these positions are somewhat analogous to professors in university departments, independent academic positions involving collegial interaction.

It is important to note that other physical anthropologists are employed in the Smithsonian in special-function positions. Ph.D.-level physical anthropologists work within the department of anthropology as the collection manager for physical anthropology, departmental statistician, and a position within another collection-oriented unit (repatriation). Others with advanced degrees in physical anthropology work as research assistants, in data collection, and with the office of exhibits. Apart from this structure, this sizable group of scholars trained in physical anthropology conducts research, lectures, teaches, manages collections, and otherwise represents physical anthropology at the Smithsonian.

The position of curator basically involves research pursuits and general participation in professional museum activities. Curators are hired largely based on their research potential within their specialty. Subsequently, they set their own research pace and direction and pursue the support needed for their work. Perhaps anomalous in a government setting, curators are given great freedom to set and pursue their own research agendas. This freedom represents a great strength of the museum research position, in my opinion. Such freedom in a nonuniversity teaching environment enables many curators to pursue long-term projects and fieldwork that may take them away from the museum for months. Of course, curators also have other obligations of committee assignments, lectures, exhibition work, collection activities, or other duties. These other activities affect research scheduling, but individuals greatly influence the extent to which they become involved.

Accountability registers in mostly two forms: an annual performance review by the immediate supervisor and a more comprehensive periodic professional review by a standing museum committee of peers. The former review largely involves discussion of the past year's accomplishments in consideration of the standards of performance that were agreed upon the previous year. This also functions as an excellent opportunity for the curator to discuss job-related issues with the supervisor, such as research support and general department problems and developments.

The more comprehensive evaluation for scientific staff is termed the Professional Accomplishments Evaluation Committee (PAEC) review. This review occurs during preemployment and at established multiyear intervals after employment. This committee consists of a delegated member and an alternate from each academic department of the museum. Those being reviewed are asked to provide information regarding their accomplishments in research, collections, public programs, and professional service and education. Additional perspectives are supplied by the supervisor and colleagues outside the Smithsonian.

Although all accomplishments are considered in PAEC review, special attention is given to those since the last review period. More specifically, the research component involves evaluation of career productivity, review period productivity, scope and originality, and research impact. The collections category includes accomplishments regarding primary Smithsonian collections, other collections, including those in other institutions, and the supervision and administration of collections.

Public program evaluation includes assessments of contributions to exhibitions at the Smithsonian, public affairs (related to public programs) and non-Smithsonian Institution public programs. The evaluation guidelines recognize the varying ways that scientists contribute to exhibitions and the variation in time involved in those commitments. Involvement can range from being asked by exhibit developers to provide some information to planning to execution of a major exhibition. The former represents an almost negligible impact on the work year; the latter can dominate a scientist's time and intellectual focus for multiyear periods.

The professional service and education category recognizes that museum scientists frequently become involved in the administration of science, and this work can comprise a significant portion of a scientist's "professional accomplishments." In this system, points are assigned for accomplishments in museum administration, committee and advisory work, the organization of symposia and workshops, serving as a society officer, journal editorship, grant and manuscript review, teaching activities, and technical and public lectures.

These criteria provide a useful overview of the diversity of activity that characterizes museum life. Each scientist finds his/her own balance of these activities, with research as the major common activity. For some scientists, this balance remains permanently tipped in one direction or another. For most others, the balance shifts during a career. One period may find a scientist engaged almost exclusively in research, whereas at other times, the same individual may become heavily involved in museum administration or exhibition work. The system is designed in both job assignments and evaluation to recognize this long-term variation. For example, department chairs are not permanent, but rotating, with an expected three- to five-year term. Similarly, exhibit participation can be minimal for many years, but if a scientist serves as the principal contact on the development of a major exhibition, the commitment can become extensive for multiple years.

My own Smithsonian career has witnessed similar variation in job priorities. Throughout my career, I have maintained an active research program in physical anthropology, including field research, laboratory science, presenting papers at scientific meetings, and publication. Also throughout my career, I have lectured regularly to both professional and public audiences, regularly reviewed manuscripts and proposals, attended scientific meetings, and otherwise participated in normal scientific activity.

Since the late 1970s, I have also served as the primary consultant in forensic anthropology for the central FBI laboratory, located just one block from the museum in downtown Washington, DC. In this capacity, I have reported on about 650 cases for the FBI and others and have testified in court on eighteen occasions (Ubelaker and Scammell, 1992).

I also have found time to teach. Since about 1986, I have held a joint appointment with The George Washington University in Washington, DC, where I teach a course in physical anthropology each spring. Each year during this period, I also have organized and taught a one-week intensive seminar in forensic anthropology, rotating the site of the course in recent years between the Smithsonian and France.

Although my research and teaching have continued year after year, exhibits work has varied dramatically. Whereas minor contributions to exhibitions have been made regularly, major exhibit activity is confined in my career to a three-year period between 1974 and 1977 when I was first a member, and then chair, of the Museum's Exhibits Committee. At that time, this committee worked closely with the museum director to plan and execute exhibitions within the museum. Because that period was a very active one of exhibition renewal, much of my time was devoted to committee meetings and associated activity.

In my experience, administrative duties also have varied considerably. Throughout my career, I have always been involved in some administration through committee assignments and so on. However, from 1980 to 1985, I served as chair of the department of anthropology at the museum, a major supervisory position over a department claiming over 100 associated persons. In addition, in 1988 I served as an assistant director of the National Museum of Natural History and chair of the PAEC from 1979 to 1980 and then again in 1997. During these periods, my balance of professional activities was weighted heavily toward administration, with compensation in time allotted to other activities.

At present, I am relatively free of administration. My performance review for this past year notes that I serve on five museum committees, consisting of the department committee for long-term strategic planning; a similar, more general effort for the entire museum; an alternate representative of our department to the Senate of Scientists (an organization of museum scientists that sponsors lectures and pursues issues of concern to scientists, independent of regular museum administration); the Scoring Committee for the NMNH Training Program (a committee to rank and select student applicants for summer internships at the museum); and the Seidell Committee (an effort to evaluate proposals and award stipends from private funds earmarked for republication of scientific information). None of these committees requires a great amount of time, but collectively they represent a significant effort.

During the past year, I completed a number of research manuscripts and submitted them to the appropriate journals. Subjects of these manuscripts vary, including historical issues in physical anthropology, forensic techniques, obituaries, a report on the skeletal biological analysis of a prehistoric sample from Ecuador, and a theory-oriented article on patterns of morbidity in the ancient Old World. Seventeen manuscripts (including published abstracts) were actually published during the year, largely reflecting work previously submitted. In addition, research was conducted on isotopic analysis of dental enamel from ancient Ecuador, an historical review of the work of T. D. Stewart, molecular approaches to disease diagnosis in forensic contexts, and long-term health changes in the ancient eastern United States. Thirteen papers were presented at professional meetings. Forty manuscripts and grant proposals were reviewed at the request of granting agencies and publications.

Collection activity was minimal during the past year, reflecting our excellent collection management staff available to deal with many collection issues. However, continual consultation is required on proposed new collections, requests by outside scholars to conduct research on existing collections, and the maintenance and accessibility of existing collections. Repatriation legislation creates some demand on curatorial time as well. Our department has a sizable staff, including several with training in physical anthropology, to address repatriation issues, but curators still become involved in evaluating reports, offering opinions on individual specimens, and general policy issues.

In this past year, I was only minimally involved with exhibition activity. I served on the department exhibit development committee and headed up an effort to plan for a future exhibition on skeletal biology. This planning phase is much less work than actual exhibition production but still involves a significant amount of time attending committee meetings and developing documents.

As in previous years, I continued major consulting on forensic cases, with the FBI and others. This involved reporting on twenty-two cases from two countries and ten U.S. states and the District of Columbia. Twice during the year I traveled to testify in murder trials.

In addition to the course taught each year at The George Washington University and the forensic anthropology course in France, I delivered five public lectures.

This information provides the reader with a one-year glimpse into my Smithsonian life, and the life of a museum curator. As noted before, the extent of activity in these various categories varies with each year and with each curator. Clearly, the opportunity exists for diverse academic involvement for the physical anthropologist in the museum environment.

TRAINING

Educational preparation for occupation in the museum environment is similar to that required for other areas of employment in physical anthropology. In filling a curatorial position in physical anthropology, museum administrators and selection committee members most likely will be searching for candidates with the best records of academic preparation and research expertise. Such a record consists not only of relevant coursework and excellent grades and letters of recommendation, but also publications and other indications of research excellence. As these same factors are important for hiring in other employment areas, students should prepare themselves well academically to compete. I feel it is important for students to follow their interests and prepare themselves broadly, rather than focus early on a specific employment strategy. Within physical anthropology, the fields of skeletal biology and paleoanthropology are especially relevant to museum work, because these fields are in part collection-based and generate considerable public interest. However, museum academic departments cover broad topic areas, so all training in physical anthropology could be not only relevant but also potentially important.

One must also keep in mind that individuals with strong training in physical anthropology may accept museum employment in areas that are peripheral to this central education. For such jobs, training and experience in computer applications and administration are especially important. Exposure to techniques of data management and conservation may prove relevant for positions in collections management or related museum areas. The complex process of generating exhibits calls for professionals with diverse backgrounds, including artistic and journalism skills.

My own training is probably similar generally to that of most museum curators. I was attracted to the field of physical anthropology early in my student life through the opportunity and experience of fieldwork and the challenge of research. When I decided to attend graduate school specializing in physical anthropology, I did not have a museum position in mind. In fact, I do not recall thinking much about future employment. At the time, I was academically involved in the subject matter and preoccupied with research. The employment opportunity at the Smithsonian came quite unexpectedly but offered an attractive opportunity to pursue my intellectual interests in an environment well known for its historical work in my area of interest. I found that my university preparation in physical anthropology not only made me competitive for this position but also provided many of the skills needed for future years of research. However, I was not well prepared for administration, having had little exposure to business or management techniques. I suspect that was neither unusual nor a major handicap, because such training is rarely acquired by academics prior to administrative assignments, and some training is offered by the employer. Administration is an area difficult to plan for by students because those following interests in science are not generally attracted to business management classes. Such training might be useful, however, because so many academics can expect to shoulder at least some administration during their careers. In retrospect, such courses would have been useful to me, as well as additional preparation in forensic science, statistics, computer science, and anatomy.

The reality is that students cannot totally anticipate what skills they will need because there is usually no way to determine the exact nature of future employment. Even those destined for museum employment likely will not become aware of this until shortly before selection. Those who desire and eventually acquire specific museum employment may not find a position opening at the time they are trained and ready for employment. Such individuals may have to accept employment in another (hopefully related) area until the desired position becomes available. This additional step in the employment process may prove useful in providing additional experience, making the later application more competitive. A good practice to follow in student planning is to concentrate on courses in the area of interest and acquire those skills needed to perform in that area at maximum level. It also is prudent for students to acquire as broad training as possible to expand their options for future employment.

Students should be aware that excellent training and exposure to museum activity can be found outside of the university experience through internships or special courses offered by museums. For example, our museum each year supports student appointments through its Research Training Program, financed through the National Science Foundation under its Research Experiences for Undergraduates Program. This program provides opportunities with stipends for students to work with a museum mentor in an area of academic interest to them. Other, more informal arrangements are made through direct contact between students and museum professionals.

THE RELATIONSHIP OF MUSEUM PHYSICAL ANTHROPOLOGY TO THE GENERAL FIELD OF PHYSICAL ANTHROPOLOGY

The distinction between "museum" physical anthropology and the more general field of physical anthropology is relatively minimal. Any physical anthropologist hired by a museum and working in that environment should have the same strong academic background as colleagues in physical anthropology working in nonmuseum environments. If a difference exists, it involves a greater percentage of museum physical anthropologists working in skeletal biology and paleoanthropology than in the profession at large. Museums have collections of human remains and related materials that need care and interpretation. This can present an argument for officials to hire physical anthropologists with academic interests that relate to those collections. On the other hand, an argument also can be made that in a well-rounded anthropology department, other areas of physical anthropology should be represented as well.

TIES TO THE OUTSIDE

From the activities discussed earlier, it should become obvious that museum physical anthropologists, like other museum scientists, usually have extensive contact and involvement with individuals and units outside the museum. The museum provides a facility, support structure, and to some extent an agenda, but museum scientists work with outside individuals as necessary to pursue their goals. This usually involves research collaboration with colleagues and specialists in other fields, as well as those presenting problems to solve and educational opportunities.

In my own research, I have collaborated extensively with archeologists and colleagues from around the world who offer complementing expertise or research opportunity. In skeletal biology, this usually involves archeologists, especially those who excavated the samples being studied or who are otherwise knowledgeable about them. Increasingly, it also includes specialists in physical anthropology or in other fields who offer greater technical expertise in an aspect of analysis. In my research in Ecuador, I may work closely with the international team who excavated the sample and who are in charge of overall site interpretation. In the same project, I may also collaborate with a specialist in chemical analysis or in a particular type of pathology. As science becomes increasingly more complex, specialized, and technological, the need for interdisciplinary work and collaboration increases. Usually, the needed expertise cannot be found down the hall in the museum, but in an outside laboratory somewhere else in the world.

With the ease of national and international travel, educational opportunities can be found outside the museum as well. Usually, this involves educational demand and public interest in the areas of scientific specialty. In my own work, the growing interest in both forensic anthropology and peoples of the past has led to regular participation in such outlets. Besides yearly teaching at The George Washington University, I also try to make myself available to assist educational efforts where appropriate. Last summer found me participating in forensic anthropology courses in France, England, and Portugal, and when I finish writing this manuscript, I must prepare for teaching in a similar course in Spain next month. Like myself, many museum scientists regularly teach university courses, offer lectures and workshops within the museum, and participate worldwide when their expertise is called for.

Outside contacts also can include public service and interagency collaboration. My best example of this, and perhaps one of the best for our museum, is our long-standing collaboration with the FBI in the analysis of forensic cases. This collaborative relationship extends back to the very foundations of American physical anthropology and the FBI itself when in the early part of this century Aleš Hrdlička began consultation (Ubelaker, 1999). This work is generally recognized as public service and interagency cooperation. It also represents an important research area. The problems presented by the cases can be quite challenging and can lead to significant research, either as part of their solution or as a result of their stimuli. A significant part of my research record, including publications, can be linked to this casework and the challenges it presents (Ubelaker, 1996). The cases also present an opportunity to apply our science for the public good. Increasingly, forensic anthropologists are drawn into forensic casework because of our unique training, especially in skeletal biology, as well as our population perspective. This knowledge and expertise can make a difference in case interpretation and ultimately in justice. Although these forensic applications and court testimonials can be stressful at times, the contribution is important and complements other, less visible, products of our work.

LIMITATIONS

Although I highly value physical anthropology in a museum environment, I recognize that it may not be ideal for everyone. The major differences between a museum format and that of a university involve teaching, collections, and exhibitions. Unlike universities, museums generally are not degree-granting institutions and do not offer physical anthropologists the usual assortment of courses to teach and students to direct. Through arrangements with universities or the organization of internal workshops and classes, teaching is possible from a museum position, but it does not automatically come with the appointment. For those who really love to teach and continually interact with students, this may be a disadvantage.

For others, the opportunity to pursue research without major teaching responsibility is welcomed. From this perspective, the museum position is like a permanent sabbatical. Museum scientists, unrestricted by teaching responsibility, are free to pursue fieldwork at any time of the year and for extended periods of time. Rather than preparing lectures, their time can be devoted to manuscript writing or laboratory work. Clearly, the museum position offers choices in time usage.

My own choice has always been a mix of teaching and research. Although I welcome the freedom from a heavy teaching load, I have always chosen to maintain substantial teaching in my yearly plans. I find that the students continually bring a fresh perspective to my work, through their inquiry and discussion. In addition, the most motivated students have collaborated with me in research or assisted through internships. Usually, such involvement brings an added dimension to the research process and can be stimulating. For scientists with no student involvement, there is a significant risk of research isolation and limitation of research perspective. Of course, this can be overcome with a vigorous, interdisciplinary research program.

Exhibitions represent a unique museum phenomenon. They represent an opportunity to present science to the public with a three-dimensional perspective. In no other format can specimens and information be integrated to instruct large numbers of the public who stroll through a facility. Exhibition production is similar to writing an academic book in organization and the desire to communicate extensive information. However, with an exhibition, the illustrations can be three-dimensional real objects, and the "reader" may be a family with three weary children and limited time.

Like motion pictures, exhibitions are expensive, complex productions that involve the creative efforts of many specialists. A scientist with primary content responsibility for a hall usually has to work with a team of other scientists, as well as designers, text writers, production people, and many others. The result is a team effort that involves considerable give-and-take on the part of participants. With strong-minded individuals, such cooperation does not always come easy and inevitably calls for compromise. Although the process can be stressful at times, the product offers an important opportunity to disseminate information and educate.

Collections also contribute in unique ways to museum scientific life. The collections represent an irreplaceable research asset that must be strengthened, protected, and utilized. Physical anthropology, as a collection-oriented science, has a strong interest in collection quality. Curators have an opportunity to build collections through their research activities and outside contacts. Hard decisions have to be made regarding prudent use of space and other resources in accepting new collections. Similar determinations apply to expenditure of resources to conserve and maintain existing collections and to make them available for research use. Such effort can intrude on the time of the museum physical anthropologist.

The collections of course also continue to offer extraordinary research opportunity in physical anthropology. Specialists in human skeletal biology, paleoanthropology, comparative primate anatomy and related areas regularly work with such collections, pursuing a wide variety of research problems. The old studies of cranial capacity and racial topology have been displaced by sophisticated research designs aimed at a better understanding of functional anatomy, the history of disease, or complex factors in human variation and evolution. Collections are increasingly in research demand and thus present special challenges for the museum curator.

SUMMARY

Students training for a career in physical anthropology should keep museums in mind for future employment opportunities. Museums offer diverse and unique opportunities for education and research. They are especially attractive to those interested in collection-oriented research and the unique educational opportunities offered by museum exhibition, and the opportunity to pursue research and fieldwork throughout the year, free from the restrictions of teaching obligations.

REFERENCES

Stewart, T. D. 1940. "The Life and Writings of Dr. Aleš Hrdlička." *American Journal of Physical Anthropology* (26): 3–40.

Ubelaker, D. H. 1996. "Skeletons Testify: Anthropology in Forensic Science, AAPA Luncheon Address: April 12, 1996." *Yearbook of Physical Anthropology* (39): 229–244.

———. 1999. "Aleš Hrdlička's Role in the History of Physical Anthropology." *Journal of Forensic Sciences* 44(4): 708–714.

Ubelaker, D., and H. Scammell. 1992. *Bones, A Forensic Detective's Casebook.* New York: HarperCollins.

Chapter 5

Paleoanthropology at Home and in the Field

Andrew Kramer

The morning of July 8, 1999, started more promising than most. By 10:00 AM we had already uncovered a few crocodile teeth, a rib, and some neck bones from an extinct water buffalo at our excavations along the Cipasang River in the Rancah District of West Java, Indonesia. However, this was only a taste of the real excitement yet to come. Just before noon, the codirector of our field project, Dr. Tony Djubiantono, noticed that Agus, our field supervisor, had arrived at the top of the rice paddies north of our site. Now this was unusual because Agus was supposed to be supervising our concurrent excavation on the Cisanca River about four kilometers away. Tony pointed out how energized Agus appeared to be; he was nearly running down the paddies and shouting something I couldn't quite make out as he descended. Finally, about two-thirds of the way down, Agus stopped and yelled for all of us to hear: "We found it! We found Rancah Man!" All of us immediately dropped what we were doing and sprinted across the stream to meet him. Agus breathlessly reported that they had just discovered a human incisor over three and one-half meters deep in our excavation at Cisanca. The moment was electric—we hooted and hollered, exchanging high-fives all around. We had found our first fossil hominid!

It was in anticipation of experiences like this that I decided to pursue a career in physical anthropology. Today, I am a paleoanthropologist employed as an associate professor of anthropology at the University of Tennessee in Knoxville (UTK). As I am writing this chapter, my forty-first birthday has just come and gone. I give you this information not to gain sympathy but

Field site next to the Cipasang River in West Java, Indonesia.

to place my educational and professional history into a chronological context. I was in college during the late 1970s, earned my graduate degrees during the 1980s, and I have held my current job through most of the 1990s. Although I may be on the wrong side of forty, I am still young enough to remember (none too fondly) the difficulties of the modern academic job market. In addition, I've now been a faculty member long enough to gain some valuable perspectives from the "other side of the fence."

The focus of this chapter is to describe my often challenging, yet always rewarding, career as a university professor and field paleoanthropologist. My first goal is to describe the necessary steps to successfully prepare for a career

Andrew Kramer proudly displaying the hominid tooth (adhering to the dirt clod between his right thumb and forefinger).

in paleoanthropology. Second, I want to convey what is actually involved in conducting paleoanthropological fieldwork. The information, suggestions, and advice that I provide derive from my own experiences as a student (I "survived" a particularly intense graduate program) and my subsequent responsibilities as a faculty member. As a university professor, my activities relevant to preparing for and securing academic employment have included (1) being our department's undergraduate advising coordinator, (2) designing and implementing our Honors' Major, (3) chairing our Undergraduate Curriculum Committee, (4) chairing our Graduate Admissions Committee, and (5) chairing our most recent Faculty Search Committee. The following are my relevant teaching and research credentials:

1. I have chaired, or am currently chairing, six Ph.D. and eight M.A. committees.
2. I have presented invited papers at international conferences.
3. I have published in the top refereed journals in my field.
4. I have generated external funding to support my international museum research and fieldwork.

However, I have one last objective for this chapter as well. I want to make certain that any potential paleoanthropologists that are reading this understand that pursuing this career requires major investments of your time, money, and hard work with absolutely no guarantees of employment on the back-end. But if you are passionate about human evolution, and you clamor to expand our knowledge of the past, and you are eager to convey this excitement to future generations of students, then this is the job for you.

EDUCATIONAL PREPARATION

Your Undergraduate Years and the Graduate School Application Process

To become a paleoanthropologist employed in a university setting, planning and preparation should ideally begin at the undergraduate level. Your performance and activities in college either open doors or limit opportunities regarding your entry into top-flight graduate programs. Devote a significant amount of time to researching graduate departments, their faculties, and the resources and funding available for their students. To find this information, consult the American Anthropological Association's annual "Guide to Departments" and the Web (a good place to start is the American Association of Physical Anthropologists' brief listing of graduate programs in physical anthropology: http://physanth.org/gradprogs/). Most importantly, identify professors whose paleoanthropological field research excites you, because these are the individuals who can most easily hasten your entry into the field.

You may consider participating in a paleoanthropological field school during the summer of your junior or senior year. These provide a great experience and would highlight any graduate school application letter. The downside is that they are not cheap, you pay your way to the tune of a few thousand dollars (minimum). Here are a few to investigate:

1. Koobi Fora Field School (administered jointly by Rutgers University and the National Museums of Kenya, http://www.rci.rutgers.edu/~mjr/HTML/indexbody.html)

2. Summer Paleoanthropology Field School at Makapansgat, South Africa (administered jointly by the Institute of Human Origins at Arizona State University and the University of the Witwatersrand, South Africa, http://www.asu.edu/clas/iho/field.htm)

3. Paleoanthropology Field School: Hungarian Miocene Hominoids (D. Begun, University of Toronto, http://www.chass.utoronto.ca:8080/anthropology/fieldlet.htm)

In order to maximize your chances of acceptance into the program of your choice, you have to maintain as high a GPA as possible, because most anthropology departments use a minimum GPA as their first filter. If your GPA falls below the departmental cut-off, no matter how stellar your other qualifications may be, your application will promptly find its way to the "Deny Admission" pile. The other "score" that matters in most grad school applications is the Graduate Record Examination (GRE). Once again, it is used as a "hard threshold" in many departments. Scoring well on all three components is important, but in my experience as chair of our graduate admissions committee, a high score on the "Quantitative" test is most impressive. It seems that many of our applicants score rather highly on the "Verbal" and "Analytical" sections, but that most of the variance is concentrated among the "Quantitative" scores. Because physical anthropology is becoming more and more reliant upon sophisticated quantitative methods, I confer greater value to a high score in this area.

Throughout your undergraduate career, and particularly during your upper-division major coursework, you should cultivate relationships with your professors. All graduate programs require letters of recommendation to be submitted with your application materials, and if by your senior year your instructors don't know you from Adam, your future as a grad student is gravely in doubt. Visit during office hours, discuss your anthropological interests with them, ask for their advice about particular graduate programs, and, above all, "wow" them in their classes.

Finally, you should devote a good deal of time and thought to your letter of intent/statement of purpose. Avoid writing a letter filled with platitudes extolling the virtues of anthropology, and any letter that begins: "I've wanted to be an anthropologist since I first began playing in my sandbox . . ." is almost certainly the kiss-of-death for your application. Instead, strike as professional a tone as possible and succinctly tell the admissions committee: (1) why you want to enroll in their program, (2) whom you would like to work with, and, most importantly, (3) what you want to do once you get there. It is not necessary to present a full-blown research agenda in this letter, nor is it expected (especially at the M.A. level), but some statement of specific research interests that relate to work done by faculty in the department would give your application a real boost. After you've written this letter, identify one of your professors who would be willing to read it for you. Their perspective and input could be invaluable.

Succeeding in Graduate School

Once you have accepted an offer of admission into a graduate program, you should now direct all of your energies toward bettering your chances at securing that faculty position after you earn your doctorate. From your first year onward, your coursework, research, and employment decisions must be made in light of this ultimate goal. After completing your required core courses, you need to choose electives that are most relevant to paleoanthropology. Because physical anthropology has become more and more quantitative over the years, a good background in statistics is required. I would recommend that you take courses up to and including multivariate statistics and become familiar with a standard statistical software package, such as SAS or SYSTAT. All paleoanthropologists should have a thorough knowledge of human osteology and anatomy, as well as having good theoretical grounding in evolutionary theory and ecology. For those intending to work in the field, geology and paleontology courses should be completed.

Besides learning the content in your graduate classes, pay attention to the effective and ineffectual teaching methods of your instructors. As a future member of the faculty, teaching will be a major part of your day-to-day responsibilities, and it is never too early to learn what works and what doesn't in the classroom and lab. If and when you earn a teaching assistantship, you may not be offered any formal instructional training. Learning to teach "on the fly" is quite often a rite-of-passage for many young graduate students. The better prepared you are for this possibility the more likely your initial forays into teaching will be successful. Toward the latter portion of your graduate training, you may be given the opportunity to teach your own class. If this occurs, take full advantage because faculty search committees place much greater value on this teaching experience in comparison to courses in which you only assisted. At every level of instruction, make sure that your performance is formally evaluated not only by your students but, if possible, by your peers and mentors as well. Depending on the evaluative instrument, the constructive criticism that you receive can be very helpful in improving your teaching effectiveness.

Although coursework and teaching are very important components of your education, your graduate training should be focused on developing your skills as a researcher. As a university professor, you will be expected to contribute to the basic knowledge of your field. Because the academic job market continues to become increasingly competitive, it is no longer adequate for freshly minted Ph.D.s to simply demonstrate research potential. Now candidates for entry-level, tenure-track positions must already have an established record of research productivity. "Publish or perish" is a truism no longer applied only to faculty; today this maxim has equal resonance for graduate students.

To maximize your opportunities, try to involve yourself in your professors' research. Ideally, this would lead to being awarded a research assistantship in which you would be assigned certain responsibilities on specific projects. Alternatively, if a research assistantship is unavailable, take advantage of the term papers in your courses. A well-conceived idea developed within the context of a course can lead to a collaboration between you and the professor. Working closely with faculty who are actively engaged in research provides an optimal environment for you to hone the skills that are necessary to become an effective researcher.

Before publishing your results, it is best to present your work at a regional or national professional meeting. For paleoanthropologists, the conferences at which your research would reach the broadest and most relevant audiences are those hosted by the American Association of Physical Anthropologists (http://physanth.org/) and the Paleoanthropology Society (http://www.paleoanthro.org/). These meetings are both held in the spring, and the latter convenes in conjunction with the former during odd-numbered years (in even-numbered years, the Paleoanthropology Society meets with the Society for American Archaeology). The value of presenting your research at these meetings, in either a podium or poster format, is the feedback you receive and the professional connections that you establish. In addition, the most current (and generally not-yet-published) research findings (including new fossil discoveries) are presented at these meetings, so it is a wonderful opportunity to become acquainted with the "state-of-the-art" in our discipline.

When you are ready to prepare your manuscript for publication, you must first choose the journal in which you would like to publish your results. Generally, it is best to select the most rigorously reviewed journals in the field. These outlets are the most prestigious and will provide the widest readership and greatest respect for your work. In paleoanthropology the top journals are the *American Journal of Physical Anthropology* (http://www.interscience.wiley.com/jpages/0002-9483/) and the *Journal of Human Evolution* (http://www.academicpress.com/jhevol). A wonderful resource for those starting their research careers as academics is *How to Write and Publish a Scientific Paper, 5th edition*, by Robert A. Day (1998). All our first year graduate students are required to read this book in our department's "Method and Theory in Biological Anthropology" core course.

Of course, the most important research project of your graduate career is your dissertation. American paleoanthropologists, owing to a quirk of paleobiogeography, are faced with an obstacle in our research that most of our Old World colleagues do not have to overcome. Because human morphological evolution was completed before the peopling of the Americas, paleoanthropologists in the United States must travel overseas to participate in fieldwork or to study original human fossils. Therefore, we need to generate rather large sums of money to support our research endeavors. A skill that will be constantly put to the test throughout your professional career is the ability to convince external funding agencies of the importance and value of your proposed research. Developing these talents must start in graduate school.

I recommend that every doctoral candidate of mine prepare and submit a National Science Foundation (NSF) Doctoral Dissertation Improvement Grant (http://www.nsf.gov/sbe/bcs/physical/physdiss.htm) to support their Ph.D. research. These proposals are submitted with your major advisor listed as the Principal Investigator (PI) and you as the co-PI. However, do not be misled by these designations—this is your project, and you are responsible for crafting the proposal. The maximum award is $12,000 and can be used to defray transportation, per diem, computer, and equipment costs. The format of these proposals is the same as that used for the standard NSF grants applied for by senior researchers, so composing an NSF Doctoral Dissertation Improvement Grant is excellent preparation for what you will be doing throughout your career. Other funding agencies that support paleoanthropological dissertation research include Sigma Xi's Grants-in-Aid of Research (http://www.sigmaxi.org/giar/guidelines.htm), the Wenner-Gren Foundation's Dissertation Fieldwork Grants Program (http://www.wennergren.org/Smallg.htm), and the L.S.B. Leakey Foundation's General Research Grants Program (http://www.leakeyfoundation.org/general_grant.html).

ACADEMIC EMPLOYMENT AS A PALEOANTHROPOLOGIST

The Job Search

It should come as no surprise that the academic job market is extremely competitive. This situation is exacerbated for human paleontologists because there are only a handful of university positions advertised each year that specifically list paleoanthropology as a desired specialty of the candidate. Therefore, these postings routinely generate upward of 100 applicants per opening. The competition is made even more intense by the fact that a large proportion of the applicant pool is not composed of new Ph.D.s. Indeed, you can expect that many of your competitors will be post-docs just completing multiyear fellowships during which they beefed-up their publication record, and junior faculty already employed at other institutions who, for whatever reason, consider the open position to be more desirable than the one they currently hold. As a result, I would not recommend entering the job market until your Ph.D. is already in hand, or, at the least, you have successfully defended your dissertation. Most search committees will not seriously consider an ABD's ("All But Dissertation") application when there are so many well-qualified Ph.D.s available.

The application process for most faculty jobs is really quite simple. All that is generally required is a cover letter, a Curriculum Vitae (CV), and names of at least three references who would be willing to provide letters of recommendation if asked. Your cover letter is a statement of research and teaching plans. Similar to your graduate school letter of intent, this document should be pithy as well. Because the search committee has, at the least, dozens of applications to review, you should avoid writing letters that exceed two pages, and personally my eyes start to glaze over after the first page and a half. Most faculty do not have the time nor the inclination to read pages upon pages of distilled dissertation results, no matter how fascinating your research may seem to you. Ideally, your letter should highlight your accomplishments and discuss, as specifically as possible, how you fit the job description and how your hiring would complement the strengths already present in the department.

Pay particular attention to the structure and content of your CV. In all likelihood, your cover letter will be read by most of the search committee and many departmental faculty, but you can be sure that every faculty member will scrutinize your CV. Not all readers will necessarily focus on the same section, so it is imperative that you present your information clearly and accessibly. The following list highlights some of the things I look for in an applicant's CV. First, where, when, and under whom did you receive your Ph.D.? If you are ABD at the time of application, have you defended your dissertation, or have you at least scheduled your defense date? What courses have you taught? In this section you must clearly distinguish for the reader the classes in which you assisted from those you had primary responsibility for instructing. Also make it clear at which level (e.g., freshman, upper-division, graduate) those courses were taught. Did you do foreign field and/or museum research for your dissertation? What external grant money did you generate and which awards did you receive? For each grant, you should list when it was awarded, its duration, the amount, and whether you were the PI.

For your presented papers and publications, I prefer to read these listings in reverse chronological order: most recent first, oldest last. For meeting presentations, distinguish between those that were invited versus those that were contributed, highlight those presented at national and international conferences (in contrast to regional and local meetings), and indicate which were refereed before acceptance. You can be sure that your list of publications will be the one section that everyone will read. Most academics sensibly place this section at the end of their vitae so it can easily be accessed. Despite its importance, the publication list is all too often a site of confusion and misrepresentation in many applicants' CVs.

Never allow your publications to appear "padded" by including such things as presented papers, manuscripts in preparation, and contract reports alongside refereed journal articles. To avoid this, I suggest explicitly listing your publications by categories of decreasing importance: (1) journal articles, (2) book chapters and conference proceedings, (3) book reviews, (4) contract reports, and (5) published abstracts. In addition, include a "manuscripts submitted" category for your papers that have entered the publication pipeline but whose formal status (e.g., accept, revise and resubmit, reject) has not yet been determined. List these as "under review" and provide the name of the journal to which they were sent. Don't bother listing manuscripts that are "in preparation" because the reader has no way of knowing at what stage of "preparation" you are referring to: it could range from a half-formed idea in your head to a paper ready to be sent off for review. For those papers that have been accepted for publication but have not yet appeared in print, list them in the appropriate category (e.g., "Journal Articles") as "in press" and enter "nd" ("no date") in the date field. Finally, always list your publications in a standard bibliographic format. Never tack your coauthors on at the end of the citation because the reader of your CV is entitled to know the actual authorship of each of your publications.

Ideally, you demonstrated a good work ethic by getting things done on time, and you maintained collegial relationships with your professors and peers during your graduate career. If so, you can expect that to be reflected in positive letters of recommendation that will be written on your behalf. If not, your letters may be less-than-glowing, and those are the last things you want read by a search committee. Working hard and being a good departmental citizen can only improve your chances of landing the kind of job you want. An excellent resource on the job search in physical anthropology can be found linked to the American Association of Physical Anthropologists' Web site (http://www.ugs.usf.edu/wienker/jobsrch.htm).

Your First Job

After completing your Ph.D., choose your first employment carefully. Of course in today's market you may justifiably consider yourself extremely fortunate to receive any offer at all. If you do not have any choices and you need the one job that was tendered to put food on your table (and start paying off your loans), then by all means take it. However, not all jobs are created equally, especially if you aspire to be a field paleoanthropologist. Your goal should be a tenure-track professorship at a research university. There, faculty are expected to pursue a vigorous program of original research and are institutionally supported to do so by a relatively reduced teaching-load, the availability of "seed" money to jump-start research projects, and an institutional track-record of generating extramural research funds.

If you land the university job right off the bat, congratulations! But what if you are faced with the following choice: a tenure-track offer from a small, liberal-arts college or a one- to two-year temporary appointment at a major university? Your first inclination may be to grab the "real" job, but be aware that you will be expected to teach six to eight courses per year (versus four at most universities). To do a good job, virtually all of your time will be spent preparing and instructing these courses. As a result you will have little opportunity, and often meager support, to prepare articles from your dissertation for publication and to initiate a research program at most small, teaching colleges. The situation may not be much more appealing at the university, especially if you were hired explicitly to reduce the teaching "burdens" of the regular faculty. If, however, it is made clear that there is a good likelihood that this temporary position will be transformed into a tenure-leading faculty "line" after one or two years, it may be worthwhile to take this job.

Use that year or two to demonstrate your instructional acumen, brilliant scholarship, and collegial warmth. As the "inside candidate," you will then have a leg-up on your competition when the time comes for the department to permanently fill that junior faculty slot.

Perhaps your best option after completing your doctorate is to use a postdoctoral fellowship as a stepping-stone to the university professorate. These positions support your blossoming research career by providing money, time, and facilities to publish the results of your dissertation, thereby making you that much more competitive once you reenter the job market. Again, a good bit of legwork is required to discover what positions are available and relevant to your interests. The following Web site, maintained by Dr. Anne C. Stone of the department of anthropology, University of New Mexico, is an excellent clearinghouse for physical anthropology post-docs: (http://www.unm.edu/~acstone/postdocs/post-doc.html).

The University Professorship

Contrary to popular perception, university professors are not valued solely on the number of articles they publish nor on the amount of external grant dollars they generate. Top researchers who cannot successfully convey the importance of their work to their students and to the public are not as prized by the university community as much as those professors who not only can "do" but can educate as well. The university professorship does not demand the sacrifice of teaching effectiveness at the altar of research productivity. Ideally, you should strive to become a "teacher/scholar" whose research informs your teaching, keeping it dynamic, relevant, and up-to-date for your students.

Of course, to be able to incorporate your research findings into your classes you must first establish a research program. As a professor at a research university, you are expected to make contributions to the expansion of basic knowledge in your field. In paleoanthropology, there are three ways to accomplish this goal. First, you can attack paleoanthropological problems by applying new methods to the interpretation of public-domain data—information on the hominid fossil record that has already been published in one form or another (e.g., in formal journal articles or posted on the Web). Second, you can secure permissions and funding to travel to the various museums and institutes around the world where hominid fossil specimens are housed to take original observations and measurements in order to resolve a particular question. Finally, you can expand the database yourself by discovering new fossils through paleoanthropological fieldwork. In the next section, I describe my own experiences establishing a field project. With the benefit of hindsight, I intend to warn you of potential pitfalls and advise you of the proper choices to make if your ultimate goal is to succeed in the field.

PALEOANTHROPOLOGY IN THE FIELD

Making Contacts and Writing Grants

My advisor was not a field paleoanthropologist so I did not have a ready-made entrée into a field site when I finished my degree. Instead, I needed to make my own connections with colleagues with whom I could collaborate in the field. My first step on this path was taken when I presented a paper at a conference commemorating the 100th anniversary of the discovery of the original "*Pithecanthropus*" ("Java Man") fossils, convened at the Senckenberg Institute, Frankfurt, Germany, in December 1991. I was invited to this meeting expressly because I had done part of my dissertation research at the Senckenberg in 1987 focusing on the evolution of the Javan fossil hominids. At this meeting I made my first professional contacts with colleagues who were active in Javan fieldwork. Further cultivation of my relationships with these Indonesian and French workers led to a 1993 publication and, most importantly, an invitation to join their team in future museum and field research.

In the fall of 1994, I wrote grant proposals to support my participation in their project, and I was awarded funds from NSF and the Wenner-Gren Foundation that allowed me to travel to Java for the first time during the summer of 1995. It is important to note that as a prerequisite to awarding funding, most granting agencies require that you have received official governmental permission to conduct research in their country. Therefore, you have to submit applications to the appropriate foreign governmental agency well in advance of your intended date of departure. Ideally, you should have these permissions in-hand before you apply for funding. In my case, the Indonesian Institute of Sciences approved my proposal and issued a research visa to me through the Indonesian consulate in Los Angeles (where I stopped on my way to Java).

Although I was unable to take part in fieldwork on this trip, I was permitted to study many of the original hominid fossils housed at various institutes in West and Central Java. During this trip, I was fortunate to be able to bring a graduate student (funded by NSF) who acted as my interpreter and cultural liaison. Having lived a couple of years in Java and being familiar with the language, he was an invaluable assistant who taught me many of the nuances of Javan culture and was able to smooth out some of the rough spots we encountered. I realize that most of you will not have the luxury of an interpreter on your first research experience in a foreign country, so I strongly recommend becoming as familiar with the local language and customs as possible. For those of you that were educated in the "four-field" approach, use your training in your contacts with your international colleagues. The more you understand and respect their society and traditions, the more likely it will be that the professional relationships you forge will be rewarding and long-lasting.

The most important contact I made during that first visit in 1995 was Dr. Tony Djubiantono, whom I introduced in the opening vignette of this chapter. Tony, as the director of the Archaeological Research and Development Center of Bandung, invited me back to codirect fieldwork in West Java the following year. We were very excited about our potential collaboration, and after discussing our various materiel and personnel needs for the project, I left Indonesia itching to prepare and submit grant proposals to fund our work.

Back in Tennessee, the fall of 1995 was devoted to grant-writing and by mid-December, I submitted ambitious proposals to NSF, Wenner-Gren, and the Leakey Foundation with high hopes of returning to Java to initiate field-work during the summer of 1996. Unfortunately, all three proposals met the same fate—a resounding "declination of support." After my righteous indignation tapered off to the point where I could read the reviewers' comments dispassionately, I came to realize that the agencies were quite justified in *not* giving me money. Up to that point in my career, I had been successful in securing grants to fund my international museum research, but I had no experience organizing a foreign field project and that was painfully

The 1997 field team: Dr. Tony Djubiantono, co-director of the project (standing far left) and Mr. Agus, the field team leader (standing second from the right).

obvious to the grant referees. Thankfully, the reviewers' thoughtful and constructive criticisms provided a road map for improvements I would have to implement and deficiencies I needed to address before this project could be competitive for funding.

Specifically, the following three reasons were consistently cited for the declination of funding: (1) not enough time was originally proposed to be spent in the field, (2) the research team required the addition of a field geologist and vertebrate paleontologist, and (3) field protocols and logistics were not adequately specified. To rectify these shortcomings, I prepared a series of more modest proposals during the fall of 1996 to fund a relatively short preparatory trip back to Java during the summer of 1997. Although both external proposals (to Wenner-Gren and Leakey) were declined, I did receive an internal summer research award from the Graduate School of the University of Tennessee. I cannot overstate how valuable this small amount of "seed" money proved to be. It not only got me back and forth from Java, where I secured the participation of Indonesia's top vertebrate paleontologist in our future projects, but it allowed Tony and me to complete preliminary excavations at two sites in West Java. One of these digs was particularly successful in that it produced large mammal fossils and exposed two volcanic layers that could be absolutely dated by extremely accurate laser $^{40}Ar/^{39}Ar$ methods.

Back in the United States, yet another fall (1997) was spent preparing grant proposals to the major funding agencies to support our next summer of fieldwork in West Java. This time, I did a bit more legwork on where and how to apply. I discovered that the Wenner-Gren Foundation had a special program that was ideal for our project. Their International Collaborative Research Grants (ICRG) are designed "to assist anthropological research projects undertaken jointly by two (or more) investigators from different countries" and "priority is given to those projects involving at least one principal investigator from outside North America and Western Europe" (quotes from the ICRG Web page http://www.wennergren.org/Icrg.htm). Tony and I certainly fit their guidelines as co-principal investigators. For the NSF proposal, electronic submissions were now being encouraged through their "FastLane" project (https://www.fastlane.nsf.gov/fastlane.htm). My university's Office of Research was offering training sessions for "FastLane," so I took advantage of this opportunity and submitted my NSF proposal over the Web, and saved a tree or two by avoiding the traditional paper route which required upward of twenty-five copies to be produced and mailed.

I was more confident in this round of submissions because I explicitly addressed the criticisms raised by my previous proposals' referees. For example, I emphasized our successful pilot project and the multidisciplinary expertise of our team, which now included a field geologist, a vertebrate paleontologist, and a geochronologist (an absolute dating specialist). I also discussed field protocols with a colleague who was directing ongoing international fieldwork and incorporated his suggestions into my proposals. And lo and behold, it worked—all three granting agencies (NSF, Wenner-Gren, and Leakey) agreed to fund our project.

Making Foreign Fieldwork a Success

As the summer of 1998 approached, my excitement grew as I anticipated returning to the field. But then, as so often happens in foreign fieldwork, circumstances completely beyond my control prevented the resumption of our project. President Suharto, Indonesia's dictator for the past three decades, was forced to step down as a result of the deadly riots that rocked Java's major cities in the wake of the Asian economic crisis that came to a head during the spring of 1998. Indonesia's political instability in combination with its powder keg potential for further violence caused the U.S. State Department to issue an advisory against "nonessential travel" there by U.S. citizens. My university interpreted this warning as a ban and effectively prohibited my return to Java that summer as a university employee. Thankfully, the granting agencies were very understanding about delaying the project and agreed to rollover the funds until the situation in Java stabilized. My Indonesian colleagues concurred that a postponement would be the most sensible course of action, and together we looked toward the summer of 1999 to resume our collaboration.

The intervening year was put to good use in preparation of mounting a major foreign field project. Materials and supplies unavailable in Java needed to be purchased, such as waterproofed field notebooks, good leather work gloves, and "hardware cloth" (metal mesh used for dry-screening sediment). In addition, field equipment, including geological rock hammers and a GPS (Global Positioning Satellite) unit, which can pinpoint your position on the landscape within 10 meters, had to be ordered. Because we anticipated collecting geological and paleontological samples for dating, we needed to secure USDA soil import permits to prevent the confiscation of our materials by customs agents upon our return. Department of Agriculture officials visited the University of Tennessee campus to inspect our laboratory facilities before the permits were issued from Washington, DC.

The grants supported the participation in the project of two graduate students from our department of anthropology and a geologist from another university whose specialty was geochronology (absolute dating). Each of us had to make individual preparations for the expedition as well. We had to ensure that our passports were up-to-date and that we had registered our contact information with the U.S. Embassy in Jakarta. The latter was accomplished on-line, and its purpose was to inform our government of our whereabouts in case an emergency evacuation became necessary. Because Indonesia is a developing country in the tropics, health concerns were a priority. Each of us needed to get, or update, our immunizations against typhoid, polio, hepatitis A and B, and tetanus/diphtheria. Prescriptions were necessary for malaria preventatives and broad-spectrum antibiotics to treat the intestinal problems inevitably encountered by most travelers to foreign lands. The Centers for Disease Control maintains a very useful Web site with information pertaining to travelers' health at http://www.cdc.gov/travel/. Over-the-counter medical supplies that I would recommend for anyone doing fieldwork in a foreign country include topical antibiotic ointment, bandages and gauze, medical tape, antidiarrheal capsules, aspirin (or some other form of pain-relief), insect repellent, sun block, cold medicine, anti-itch ointments for insect bites, and antihistamine tablets for allergies. Make sure to keep all of your medications in their originally prescribed vials and store-bought packages so as not to raise the suspicions of foreign custom-control agents that you are bringing illicit drugs into their country.

Regarding money, I suggest taking as much in traveler's checks as possible. If you need to take cash, be aware of a peculiarity I have encountered in Javan banks and official "moneychangers": they refuse to accept U.S. bills that are not in crisp and uncirculated condition. If you are directing the field project and responsible for its finances, it would not be unusual for you to bring a lot of currency with you to pay for labor, ground transportation, lodging, and food in countries where credit cards are not widely used and accepted. If you are carrying over $10,000 (in any combination of cash and traveler's checks), you must declare this amount before you leave the country by filing Form 4790 with the U.S. Customs Service. Transportation of currency out of the country is legal, regardless of the amount, as long as you complete the required paperwork. In addition to registering your money, make sure to register your equipment (e.g., camera, laptop computer, GPS unit) with customs as well. This prevents import duties being charged to you on your return by a customs officer who erroneously presumes that you purchased this equipment overseas.

Finally, on June 14, 1999, we left for Indonesia. The next six weeks were wonderfully productive. Excavating at two sites, and surveying in their vicinities, we collected datable volcanic sediments, recovered many animal fossils, and, as described at the beginning of this chapter, discovered the first fossil hominid from West Java. There were many keys to the success of our project. In the first place, the necessary and appropriate preparations were completed before we started to dig. For example, we met with local political leaders and secured their cooperation before we began our project. This process was expedited by the sponsorship of our research by a university in the Central Javan city of Yogyakarta. This university and my own entered into a relationship that was formalized in April 1998 by a mutual "Memorandum of Understanding." This document, which codifies interinstitutional research collaboration, professional and educational exchanges, is very important because it provides an official Indonesian "umbrella" under which our research can be carried out anywhere in Java.

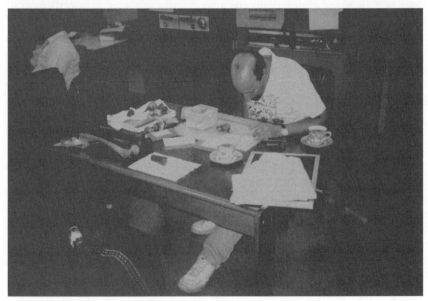

Studying fossils in the field and in the lab.

Our field crews were hired from amongst the farmers and land-owners in and around our excavation areas. These men were enthusiastic to work with us because, like many residents who had collected fossils from their fields and streams since their youth, they were interested in the prehistory of their area. The day-to-day field operations ran smoothly because Tony's institutional assistants directed the excavations. Although some of the Indonesian field techniques differed from methods Americans employ, it would not have been appropriate (and it likely would have been counterproductive) to impose our protocols upon theirs. Agus, our field supervisor, was critically important in coordinating the activities at both sites and providing an interface between the Indonesian laborers and the American components of the team.

To succeed, any modern paleoanthropological field project must be multidisciplinary. No single individual has the expertise to be able to accomplish the various tasks and interpret all of the relevant data that are produced during a typical season of fieldwork. We were fortunate in that all of our experts did their jobs, and did them well. Our geologists identified the most promising areas to excavate based on their knowledge of the local stratigraphy, our geochronologist collected numerous volcanic samples to be dated back in the States, and our vertebrate paleontologist and zooarchaeologist classified the often fragmentary animal fossils into their appropriate taxonomic categories. One of these bone fragments provided an excellent object lesson in the self-correcting nature of good science. On July 1, I happened upon a partial long-bone shaft that I thought was a femur of *Homo erectus* based on its diameter and cortical bone thickness. Everyone on the team agreed, although our zooarchaeologist (UTK doctoral candidate Dan Weinand) was never completely convinced based on one muscle scar that seemed out of place. Without access to an adequate comparative collection while we were in the field, the final verdict had to wait until we returned to the vertebrate paleontology laboratories back in Bandung. There Dan's suspicions were confirmed when he saw an unusually small bovid (cowlike animal) femur that looked very familiar. Upon comparison to our "hominid" thigh bone, the two proved to be a perfect match: their surface morphologies and their cross-sections were identical. By taking the time and undertaking the appropriate comparisons, we avoided making what would have proven to be an embarrassing announcement.

CONCLUSION

In retrospect, my advice to anyone who ultimately wants to direct a paleoanthropological field project is to surround yourself with excellence. Ideally, the individual experts that form the team will eventually meld into a fully functioning whole that truly is greater than the sum of its parts. Remember, also, that you are the "foreigner." It is especially critical that you respect the attitudes and conform to the work habits of your collaborators and hosts. Any imposition of an American mind-set is likely to be disastrous to your relationships with your colleagues and for your project's success. In general, the American "Type-A" personality does not travel well, so if this describes you, try to rein-in those aggressive tendencies before getting off the plane.

It is hard to overstate the excitement and fascination that I feel for paleoanthropology. Even today, three months after I have returned from the field, I am on pins and needles waiting for our various analytical results to start coming in. Laser ^{40}Ar/^{39}Ar dating of the volcanic material is being done at the Berkeley Geochronology Center, neutron activation analysis (chemical correlation) of the sediments from our two West Javan sites will be undertaken at the Archaeometry Laboratory of the University of Missouri's nuclear research facility, and electron spin resonance dating of fossil bovid teeth is slated to begin at the Oak Ridge National Laboratories here in east Tennessee. Once the analyses are completed and the results interpreted, our team will write various manuscripts for publication. After that, it will be time to start preparing proposals again to fund our return to Java and re-start our fieldwork. This job is not for everyone, and it was a long, hard road to get here, but I wouldn't trade it for the world.

REFERENCES

Day, R. A. 1998. *How to Write and Publish a Scientific Paper*, 5th ed. Phoenix, AZ: Oryx Press.

Howells, W. W. 1993. *Getting Here: The Story of Human Evolution, New Edition*. Washington, DC: Compass Press.

Johanson, D. C., and M. A. Edey. 1981. *Lucy: The Beginnings of Human Kind*. New York: Simon and Schuster.

Leakey, R., and R. Lewin. 1992. *Origins Reconsidered: In Search of What Makes Us Human*. New York: Doubleday.

Willis, D. 1989. *The Hominid Gang: Behind the Scenes in the Search for Human Origins*. New York: Penguin Books.

Chapter 6

Primatology as a Career

Kevin D. Hunt

POPULAR IMPRESSION OF PRIMATE RESEARCH

Primatology is a field of scientific inquiry burdened by such heavy expectations of romance and excitement that it is almost certain to disappoint a neophyte. Rather than warming to the theoretically interesting evolutionary questions of primatology in a classroom setting, many potential primatologists start right out with the best stuff. Most students who walk into my primatology class have already seen spectacular images of primate behaviors, films of such behaviors as infanticide, meat eating, tool use, and crippling male-male conflicts. Even as a wizened veteran of primate field research, I still marvel at how intimately—and accurately—primatology films have documented primate behavior. Some of these film depictions are even richer than firsthand observations. Film depiction of the *study* of primates, however, is a different matter.

Primatologists are introduced in films with a voice-over that has an almost eerie constancy, running something like, "Here in this wild and remote corner of the Amazon (or the Congo, or Malayasia . . .), a lone dedicated scientist pursues her (or his) solitary quest to document the behavior of these timid but remarkable primates. . . ." As this well-modulated voice generates scholarly ambiance, the viewer is treated to a sumptuous visual image. A sun-dappled figure, partly obscured by a shimmering curtain of emerald-green foliage, stands alternately jotting notes and peering up at a forest canopy teeming with primates. We see that the romantic primatologist, at home in the forest, lives and works far from the crush of humanity, unconcerned by the everyday worries that nag such mere mortals as us.

PRIMATOLOGY IN THE REAL WORLD

It isn't like that. Primatology through the camera lens is all about observing primates in gorgeous surroundings. Contrary to this pleasing image, most of the time researchers spend "in the field" is eaten up by everything *but* primate watching. Drudgery, tedium, and hard work are the price the primatologist pays for a few hours of primate watching per day.

Simply getting to a primate field site can be an adventure. Most primates eat fruits, leaves, insects, and other tree resources. Unfortunately, the huge trees in which primates are most likely to be found are also those most prized by a logging industry that shows no signs of having slaked its appetite for old-growth forests. Because primates cannot live without the trees that produce their food, undisturbed forests that support primates are found in ever more remote areas. Nor is industrial logging the only threat nibbling away at primate habitats. As African economies blossom, the need for building timber increases, and local, small-scale harvesting of building-grade trees has increased. An exploding population in many tropical nations requires firewood for cooking, too. Whereas thirty years ago Shirley Strum could observe wild baboons at Gilgil, nearly in sight of the skyscrapers of Nairobi, nowadays primates that still live in natural habitats and feed on their natural foods are found in much more remote settings. It is typical to find primate research sites in the most inaccessible corners of the least developed countries in the world, places where poor roads or political instability mean it is not yet profitable to harvest timber.

Transportation to such remote areas is often a protracted, uncomfortable affair that begins in the first world and ends in the third. One lands at a modern airport on a gleaming Boeing 767, and things get earthier from there. Travel to a field site might begin with bus travel, but not on an air-conditioned, restroom-equipped coach. I often travel squeezed into the seat of a public bus designed for people a head shorter than me. Mostly the open windows (or complete lack of same) provide welcome access to the outdoors, but I never seem to be able to remove the coating of fine, red dust on my luggage. At times I'm actually relieved when circumstances force me to travel in the back of an open pickup truck. During your hours-long travel, if you are from North America or Europe, your western preferences for privacy and cleanliness are likely to be challenged. As you journey nearer the primates, infrastructure rolls away behind you. Primates are found at the end of the trail, after asphalt has trickled to gravel, and gravel has given way to rutted dirt tracks. Most researchers approach travel in these remote regions with a spirit of adventure, but at times the risk to equipment, data, and personal belongings makes the often-slow progress more tedium than adventure.

Kevin Hunt negotiates dense foliage at Mahale, Tanzania, while on a target-follow of a chimpanzee. The smaller, quadrupedal chimpanzees can pass underneath such foliage, while a human follower must push through or walk over. Photo by Marion Hunt, 1987.

Nor has the drudgery ended once the primatologist has landed at his or her field site. One imagines a field stint beginning with a solitary primatologist emerging from a battered but functional Land Rover, stepping into a pristine, unpopulated tropical paradise. In reality, primatology is a team effort, and privacy is at a premium. In many field situations, you will sleep in a tent fifteen feet from various cooks, launderers, porters, and fellow researchers, listening to them variously sneeze, snore, and cough. When field sites have permanent structures, the buildings are likely to be tiny, primitive, and crowded, but at least they tend to be dry.

It is somewhat counterintuitive that more remote field stations can require a larger support staff than more accessible sites. Remote locations often lack refrigeration, electric lights, cooking stoves, and running water, and although you might view dispensing with these first-world conveniences as a blessing rather than a curse, you also might change your mind once you get there. Few novice field workers fully appreciate how much time can be consumed in daily maintenance tasks when running water and electricity are absent. Without staff, fieldwork would devolve into laundering, clothes repairing, cooking, carrying water, starting fires, shopping, and washing. In short, less infrastructure means more employees are needed to help out.

One always dreams that with enough experience, one will find the knack of supervising staff, so that the task is hardly noticed. I haven't yet found that knack, and I suspect few do. Much time in the field is consumed by monitoring the work of your research assistants, patiently listening to their complaints about work schedules, solving their transportation difficulties, creatively dealing with equipment inadequacies, coping with health problems, negotiating requests for salary adjustments, entertaining pleas for expanded benefits, and politely rebuffing recommendations of friends and relatives for jobs. Although the college-educated primatologist may see a data collection protocol as uncomplicated and straightforward, an assistant who is not responsible for the sanctity of the data and who is only grammar-school educated must be thoroughly trained and constantly supervised.

Sustaining a functional field site means supplying it. Part of the primatologist's weekly routine must be scheduled trips to town to placate bureaucracy, buy food, replenish supplies, and run other errands. In remote locations, medical care is rarely near at hand. A visiting scientist lucky enough to have a vehicle inevitably becomes the local ambulance, likely to be called upon at any hour of the day—or more likely, night. You, relatively wealthy, college-educated, will often find your medical supplies and medical training, such as it is, are the best available. I have served as an emergency doctor many a time when there was simply no alternative, twice in life-or-death circumstances (results: one recovery, one death[1]). If you are at all sympathetic, you will enter the forest many a day preoccupied with a serious health problem of one or another of your associates or his or her family.

The Semliki Wildlife Reserve is among the driest chimpanzee habitats known. Hunt and research assistant Rachel Weiss stand on a slope overlooking more forested areas that are the preferred chimpanzee habitat.

Your own health, despite modern medicine, is not guaranteed. Malaria is very difficult to avoid, and it is a particularly annoying inconvenience. Antimalarials themselves can have significant and unpleasant side effects. There are also the less serious but still disconcerting bouts of amoebic dysentery, typhoid, and flu. No matter how healthy you are, eventually you will get sick. If you fall ill in the field, the nearest hospital may not be the medical delight you'd welcome. I've been treated in hospitals where the sanitary condition would repel me if they were bus stations.

It's easier than most would imagine allowing one's focus to shift from primate research to improving your own or someone else's living conditions. I know of field workers who are so distressed by local poverty, disease, or poor medical care that they find it impossible to do their work (for some reason my American assistants have succumbed to this much more often than my European assistants). To avoid succumbing to these distractions, I must continually remind myself to focus on my research. I have seen others become full-time social workers.

These are just the distractions. Many aspiring primatologists find that even the primates are disappointing. On television primate society is one drama after another. In the wild, primates chew. They chew while gathering food, they chew while glancing around for more food, and they chew while climbing to a new perch, while walking, while grooming, and even while having sex. Half of the chimpanzee day, for instance, is taken up in feeding. The next most common behavior is resting. Films naturally edit out all this boring stuff, so that even though a novice might very well have a good idea of what a chimpanzee fight looks like, they are less likely to realize that aggression, hunting, and complex social behavior are rare events that take up a few minutes in a long day. Most field primatologists I know derive great pleasure from the peaceful ambience of the forest, not just primate behavior.

FORGET THAT! WHERE ARE THE MONKEYS?

Even with these admonitions and qualifications, primatology may be just as appealing as ever, so your next question is, How can I get into the field fastest? You can't. Perhaps there was a time when primatologists needed field assistants so desperately that they were willing to hire untested but enthusiastic young volunteers. If so, that time has passed. Directors of field projects are typically very cautious in hiring or accepting volunteers. At first blush, it may seem that a primatologist has nothing to lose in taking on an unpaid volunteer. After all, if the volunteer is unhelpful, he or she can be asked to leave. True enough, but by the time a team member is expelled, much may have been lost. A research initiative can be successful only if team members cooperate in working toward established objectives. Members must subjugate their personal needs and their particular research program to the objectives of the larger research project. Daily research initiatives must be sustained

Habituated chimpanzees ignore researchers. Here, Hunt sits next to Mahale chimpanzee brothers Toshiba and Kasengazi at Mahale, Tanzania. Photo by Marion Hunt, 1987.

regardless of the health or emotional state of team members. When one worker is negligent or ill, others must pick up the slack. A good team has a certain chemistry and esprit de corps that helps to balance workloads to the satisfaction of all. A single individual distressed by the poor food, or close quarters, or homesickness, or any one of a dozen things can make life miserable for an entire field crew. When one team member consistently shunts work onto others, resentments build, commitments fray, and project tasks are not given the attention they need. When a project director takes time to mediate squabbles between team members, precious research time is lost.

In order to minimize these difficulties, most research directors prefer to draw their assistants from a pool of field-tested primatologists from which the disgruntled and disappointed have been culled. If an experienced hand is not available, a researcher is often able to pick from a long list of willing and competent candidates known personally. Even a volunteer who is able to pay his or her own way is unlikely to find a field position without knowing a field director personally. Without experience, the only thing a first timer has to offer is that they can pay their own way, and often that's not enough.

HOW *DO* PEOPLE GET STARTED, THEN?

The barriers may seem insurmountable. They are not, but they are imposing enough that they discourage all but the most dedicated. Although there are many routes into the field, the common thread among the stories of primatologists I know is that they simply refused to be told no. Virtually anyone who is willing to make sacrifices and persevere through a number of false starts and rejections can succeed.

Scholarly ambitions determine one's best course of action. Attending college probably gives the budding primatologist the most options, but for those who do not plan on college, or those who will put off college, making contacts and getting experience are the first order of business.

You can gain experience and perhaps make that all important first contact by volunteering at a zoo, taking a noncredit primatology class at a local university, volunteering at a sanctuary, or involving yourself with a primate conservation organization. These routes are effective because, although research may require genius to conceive, in execution it is rarely intellectually challenging; instead, passion, persistence, and reliability are the qualities most valuable in the field worker. You can demonstrate those in a volunteer position.

Determining which of the dozens of eager volunteers clamoring around a project director have these qualities and at the same time might be able to function under field conditions is difficult. In my experience, the only true test is experience. This means that as a primatology aspirant, perhaps the single best credential you can give yourself is a certificate from a primatology field school. As foreshadowed earlier, it will cost you probably $1,000 to $2,000 plus airfare. But field school is perhaps the soundest investment you can make.

For most, the field school itself will be a rich enough experience to satisfy their interest in primates, and for most, regardless of how passionate they feel beforehand, it will be more than enough. You probably think you're not in that group, or you wouldn't be reading this. Yet field school students who find they want to return to field life are less common than one might expect. Primatology is a field with a huge attrition rate, which means that an applicant for a field position who has been to the field even a single time and wishes to return has at least demonstrated that they can cope with the field experience. Compared with someone who has never observed a wild primate, a field school graduate is a tested veteran, and much more likely to be hired for a paying job.

That paying job, the entry-level position, as it were, is the "field assistant" position. A field assistant often works in the context of a large project, and s/he will likely be hired for a well-defined, relatively brief period of time from six months to two years or so. By the end of that time, you will be a primatologist, regardless of your educational background.

CAPTIVE PRIMATE RESEARCH

A compromise credential on the road to a field job, and for many an end in itself, is experience with captive primates. Although most aspiring primatologists envision working with wild primates, working with captive primates can be very rewarding. It is easier to get a job at this level in a laboratory or sanctuary than in the wild, leaving these captive jobs as the first experience of many assistants.

Lab positions commonly entail feeding, cleaning, and other rudimentary care of primates. As the assistant gains experience and earns the trust of his or her supervisors, the assistant may graduate to data gathering and even helping with experimental design. These days many if not most captive primates are treated to "enrichment" activities. Enrichment engages primates in activities that are similar to those they engage in the wild. These activities increase their sense of well-being and decrease their stress level, presumably leading to greater psychological and physiological normalcy. Primates in captivity must have medical examinations and may have to endure medical procedures. Assistants will help to sedate, transport, and care for animals after medical procedures. In the past almost all of such assistant positions were in laboratories, but these days an increasing number of primates are found in sanctuaries or retirement facilities. These primates are retired from experimentation, rescued from poor or unacceptable captive situations, or are failed pets.

Even if your area of study is primatology, persistence is important as a position may be hard to come by. Taking classes from the researcher who runs a primate lab will both familiarize you with the research conducted at the lab, and give the lab director a chance to know you.

CAREER ASSISTANT TRACK

Once you have that first job, you're on your way. Even while in the field on that first field job, many of my assistants have been offered positions with better pay and more responsibility. Both in the lab and in the field, it is possible to make a career as an itinerate and freelance assistant, perhaps staying with the same situation for years, but more likely moving from one project to another. Yet few choose to remain at this level forever.

"ASSISTANT TRACK" DRAWBACKS

Although an experience as an assistant will be satisfying to some, as one acquires more experience and expertise, the position may become less rewarding. The disadvantages of the assistant position will be merely part of a trade-off equation for a career assistant, but for others they may make pursuing a Ph.D. a better career choice.

The assistant faces some frustrations that a research team leader, most likely to be someone with a Ph.D., does not. The direction of the research is largely in the hands of a project director, not the assistants, and this lack of control is frustrating for some people. An assistant who thinks the scholarly direction of a research project is not ambitious enough, or whose experience gives them a confident yet indefinable feeling that the research subject is a dead end, or who would design a different data collection protocol can only make suggestions to the team leader. If the principal investigator chooses to ignore the suggestions, the assistant must fume in silence.

Pay is low for assistants. Without an advanced degree, assistants are easily replaced, and therefore not in very high demand. The career assistant is subject to the vagaries of funding. There are only a few projects that continue for decades without interruption in funding. Although the professor who directs a project may fall back on teaching for a year or two when funding is scarce, the field assistant suffers either temporary unemployment or a job change.

The inclusion of assistants in the analysis of data and writing of scientific papers is at the whim of the principal researcher. And when all the work is done and published, most of the credit will go to the team leader, and assistants may not even appear in the roster of authors on the publication. It is more stressful than most people realize to be doing a similar job as your employer, yet receiving a quarter of the compensation and recognition.

There are advantages, however. While the project director is writing grants, analyzing data, presenting papers at scientific meetings, writing journal articles, and coping with a full-time teaching load back home, his or her assistant is in the field or lab actually watching the primates. Although some will find these frustrations more than they can bear, even those who find the assistant routine constraining will have a helpful credential.

The alternate path, and really the more conventional route, is that of working toward a college degree. Attending a college with a strong primatology program means that finding some sort of a position requires less initiative, and it comes many times of its own accord, if a student works hard and takes the right classes. A bachelor's degree makes one much more likely to be hired as an assistant, and it raises the ceiling of advancement a little. It also provides you with a credential that is valuable whatever job you apply for later in life. That cannot be said of most primatology jobs.

Although a bachelor's degree can open some doors, for the most part significant advancement requires a Ph.D. Primatologists who see their studies through to a Ph.D. are likely to become professors, where one's job then becomes teaching about primates and continuing to do research. There are other positions, though very few, in zoos and conservation organizations. The method of entering primatology relies less on luck, and more on just putting your head down and getting your schoolwork done—with distinction. It requires more sacrifice, however, than many realize. More on that later.

CHOOSING THE COLLEGE ROUTE

The most conventional way of entering primatology, then, and certainly the most common way, is to study primates and animal behavior on the way to earning a bachelor's degree at a university where there is at least one primatologist. In this context you'll have gotten a well-rounded education, learned about primates, and made contact with a primatology insider. The Wisconsin Regional Primate Center's Web page lists a number of distinguished primatology programs (http://www.brown.edu/Research/Primate/dir98.html). Choosing among these programs depends in part on which primate and which issue within primatology interests you most. If you allow your interests to direct your choice of a university, you are much more likely to succeed in college. You'll work harder because you enjoy it more, and your grades will reflect that. Identifying the area of research that interests you most, however, is no small matter.

THE FIELD OF PRIMATOLOGY

If you have heard of a primatologist, it is likely someone who studies social organization or social behavior. This is partly because the study of primate societies is relatively new and exciting, and newsworthy discoveries are still being made. It is also due to the fact that social behavior looks good on film.

Despite its prominence, the study of primate social behavior is only one component of a large field, and one that flowered long before social behavior became a focus. In the 1860s, only a few years after Darwin's *Origin of Species* appeared, Thomas Henry Huxley was using research on ape anatomy to argue that humans had evolved from an apelike being. This human evolution focus explains why primatology is a subfield of physical anthropology rather than biology, where the study of the ecology, morphology, and behavior of most animals is found.

Primatology found a home in anthropology partly because biologists know that primates are a particularly unrewarding group of animals to study. Large brains, long life spans, long growth periods, large body masses, and low population densities carry with them a long list of discouraging consequences. Primates grow and reproduce slowly, and their social relationships tend to be complex and deep. This means that killing an individual to sample its stomach contents, to examine its morphology, to determine its body weight, to quantify its parasite load, or to run up its body chemistry alters the group's ecology and behavior in a devastating fashion, not to mention that most of us would have ethical qualms about such research. Collecting individuals to rear in the lab is equally impractical, and when it is worth considering, sustaining wildlike conditions in the lab is expensive and difficult. Add to this that primates are often found in remote areas, that many species move and interact high in the forest canopy, and that many species are difficult to habituate to human observation, and we see why most scholarly questions can be answered more easily studying species other than primates. In short, the study of primates is profitably undertaken only when there is no other alternative.

Anthropologists have reason to overlook all of these drawbacks, chief among them that primates are our closest relatives. This genetic propinquity means that *ceteris paribus* assumptions, assumptions that include "all other things being equal" arguments, are better bets with primates than other animals. In years past, perhaps through the 1960s, anthropologists made the simplifying assumption that living primates were primitive versions of our own primate ancestors. It was acknowledged as a simplifying assumption then, and it is viewed as overly simplistic now, given what we know about how variable primate societies are. Still, when a field of inquiry requires a living model for hominid ancestors, primates are the best choice. Well-conceived reconstructions of fossil behavior choose as models species that share ecological, brain size, body mass, and life history states with the ancestor of interest. When the dead and living species are closely related, it is reasonable to assume that other variables such as physiology, neuroanatomy, organ structure, and the capacity for social complexity are more or less "equal." It is anthropologists studying early humans who need to study our closest relatives.

All primatologists are not anthropologists, though, and in fact even primatologists trained in anthropology departments may find themselves employed in allied disciplines. Primatologists in psychology departments often study cognition. Their interests may be in the anatomy of the brain, the physiology of the brain, or quirks of information processing that influence how an animal learns and behaves. Communication is commonly studied in the wild, but there is often a strong laboratory component to such research. Primate ecology, or how primates interact with other species (particularly those they eat), is an area of study that fits comfortably in biology, even though the objections discussed earlier make an anthropology home more likely. The study of primate physiology and reproduction, that is, the study of body chemistry including hormonal systems, is one often engaged in biology departments or medical programs. Primatologists who study diets may be found in nutrition programs or in medical schools. Anatomists and functional morphologists (they add a physics-like mechanical edge to their study of anatomy) study humans or primates in dissection labs, and are typically anatomy teachers in medical schools. Some of those morphologists (like me) specialize on the field study of locomotion and posture rather than quantifying anatomical variation. Field workers are somewhat more likely to be in anthropology departments than are anatomists. Research on primate growth and development is often located in anthropology departments, but may be found in medical schools, too. Studies of phylogeny (relatedness of species) and genetics are largely laboratory pursuits, most often in anthropology departments. Primate paleontologists are often anatomists and functional morphologists as well, and may not study behavior at all. These researchers may be in medical schools or anthropology departments.

Determining which of these areas is of interest to you will allow you to choose an appropriate graduate school, so this is one of your undergraduate missions. Another of those missions is acquiring skills and expertise that will make the path to your Ph.D. smoother. Although it is true that primatology was, at one time, a field that depended on a scientist's knack for detecting patterns in behavioral data, it has now become both more prosaic and more scientific. If you enter primatology with the impression that you are cleverly dodging the need for quantitative skills, you will be disappointed. Primatology is a heavily quantitative field. It requires the same scientific method and rigor as chemistry and biology (that's not to say it always gets it). An undergraduate class in statistics will help you understand what you are doing as a field assistant engaged in some sampling technique or another, and it will give your application to graduate school a boost. Courses in scientific method and history and philosophy of science will provide you with a depth of knowledge and maturity of perspective that will help you later. All of primatology, even the study of social behavior, is based in evolutionary theory; a class in evolution is essential.

Primates eat, most of them most of the time, plants; a practical botany class is a good credential. Primates differ in their physiology according to their diet, among other things, and a class in physiology will give you some perspective on these issues. Classes in animal behavior, whether the animal is a fish, an insect, or a mammal, are very useful. If you are extremely lucky, you may be at a university that offers a course in behavioral observation methods; if so, you'll be at an advantage if you take it. Introductory physical anthropology classes typically cover elementary primate anatomy and phylogeny. The most apropos class, of course, will be primatology. I have had graduating seniors come to me asking for help applying to Ph.D. programs in primatology, whom I discover have not even taken the one primatology class we offer here. I don't take these inquiries very seriously. As an undergraduate student, you will become familiar with the names of active primatologists whose research you find appealing. The dedicated student will begin to read scientific journals early in his or her undergraduate career. As you begin to identify the area of primatology that interests you most, you will be able to identify programs where one or more of these scholars are established.

MASTER'S DEGREE

It may seem curious that I have mentioned the bachelor's degree and the Ph.D., but I have ignored the master's degree. Some students consider pursuing a master's degree in anthropology as a way of gaining a little more control over their fate and commanding more clout in scientific circles. Many assume an M.A. will give a candidate a boost when competing for field positions over a B.A.-qualified candidate. In fact, this is not a good track. Field school expenses are much lower than the cost of an M.A. degree, and field school requires a much lighter time commitment—a month or two, versus two years for an M.A. It is also a better credential than an M.A., if fieldwork is your goal. Few students fail under field conditions because their academic preparation is weak, but many fail because field conditions are too stressful for them.

PH.D. TRACK

If you are considering primatology as a lifelong career, obtaining a Ph.D. under supervision of a primatologist is perhaps the most reliable entrée to the field. It is the track I pursued, and one that arguably gives one the most control over one's fate, though it also entails shouldering the greatest amount of responsibility. Perhaps the best introduction to what Ph.D. work entails is to note that finishing the degree, once you've reached graduate school, is dependent more on good work habits than luck, innate intelligence, creativity, or connections. Perhaps reviewing my career path will provide some insight into this track.

I am an ecological morphologist. I study chimpanzee posture, locomotion, and food-getting practices in order to better understand why apes have their peculiar anatomy. I use this knowledge to reconstruct the lifeway of our earliest ancestors after we branched off from the apes. I came at primatology from an unconventional direction. As early as high school, I was interested in human evolution, and in a vague way the evolution of bipedalism. As an undergraduate I centered my interests on locomotor and masticatory morphology. Primatology never occurred to me as a career track, because I was interested in evolution, and I was not aware until graduate school that primatology is an evolutionary field. I took five years to finish my B.A. at the University of Tennessee, most of the last year spent writing my honors thesis on the elastic modulus of human cortical bone. Early in my undergraduate career, I had planned to study the body from micro to macro. I had the naïve plan that I would begin with a study of the physical properties of bone—study in a physics department—continue with the study of the physical properties of tendons, ligaments, and muscles, and proceed to construct a quantitative mechanical model of the human body. I spent over a year obtaining the most rudimentary knowledge of bone properties. To acquire a minimally extensive understanding of bone, I might have required another five years. I soon realized my plan was ridiculously overambitious.

I went to graduate school at the University of Michigan intending to study the evolution of human locomotion. In my first year of graduate school, a faculty member handed me Richard Wrangham's doctoral dissertation. Wrangham, a primatologist specializing on chimpanzees, was a candidate for a primatology position at UM. It is not exaggerating to say it was a revelation. I realized that primatology was a rigorous, quantitative, and evolutionary field that was more similar to my own interests than I had imagined. Although I had never intentionally meant to begin to emphasize primatology in my studies, I subsequently took every class Wrangham offered at Michigan. By my second year of graduate school, I applied for a field assistant position studying baboons. It went to a more experienced candidate. The fall of that year I was assigned as an assistant in Wrangham's evolution of primate social behavior class, and I learned the basics of primate sociality just one step ahead of my students. I found primate ecology and evolution fascinating, but I still viewed it as tangential to my research interests.

As I progressed in my studies on the evolution of bipedality, I found myself returning again and again to data on primate locomotion and posture, as I attempted to reason through various models for bipedalism origins. I pestered Wrangham with little lists of questions about chimpanzee locomotion and posture. I began to read journal articles on locomotion in primates, particularly chimpanzees. I was surprised to learn that some important questions about chimpanzee locomotion and posture had not yet been the subject of quantitative studies. One day while annoying Wrangham with another of my lists, he asked whether it might be best for me to actually go out and get some of the information I kept asking for. At last I began to see that my interest in primates might be combined with my interest in australopithecine bipedality.

Wrangham had connections of the very most valuable kind. He generously arranged with Toshisada Nishida for me to conduct research at Mahale, and with Jane Goodall to work at Gombe. Hard work almost always pays off, but sometimes you can't beat dumb luck.

I spent a year reading, crafting a dissertation proposal, writing grants, and planning my fieldwork. At the end of that year I took my Ph.D. exams and left for Tanzania just a month later to study chimpanzees at Gombe and Mahale. I spent a year in East Africa in 1986 and 1987. I spent nearly two years writing my dissertation, finishing my Ph.D. in 1989. When I failed to land a job, Wrangham came to my aid once again, offering me a two-year post-doctoral fellowship. For the second time in five years, Wrangham's initiative changed my career trajectory. During my post-doc I was part of a team that Wrangham directed in a study of chimpanzee and monkey diets at the Kibale National Park, in Uganda. I learned during that time most of what I know about primate ecology, food chemistry, and perhaps, equally important, directing a large research station. The lessons I learned watching Wrangham manage his team at Kibale was the training ground that allowed me to begin my own chimpanzee research initiative in 1996. Ironically, this essential part of my education was completely accidental, at least from my own perspective; in my own mind my work at Kibale was simply putting food on the table while I searched for a tenure-track job, and I thought at the time that my real career effort was the work I did writing up my results from my Mahale and Gombe research.

My experiences at Gombe, Mahale, and Kibale helped me to envision how I might conduct research at a new field site. It was becoming apparent to me that my research on australopithecines required study at a drier site than Kibale, where I had continued to work several years after moving to Indiana University. I began searching for an appropriate site in 1993, and gradually chimp researchers learned of my interest. I inquired about several possibilities, in Mali, Senegal, and D.R. Congo. Wrangham thought a site in Uganda might be appropriate, at the Semliki Wildlife Reserve (or "Toro Game Reserve," as it had been known). I applied for a research permit in 1995, and I started fieldwork at Semliki-Toro in July 1996. If called upon to summarize my training in a sentence, it might be that from early 1980s through 1994 I apprenticed under Wrangham, and only in 1995 did I begin my own primate research career.

GRADUATE SCHOOL

Many of you will consider following a similar course, but be forewarned that pursuing a Ph.D. is a long row to hoe. These days a Ph.D. requires at the very least six years of graduate school, and I know of very few people who have managed it in fewer than eight (I didn't). Graduate school is a long, expensive, frequently ego-diminishing experience that is worth it only if you wouldn't be happy doing anything else. Before deciding to pursue a doctorate, you should be very honest with yourself about your intellectual abilities, your work ethic, your tolerance of poverty, and most of all your passion for primatology. If there is another career where you'd be just as fulfilled intellectually, choose it. I, for one, had no choice. I'm squeamish about prodding sick and injured people, so a career in medicine was unattractive. My interest in human evolution seemed to rule out law and business. Being a veterinarian seemed to have too much to do with cows and cats. The potential primatologist should consider very carefully, then, that becoming a doctor or a lawyer requires less time in school (six years after college for a doctor, part of that with a salary, only three for a law or business degree, versus around six to twelve years for a Ph.D., eight years average). Doctoring and lawyering not only take less time to achieve, but they also pay better. Then there are the lifestyle sacrifices. If you plan on having kids, you'll be having them very soon after graduate school, because your biological clock (or your wife's) will be ticking. And if you have kids, you'll be working your field research around them for years. Before you seriously consider a career as a primatologist, weigh the toll these sacrifices will make on your life.

HOW TO GET INTO GRADUATE SCHOOL

The essential first step is to make the best possible grades you can as an undergraduate, so that a good graduate school will be in reach. Some students begin to think of entering a Ph.D. program late in their undergraduate career as law and medical schools begin to seem out of reach. These students often have the impression that graduate school admission requirements will be lower than those for medical school or law school. From what I've seen of applicants to IU, it may very well be the other way around; competition is intense for the few grad school slots available. This is largely because primatology is not a mainstream academic discipline, and that means there are few tenure-track jobs. As a consequence, graduate programs very responsibly limit the number of primatology Ph.D.s they produce. Your grades will have to be equivalent to those required to enter law school or medical school, if not better.

If you have maintained a high grade point average for three years, piled up the sorts of classes that make you attractive to a graduate program, and managed to get some field experience, choosing the appropriate graduate program—and getting admitted—is the next step. There are perhaps twenty universities in North America where a primatologist can hope to get the expertise they need to get a tenure-track job specializing in primatology. Narrowing the field is largely matching your interests to the specializations of faculty at these Ph.D. programs, and forging some preliminary direction to your graduate work. Most aspiring primatologists will have read a number of primatology books such as *In the Shadow of Man* (Goodall, 1971), *Almost Human* (Strum, 1987), *Sex and Friendship in Baboons* (Smuts, 1985), *Gorillas in the Mist* (Fossey, 1983), and *Kanzi* (Savage-Rumbaugh and Lewin, 1994). More scholarly and rigorous works are in order after an introduction to primatology from these sources. Some excellent books are *The Woman That Never Evolved* (Hrdy, 1981), *Chimpanzee Politics* (de Waal, 1982), *How Monkeys See the World* (Cheney and Seyfarth, 1990), *Demonic Males* (Wrangham and Peterson, 1997), and *The Chimpanzees of Gombe: Patterns of Behavior* (Goodall, 1986). As you become familiar with issues in primatology, and as you narrow your interests, you will benefit from reading abstracts of articles in scientific journals such as *International Journal of Primatology, American Journal of Primatology, American Naturalist, Primates, Behavioral Ecology and Sociobiology,* and *Animal Behavior.* And of course, it is important to read the articles themselves in the areas on which you begin to focus. From these sources you will be able to identify an area of specialization that you find most interesting.

All this research has a purpose. As you work through first the books and then the articles, you will find that as you read about primatological issues that interest you, some names recur again and again. Scientific articles list the host institutions for the authors, and you can use this to investigate Ph.D. programs. The American Association of Anthropologists (AAA) publishes a guide to anthropology departments. In this guide you will find a list of every faculty member in any North American anthropology department. The guide also gives some information about whom to contact to apply to graduate school. Using these resources, and the advice of your undergraduate advisor, you will be able to identify several programs that suit your interests.

My experience on graduate school admissions committees suggests that few applicants to graduate school understand the importance of their "personal statement." The statement is your chance, your only chance, to express your goals to the Ph.D. admissions committee in your own words. Most applicants often feel strongly about their chosen field, and the impulse is to use the statement to express that passion. Field school attendance is a better demonstration. It assures the admissions committee that you have experienced field conditions and are applying to graduate school aware of its foibles, and it shows you have taken the initiative to learn about primatology. A passionate expression of interest in primates will not substitute for this experience. Bursts of emotion are almost without exception either useless or counterproductive. Taken most charitably by an admission committee reader, passionate words only state the obvious: This person wants to get into graduate school. To some readers, they make the candidate seem desperate, hysterical, or scheming. When I tell applicants this, many fret that they have nothing else to say, but they do—and it's worth saying.

An application to graduate school presents four credentials: your Grade Point Average, your GRE scores, letters of recommendation from professors, and your statement. By the time a candidate is composing applications, there is very little to be done about three of the four areas. Your grades, GREs, and the opinion of your instructors are long since determined. The fourth area, the personal statement, is your only opportunity to boost your chances for admission. The strongest candidates for admission use their statement to *demonstrate,* not just to *state* that the program to which they are applying is a good fit. The best way to do this is to use what you learned from all the reading I've outlined earlier to narrow your interest in primatology to a dissertation-research-sized project. The importance of being specific cannot be overestimated. Defining a viable research project shows off your scientific training, gives evidence that you can identify an important research question, demonstrates that you are current in the field, highlights your ability to delimit a problem without meandering into side issues, and perhaps, most important, allows your potential advisor to see why you have chosen him or her to direct your graduate career.

THE JOB OF PROFESSOR

Once you obtain your Ph.D., your most likely career path is as a professor, so it is worth a long and thoughtful consideration of whether that job is for you. Even though it was my career aspiration to be a professor from my earliest days as an undergraduate, the job itself was more than a little mysterious to me. Although I was aware that professors taught and did research, I knew little more than that. I might have estimated that professors spent half their day teaching and half their working hours "doing research." It might be worth knowing that, at a research university, it's more like one-quarter teaching; one-quarter in "service" work such as reviewing other people's grants and articles, giving talks to people outside of academic circles, serving on university committees, and other university administrative duties; maybe one-eighth writing grant proposals or administering the grants you've already gotten; one-quarter "doing research"; and one-eighth writing scientific papers.

Perhaps the most appealing aspect of the job of professor is the least concrete. I think job satisfaction is very high. Although my knowledge of careers in medicine, law, business, government, and engineering is secondhand,

I consider my job to be among the handful of jobs that remain rewarding, interesting, and challenging to most professors at midcareer and beyond. I cannot imagine a career that would be more satisfying for me.

Part of the appeal of being a professor is the variety. Typically, from September to mid-May I spend half of each day lecturing, composing lectures, preparing labs, writing and grading exams, and interacting with students. I divide up the rest of my time approximately equally among reading professional journals, directing Ph.D. students, directing my field project, writing research articles, and serving on university administrative committees. It is rare for two days to be the same. I am fortunate that I am able to teach advanced classes that require that I keep current with my field. The mix of teaching and research is a pleasant one, though if I could change one thing it would be to reduce my teaching load.

Although no two years have been the same, I spend most of the North American summer at my field site, directing research firsthand. I usually make one other trip to Uganda during the school year (last year during spring "break"). Since I have begun at Semliki-Toro, I have spent three months a year in Uganda.

Being a university professor is really four different jobs: teaching, doing research, writing research papers, and administration. If all four appeal to you, professoring is a wise career choice. If all but administration appeals to you, you're probably like the typical professor. I don't often enjoy my administrative duties, though there have been times when accomplishing a tough job I've been saddled with has been deeply satisfying. If only two of the four fit your personal style, perhaps that should not in and of itself disqualify research-university teaching from your career options, but certainly you should consider other callings. Teaching at universities where research is not a priority, such as some private universities and most community colleges, absolves you from intense research, but requires a heavier teaching load. Administration is about the same. If two of the three are unappealing, you will probably find another career more rewarding.

Among the pleasures I take in teaching is sharing my wonder in evolution and animal behavior with people of like mind. Teaching, in this sense, is like having a conversation about something you find enthralling, albeit a fairly one-sided one. I find the job of marshalling my thoughts, plugging in stray details, thinking of good examples for principles I'm trying to convey, making illustrations that convey some image I need to teach, and reviewing articles and texts to keep up with collateral fields of study very rewarding. Lecturing has an entertainment component, especially at the lower levels, that happy professors find pleasing at some level. The public speaking aspect is harrowing for me at times, but pleasant on the whole. If you cannot imagine yourself talking about Linnaean taxonomy or protein synthesis to 300 freshmen, you are considering the wrong profession. I also enjoy discussing primatology and human paleontology with people who are just discovering it. I find my work with graduate students pleasant on a personal level, but also it is intellectually stimulating talking about innovations and new discoveries with them.

I find travel exciting. I find primates fascinating. I enjoy walking in a forest. I can't help but think about the relationship between body shape and locomotor abilities. Research on chimpanzees is exciting to me because it demands all of these things.

Writing research papers is a chore to many professors. It is often a chore to me as well, but as I've written every paper I can think of, I have discovered something new and exciting that I didn't know just from having collected the data. When I am forced to limit my analysis to relationships that I can demonstrate statistically, and not just relationships I've seen while I collected the data, I learn something. I enjoy the attempt to write concisely. If you find writing a bore, find blocking out illustrations excruciating, hate even thinking about making long tables, part of the joy of professoring will be denied to you.

One of the frustrations I found in my McJobs in high school and college was supervisors whom I found to be high-handed, capricious, thoughtless, and alternately hovering and inaccessible. There were times when I spent more time explaining my work plan than actually doing the work. For an independent person like me, the most rewarding thing about the job of being a professor is its freedom. If I put in a half day during the week and choose Sunday afternoon to catch up, it matters little if at all to my colleagues. If I need to stare into space for half an hour to resolve some tricky issue, I can shut my door and do it. If I need a walk to clear my head, I can take it. Rather than a manager attempting to manage me and motivate me daily, the university does little checking on my productivity beyond assessing the yearly "summary report" I file in January. If I have taught my classes, published my two or three articles, and sustained some grant support, I need not account for how I did it. Precious few careers offer similar freedom. This freedom does, however, require that you be self-motivated and a good time-manager.

CONCLUSION

Primatology is not much like it seems from watching a video or two on the Discovery Channel, where something always seems to be happening. Rather than quick reflexes, primatology requires patience and persistence—while waiting for that first job to appear, while grinding away toward a degree, or while following primates in the forest. Yet, for those who possess these traits, primate observation is profoundly rewarding. Primatologists are often called upon to teach, to administer bureaucracies, to write articles, to plan research programs, and to supervise doctoral students. Travel is essential. The job provides a measure of freedom few careers can offer. For most potential primatologists, determining whether the inventory of activities subsumed under the label of primatologist suits them will be a long journey. Your way will be clearer if you attend a field school, make good grades, and read about primates. Journey safely.

NOTE

1. In one case I was called in the evening to my driver's house. His three-year-old boy had an extremely high fever and was dehydrated. The boy's parents were attempting to cool him down by giving him cold water, but he was throwing it up. I mixed some sugar, salt, and a little bit of Tylenol in a warm solution for him to drink, and had his parents bathe him with a damp cloth to cool him down. When his fever subsided and he appeared better hydrated, I treated him with antimalarials. He survived. In another case I was called near dawn to the assistant warden's house. His two-year-old was comatose, suffering seizures, and seemed very dehydrated. We did not have an IV, and thus there was no way to rehydrate him. We asked that a boat be prepared to take him to a clinic as quickly as possible. He died before we could get the boat in the water. I later learned his father had injected him with chloroquine before I was called.

REFERENCES

Cheney, D. L., and R. M. Seyfarth. 1990. *How Monkeys See the World.* Chicago: University of Chicago Press.

de Waal, F.B.M. 1982. *Chimpanzee Politics.* New York: Harper and Row.

Fossey, D. 1983. *Gorillas in the Mist.* Boston: Houghton Mifflin.

Goodall, J. 1986. *The Chimpanzees of Gombe: Patterns of Behavior.* Cambridge, MA: Harvard University Press.

Goodall, J. van Lawick. 1971. *In the Shadow of Man.* London: Collins.

Hrdy, S. B. 1977. *The Langurs of Abu.* Cambridge, MA: Harvard University Press.

———. 1981. *The Woman That Never Evolved.* Cambridge, MA: Harvard University Press.

Hunt, K. D. 1991a. "Mechanical Implications of Chimpanzee Positional Behavior." *American Journal of Physical Anthropology* (86): 521–536.

———. 1991b. "Positional Behavior in the Hominoidea." *International Journal of Primatology* 12(2): 95–118.

———. 1992a. "Positional Behavior of *Pan troglodytes* in the Mahale Mountains and Gombe Stream National Parks, Tanzania." *American Journal of Physical Anthropology* 87(1): 83–107.

———. 1992b. "Social Rank and Body Size as Determinants of Positional Behavior in *Pan troglodytes.*" *Primates* 33(3): 347–357.

———. 1994. "The Evolution of Human Bipedality: Ecology and Functional Morphology." *Journal of Human Evolution* (26): 183–202.

———. 1996. "The Postural Feeding Hypothesis: An Ecological Model for the Evolution of Bipedalism." *South African Journal of Science* (92): 77–90.

———. 1998. "Ecological Morphology of *Australopithecus afarensis:* Traveling Terrestrially, Eating Arboreally." In E. Strasser, J. G. Fleagle, H. M. McHenry, and A. Rosenberger, eds. *Primate Locomotion: Recent Advances.* New York: Plenum, pp. 397–418.

Hunt, K. D., J.G.H. Cant, D. L. Gebo, M. D. Rose, S. E. Walker, and D. Youlatos. 1996. "Standardized Descriptions of Primate Locomotor and Postural Modes." *Primates* (37): 363–387.

Huxley, T. H. 1863. *Evidence as to Man's Place in Nature.* London: Williams and Norgate.

Savage-Rumbaugh, E. S., and R. Lewin. 1994. *Kanzi: The Ape at the Brink of the Human Mind.* New York: Wiley.

Smuts, B. 1985. *Sex and Friendship in Baboons.* New York: Aldine.

Strum, S. C. 1987. *Almost Human: A Journey into the World of Baboons.* Norton: New York.

Wrangham, R. W., and D. Peterson. 1997. *Demonic Males: Apes and the Origins of Violence.* London: Bloomsbury.

Chapter 7

The Post-Doc Experience: Is There a Light at the End of the Tunnel?

Anne C. Stone

WHAT IS A "POST-DOC" AND HOW DO I BECOME ONE?

A postdoctoral fellowship is typically a one- to three-year research position that is begun after finishing the Ph.D. In biological anthropology, participating in post-doctoral training is less common than in the life sciences but more common than in the other subfields of anthropology. Many opportunities for such positions exist (in all subfields within physical anthropology), and being a "post-doc" is a terrific chance to expand your dissertation research in novel directions or to start a new line of research. Some post-doctoral positions also include teaching or planning a conference. In order to get a post-doc, however, you typically need to lay the groundwork at least a year in advance (Figure 7.1). This gives you the time to investigate the opportunities that are available and discuss potential projects with those that you would be interested in working with. In addition, many award applications such as those through the National Science Foundation (NSF) or the National Institutes of Health (NIH) require six months for review and notification. In general, it is best if you begin thinking about potential post-doctoral posts early in your graduate career and if you establish networks early through your graduate advisors, professional meetings and other contacts with individuals in the field. Even if you do not ultimately take a post-doc with a particular person, he or she may be able to point you toward other opportunities.

Figure 7.1
Post-doc Search Timeline

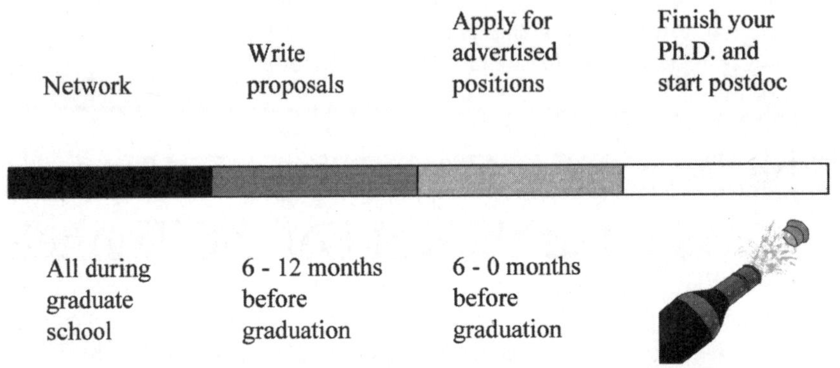

Network	Write proposals	Apply for advertised positions	Finish your Ph.D. and start postdoc

| All during graduate school | 6 - 12 months before graduation | 6 - 0 months before graduation | |

When thinking about potential projects and post-doc opportunities, there are several questions to contemplate. The first of these is what are your research interests? In the process of working on your dissertation, was there an interesting issue that you did not focus on and would like to address? Did your dissertation suggest other avenues of further research? Many people would like to continue working on issues raised during their graduate training and want to take advantage of new techniques or perspectives developed outside of their graduate department. Others would like to investigate a new topic that has intrigued them and diversify their research interests. A post-doctoral position allows a new Ph.D. to go to a new place, learn new techniques, work with new people, and focus on his or her research. After being in a graduate program for five or more years, most people benefit by going somewhere new simply because they are exposed to different people and ideas.

Another question to consider is what are your research strengths and weaknesses? Do you want more training in areas of weakness? How can you build on your strengths? Any particular graduate program does not cover every aspect of the field of physical anthropology. Thus, in the process of evaluating your graduate and research experience, you may realize that there are certain topics or methodologies that, with a deeper understanding of them, would improve your ability as an independent scholar.

Finally, you should think about what you would like to be doing in three to five years. If you would like to go into academia, particularly at a large research university, your time as a post-doc lets you start new research projects and publish; both these activities are difficult during your last year as a graduate student and during your first year as a new faculty member. If you wish to work for the government or for industry, a post-doc in a government laboratory such as the NIH or Centers for Disease Control or a post-doc in industry allows you to make important contacts, experience that environment, and decide if that is indeed the place for you.

After considering these questions, think of several potential projects or areas of interest. You should be somewhat flexible in this, because you will have to find an advisor who is also interested in your proposed project. It is important, however, to think of your overall project in terms of a collection of well-defined smaller projects that each lead to a paper. Contact several people about your ideas and talk to them about the possibility of being a post-doc in their laboratory or under their direction at a university, museum, or foundation. Be sure to give them plenty of lead time before applications are due because they will need to write letters of support for your proposal, or, in some cases, they may need to write a grant to hire you as a post-doc.

There are several different types of post-doctoral fellowships that are available. The first type provides the most independence for you to do exactly what you want to do, but this type is also usually the most competitive. These are fellowships that allow you to work with the person of your choice at the place of your choice. These fellowships may include those where you write the application to go to a specific place to do a specific project (but this place could be anywhere in the United States or even in the world), and they can include those that can only be used at a specific institution, which is perfect if that is where you really want to be. Such fellowships include the NIH National Research Service Award (NRSA), which can be taken anywhere in the United States; NSF-NATO fellowships to work in NATO member countries; Smithsonian Fellowships that require working at the Smithsonian Institute in Washington, DC, or at one of its research stations; or fellowships at one of the American Schools of Oriental Research. Depending on your research plans, and depending on whether the fellowship only covers your salary or provides only a small research budget in addition to your salary, you may also have to write a grant proposal to cover research costs. Another option is to write a regular grant proposal as a co-PI with your future advisor that includes your salary as a post-doc, as well as the other research costs. In the latter case, you must sell the idea to him or her in plenty of time to write the proposal.

In the second type of post-doctoral fellowship, your future advisor obtains a grant, and you answer his or her advertisement to be a post-doc on that project. In this case, you may be lucky to find a post-doc that matches your interests perfectly, or it may not be your first choice of what you would like to do but it allows you to work with a particular person and learn new methods. Although these postdoctoral fellowships do not provide as much research independence as the first type because you are hired to work on a specific project, you can often arrange to work on some of your own research as well. Such post-docs are also good to apply to as a backup if you are also applying for an independent post-doc award.

The third type of post-doctoral award typically requires more than just pure research. For example, you may be required to organize a conference or program or to teach a certain number of classes, and usually you also have sufficient time to work on your research. Organizing a conference can have the advantage of enabling you to meet many people in your field of interest, and it can lead to the publication of a volume that you edit. Teaching a class or two allows you to develop new classes without the pressure of a full teaching load and may make you particularly attractive to universities and colleges that emphasize undergraduate teaching when you begin looking for a "real" job.

If you are applying for an individual post-doctoral fellowship, it is a very good idea to send your future advisor a copy of your proposal for comments and suggestions. In general, it is good practice to get comments on your proposal from as many people as possible. Remember, you have to sell yourself, first to your potential advisor and then to the granting agency. However, do not hesitate to approach someone about working with him or her as a post-doc. Most people are very happy to have post-docs, especially if they bring their own money, as post-docs are typically quite motivated and productive in their research. From the advisor's perspective, post-docs usually do not require that much hands-on help to begin a project because they have become trained researchers while working on their Ph.D.s. In addition, post-docs can take on all or some of the job of managing a busy laboratory, and they often help train and mentor students.

In my own case, I completed two years as a post-doc studying Y chromosome variation in chimpanzees in the laboratory of Dr. Michael Hammer at the University of Arizona. My dissertation research at the Pennsylvania State University involved ancient DNA from a prehistoric Native American community, and in working on this project, I realized that if I ultimately wanted an academic job, I could not just specialize in ancient DNA for two reasons. First, ancient DNA is very slow work and doing it alone would not result in enough publications for tenure. Second, students in my lab would need to train on modern projects before beginning the technically challenging work required for ancient DNA, and it is likely that many students would choose to work on a project involving modern populations rather than ancient ones. In addition, I wanted to use my post-doc to learn new techniques. During my dissertation work, I developed a method to sex skeletons based on DNA. While working on this method, I became interested in the evolution of the Y chromosome. My advisor put me in touch with Michael Hammer about a year prior to my graduation, and we discussed several potential projects that I might work on if I became a post-doc in his laboratory. After spending some time in the library and talking again with Dr. Hammer, we decided that one project would be particularly interesting, and I wrote two post-doctoral fellowship applications. I was successful in obtaining an NIH National Research Service Award and started my post-doc in his lab in January 1997.

THE ADVANTAGES AND DISADVANTAGES OF BEING A POST-DOC

A post-doc can serve as a launching pad for a job, whether that job is in academia, industry, or government. It gives you time to produce publications from your dissertation, as well as start new avenues of research. In addition, successfully obtaining a post-doctoral fellowship and/or research grant for your post-doctoral research is an attractive feature to potential employers. A post-doc may also provide the opportunity to work with a specific person who is well known and well connected in your field of interest. Most post-doc positions also enable you to concentrate on your research without the distractions of teaching. Advantages also exist in interacting with others outside of your advisor's laboratory or workgroup at a new institution through advanced seminars and journal clubs. Although you will probably not remain at that institution for more than two to four years, you will have the opportunity to develop new networks or even collaborations.

Although being a post-doc can provide many advantages, there are disadvantages as well. A post-doc is a temporary position, so it is difficult to feel settled. To start your post-doc, you may have to move across the country and leave your support network of fellow grad students and friends. As a post-doc, you are often in a sort of limbo. That is, you are not a grad student and you are not faculty, so you do not quite fit into the usual categories. If your department has few other post-docs, you can feel somewhat isolated. Finally, it is always possible to end up with a poor advisor if you do not investigate the environment sufficiently. Be sure to ask current graduate students and post-docs what it is like to work with a particular person before you apply. Try to visit before starting as a post-doc. Does your prospective advisor have an active and lively research group? Is he or she available to students, and does he or she provide good guidance? Is the prospective supervisor competitive or supportive with his or her students and post-docs? Is he or she active in professional societies, and does he or she have good connections in your field?

HOW DO I FIND OUT ABOUT POST-DOCTORAL OPPORTUNITIES IN ANTHROPOLOGY?

Anthropology is a very interdisciplinary field. As a result, post-doctoral fellowships or positions may be available from a broad spectrum of agencies and institutions. The best way to begin looking for post-doc funding is to talk to your advisors and to others in your particular subfield who have had a post-doc, to visit your university's office of research services, and to investigate possibilities on the Web. University research offices maintain databases of funding opportunities for all types of projects and, thus, are an excellent source of information. On the Web, several sites include post-doctoral position announcements from a broad range of disciplines. These include http://nextwave.sciencemag.org and http://www.nature.com/jobs/index.html which are sponsored by the journals *Science* and *Nature*, respectively. Within anthropology, the American Association of Physical Anthropologists' Web site, http://physanth.org, the American Association of Anthropologists' http://www.aaanet.org, and the Primate-Jobs listing, http://www.primate.wisc.edu/pin/jobs/listings-avail.html at the Wisconsin Regional Primate Research Center list post-doctoral, academic, and nonacademic job openings. I have also put together a Web page listing post-doctoral opportunities in anthropology (http://www.unm.edu/~acstone/postdocs/post-doc.html). Do not limit your search to these pages, however!

Finally, in planning a post-doc, or indeed any phase of your career, it may be helpful to take a look at the books listed in the references section of this essay.

REFERENCES

Feibelman, P. J. 1993. *A PhD Is Not Enough*. Reading, MA: Addison-Wesley.

Fisk, P. S. 1996. *To Boldly Go: A Practical Career Guide for Scientists*. Washington, DC: American Geophysical Union.

Reis, R. M. 1997. *Tomorrow's Professor: Preparing for Academic Careers in Science and Engineering*. New York: IEEE Press.

Chapter 8

Krogman, His Cleft Palate Collection, and Me: or, What Can an Auxologist Do Today?

Evelyn J. Bowers-Bienkowski

One of the nonacademic settings where physical/biological anthropologists sometimes find a role is as an auxologist in conjunction with children's medical facilities. This can be in a center for the study of children's growth, or a cleft palate center, or a variety of other capacities. Pivotal in my career development was time spent at Children's Hospital of Philadelphia, first with the W. M. Krogman Center for Research in Child Growth and Development, and then with the Philadelphia Facial Reconstruction Center. For some of that time, I also was a part of the Southern New Jersey Cleft Palate Center. The role of a growth specialist on a cleft palate team is one that was pioneered by Wilton Marion Krogman, Ph.D. (Cooper et al., 1979). Krogman came to Philadelphia in 1947, taking a position with the Graduate School of Medicine of the University of Pennsylvania. One of his interests was to develop a set of longitudinal anthropometric and cephalometric measurements documenting how the human face grows. To facilitate this work, he established the Philadelphia Growth Center, now the W. M. Krogman Center for Research in Child Growth and Development (Katz, 1973; Stewart, 1973). At Children's Hospital, surgeon Henry Royster was developing a team to treat children with clefts of the lip and palate, of which Krogman became a part (Randall, 1999). These children were seen at the Growth Center to document their growth, which needs to be tracked for clinical reasons, as well as being of comparative interest. Krogman brought a pioneering interest in the dynamics of human growth to the study of the maturation of the head, face, and dental apparatus. Having studied with

T. Wingate Todd, known for his pioneering work on the use of hand-wrist radiographs for assaying biological age (Todd, 1937), Krogman included serial hand-wrist x-rays in his data collection. In 1970, he published his long term observations in a monograph titled "Growth of the Head, Face, Trunk and Limbs in Philadelphia White and Negro Children of Elementary and High School Age," *Monographs of the Society for Research in Child Development*. I had the good fortune to take Dr. Krogman's graduate course in child growth and development the last year he taught it prior to retiring from Penn.

I am now, somewhat unexpectedly, a teacher-scholar: a tenured associate professor in the anthropology department at Ball State University, a major teaching university, in Muncie, Indiana. The road to Muncie was long and convoluted, but perhaps it can teach you what is better avoided, as well as "how to make lemonade when life gives you lemons" as it were. But I would not be able to do the research I do without the complexities in my career path, and I find today to be a very exciting time for studies of the growth of the head and face. With the emergence of studies of the genetics of development (Gilbert, 1997; Raff, 1996), scholars are very close to developing a genetic model for the embryogenesis of the head and face. This will be of great importance to anthropology, and physical anthropology may be of great importance to it. David Leaf, in a review of the Cold Spring Harbor Symposium *Pattern Formation during Development*, wrote that the analysis of development will eventually "provide the proximal explanations of human evolution" (Leaf, 1999:4422). Peter Thorogood of the Institute of Child Health at Great Ormond Street Hospital in London has written, "[A] unified model of craniofacial development . . . should be able to explain not only normal development of the head and face, but also the range of craniofacial phenotypes seen phylogenetically and the dismorphologies seen by the clinician" (Thorogood, 1997:224). My long and convoluted preparation puts me in a position to understand and perhaps contribute to this area (Bowers et al., 1987, 1988; Bowers-Bienkowski, 1993, 1998, 1999a, 1999b). I am currently reanalyzing serial growth data, including hand-wrist x-rays, from children in the Krogman Cleft-Palate Series. In a preliminary analysis (Bowers-Bienkowski and Hurst, 1996), I have found that they support a systemic effect of the processes that produce clefts.

I grew up in rural New England, the only daughter of a self-taught industrial safety engineer, who was an instructor trainer for the American Red Cross; and an artist/craftswoman, who had also certified in the YWCA Trained Attendant's program in home nursing. I think I earned my first American Red Cross Junior First Aid Card when I was ten, and volunteered with the Scituate R.I. Accident and Rescue Corp from age sixteen to twenty. I had the good luck to attend Providence (RI) Classical High School, because my home town had not then built a high school. There I studied biology under Angus Thompson, who had earned his master's degree under

Herman Muller, at Indiana University. I found biology, especially human biology, fascinating. My parents considered the ability to earn a living essential for any person, male or female, so I applied for and won a full tuition university scholarship to the University of Pennsylvania in Philadelphia. I graduated with a degree in natural science, which has proved to be invaluable for a career in physical anthropology, because it encompassed introductory work in botany, zoology, psychology, chemistry, and physics. My upper division work was focused on genetics. I had the good fortune to take population genetics with the ecologist Robert MacArthur, and genetics of microorganisms with John Preer, who had done some of the early work on movable genetic elements. One benefit of this broad early training is an understanding of basic biological processes, which contemporary anthropologists sometimes lack. For anyone contemplating the study of human ontogeny today, I strongly recommend preparation in comparative anatomy, physiology, and development, as well as the usual undergraduate anthropology courses. The anthropological training is, however, important in that training in biology alone makes for a lack of understanding of the impact of cultural variation on human biology.

When I finished my B.A. I did not immediately go on to graduate school, as my first born was three months old. I had married at the beginning of my junior year, having naively absorbed what I understood was the European idea that if I planned to combine marriage and scholarship there was no reason to put off marrying. When my son turned out to have progressive spinal muscular atrophy and died at the age of nine months, I found comfort in a job as a research assistant with a physician on the cardiovascular service of the Hospital of the University of Pennsylvania. I also applied to, and was accepted by, the Graduate School of Arts and Sciences of the University of Pennsylvania as a special or unclassified student, and took my first course in physical anthropology. The year was 1960, and the course was Anthropology 604, "Races," with Carlton Coon. As I remember, Coon was very interested in the genetic variation some of the medical students in the class were talking about, in particular the haptaglobin variants. In the classroom Coon presented the view that human gene pools had been isolated for various periods in the past, probably by expansions of the Kalihari, Sahara, and Gobi deserts, as well as water barriers, and had accumulated genetic variations adapting people to their differing environments, just as my undergraduate evolution course, using Dobzhanski's *Genetics, Evolution and Man* (1955) as text, had suggested.

I did not continue in graduate school at that time, but spent the next several years having children and working part time. By the time I was twenty-eight I had buried two children and one marriage, and taken over the responsibility for earning a living for myself and my two remaining children. I became a bibliographer on a research project, directed by my undergraduate advisor. As a single mother, I knew I needed a stable income, promptly. Career planning was, I thought, a luxury beyond my means. But then I discovered my job carried part tuition at Penn, and that 1960 admission carried the phrase "admission valid until withdrawal." I knew I still wanted to study morphological genetics, but the questions were with whom and in what department? My initial genetics professor, Conway Zirkle, had died. Morphological genetics was thoroughly out of fashion. It was the late 1960s, and biochemical genetics held the spotlight, but it was not what really interested me. I was distinctly inner directed; some would say stubborn. Perhaps idealistic would be more accurate. I understood science as a search for answers. I arranged with my supervisor to take two hours for lunch and work an hour later in the afternoon. I hired a neighbor to look after my daughters when they got home from nursery school, and I presented that old admission form to the graduate school and said I wanted to register. Their response was that I might register if I could secure the approval of my department chairman. As the original admission had been to the department of zoology, I made an appointment to talk to John Preer, who was at that point the acting chairman of a joint department of biology, and the director of admissions of the Graduate School of Arts and Sciences. We talked about the kind of research problems I wanted to study, and he approved the reactivation of my admission. Because I was interested in humans, he sent me to Rupert Billingham, the chair of the department of genetics in the Medical School. This was about 1967, at which time genetics was becoming increasingly biochemical. Professor Billingham told me to talk to Barry Blumberg, who was then teaching in the department of anthropology, as well as conducting research at the Institute for Cancer Research. Dr. Blumberg, the discoverer of Australia antigen work for which he later shared a Nobel Prize, was then also doing biochemical genetics which was about to become molecular genetics. We found that my interests were not a good match with his, but he sent me to the new professor of physical anthropology, Solomon Katz, who was to become my academic advisor and dissertation supervisor. Katz had done a master's in the new genetics, then come to study child growth under Krogman in Philadelphia, with interests in the role of endocrine hormones in child growth, development, and behavior. It took me two months to get to see Dr. Katz, but when we finally met, there was great rapport. He was full of ideas and we talked for several hours. Meanwhile I had enrolled in genetics with Dr. Suyama, and ecology with Bob Ricklefs and Henry Hespenheid in the biology department. Ricklefs' text *Ecology* (1973) was the first to combine consideration of genetic variation with ecological variation. On completing those courses, I started to enroll in anthropology courses. I took a two-semester introduction to physical anthropology with Christopher Mickeljohn and was hooked. Then came the matter of transferring to the anthropology department and changing from unclassified student to degree status. My initial application, as an M.A. candidate, was turned down. I did not then know that universities such as Penn, with major Ph.D. programs, wanted the commitment of an application for a Ph.D. I next made an appointment with the new head of anthropology's admissions committee, Bernard Wales, and found myself being interviewed by a tall archaeologist in a basement office equipped with an impressive, battered, antique rolltop desk. This interview proved successful, and I was allowed to transfer to Penn's four-quadrant anthropology department and was admitted to degree status. Wales was a Cambridge-trained European archaeologist, and was to be very important to my development as an anthropologist. He dared me to take my foreign language exam, when I thought I could not possibly pass. He pointed out that I would be no worse off if I took the exam and failed, and I might pass and be that far ahead. I passed. I took courses that interested me, courses that were required, and whatever was offered in physical anthropology. One required course was sociolinguistics with Dell Hymes. Dr. Hymes wanted a research paper on an area on which there was little anthropology published. I chose Iceland, and went to Dr. Wales and asked to borrow material on the Viking Expansion. Dr. Wales piled about two feet of books into my lap, then asked why I wanted the material. I said I was interested in Iceland because it was an island. One knows who is and is not a part of the population of an island. His reply was to say something along the line of he had a friend "who was a bit of a nut on islands," and would I like an introduction? Perhaps there would be a project I could undertake. I said yes, but not yet. About a year later I asked Dr. Wales to write his friend. The friend turned out to be Don Brothwell who was, at that point, the head of the sub-department of anthropology in the British Museum (Natural History) and was then working on a population study of the Orkney Islands. Over the year-end break, I made my first trip abroad. I flew to London and met Brothwell. He decided I would be compatible as part of a field team and that I had some useful skills and interests. I found that he was someone I thought I could work with. Brothwell then sent me off to look at Orkney. I went by train up most of the length of Britain, from London to the rail head at Thurso, in the north of Scotland, then by ferry to Stromness on Mainland, the largest of the Orkney Islands. And I thought the Orkney Islands were wonderful. I arranged with Brothwell to come back in the summer when my daughters would be spending time with their paternal grandparents, and to develop a project to look at shifts in the patterns of mortality in Orkney over time, based on the Scottish Registers of Mortality which start in 1855. I would help with the anthropometric survey of current Islanders, but my dissertation would be based on the Registers. And so it was. The biggest surprise in the data was the high modal age at death of the Orcadians, right from the beginning of the Registers. The most frequent ages at death for Orcadians who survived infancy from the Parishes I studied were between seventy-five and seventy-nine for men and between eighty and eighty-four for women, and did not differ much whether I looked at 1860–1889, 1890–1919, 1920–1949, or 1950–1964, even though there were major cultural changes among the different periods.

I think one lesson to be drawn from this meandering pattern is the importance of networking. The other is to be true to yourself. Keep yourself open to learning from those around you. You never know when a skill will prove useful. And keep looking until you find a place that is intellectually comfortable. Be willing to do the extra bit. You never know who you will meet and what interesting ideas and projects they may have.

It took a very long time to analyze and write up my data, much longer than the collection. I received my master's degree in 1975 and finished my Ph.D. in December 1983. This was possible because at Pennsylvania, at least when I was there, the seven-year rule applied to passing the oral examination, which was based partly on general competence and partly on the dissertation proposal rather than the finished dissertation.

In 1971 Krogman retired from the University of Pennsylvania and became director of research at the Lancaster (PA) Cleft Palate Clinic, and Solomon H. Katz became the new director of the renamed W. M. Krogman Center for Research in Child Growth and Development. One of the first projects the Growth Center undertook under Katz's direction was a semilongitudinal study of the changes in blood pressure over the course of adolescence (Katz et al., 1980). This was one of a number of projects funded by the National Heart Lung and Blood Institute as part of a major push to understand the relationships between the development of elevated blood pressure and cardiovascular diseases in adults and any childhood precursors. The Philadelphia Blood Pressure Project had four codirectors contributing various sorts of expertise. These included auxologist Phylis Eveleth. Dr. Eveleth was responsible for training a set of graduate students in anthropometric methods, because cross-sectional studies had suggested that body size had an influence on blood pressure, even in adolescents, although changes with age were known. The project was to employ students as technicians. I was in the process of writing up my dissertation and was only too happy to be offered a position as a research technician. My previous experience with the Orkney Population Survey and working with the cardiologist made me a good candidate. Eveleth had previously worked with James Tanner at London's Institute of Child Health (Eveleth and Tanner, 1976, 1990). She trained the graduate students who were to act as anthropometry technicians, and trained them rigorously. I was also chosen to learn to read hand-wrist x-rays for the biological age, using the Tanner-Whitehouse II system (Tanner et al., 1983). I have found this a very useful skill (Bowers, 1986). I read all the hand-wrist x-rays from the project and subsequently acted as a consultant for the Growth Center as long as I was in Philadelphia.

One afternoon, while I was working on the Philadelphia Blood Pressure Project at the Growth Center, which was then at Children's Hospital of

Philadelphia, Rosario Mayro asked me if I wanted to attend rounds at the Facial Reconstruction Center. Dr. Mayro was the orthodontist on the Philadelphia facial reconstruction team, then directed by Peter Randall. Having studied child growth and development with Professor Krogman, she understood the value of an accurate assessment of biological age in orthodontics patients, especially those undergoing repair of clefts of the lip and/or palate, or more extensive facial reconstruction. On a number of occasions, Dr. Mayro had brought me hand-wrist films of her patients for reading. Adding these to the ten or so from the Philadelphia Blood Pressure Project I read on an average workday was no problem, and I was happy to accommodate her. The teeth of many children with clefts emerge at abnormal angles and positions. Sometimes this malpositioning can be corrected by orthodontia, but sometimes it requires orognathic surgery. If an orthodontist knows how much growth a particular child can expect to have remaining, more satisfactory treatment planning is possible. Thus reading hand-wrist radiographs for skeletal age is one of the things a physical anthropologist trained in auxology (child growth and development) can provide as part of a facial reconstruction team, in addition to precise somatic measurements.

At the time Dr. Mayro made this offer, I was still working on my Ph.D. in addition to participating in the project at the Growth Center and doing some teaching of both anthropology and biology at Community College of Philadelphia. In December 1983 I received my Ph.D. and set about looking for work. I knew Dr. Krogman had been a member of the Philadelphia Cleft Palate Team and had seen patients being treated for clefts of the lip and palate by the surgical staff of Philadelphia Children's Hospital. His role was to monitor the growth of these children, to see that they were big enough to undergo their initial surgery, and that they continued to grow normally in spite of the stress of the necessary repeated surgeries. He also observed the growth of the face, as well as the whole body in these children. The growth of the face in children is complex. Different regions of the face follow different growth trajectories: the upper face follows the pattern of growth of the brain, which is extensive in the early part of life, as Scammon showed many years ago (Scammon, 1930). The mandible is influenced by both the factors regulating somatic growth in general and by those influencing the reproductive system. This is clearly seen in the more robust mandibles found in most adult males. The midface links the other two regions, but also appears to be responsive to the factors that produce the midchildhood growth spurt (Minugh Purvis et al., 1989). Because I knew of Dr. Krogman's work on the Philadelphia cleft palate team, I decided to ask Dr. Mayro if I could now accept her invitation and attend rounds at the Facial Reconstruction Center. The idea of participating in the habilitation of children with clefts and other facial anomalies appealed to me. Team leader Peter Randall had worked with Krogman. Randall and the other team members were amenable to having an anthropologist on the teams again.

Initially I worked as a volunteer, but when I demonstrated my usefulness I was made a member of the team and placed on the payroll as an ancillary professional. I was a member of the Philadelphia cleft palate and facial reconstruction teams from 1984 until I left the Philadelphia area to take my current position in the anthropology department of Ball State University in 1987. I also served as a member of the Southern New Jersey cleft palate team working out of Cooper Hospital in Camden, NJ. I have continued to work intermittently with data I collected while in Philadelphia ever since.

Children with clefts of the lip and palate, alone or in combination, often grow in an atypical pattern (Bowers et al., 1987, 1988a). Their early difficulties with feeding, and the repeated surgeries involved in repairing clefts, had often been thought to account for any deficits. Krogman had emphasized that children with clefts usually end up with adult heights within the normal range, which is an important fact for parents to know. My work with the Philadelphia team, however, showed that children with clefts are shorter than other children, on average, in certain age ranges, suggesting that clefts are, in part, the result of altered growth processes affecting the whole body (Bowers et al. 1987, 1988a). Average heights and weights of children with clefts do not differ significantly from those of other children in the period from two to six years of age. Boys, however, have weights that are significantly different thereafter (Bowers et al., 1988a). Although the face is subject to the circulating hormones and growth factors that govern the growth of the postcranium, growth of the face is distinct from the body. Alterations in facial growth in children with clefts are clear (Krogman et al., 1975). What has not been clear is whether these were effects of surgery or of a continuation of the abnormal growth processes that gave rise to the cleft initially. While at the Facial Reconstruction Center, I collected a variety of anthropometric data in different years. These included triceps and subscapular skinfolds; biacromial, bi-iliac, and biepicondilar humeral breadths; and sitting height, as well as head length, breadth, and circumference, and bigonial and bizygomatic diameters. These data have been analyzed in a preliminary fashion and presented at professional meetings, but remain unpublished (Bowers, 1990; Bowers et al., 1988b, 1989, 1993a, 1993b; Bowers-Bienkowski and Hurst, 1996; Bowers-Bienkowski et al., 1995).

Before I left, I introduced Nancy Minugh Purvis to the Philadelphia teams. Minugh Purvis is an anthropologist especially interested in the growth of the head and face. She studied under Alan Mann and wrote her dissertation on the growth of the face in Neanderthals. When I left Philadelphia, she replaced me on the teams there, and she continues to be a team member.

While working with the Philadelphia group, I found there were people with similar interests in a few other places in the United States. In 1989 John C. Kolar chaired a symposium on the work of anthropologists in facial anthropometry at the annual meeting of the American Association of Physical

Anthropologists. Kolar is with the Columbia Craniofacial Center of Columbia Hospital at Medical City in Dallas, TX. He has been especially active in designing models for surgical construction of facial features such as the nose, either for habilitation of congenital defects or reconstruction after cancer (Kolar and Solar, 1997). In 1993, Richard E. Ward and K. M. Kelly put together another symposium for these meetings on anthropometry in the Cleft Palate Clinic. Kelly is with the Humana Advanced Surgical Institute in Dallas, TX. Ward holds appointments in oral facial genetics, as well as anthropology at Indiana University in Indianapolis. Ward has written on the importance of anthropometry in the study and habilitation of facial dismorphology patients (Ward, 1989, 1994; Ward and Jamison, 1991; Ward, Jamison and Farkas, 1998; Ward and Sadove, 1989). Minugh Purvis and I both contributed to these symposia based on work from the Philadelphia teams (Bowers et al., 1993b; Minugh Purvis et al., 1993).

There are several hundred cleft palate teams in the United States. Some of them have anthropologists as members; many do not. The anthropologists who are members of these teams have presented at professional meetings held by the surgeons, physicians, dentists, and speech pathologists who are responsible for the clinical care and habilitation of people with clefts. As a result there is some awareness of what anthropologists can contribute to their work. The difficulties with developing anthropometrists' and auxologists' positions in clinical settings come partly from working out how to compensate their holders and partly from the numbers of individuals that the teams serve. In general, even in very large metropolitan areas, patient loads are too low to support full-time positions. Nevertheless there are opportunities for useful work on cleft palate and craniofacial teams for anthropologists trained in growth and development. With the growing interest in the evolution of development, such positions may be seen to fit well with frontier interests in genetics.

For me, certain skills and attitudes have been important in building a satisfying career in physical anthropology/human biology. In a world that is changing as rapidly as today's, I think training for a very specific kind of position is not wise. In some ways, I am an unlikely role model. I am part of the good gray generation of the fifties; part of the generation of women whose upper middle-class members expected to marry the man in the gray flannel suit and raise the ideal four or so children. But then life expectancy went up, expectations went up, and the income it takes to be upper middle class went up, too. And my life experience, which looks more like that of the scrappy women scholars of the 1890–1919 period than it does that of more recent academic women, becomes more relevant. My career is built on certain attitudes, which led to the acquisition of certain skills, and to finding the opportunities to use them. This includes knowing what sort of things I want, what I can and cannot do, plus patience, persistence, flexibility, and faith in myself. I've used networking to find opportunities, and volunteered in order to convince people that I had something valuable to contribute. I've also made mistakes from which others might profit by misbalancing teaching and service, with research and its publication and by not being fully clear and focused on the mechanics of task definition and accomplishment. Jobs may be scarce, but opportunities are numerous. With the emergence of evo-devo studies, there are numerous questions for physical anthropologists to answer and problems to solve, although you may have to build or modify some structure in which to answer them before you can get on with finding solutions. And you may have to convince people that a physical anthropologist is what they need when they don't know it. If you don't have the drive to shape opportunities to your needs and desires, perhaps you should consider moving in the direction of a more structured profession such as medicine or public health or physical therapy, or toward something for which there is an obvious greater demand, such as genomics or operations research. I am an unlikely person to be an academic, because I come from an upwardly mobile family. Although my father was an engineer, he did not have a degree, and I grew up in the ambiance of my mother's family who were blue collar. But that was long enough ago that it meant that I knew that women worked. My mother had graduated from the Rhode Island School of Design on a city scholarship, planning to become a school art teacher. She gave up that dream to marry my father, but she worked as a bookkeeper before I was born and while my father was away during World War II. Later she used her training in design to make rugs and teach rug hooking from home. Her mother was a seamstress, and her mother a storekeeper. My paternal grandmother, her mother, and mother-in-law had been self-supporting Salvation Army workers. None of them made a lot of money, but they were able to manage. So I knew women worked when they needed to, and being poor did not mean being ignorant. I grew up in the country with no siblings in an area that sent only 20 percent of its children to high school. I am the first of my set of cousins to go to college. I have Girl Scout Camp to thank for the first academics I met. The camp counselor we called Mrs. Mac turned out to be Dean Millicent Mackintosh of Barnard College. And the nature counselor, who slept in the camp grounds when State U's dorms were closed—because she had no other home—earned her Ph.D. and joined the botany department of an ivy league college before I ceased to be a camper. Accordingly it never occurred to me that working one's way through college wasn't possible.

So what ideas, besides the use of sheer stubborn persistence and willingness to work very hard, can I offer you? I would suggest that, first off, you figure out what you really want to do. What do you love? What can you not stop asking questions about?

Trying to answer those questions is a foundation for a good life and a satisfying career.

REFERENCES

Bowers, E. J. 1986. "The Use of Hand-Wrist Radiographs for Age Assessment in Diseased Individuals." In M. R. Zimmerman and J. L. Angel, eds. *Dating and Age Determination in Biological Materials*. London: Croon Helm, pp. 221–239.

————. 1990. "Body Proportions in Children with Clefts of the Lip and Palate." Program and Abstracts, Seventh Congress of the European Anthropological Association, p. 74.

Bowers, E. J., R. M. Mayro, L. A. Whitaker, P .S. Pasquariello, D. LaRossa and P. Randall. 1987. "General Body Growth in Children with Clefts of the Lip, Palate and Craniofacial Structure." *Scandinavian Journal of Plastic and Reconstructive Surgery* (21):7–14.

————. 1988a. "General Body Growth in Children with Cleft Palate and Related Disorders: Age Differences." *American Journal of Physical Anthropology* (75):503–515.

Bowers, E. J., C. M. Staley, N. Minugh Purvis, R. F. Mayro, L. A. Whitaker, D. LaRossa, P. Randall and P. S. Pasquariello. 1988b. "Alterations in Muscle and Fat Mass in Children with Clefts." Fifth International Auxology Congress Abstracts, p. 89.

————. 1989. "Cleft Lip and Palate, Morphology and Androgens." Abstracts of the 1990 AAAS Annual Meeting, p. 254.

Bowers, E. J., C. M. Staley, N. Minugh Purvis, R. F. Mayro, D. LaRossa, P. S. Pasquariello, L. A. Whitaker, P. Randall, and R. D. Bock. 1993a. "Analysis of Growth in Children with Oral Clefts." *American Journal of Physical Anthropology* Suppl. (16): 59.

————. 1993b. "Analysis of Growth in Children with Oral Clefts." Presented in the Symposium on Anthropological Perspectives on Cleft Lip and Palate at the American Association of Physical Anthropologists.

Bowers-Bienkowski, E. J. 1993. "Growth in Children with Oral Clefts." International Symposium on Anthropometry in Medicine and Surgery.

————. 1998. "How Would You Make a Neandertal?" Dual Congress of the International Human Biology Association and the International Association of Human Paleontologists, Abstracts.

————. 1999a. "How Would You Make a Neandertal Face?" Program, 24th Meeting of the Human Biology Association. Abstract 107, p. 105.

————. 1999b. "Implications of Developmental Genetics for Hominid Phylogeny." *American Journal of Physical Anthropology* Suppl. 28.

Bowers-Bienkowski, E. J., E. G. Brocken, and C. M. Staley. 1994. "Genetics, Teratogenesis and Vitamin A Metabolism." Ninth Congress of the European Anthropological Association. Abstracts.

Bowers-Bienkowski, E. J., and S. D. Hurst. 1996. "Homeobox Genes and Maturation of the Hand and Wrist in Children with Clefts of the Lip and Palate." Tenth Congress of the European Anthropological Association. Abstracts.

Bowers-Bienkowski, E. J., C. M. Staley, E. G. Brocken, M. Sedam, C. V. Nelson, N. Minugh Purvis, R. F. Mayro, D. LaRossa, P. S. Pasquariello, L. A. Whitaker, and P. Randall. 1995. "Altered Sex Differences in Growth Patterns of Children with Cleft Lip and/or Palate." *American Journal of Human Biology* (7):117.

Cooper, H. K. Sr., R. L. Harding, W. K. Krogman, M. Mazaheri, and R. T. Millard. 1979. *Cleft Palate and Cleft Lip: A Team Approach to Clinical Management and Rehabilitation of the Patient.* Philadelphia, PA: W. B. Saunders Company.

Dobzhanski, T. 1955. *Genetics, Evolution and Man.* New York: Wiley.

Eveleth, P. E., and J. M. Tanner. 1976. *World Wide Variation in Human Growth.* 1st edition. Cambridge: Cambridge University Press.

———. 1990. *World Wide Variation in Human Growth.* 2nd edition. Cambridge: Cambridge University Press.

Gilbert, S. F. 1997. *Developmental Biology,* 5th ed. Sunderland, MA: Sinauer Associates.

Katz, S. H. 1973. "The Wilton Marion Krogman Center for Research in Child Growth and Development." *American Journal of Physical Anthropology* (38):57–58.

Katz, S. H., M. L. Hediger, J. I. Schall, E. J. Bowers, W. F. Barker, S. Aurand, P. B. Eveleth, A. B. Gruskin, and J. S. Parks. 1980. "Blood Pressure, Growth and Maturation from Childhood Through Adolescence, Mixed Longitudinal Analyses of the Philadelphia Blood Pressure Project." *Hypertension* 2 (Suppl. I): 155–169.

Kolar, J. C., and E. M. Solar. 1997. *Craniofacial Anthropometry,* Springfield, IL: C. C. Thomas.

Krogman, W. M. 1970. "Growth of the Head, Face, Trunk, and Limbs in Philadelphia White and Negro Children of Elementary and High School Age." *Monograph of the Society for Research in Child Development,* 35.

Krogman, W. M., M. Mazaheri, R. L. Harding, K. Ishiguru, G. Barini, J. Meier, H. Canter, and P. Ross. 1975. "A Longitudinal Study of the Craniofacial Growth Pattern in Children with Clefts as Compared to Normal, Birth to Six Years." *Cleft Palate Journal* (12):59–84.

Leaf, D. 1999. "Review of Pattern Formation during Development." Cold Spring Harbor Symposium. *American Journal of Human Biology* (11):4421–4422.

Minugh Purvis, N., D. LaRossa, P. Randall, L. A. Whitaker, R. F. Mayro, P. S. Pasquariello, S. H. Katz, and E. J. Bowers. 1989. "A Comparison of the Mid-Childhood Growth Spurt in the Normal and Cleft Palate Face." VI International Congress on Cleft Palate and Related Craniofacial Association. Abstracts.

Minugh Purvis, N., J. Lewandowski, D. LaRossa, P. Randall, R. E. Mayro, D. McDonald-McGinn, and E. Zackai. 1993. "A Comparison of Lower Facial Growth in Pierre-Robin, Stickler's and non-Stickler's Cleft Palate Children." *American Journal of Physical Anthropology* Suppl. (16):147.

Raff, R.A. 1996. *The Shape of Life: Genes, Development, and the Evolution of Animal Form.* Chicago: University of Chicago Press.

Randall, Peter, 1999. Personal communication.

Ricklefs, R. E. 1973. *Ecology,* 1st edition. Newton, MA: Chiron Press.

Scammon, R. E. 1930. "The Measurement of the Body in Childhood." In J. A. Harris, C. M. Jackson, D. G. Patterson, and R. E. Scammon, eds. *The Measurement of Man.* Minneapolis: University of Minnesota Press, pp. 173–215.

Stewart, T. Dale. 1973. "Wilton Marion Krogman: A Resume." *American Journal of Physical Anthropology* (38):53–56.

Tanner, J. M., R. H. Whitehouse, N. Cameron, W. A. Marshall, M.J.R. Healy, and H. Goldstein. 1983. *Assessment of Skeletal Maturity and Prediction of Adult Height (TWII Method).* London: Academic Press.

Thorogood, P. 1997. "The Head and Face." In P. Thorogood, ed. *Embryos, Genes and Birth Defects.* New York: John Wiley and Sons, pp. 197–229.

Todd, T. W. 1937. *Atlas of Skeletal Maturation.* London: Kimpton.

Ward, R. E. 1989. "Facial Morphology as Determined by Anthropometry: Keeping it Simple." *Journal of Craniofacial Genetics and Developmental Biology* (9):45–60.

———. 1994. "Anthropometry and Clinical Genetics." In L. G. Farkas, ed. *Anthropometry of the Head and Face,* 2nd ed. Philadelphia: Lippencott-Raven Publishers.

Ward, R. E., and P. L. Jamison. 1991. "Measurement Precision and Reliability in Craniofacial Anthropometry: Implications and Suggestions for Clinical Applications." *Journal of Craniofacial Genetics and Developmental Biology* (11):156–164.

Ward, R. E., P. L. Jamison, and L. G. Farkas. 1998. "The Craniofacial Variability Index: A Simple Measure of Normal and Abnormal Variation in the Head and Face." *American Journal of Medical Genetics* (80):232–240.

Ward, R. E., and A. M. Sadove. 1989. "Biomedical Anthropology and the Team Approach to Craniofacial Surgery." *Medical Anthropology Quarterly* (3):395–404.

Chapter 9

Teaching Anatomy at a University

Mark F. Teaford

At first glance, teaching anatomy at a university may seem like a break with tradition, or a new option, for a person with a Ph.D. in physical anthropology. Such a perspective might be reinforced by the relatively recent rise to prominence of training programs with close ties to anatomy departments, such as those associated with the medical schools at Duke, Johns Hopkins, Northwestern, Stony Brook, and Washington University. But closer examination reveals that the ties between anatomy and physical anthropology run as deep as any. Many of the founding fathers of physical anthropology (e.g., Blumenbach, Broca, Flower, and Morton) were anatomists, and when Hrdlička wrote about the ties between anthropology and medicine in 1927, he noted that "the leaders in [physical] anthropology at the present time, with very few exceptions, are . . . anatomists" (1927:2). The inaugural meeting of the American Association of Physical Anthropologists in 1930 was actually held jointly with the American Association of Anatomists, and "the vast majority" of the charter members of the AAPA were anatomists (Spencer, 1981). In short, physical anthropology and anatomy "go back a long way" together. So, in today's tough job market, what does it take to get a job teaching anatomy? Like most career options for physical anthropologists, it takes more hard work than you can imagine, plus a little luck! But what might help you in the quest for such a job?

USEFUL TRAINING AND SKILLS

It all starts with coursework. A breadth of courses is needed beyond those offered in traditional anthropology departments. In fact, certain classes can only *help* you obtain a job in anatomy. These would include anatomy, comparative anatomy, osteology, histology, and embryology. Given current trends in biomedical research, courses in cell and molecular biology, genetics, and statistics are now also invaluable, and a familiarity with computers and at least one foreign language is essential. Other coursework depends on the job opportunity at-hand. For instance, in a medical school, courses in pathology and medical imaging might be very useful, whereas, in a zoology department, courses in evolution, paleontology, ecology, and ethology might be more useful.

Even more crucial than a list of courses, however, is a keen interest in them. The courses by themselves are not a cookbook-like recipe for success—for example, "If I take this and this (even though I don't *want* to!), I'll be guaranteed a job." Each and every course should be approached with the expectation that they will somehow help you in the future. All too often, a job applicant's candidacy is derailed by a professed, or intimated, lack of interest in associated areas of study. In this age of collaborative research, you never know from where your next insight will come. Thus, use your coursework to keep open as many options as possible.

It used to be that a new Ph.D. could be either a good researcher or a good teacher and still get a job in physical anthropology. That's no longer the case. Oftentimes a person's research is what "tweaks" the interest of a search committee, as they are ultimately looking for a colleague who will be a source of exciting ideas for years to come. However, there is so much good research being done today, that that alone won't guarantee success in the job market. If a candidate doesn't come with a complete package of teaching and research skills, he or she will be at a disadvantage—it's as simple as that.

So, how to develop such skills? As in everything else, don't wait for opportunities to fall in your lap—seek them out! Certainly every student must take full advantage of the teaching and research opportunities presented by graduate and undergraduate programs. For instance, if there are options of doing research rotations, or independent studies as follow-ups to introductory courses, they should be put to maximum use as they can serve innumerable purposes. Obviously, research rotations or assistantships can teach a student new skills, ultimately giving the student a chance for publications, paper presentations at scientific meetings, and exposure to a wide range of people and programs. They will also allow a student to decide whom they might work with and who might serve on their dissertation committee—no small concerns when starting in graduate school. Another point to keep in mind is that, if given the chance, cultivate multiple research interests. All too many people lock themselves into research "blinders," insisting that they will only work on certain circumscribed (obscure!) topics. Initially such a strategy allows one to master a particular segment of literature. In the long run, however, it can be disastrous, as limited research opportunities readily translate into limited research funding.

Likewise, in teaching, seek out new opportunities. Don't just teach "introduction to physical anthropology" ad infinitum! Try to develop a broad range of courses that you can teach, because you never know when the ability to teach an extra course will help you get a job. Even in anatomy departments, the teaching of extra courses can be a plus, as the proliferation of multidisciplinary programs and connections between medical schools and undergraduate campuses is now beginning to foster more support for teaching in a variety of courses.

Just like coursework, teaching must be approached with palpable, unrestrained enthusiasm. At many institutions, teaching is your raison d'être. Yet many people still talk of teaching "loads," as if teaching were an oppressive burden firmly planted on their shoulders. Never think of it that way, and never pay it short shrift. Also, remember that teaching opportunities come in many forms—for example, talks to students in college, secondary school, and primary school, and talks to the general public in many settings (e.g., public libraries). Audiences are extremely perceptive, and they can easily tell if someone is begrudgingly lecturing to them. If you do not make good use of your teaching opportunities, you will miss a golden chance to educate, and to incite, new people. The future health of any scientific discipline depends on eager young minds, and physical anthropology is no exception. If we don't help to stimulate the interests of students and lay people alike, we will miss innumerable, unforeseen opportunities to make connections that can only help us in the future.

HOW PHYSICAL ANTHROPOLOGY RELATES TO THE TEACHING OF ANATOMY

There are five main insights that a physical anthropologist can add to the teaching of anatomy. The first is an appreciation of, or love for, human variation. When a group of students begins dissecting a human body, one of the first realizations is that their cadaver "doesn't look like the book." At first, this is often a disappointment for the students. But as the course progresses, the physical anthropologist can help them appreciate the marvelous variations that lie within us. By the end of the course, the students should understand that anatomical "norms" are merely rough guidelines of what to expect in real life.

A second type of insight that a physical anthropologist can bring to the anatomy lab is an appreciation for the growth of the human body. Granted, most cadavers are older individuals. But occasionally, younger bodies add new perspectives to the lab. If that is not the case, then the physical anthropologist can add insights into both the growth of the juvenile into an adult, and the growth of a fetus into a newborn, where classical embryology helps to explain innumerable idiosyncrasies of the adult human body.

A third area of physical anthropological interest is in comparative anatomy. Students in medical school anatomy classes (especially with the emphasis of cellular/molecular training in premed curricula) often view the human body as a blueprint for all other organisms. Again, although the physical anthropologist can point out the common elements between humans and other animals, he or she can also mention the differences.

A fourth area of insight concerns normal function. Most physical anthropologists obtain a good background in certain aspects of the normal, everyday functions of the human body, particularly those related to gait, chewing, climbing, and so on. Thus, although many physical anthropologists don't receive as much training in other topics (e.g., GI tract physiology), they can still make valuable contributions to the understanding of topics that are sometimes given short shrift in anatomy texts.

Finally, knowledge of our evolution always adds new insights to the study of anatomy. Admittedly, our fossil record is but a patchwork quilt of glimpses into the past. Still, it can often pick up where comparative anatomy leaves off. For instance, consideration of the evolution of our earliest ancestors can yield many insights into the anatomical gaps between humans and our closest living relatives.

WHAT ROLE HAS PHYSICAL ANTHROPOLOGY PLAYED IN MY TRAINING AND CURRENT ACADEMIC ENVIRONMENT?

I have always been interested in fossils, but when I entered college, I never thought of anthropology as a possible career. Very few students from my high school attended college. Like most of those who did, I entered business school, figuring I'd ultimately get a job in the "private sector." However, I quickly got bored with the intro business classes, and decided to switch into something I liked: anthropology. I was lucky because my undergraduate institution (the University of Pennsylvania) had an outstanding anthropology department. Still, my previous undergraduate record wasn't stellar due to my boredom with business. So when I applied to the top graduate programs in the country, I got few acceptances and no offers of financial support. So I took a year off, made some money, and helped teach a course at a community college. When I applied to graduate schools the next year, I applied to a more realistic range of programs and decided to go to the University of Illinois, where the graduate program gave me the flexibility I thought I needed for my future studies.

When I began thinking about thesis topics, I naively thought I might be able to discover and describe some new fossils as part of my thesis. I was quickly, and tactfully, shown the lack of wisdom in such a perspective, and began focusing on teeth because they were the most common elements in the fossil record. That led me into a thesis topic. As I wrote my dissertation, under the guidance of Gene Giles at Illinois, I also had to send chapters to other advisors off-campus. As I was finishing up the last chapters, one of those advisors, Bill Jungers—who had recently moved to Stony Brook—insisted that I apply for a post-doc at Johns Hopkins, because he had heard that Alan Walker needed someone to help teach anatomy there. After much hemming and hawing, I did, and the rest is increasingly ancient history!

Once at Johns Hopkins, I rapidly realized that fossil teeth could not tell me everything I wanted to know. So I began working on a variety of other projects, and now alternate between projects involving fossils, live primates, archeological samples, and dental patients. Some are funded by the National Science Foundation (NSF), some by the National Institutes of Health (NIH), and some are true patchwork affairs, held together by the funding equivalent of paper clips and bailing wire! Underlying all these projects is an interest in teeth, dental function, and evolution. The key to success in such a strategy is flexibility in research interest. Certainly, there are rare times when multiple projects are funded unexpectedly, and one is forced to scramble to get the work done. But we should always have such "problems!" More often that not, some proposals are turned down, and others are funded.

The funded projects have allowed me to realize a number of dreams, including paleontological fieldwork in Africa, museum work involving all the early hominid fossil material in Africa, and studies of wild primates in Costa Rica. When I'm not in the field, I'm either teaching (anatomy to first-year medical students, and undergraduate and graduate courses in biological anthropology), or doing research—usually involving data I've collected in the field. I'm always on the lookout for new projects, and I'm currently moving into some preliminary work on the physical properties of enamel that (I hope) will be of clinical and paleontological importance.

TIES TO OTHER DEPARTMENTS, UNIVERSITIES, AND INSTITUTIONS

It used to be that people in academia could exist in their own little "ivory tower," isolated from the rest of the world, if they chose to do so. Now, with the advent of personal computers, the Internet, on-line databases, and so on, that is becoming increasingly difficult. We are constantly being bombarded with information, and virtually everyone can be located and contacted somehow. Although some people dislike these disruptions of privacy, the plain fact remains that they open up infinite possibilities for communication and collaborative research. A case in point is provided by communications with colleagues overseas. It used to take four weeks to exchange letters with some colleagues (even if they responded promptly). Now it can be done overnight, if not in an instant, depending on time zone differences. With such capabilities at our fingertips, we have no one to blame but ourselves if we do not communicate widely and regularly with colleagues around the globe. This is especially important for graduate students and young Ph.D.s, who need to get to know people and need to get known. With this in mind, seek out people doing research in your field. If you read something of interest, and have questions or comments about it, contact the author(s). You will probably be pleasantly surprised by the valuable feedback you can get. As you proceed through your career, also remember the help you've been given, and always try to return the favor when students begin contacting you with questions.

Certainly, with the plethora of research being done in so many areas, the volume of research information available may seem quite daunting. However, the key to making effective use of that information is once again technology. Know what you can and cannot obtain on-line: databases, journal contents, citation indices, full-text articles, reviews, guideline for authors, and so on. Most on-line databases gather information from a range of sources impossible to duplicate on-site in a library, and most come with impressive search capabilities. Thus, keep a list of a wide range of topics or keywords that you can use to search for information. You will be amazed at the range of sources you will encounter, and when you do, make use of them by not only reading the articles, but assiduously checking the bibliographies (often the most valuable part of an article), contacting authors, and so on. The information age is upon us. Keep abreast of it, and it will help you keep abreast of current research.

Another way to maintain ties and keep abreast of research is through professional service. This may seem like an unorthodox way to do so, and, in fact, many people (at any and all stages of their careers) think they have too much research and teaching to be able to offer their time for anything else. Such perspectives are selfish and do our field a grave injustice, because the health of physical anthropology, like any discipline, is dependent on the quality of the papers and research projects generated by its investigators. If you cannot find time to aid with tasks such as the refereeing of papers and grants, you run the risk of letting poor work get published or funded. At the same time, it keeps you out of touch with what's going on, and it cannot help you on the job market.

PLUSES AND MINUSES OF TEACHING ANATOMY IN A MEDICAL SCHOOL

One thing to keep in mind, as you enter the job market, is that no academic appointment is without its drawbacks. That may sound naive or trite—especially when *any* tenure-track job looks attractive. But the fact remains that any appointment has its pluses and minuses. In a medical school, a new faculty member will often have a higher salary and better research facilities

than someone in a traditional anthropology department. Teaching requirements may also be less. It may, in fact, be an academic "chance of a lifetime."
However, if you are given such a chance, you will be expected to produce
at an exceptionally high level. For promotional decisions, you will be in competition with other researchers with far more grant support, usually through
agencies such as the National Institutes of Health. As a result, they will have
the facilities and personnel to churn out vast amounts of research. You may
even be required to obtain a certain percentage of your salary from grants,
something that's virtually impossible if you're pursuing a more traditional
research program in something like paleoanthropology. Also, given the emphasis on the "bottom-line" in many medical schools, the intellectual climate
may suffer, because your intellectual contacts with other departments, such
as biology, anthropology, and geology, may be held to a minimum by the
school's overwhelming emphasis on fundable research projects.

The take-home message is that you need to know what you're getting into
before you wade into it. A faculty appointment in a medical school is not a
guaranteed ticket to academic fame and fortune. It requires an exceptional
amount of dedication and effort. If you can handle the pressures, you can
excel. If you can't, it will eat you alive!

MAINTAINING A REALISTIC PERSPECTIVE

Once you have a job, one of the toughest things to do is to maintain a
realistic perspective on how you are progressing in your career. Often there
is a tendency to keep doing whatever you are doing and naively think "I'm
in great shape" for promotion. Don't succumb to such urges. Always retain
the ability to step back and take a good look at yourself. Always ask yourself "What could I do to broaden my perspectives?" Have the eagerness to
pursue new options.

One change that has swept through physical anthropology in the past
decade is that most of the best jobs in the country are filled by people with
at least one year of post-doctoral experience. Some people regard post-doctoral fellowships as a poor substitute for tenure-track jobs, and in some situations that is true. After all, post-doctoral fellowships certainly don't offer
the same long-term job security as tenure-track jobs. But they do give you
a chance to work with new people, gain new teaching and research experience, and set yourself in a better position for the prime jobs in academia. If
you have a choice between a post-doc at a major research institution and a
tenure-track job at a college where you will have little time for research, you
will need to think long and hard about your priorities. If your goal is a faculty position at a major research institution, you may be better served by
the post-doc.

So, as you move into the job market, keep your eyes open and be honest
with yourself. There are few guarantees in academia. But one thing is cer-

tain, if you do the bare minimum and stay isolated in your own little world, you won't stand a chance. If you work hard, stay flexible, and view the world with a healthy dose of realism, you could end up like a professional athlete—being paid to do something you love.

ACKNOWLEDGMENTS

I'd like to thank Al Ryan for his patience and encouragement throughout the gestation of this chapter, and I'd like to thank Curtis Wienker and the rest of the AAPA's Career Development Committee for their encouragement as well. This work was supported by NSF grant 9601766.

REFERENCES

Hrdlička, A. 1927. "Anthropology and Medicine." *American Journal of Physical Anthropology* (10): 1–9.
Spencer, F. 1981. "The Rise of Academic Physical Anthropology in the United States (1880–1980): A Historical Overview." *American Journal of Physical Anthropology* (56): 353–364.

Chapter 10

Research Faculty in Medical, Nursing, and Public Health Schools

Stephen T. McGarvey and Gary D. James

Not all biological anthropologists choose or are able to find employment within departments of anthropology. Because of their training in human biology and quantitative methods, many biological anthropologists have the potential to contribute to basic research, teaching and even interventions in the disciplines concerned with human health. The inclusion of epidemiological and community health perspectives in biological anthropology training programs will make these health-related research and teaching activities more common and possible. The present and likely future increase in the employment of biological anthropologists in medical, nursing, and public health schools is related to the continuing overproduction of Ph.D.s in biological anthropology relative to the growth in faculty positions within anthropology departments. At the same time, there has been an increase in research faculty within the various departments and schools dedicated to research and training of human health professionals.

We view these trends in employment for biological anthropologists as inevitable and continuing in the future. We are happy to argue that there should be more tenured faculty positions for biological anthropology within anthropology departments, and do not wish to be overly accommodating to the political, economic, and academic factors behind the waxing and waning of disciplines in the American universities and colleges. Nevertheless, the employment patterns we experienced and observed in the last two decades indicate that bioanthropologists should anticipate and plan for potential employment as research faculty in biomedical research and teaching institutions.

The purpose of this chapter is to describe briefly and somewhat idio-syncratically some issues related to biological anthropologists working as research faculty in medical, nursing, and public health schools. This chapter is aimed at students currently enrolled in graduate study in biological anthropology or who are about to undertake graduate study in biological anthropology. We assume that young scholars would like to remain active and contribute to teaching and research in biological anthropology. We believe that they will be faced with a range of job possibilities, including as research faculty in medical, nursing, and public health schools. In light of the trends we described, this chapter will have been worthwhile if we can influence biological anthropology students to plan for the potential that they might not be anthropology faculty. We make no attempt here to report quantitative data on these employment trends because there is little information readily available on biological anthropologists' career tracks after completion of Ph.D. study. Thus, we rely on our own observations and experiences as biological anthropologists who have worked in health-related schools and departments for thirty-six person-years.

We have both attempted to remain connected to biological anthropology by attending annual meetings, publishing in bioanthropology journals, and maintaining our own networks of collaboration and mentoring with colleagues and students. Thus, this chapter has an encouraging tone about the possibility and rewards for biological anthropologists to thrive as research faculty within biomedical and public health academic institutions. Close colleagues and family may have different stories to tell, but here we have decided to light a candle rather than curse the darkness. We are unable to comment on biological anthropologists working within medical or public health schools who no longer participate in the professional activities of their original discipline due to adaptive changes in interests and activities after exposure to these new environments. In situations and institutions where external financial support is the final arbiter of long-term employment despite the putative intellectual value of ideas and approaches, we have learned to not judge others' career decisions, and to feel fortunate.

SCIENTIFIC QUESTIONS OF INTEREST

Scientific interests in biological anthropology must be primary and satisfying for biomedical research faculty who want to continue to contribute to their parent discipline. It is crucial to pursue scientific questions related to biological anthropology as part of establishing intellectual autonomy and relative career and financial independence. In biomedical institutions there are many dynamic, exciting, and well-supported domains of investigation and departments in which research and teaching occur. These traditional biomedical departments and new interdisciplinary centers, institutes, and programs obviously have far greater power and resources than most biological anthropologists have experienced. But it is necessary for biological anthropologists in such environments to show their nonbioanthropological colleagues our parent discipline's theoretical and methodological innovations. The traditional adaptive, ecological, and population genetic perspectives of biological anthropology, along with more recent work on biopsychosocial context and political economic analyses of health and function, have much to offer contemporary health research and teaching in biomedical institutions. At a minimum, biological anthropologists can resist the vacuous biological race interpretations about ethnic group differences in health or risk factor research in schools of medicine, nursing, and public health. Instead we can offer measurable concepts and approaches to putative family and population genetic influences and their salient interactions with specific environmental exposures on human biology and health. Research faculty outside of anthropology departments who can combine the adaptive, evolutionary, and ecological perspectives of human population biology with the conceptual and methodological innovations from biomedical and health studies appear to have an excellent opportunity to participate in the growth of our parent discipline. For example, the elaboration in studies of psychosocial stress and genetic epidemiology provide only two illustrations of research areas in which biological anthropologists are actively pursuing new findings and methods, and developing middle-range theories with substantial financial support (James and Brown, 1997; McGarvey, 1999; Rogers et al., 1999). Finally, research findings by biological anthropologists, regardless of their jobs, will be an influential part of the progress in the parent discipline through contributions to our journals, meetings, and graduate training programs. We discuss later the context of the decisions about what journals may be best for publishing the work of bioanthropologists working outside of anthropology departments.

PREPARATION FOR BIOMEDICAL CAREERS

Can a Ph.D. student in biological anthropology actually prepare for a career or employment as a research faculty in biomedical institutions? Despite the fact that neither of us have done so, it seems clear that it could and should be done by contemporary and future graduate students. As we asserted earlier, it appears that there will be more Ph.D.s granted in bioanthropology than there will be tenure-line anthropology faculty positions in the future. If that scenario occurs, it will be prudent for students to expect to apply for jobs with a wide range of available vocational possibilities after completion of the Ph.D.

The specialization within bioanthropology and the specific Ph.D. thesis topics must primarily follow the intellectual interests and motivations of individual scholars, as they are the only truly sustaining forces behind scientific research and teaching. Second, learning specific content areas and acquisition of special skills should be chosen in light of potential employment. This advice presents no conflict as the variety of questions, concepts, and methods currently pursued by biomedicine, nursing, and public health has widened to embrace many of the pursuits of biological anthropology. The exposure to new concepts and measures about human biology can refresh bioanthropologists' research ideas, and the applied health perspective can help us avoid Weber's admonition about "specialists without spirit" among academics.

The expansion of theoretical perspectives in human biology and health among schools of medicine, nursing, and public health and the increase in U.S. federal funding for biomedical and health research has broadened the types of research supported by the National Institutes of Health (NIH). As evidence we urge readers to review the listing of Requests for Applications, Program Announcements, and other fundable research opportunities published weekly in the NIH Guide, available at the NIH Web site. Investigator-initiated research has also expanded to include many areas completely within the contemporary definitions of biological anthropology.

During the early stages of one's career in schools of medicine, nursing, and public health, it is important to be active in maintaining one's identity as a professional biological anthropologist. The usual history, hierarchies, and internal politics of academic biomedical institutions can make it difficult for Ph.D.s in anthropology to be recognized as independent scientists and not merely interesting scholars or worse, supertechnicians. Despite research activity, independent funding, publications, and fruitful collaborations, it is amazing to us both how many nonanthropologists in such institutions assumed that all types of habits of thought and inquiry were natural to us as anthropologists. The perception of anthropologists as generalists can be advantageous sometimes as it allows bioanthropologists entrée to potential collaborations. Unfortunately more rigid stereotypes of anthropology as nonscientific can lead to less attractive adaptive traits such as overvigorous explanation, self-assertion, and playing the power and money games. Educating and disabusing biomedical faculty of their ignorance and stereotypical views of anthropology research must be considered part of the job description for biological anthropologists in such institutions.

Developing and teaching courses and giving lectures in other faculty's courses is an excellent way to establish a recognizable intellectual perspective and content area. This requires active engagement with other faculty and administrators, and the rewards include recruitment of students to assist in your work, informing students and faculty about your ideas and findings, and, perhaps, some salary support for such teaching duties. Of course, the short-term and midterm goal of establishing independent external financial support by investing the time and effort necessary for publications and grant submission can conflict with the significant effort required for regular teaching. But the immediate psychic rewards of teaching and the acquisition of the social label as a "biological anthropologist" should be considered when weighing the advantages and disadvantages of teaching as a research faculty member.

PERSONAL VIGNETTES OF THE AUTHORS' CAREER TRACKS

The following sections are a summary of our respective experiences as research faculty in biomedical institutions. We try to emphasize the positive experiences and the combination of chance and opportunity that led to our past and current employment. We apologize for what might be perceived as a self-aggrandizing tone and recognize that both of us have been very fortunate in establishing ourselves as independent investigators outside of anthropology while keeping a presence within biological anthropology.

Both of us applied over the years to anthropology faculty and other positions but for various reasons remained as research faculty. We do not describe the jobs we did not get and the stimulating effect that had on our grant-writing, although we freely admit such experiences were powerful stimuli to continue establishing and finding independent financial support for our research interests. In short, after completion of the Ph.D.s, or even our respective post-doctoral posts, we did not plan the career paths we describe. Both narratives focus on how we developed autonomous interests, found ways to financially support them, and made them fit into institutional realities and priorities.

In the spirit of telling honestly our stories to younger scholars, it is hard to underemphasize the occasional acute feelings of unpredictability, uncontrollability, and undesirability we both had about our long-range job future. What allowed us to continue was a mixture of personal stubbornness, adaptive optimism, family support, both instrumental and affective, and dedication to the scientific ideas and methods in which we had been trained. We both felt also at a basic level that we knew at least as much, and were just as capable, if not more than, the majority of other faculty we encountered in the institutions where we worked.

The Experience of Stephen T. McGarvey

Three months of research in high altitude Peru after the first year of graduate study was the salient intellectual and physical experience that led to my commitment to biological anthropology. Those revisited and refracted field experiences endured and remained influential at the times I was making career decisions. After finishing my master's thesis on a longitudinal study of a small cohort of infants from Nunoa, Peru, a site visit team from NIH came to Pennsylvania State University's department of anthropology human biology laboratory to review the Human Biological Adaptability interdisciplinary training grant directed by Paul T. Baker. The training grant was funded by the National Institute for General Medical Sciences (NIGMS), and the visitors consisted of NIH staff and a few faculty from other universities. The visitors met with all the trainees as a group, and after pleasantries and initial discussions, one of the NIGMS staff asked if anyone was interested in epidemiology. This is my best recollection of when the idea for most of my later research was reified. It was also the first time I became aware of the powerful role that NIH funding played in setting the agenda for human biology and health research and training. I never thought I would not be a biological anthropologist, but that event, my preexisting interests, the intellectual, career, and employment contexts of the late 1970s and early 1980s, and personal factors interacted to produce my (initially unplanned) employment pattern.

For my Ph.D. thesis research, I chose to perform a cross-sectional survey of cardiovascular disease (CVD) risk factors, focusing on blood pressure, among adult American Samoans and Samoans residing in Hawaii. The doctoral experience of data collection, analysis, and writing about CVD risk factors brought me closer to epidemiology and public health and further influenced my scientific interests. Many of the themes of my doctoral work remain central to my research now. While still a student, I led a corollary preliminary analysis of familial resemblance of blood pressure in the Samoans, which foreshadowed my current involvement in genetic epidemiology of fatness and diabetes. After my Ph.D. I was a post-doctoral fellow at the University of Hawaii in a joint anthropology and medicine training program, during which I spent six months in American Samoa conducting a follow-up study of participants from my earlier doctoral study.

While in American Samoa and working with their Public Health Division, I decided to pursue further study in epidemiology and public health for several reasons: (1) to learn the corpus of epidemiology theory and methods; (2) to increase my quantitative skills through biostatistics courses; (3) to obtain another degree that might be more marketable outside of anthropology departments; and (4) to determine if I wanted to work in more applied public health settings. Fortunately, I received a Wenner-Gren Foundation for Anthropological Research fellowship for M.P.H. study in epidemiology and public health at Yale University. It is worth noting this key foundation in the history of our parent discipline anticipated that such further study was going to be necessary for the development of biological anthropology!

The M.P.H. degree and public health school experience opened greater opportunities outside anthropology but did not lead to the sought-after tenure line anthropology faculty position. My wife received an offer to join Brown University as a clinician and researcher, and soon after making that family decision, I found an opportunity also at Brown. I came as a hospital-based assistant professor (research) working 50 percent of the time to help conduct an epidemiological study of infant and early childhood blood pressure that had recently been funded by NIH. This work used my extant interest and skills in blood pressure studies and the dietary, biological, and social influences within families. Because of Brown's relatively small size, its entrepreneurial context, and the need to increase my salary percentage, I began to explore opportunities for other research. I became involved in epidemiological studies of community-dwelling geriatric patients, caretaking burdens of their families, and a randomized study of innovative clinical treatments for these patients.

These activities sufficed as employment and intellectual stimulation for about two years, when I became concerned about maintaining my active links to biological anthropology. Brown did not have any courses in biological/ physical anthropology, and I developed an introductory course. I taught it for three years with increasing enrollments, due to the natural curiosity among undergraduates in the basic scientific questions of our discipline. There were immediate rewards from instructing students in human evolutionary and population biology, but the crucial long-range benefit was renewing my allegiance to the evolutionary and adaptive questions we ask.

During the time of teaching and conducting the research, I was learning the formal and informal techniques of trying to obtain external financial support for research. The funding for the infant blood pressure studies was not renewed, and after several difficult and unsuccessful attempts, it became clear that my salary support was disappearing, despite my and others' best efforts. Personal and professional autonomy became extremely important also then to me as I had heard enough comments, generally well intentioned, such as "Oh you work *for* Dr. . . .," or "I hear you are good at statistics, could you run this t-test for me by tomorrow?" I decided that if I was going to keep applying for financial support, I wanted to do so to support my own research ideas. The thrill of knowing that the decision to pursue funding for my independent ideas in biological anthropology was the correct one did not forestall fears of not obtaining financial support or becoming another Ph.D. without independence in a medical school.

After more than one attempt, I was able to secure an NIH grant to study longitudinally the constellation of CVD risk factors among adult Samoans from American Samoa and (Western) Samoa. I moved the NIH grant from one Brown-affiliated hospital to another hospital because a group of physicians and immunologists conducting parasitic disease research in China and the Philippines had begun to form at the second hospital. This allowed the professional and personal contacts that fostered collaborations on *Schistosomiasis japonica* and my leading the efforts to study schistosomiasis-associated malnutrition, child growth, and cognition. This collaboration led to external funds from the World Health Organization, NIH, and several foundations over the next six years.

I also was invited to give several lectures in an introductory international health course on biological anthropology perspectives and research, including child malnutrition and morbidity, demographic trends in mortality, and changes in the burden of disease with economic development and modernization (whatever that really is!). I also became more closely allied to the Brown Population Studies and Training Center that had several sociologists and economists doing international demographic and health research. Regrettably, at the same time, there was a loss of support for my teaching introductory biological anthropology, and I stopped that teaching. I had to practice what I learned the prior five years as a research faculty member: if I was not going to be paid fairly for doing something others wanted, I would not do it for nothing.

Most recently the funded Samoan research has focused on genetic epidemiology of CVD risk factors made possible through collaborations with geneticists at other universities. The emphasis has been on understanding the specific interactions between candidate genes and putative susceptibility loci and other biological, behavioral, and genetic factors. This has allowed as much concentrated conceptual and methodological efforts on measuring the environment as on exploiting the innovations in population and laboratory genetics. My parasitic disease activities also continue with new emphases for which we are seeking external support, including interactions between hormonal events of puberty and the development of partial resistance to re-infection and ecological studies of nonhuman mammalian and snail transmission of infection and agricultural and water management practices. I also became the instructor/course leader for the international health course, which brought me in contact with undergraduate, graduate, and medical students who began to work with me on my research.

The record of external funding has led Brown biomedical institutions to support some of my salary and to provide reserve funds to provide some short-term stability when external grant funds are low. I remain a faculty, and the basic lack of long-term stability in my academic appointment has not changed. A recent position as director of the International Health Institute at Brown will allow me greater opportunity to form collaborations, move in new directions with start-up funds, and improve my own job security. I view what I ask questions about and what I teach as inherently based in biological anthropology. The excitement remains for its traditional focus on detecting the signatures of past evolutionary and adaptive events on human population biology in all its contemporary multidimensional ecological complexity. The interdisciplinary nature of my doctoral and post-doctoral training obviously make it possible for me to have survived and thrived in a medical school environment, despite the soft money nature of being a research faculty.

The Experience of Gary D. James

For my dissertation, I examined how differences in lifestyle (more traditional Samoan vs. more modern Western) affected the biological stress response (blood pressure and urinary catecholamines) of Western Samoan men. Despite an impressive literature review (at least I thought so) and the experience of living in a different culture collecting urine specimens and taking blood pressures, it was amazing how much I didn't know about the topic of stress. I learned this lesson when I accepted a post-doctoral traineeship in the Cardiovascular Center at Cornell University Medical College after I completed my Ph.D. The post-doc was my entrée into the world of soft money research positions in Medical Schools. I became aware of the position while attending the physical anthropology meetings the year I defended my dissertation. It wasn't posted; I was just doing the usual hanging around in the bar and talking to people. It just goes to show that it does pay to go to professional meetings when you are in graduate school and that some of those conversations you have while you are relating your drab and wretched life at 2:00 AM actually do lead to something.

My wife and I packed up from Penn State (actually Bellefonte, PA) and headed off to New York City. We realized at once that we could not afford to live in Manhattan (where the Medical School is) on a post-doctoral stipend (which was and generally still is paltry) so we rented an apartment in Lodi, New Jersey, and I became a straphanger. When I began at the Medical School in the fall of 1984, I was given a desk and assigned to work with two other researchers, one an experimental psychologist and the other an electrical engineer. They were using and developing a new-fangled device that was being introduced into cardiovascular medicine: the automatic ambulatory blood pressure monitor. What was exciting about working with this technology was that there was relatively little known about it, so that I had the opportunity to develop its use in biological anthropology and explore what I could do with it. I was extremely lucky because I was plunked down in a research group that was on the cutting edge, and creativity was encouraged and demanded. The fact that I came from a discipline that had a different perspective from both the Ph.D.s and M.D.s at the Medical College meant that I immediately had a niche. To them (the researchers with which I worked), at that time, I embodied anthropology, and it was important to them for me to be a collaborating investigator because having a diverse, interdisciplinary research team improved their chances of getting large NIH grants.

The research group I worked with was actually one of several that were knit together into a larger entity that was funded by NIH as a Special Center of Research (SCOR) in hypertension. This larger entity included clinical M.D.s, endocrinology labs, molecular biology labs, and invasive (catheterization) and noninvasive (echocardiography) cardiology labs.

Research involved both human and animal models. Amazingly, in this rich clinical setting, there was a complete lack of statistical skills. I made it known that I could analyze data, and I was immediately included in a rainbow of related cardiovascular projects, ranging from pharmacological studies of hormone regulation to the impact of heart failure on vascular biology. The skills I learned in biological anthropology that were developed for field and epidemiological settings were easily transferred to the clinical setting. This added to my indispensability to the group. It also helped me maintain my anthropology identity, in that in this clinical setting, I was unique in terms of my skills set.

As my post-doc was ending, I was encouraged to write for an NIH New Investigator Research Award, which I got. Once I had my own funding, I was given a faculty title and thus began my "professional" odyssey in soft money funding in a Medical School. Over the next twelve years, I collaborated with numerous medical researchers at Cornell Medical College, NYU, Sloan-Kettering Cancer Institute, The Albert Einstein School of Medicine, and Mt. Sinai School of Medicine, such that I was a 10 percent-to-20 percent investigator (getting that proportion of my salary) on three to four grants at any given time.

Why did I have to be involved in so many projects at once? It was necessary because the Medical School did not directly fund my research group, which is the case with many other major research groups in Medical Schools. The Medical School basically provided us with the research space, but the members of the group had to provide the money for the support and conduct of the research. It is also important to emphasize that although I was in a medical school, I was not paid anywhere near the salary of the physician researchers. However, I was paid a lot more than I would have been had I taken a tenure track academic position in a department of anthropology. Thus, the trade-off between soft money and hard money positions is that you get a higher salary and perhaps greater research freedom but no safety net (tenure). Put another way, if you don't get the grants, you don't have a job.

Finally, my ability to succeed in the biomedical environment at Cornell Medical College was based on the fact that I did have training in a biomedical area. My doctoral coursework was interdisciplinary and included many non-anthropology Ph.D. level courses in medical physiology and statistics. I did have some idea about what I was getting into when I began my post-doc at Cornell Medical College. Without the interdisciplinary training, it would have been much more difficult to fit in and survive.

As I noted earlier, at Cornell Medical I was part of a large, loosely federated research group. As with most large loosely tied entities, the research group began to slowly break up and fragment as many of the senior researchers retired, and the leadership and reputation they provided evaporated. So you know, physicians monopolize positions of power and influence in medical schools. Thus, researchers such as me with a Ph.D. are peripheralized and shut out of leadership positions when research groups crumble and re-assemble. Realizing that the handwriting was on the wall, I used the large network I had developed over my years in research to find another job. In-terestingly, it was contacts from anthropology that allowed me to garner my current position at Binghamton University, as director of their newly cre-ated Institute for Primary and Preventative Health Care. I am also a research professor in the School of Nursing and have an adjunct professorship in the department of anthropology. My position at the university is partially sup-ported by hard money, although I am not tenured. The ultimate goal of the work at Binghamton is to make the new Institute self-sustaining through the acquisition of federal and private grants. In this scenario, I am also supposed to cover the bulk of my salary.

Finally, when I left the Medical College, I did so on good terms with my medical colleagues, such that I continue to collaborate with them on sev-eral projects related to the effects of stress on hypertension, cardiovascular disease, and cancer. I am fortunate in that I am now in a position where I can create new research directions with both my past and current colleagues. Still, I have continued to sacrifice the safety net of a tenured position in an anthropology department for the lure of unrestricted and unfettered scien-tific creativity (e.g., not hampered by heavy teaching loads) in biomedical research.

CONCLUDING LESSONS AND STRATEGIES

Keep your identity as a biological anthropologist. This may be difficult especially if one is the only such scientist in a whole school or department, but in the long run, it is worth it because you have the chance to broaden the intellectual and methodological horizons of your parent discipline. De-scribing and reminding others of this identity also allows for accurate social labeling of your interests and skills by physicians, epidemiologists, nurses, and other faculty, researchers, and administrators in biomedical institutions. Maintaining and promulgating your identity is crucial for the processes of promotion because such committees need guidance in inviting external re-viewers. The pattern of publication in certain journals also becomes impor-tant to consider for biological anthropologists in biomedical institutions. Review committees for promotion and for grants evaluate the quality of the journals and the number of publications. Thus, maintaining one's identity as a bioanthropologist for research faculty in schools of medicine, public health, or nursing does not mean publishing all your findings in biological anthropology journals. The name recognition and putatively higher value to review committees of more mainline biomedical journals compared with biological anthropology journals is a reality, whether we like it or not. It is difficult to change the journal preference of the biomedicine disciplines.

Distinguish yourself and what you do from medical anthropology. Evolutionary and adaptive perspectives on human population biology using quantitative methods define us. We are all trained in the importance of holistic concepts about human populations, and we and many bioanthropologists use methods of social science and qualitative methods as part of our human biology and health studies. However, we do not focus solely, or place at the center, concepts and methods about sociocultural phenomena. We mean no disservice to our cultural anthropology colleagues who investigate social, cultural, and behavioral factors about health, medical care, and medical institutions. We suggest that using biological rather than medical anthropologist as a term will help nonanthropologist colleagues see the commonalities about biology. One of us is comfortable with the term biomedical anthropologist and the other prefers biological anthropologist.

In the biomedical setting, find out what niche is missing and fill it. You need to establish yourself as a peer, not an underling. Make a point to publish as much of the work that you do as you can. This will establish your reputation and make it easier to get future funding; you will also gain the respect of your colleagues.

In biomedical institutions there are many similarities between what biological anthropologists do and those things done by epidemiologists. The use of populations as the unit of study, the reliance on quantitative methods, an inclusive biosocial perspective, and an emphasis on the poor and underserved segments of societies are only a few. There are also differences in that epidemiologists tend to have more experience in research design for studies of health and on the relationship of their work to public health policy and decisions. As biological anthropologists seeking and receiving public money to do human biology and health research, it is incumbent on us to learn from epidemiology colleagues how to make the closer links between our research and national, regional, and local public health needs and programs. In terms of one of our major differences with epidemiology, it is important to maintain the evolutionary emphasis in our research. It allows bioanthropologists to justify looking further into human biology, including genetics, in an adaptive framework into why some risk factor or health condition exists at a certain level in populations.

It is important to contemplate joining a research team, ideally a multidisciplinary group. This provides a basis for continuing growth of collaborations and search for innovative sources for external funds. One's research skills should be flexible and complement potential colleagues' skills. One should be open to identify how you can best contribute in a creative way that shows your independent contributions. Know what biomedical faculty need and are doing by attending departmental lectures, guests' colloquia, and by seeking out other faculty. The multidisciplinary training of biological anthropology is an enormous advantage. We argue strongly that bioanthropology graduate programs need to continue and embrace other human biological disciplines by encouraging courses in other departments, inclusion of other faculty on committees, and so on. Because of the tenuous nature of externally supported soft money jobs, you may need to collaborate doing tasks that you can do best, but that are not central to your extant or developing interests. Try to turn this base financial reality into an opportunity for entrepreneurship and learning new concepts and methods.

If there is only one message readers should take from this chapter, it is that biological anthropologists working in academic biomedical institutions must write grants for external financial support to become as independent as possible. Whatever career stability might exist is only obtained this way, not to speak of some relative peace of mind about what topics you are spending your workweek thinking about.

Finally, research faculty in biomedical institutions often ask themselves, Is what I'm doing anthropology or bioanthropology? Even if one stays connected to biological anthropology, the daily environment can distance research faculty from the core and peripheral events within our academic parent discipline. One coping skill is to remind oneself that anthropology has roots as an applied discipline and that those research perspectives can have impacts outside the walls of the academic setting. Biomedical colleagues will understand more about what anthropologists do when they learn from us how it blends with disciplines with which they have everyday experience, such as medicine. Biological anthropologists can contribute to the increased emphasis in schools of medicine, public health, and nursing on a more community, multidisciplinary, and historical perspective on what brings citizens and patients into contact with their institutions.

ACKNOWLEDGMENTS

We recognize the influence of Paul T. Baker in our training and careers. We thank him for teaching us that the excitement of the ideas is the only true motivation for a scientific career and that exposure to many other disciplines sustains curiosity and expands skills. We are happy to dedicate this chapter to him.

REFERENCES

James, G. D., and D. E. Brown. 1997. "The Biological Stress Response and Lifestyle." *Annual Review of Anthropology* (26):313–335.

McGarvey, S. T. 1999. "Modernization, Psychosocial Factors, Insulin and Cardiovascular Health." In C. Panter-Brick and C. M. Worthman, eds. *Hormones, Health and Behavior: A Socio-Ecological and Lifespan Perspective*. Cambridge: Cambridge University Press, pp. 244–280.

Rogers, J., M. C. Mahaney, L. Almasy, A. G. Comuzzie, and J. Blangero. 1999. "Quantitative Trait Linkage Mapping in Anthropology." *Yearbook of Physical Anthropology* (42): 127–152.

Chapter 11

Physical Anthropology, Medical Genetics, and Research

Bert B. Little

The title of this chapter was originally "Teaching Genetics in a Medical School." I changed the title because I thought it should reflect the content of the chapter, and this chapter contains more than just the medical school teaching experience. The aim of this volume is to highlight careers in physical anthropology, and this chapter contains academic experiences during my career.

Three issues are vitally important to career development in any academic field. First, collecting the skill sets that will be useful is crucial, although often they are difficult to determine. Second, get involved in the work (research and publication) of the field early, even if it means accepting very humble assignments to gain experience. Third, learn the mechanics of obtaining funding for research and publication activities, as this is an essential ability directly related to surviving in academia. Grantsmanship is certainly an integral component of establishing an independent research program.

Possessing the skill set needed to do research, having research and publication experience, and grant funding expertise makes an academic professional attractive to potential employers, inside and outside academia. This collection of experience and abilities is especially valuable in physical/biological anthropology because it is important to be self-sufficient professionally and an asset to your colleagues. Purists may say that it is diminutive to the field to be so practical as to plan to be employable, but it is personally diminutive not to be professionally employable, and even worse not to be employed.

Perhaps the greatest benefit of physical/biological anthropology is diversity. It is an eclectic field with sound training in social science, biology, research methods, statistics, and databases. Archeology, primatology, human biology, human genetics, mathematics, and statistics are an unusual combination outside anthropology. But such a combination is common in physical anthropology. The advantage of anthropology in my career is the ability to be involved in research from many different areas. Very early in my education, I tried to be involved in as many research projects as possible. As early as high school, a friend (H. Kenneth Stephens IV, Esq.) and I did research on a 1690 water mill site near the high school on the Cape Fear River in North Carolina for academic credit.

While an undergraduate at Appalachian State University in Boone, North Carolina, I took over sixty semester hours of anthropology, primarily with Drs. Burton Purrington and Harvard Ayers. They took me, at age nineteen, to the first professional meeting I attended and assigned me to be a crew leader on the 1976 summer archeological field school. Dr. Pat Beaver gave me the opportunity to do independent study courses such as mini-ethnographies of prison subculture, the Ku Klux Klan, and anthropological linguistics. Through these experiences I first came into contact with research, research methods, and statistical analysis. This piqued an interest in research. More than a third of my anthropology hours were comprised of independent study credit for field archeology research, field experience, laboratory work, and computer analysis. During this time the importance of statistics was clear, and I took four semesters of it. I graduated in 1976.

My father had foreseen that a bachelor's degree in anthropology would not qualify me for much of a job when I graduated. He worked for the N.C. Department of Corrections and Cape Fear Technical Institute (now Cape Fear Community College). He arranged, through the college, employment for me at the prison. For two years I worked in a medium security prison in rural North Carolina teaching G.E.D. classes, health, physical education, and drug education. It was, however, serendipitous that I had taken rudimentary notes while working in the prison. I later used this experience in my master's and doctoral programs, writing manuscripts on sociolinguistics for required "core" classes and finally publishing a composite of these (Little, 1982a).

GRADUATE SCHOOL

Upon entry into the M.A. program at Ball State University in Muncie, Indiana, I intended to concentrate in archeology. I worked (for money!) as an archeologist in the Cultural Resource Management (CRM) Service. I had the opportunity to create a database on hengiforms in the British Isles from the dissertation data of one of my professors (Dr. Ron Hicks) that I continue to update and analyze. Interested in osteology, I took physical anthro-

Table 11.1
Important Things to Learn as an Undergraduate

Geology
Chemistry, through Organic
Math, through Calculus
Statistics, through multivariate
Computer Science, through database theory
Technical writing
Molecular biology/genetics and biochemistry
Accounting
Research Methods
Fieldwork
Humble basic work
Oral presentation

pology and multivariate statistics. During 1978–1979 I had five part-time jobs: working for the University computer center as a statistical and computing consultant, as teaching assistant in Anthropology, a research assistant on the Middletown III sociological fifty-year follow-up study of Muncie, and a statistical research assistant for the National Center for State Courts (Hewitt and Little, 1981). Concurrently I continued as an archeologist with the CRM Service.

It was through Dr. Jack Whitehead that I became interested in the phylogenetic relationships of primates and collected data on morphological, molecular genetic, and cladistic classifications of the order. The coursework and research culminated in a M.A. thesis entitled "A Numerical Taxonomy of the Order Primates" (Little, 1982b) with a committee chaired by Dr. Jack Whitehead. A subset of data from my master's thesis was the basis for a publication on the epigenetic relationships of body and brain weights among the primates (Little, 1989). Because Dr. Whitehead personally paid for my travel, I was able to make my first presentation at the Midwestern Anthropological Society Meeting in Milwaukee.

While I was at Ball State University, Dr. Whitehead learned of a research position at Wright State University School of Medicine's Fels Research Center in Xenia, Ohio, and arranged an interview for me. The Center's director, Dr. Alex Roche, told me that I would have to "focus on humans to go anywhere in the field." During the interview process, I met Dr. John Himes (professor of Epidemiology, School of Public Health, University of Minnesota), and we became friends instantly. Dr. Himes said that if I wanted to get a Ph.D. I should pursue it immediately because if I waited "Ph.D.s are not going to get any easier or cheaper." John Himes telephoned his Ph.D. advisor at The University of Texas at Austin, Dr. Robert Malina. The condensed version is that instead of following a "rabbit trail" at Wright State reading and scoring hand-wrist x-rays, three weeks later I was admitted to the Ph.D. program at UT-Austin with a doctoral fellowship. I left Ball State in August 1979, and in September enrolled at UT-Austin in the physical anthropology Ph.D. program.

At the University of Texas-Austin, I had three curricular anthropology mentors: Dr. Ellen Brennan (human genetics), Dr. Robert Malina (human growth and development), and Dr. Henry Selby (mathematical anthropology). While only in my second week at UT, Dr. Malina asked me to write a computer program to analyze the differences between Tanner-Whitehouse I and II hand-wrist skeletal aging methods in Zapotec Indian, American White, and African-American children. I naively thought it would be a task completed quickly. I finished the project a year later, presented the results at the next annual AAPA meeting, and finally published the results (Malina and Little, 1981). The next project with Dr. Malina was the National Science Foundation (NSF)-funded Valley of Oaxaca project, part of which would become my dissertation. My first Oaxaca project was on skeletal age research. A concurrent project, with Dr. Henry Selby and a group of graduate students, was a computer simulation model of the ecology and human biology of the study village in the Valley of Oaxaca. This became the master's thesis of my friend Dr. Michael Fischer (University of Kent-Canterbury, founder and director, Social Anthropology Computing Centre) (Fischer, 1980). The next project was assortative mating of Zapotec Indians of the same village (Malina, Selby et al., 1983). Dr. Malina also involved me in the San Antonio Heart Study project, allowing me to earn money (something graduate students always appreciate) and a publication (Malina, Little et al., 1983). In addition to physical and other anthropology coursework toward the Ph.D., I took several courses in the mathematics department, including matrix theory, matrix algebra, biostatistics, multivariate statistics, multivariate analysis, sampling theory, probability theory, statistical theory, and mathematical statistics to support my work in human genetics (quantitative, theoretical, and population). While still a graduate student, the University of Texas funded a two-year grant to develop a relational database in physical anthropology that survives today. It was refreshed when Dr. Malina returned in the fall of 2000 to the Valley of Oaxaca for an NSF-sponsored thirty-year follow-up study of the same Zapotec Village.

During my first year at UT-Austin, I also worked at Balcones Research Center for Dr. Claud Bramblett. Daily, I fed and cared for about 150 monkeys in Dr. Bramblett's Vervet colony. This closed the loop in my interest

Table 11.2
Important Skills to Develop in Graduate School

Grantsmanship

Biostatistics

Data collection and analysis

Database design and administration

Manuscript publication, writing and editing skills

Public speaking as in professional meeting presentations

---

in primatology after scraping monkey feces in the hot Texas sun everyday. The experience gave me a well-rounded appreciation for the master's degree concentration in primatology, but not one I care to repeat. It also gave me the practical experience in animal handling and survival surgery that would later be needed in research at the medical school.

My dissertation project was the analysis of the genetic and environmental determinants of child growth among the shortest peoples in the Americas, a genetically isolated group of Zapotec Indians in the Valley of Oaxaca (Little, 1983). Although I did go to southern Mexico, the real work in researching my dissertation was constructing families and households in Austin in the databases, integrating information from many different sources (biological, agricultural, dietary, sociocultural, genealogical, meteorological) for analysis. The first publication utilizing the crude relational database was written after my dissertation was completed. Diverse information is available for households and individuals in the village. In the publication we analyzed socioeconomic determinants of child growth in a subsistence agricultural community assumed to be classless (Malina, Little et al., 1985). The next publication (Buschang et al., 1986) was a collaboration with my "big brother" (Dr. Peter Buschang, professor, Texas A&M Baylor College of Dentistry) who was completing his dissertation fieldwork during the semester I arrived at UT-Austin. The other projects I worked on during this time included the dissertations of ABD faculty in anthropology, sociology, and zoology. With "Uncle Jim" (my graduate advisor, professor James Neely), I was able to pursue my interests in archeology.

AFTER GRADUATE SCHOOL

After I completed the Ph.D. in July 1983, I was appointed lecturer, teaching physical anthropology (human genetics, introduction to physical anthropology, sex and evolution) for two years at UT-Austin. I replaced Dr. Ellen

Brennan, one of my dissertation committee members, who was killed in March 1983. I enrolled in the M.A. program in mathematics. I was able to include twenty-four semester hours of graduate credit to fulfill requirements for the mathematics master's degree. However, it was my interest in databases and human growth and development that led to a faculty position (research assistant professor) at UT Southwestern Medical School in Dallas (UTSWMC). Dr. Jan Friedman (Division of Clinical Genetics) hired me to develop a computerized medical knowledge base system of expert information for clinical use by physicians on the effects of specific drugs on human prenatal development (TERIS–Human Teratology Information System, ©University of Washington, 2001). It was funded by a maternal and child health (USPHS) grant, of which I later became PI. TERIS was a practical demonstration that databases useful for research can be compiled from published information (Friedman et al., 1990), and could be a valuable clinical resource.

After graduate school, I continued to collaborate with my major professor, Dr. Robert Malina, on several projects: child growth and development (Malina, Shoup et al., 1987), childhood obesity (Malina, Zavaleta et al., 1986, 1987a, 1987b; Malina, Skrabanek et al., 1989), menarche/ menstruation (Little, Guzick et al., 1989), admixture and body size in Meso-America (Little and Malina, 1986), and genetics of Zapotec Indians in the Valley of Oaxaca (Little, Malina et al., 1986, 1987, 1989; Little and Malina, 1989).

THE MEDICAL SCHOOL EXPERIENCE

The work on TERIS involved database content authoring, indexing, query structure, and taxonomics for physician end-users in human teratology. One of the people who interviewed me at UTSWMC was the chief of toxicology for the Dallas County Medical Examiners office, Dr. Robert Bost. Bob knew of my interest in anomalies in child/fetal growth and development. He told me of an unusual finding: a gas chromatograph peak that occurred in approximately 20 percent of cases in postmortem SIDS toxicology. The peak was a C-12 fatty acid known as lauric acid. With support from an NIH small research grant, we analyzed this historically, and explored prospectively and confirmed the finding of MCAD (medium chain acyl co-A dehydrogenase) deficiency with GC/MS and external laboratory blinded analysis (Kemp et al., 1996). I presented these findings at the American Society of Human Genetics in New Orleans in 1988. Those findings generated much interest and several ongoing collaborations.

Soon after my arrival in Dallas, Dr. Friedman (Chair. Medical Genetics, University of British Columbia) asked if I would also like to counsel genetics patients in his clinic. For the next fourteen years, I did medical genetic counseling, laboratory and clinical research, and taught human teratology to medical students, residents, and fellows. I did medical genetic counseling at Parkland Memorial Hospital's obstetrical complications clinic and at St. Paul Hospital's maternal-fetal medicine (MFM) unit.

During the first few months of counseling patients exposed to potential teratogens I noted that there were a "bunch" of women who used cocaine during their pregnancies. At this time in mid-1985, the only publication regarding cocaine use during pregnancy was a 1983 case series of eight women who had a placental abruption following cocaine use. I began collecting information on birth outcomes of cocaine-exposed pregnancies (Little, Snell et al., 1988, 1989; Little, Jackson et al., 1996; Little and Snell, 1991). Later included were methamphetamine (Little, Snell et al., 1988), alcohol (Little, Snell et al., 1990), T's and blues (Little, Snell, Gilstrap et al., 1990), and heroin-exposed (Little, Snell, Klein et al., 1990) pregnancies.

The first international paper I presented on the topic was "Congenital Anomalies and Substance Abuse in Pregnancy" at the Fifth International Auxology Congress, Exeter University, England, 1988. The University of Texas would not prepay for the trip, and advance payment was required. Professor Jim Tanner advanced the funds for the trip, and told me to repay him when I could. I attended the conference, was reimbursed, and paid the loan from this sterling gentleman.

We also investigated the prevalence of HIV among pregnant intravenous drugs users (Little, Snell, Wendel et al., 1991). We published the perinatal outcomes, and postnatal growth and development of infants and children born to substance abusers (Little, Snell, Gilstrap, and Johnston, 1990; Little, Snell et al. (in review); VanBeveren et al., 2000). In 1990 I was awarded a five-year multimillion dollar federal grant to investigate substance abuse during pregnancy.

In 1990 I also received a four-year grant from the American Heart Association to investigate effects of prenatal cocaine exposure on prenatal and postnatal cardiovascular development. In 1992 I received a four-year grant from the Hogg Foundation for Mental Health to investigate the effects of prenatal cocaine exposure on postnatal growth and neurobehavioral development. The Hogg Foundation also funded our two-year-long investigation to determine whether prenatal exposure to cocaine was associated with a fetal cocaine syndrome (Little, Jackson et al., 1996). In 1990 a student in the Graduate School of Human Development at UT-Dallas who was interested in early childhood development and prenatal cocaine exposure contacted me. Dr. Toosje Van Beveren spent six years with me researching her dissertation and completing her doctorate in 1996. Her dissertation was a study of the effects of prenatal cocaine exposure on infant mental development of adopted infants versus infants remaining with their biological parent (VanBeveren et al., 2000). My work with Dr. VanBeveren indirectly led to my appointment as professor of human development at UT-Dallas.

In 1995 we received funding from the Texas Commission on Alcohol and Drug Abuse in excess of a half-million dollars annually to continue the federally funded project. The purpose of the state funded project was to provide clinical assessments of infants and children prenatally exposed to substances of abuse, design a specific intensive intervention, deliver the intervention, and assess infants posttreatment for positive effects of intervention. This program continues today (July 2001) with funding in excess of $600,000 annually. The ongoing study continues the research begun with a Hogg Foundation grant and is the long-term follow-up of substance-exposed children after an intensive intervention period compared to controls.

At the medical school, there were other opportunities in addition to developing the content and architecture of the clinical teratology computerized knowledge base, and doing medical genetic counseling. In 1992, my "boss," Dr. Larry Gilstrap (Chair, Obstetrics and Gynecology, UT Medical School-Houston), and I published a textbook for obstetricians, *Drugs and Pregnancy* (Gilstrap and Little, 1992). A current second edition was recently published (Gilstrap and Little, 1998), and is in its fourth printing. I was also able to do research in clinical genetics, collecting and analyzing a decade's (1980–1989) births at Parkland Memorial Hospital, and using the 120,000+ births to compute population specific risks for chromosomal abnormalities (Little, Ramin et al., 1995). It was also possible to teach my "specialty area," drugs and pregnancy, to medical students, obstetrics and gynecology residents, and MFM fellows. It is important to point out that teaching in a medical school differs from the traditional university. Courses in medical schools are very frequently team taught with the course director directing, but not teaching every lecture. In contrast, at the traditional university, the professor teaches nearly every lecture.

Working with students, residents and fellows was quite rewarding. Frequently these individuals needed assistance in research design, sometimes they were in search of a research topic, and in other instances they needed assistance with data structure, statistical analysis, statistical interpretation, and manuscript preparation. The outcome was a number of collaborations that resulted in the following publications in a variety of areas: Cancer cytogenetics (Kessler et al., 1988), sexually transmitted diseases in pregnancy (Christmas et al., 1989), acid-base status in premature infants (Ramin et al., 1989), intrauterine transfusion (Christmas et al., 1990), drug teratology (Harstad et al., 1990), teratogenic effects of hyperthermia in pregnancy (Little, Ghali et al., 1991), pelvicalyceal dilation in pregnancy (Twickler et al., 1991), intraamniotic infection (Maberry et al., 1991), hepatitis C in pregnancy (Bohman et al., 1992), episiotomy dehiscence (Ramus et al., 1992), operative vaginal delivery (Ramin, Little et al., 1993), pre-labor meconium staining (Ramin, Gilstrap et al., 1993), GnRH effects of hormone metabolism (Wilson et al., 1993), meconium aspiration syndrome (Hernandez et al., 1993), ultrasound anthropometric reliability (Harstad et al., 1994), surgical suture practices (Bohman et al., 1994), cord blood methamphet-amine and perinatal outcome (Ramin et al., 1994), blood flow and neuro-logic effects in cocaine-exposed term infants (King et al., 1995), clinical trial of suture vs. staples for Cesarean section (Bohman et al., 1995), metabolism of cocaine during pregnancy (Stettler et al., 1995), and preven-tion of herpes in pregnancy (Dobson et al., 1998).

My "lab" neighbor to the west (Dr. Roger Bawdon) was a microbiologist. He involved me in work in animal experiments that he conducted with rabbits and acute phase reactions in a model of bacterial C-section infections (Bawdon, Fiskin et al., 1989; Bawdon, Davis et al., 1989). Later we collabo-rated on studies on teratology and pharmacokinetics of HIV therapies, AZT (Little, Bawdon et al., 1989; Christmas et al., 1995), and pentamidine (Little, Harstad et al., 1991; Harstad et al., 1990). During this time I became in-terested in quantitative chemistry techniques after working with Bawdon and established a gas chromatography (GC) laboratory for drug metabolism studies. Eventually, in 1990, I acquired a Finnegen gas chromatograph-mass spectrometer (GC/MS) laboratory from the department of molecular genetics because my department was willing to guarantee maintenance sup-port of $20,000 per year for its operation. Over the ensuing decade, the ma-chine earned its own income. We performed studies of new contrast media for MRI imaging, novel pathways of glucose metabolism, cocaine metabo-lism, and pharmacokinetics of new antineoplastics. However, equipment is more demanding than raising children. One must spend significant amounts of time not only maintaining the equipment, but also soliciting projects to monetarily support it because a single funded research project cannot pro-vide all the support needed for routine maintenance. My lab neighbor to the east was Dr. Ayalla Barnea. She and I collaborated on several projects, in-cluding a $1.2 million NIH grant to research cocaine and HIV interactions in fetal brain culture (Aguila-Nelson et al., 1997).

During the time I was at the medical school, I had the opportunity to work with many medical students. Some would accompany me during pa-tient consults; others would have specific questions and be referred by their attending physicians. Still others would choose to work with me for elective credit. However, most of these students needed paid work during the sum-mers. I was able to get a Chilton Fellowship to pay the medical students to work with me. One summer I had as many as four students on fellowships. That was very demanding because they were so eager to learn, but they did not have the specific training for the lab procedures, and required nearly constant attention. However, there were great rewards. Probably the most rewarding and productive experience was the work one summer with three medical students. I was developing the basic science aspect of my interest in cocaine use during pregnancy. I had already published the preliminary estimates of prevalence of cocaine in pregnancy, and clinical findings of pregnancy complications and infant outcomes. I was also interested in pharmacokinetics of cocaine in pregnancy, and was reading what little information was available. The generally accepted dictum was that the human placenta transferred cocaine without metabolizing it. I studied the papers that asserted the placenta could not metabolize cocaine and identified several laboratory procedure errors that may have affected the studies' outcomes. One study used frozen placentas, another used a buffer with pH that was far too low for enzyme activity, and another used very old tissue that was frozen. In yet another study, incubation techniques were not correct. During the summer of 1988, the students and I repeated the experiments, and corrected the errors. We were in a research building attached to Parkland Memorial Hospital where nearly 15,000 babies were delivered annually. We obtained placentas and began incubation within forty-five minutes of delivery. By the end of the summer, in spite of the aforementioned papers, we had demonstrated conclusively that the placenta could, indeed, metabolize cocaine (Roe et al., 1990).

In later experiments with other medical students, we documented a new placental enzyme system for the metabolism of cocaine (Little, Roe et al., 1995). All medical student work was presented at the local and national medical student research fora. Medical students also worked along side me in animal experiments, assisting in everything from injecting cocaine, AZT, and other drugs to chemical extractions and GC/MS analysis, and manuscript preparation. Importantly, all medical students were included as authors on publications of the projects on which they worked.

Child development has remained a research interest throughout my career, and the research I did—even on drug metabolism—was related to growth and development. I continued to publish work from my dissertation research while at the medical school (Malina, Little et al., 1986; Little, Malina et al., 1986, 1987, 1988, 1990; Little, Knoll et al., 1991). My other child growth investigations were very specialized, such as childhood lead poisoning (Little, Snell, Johnston et al., 1990), substance exposure during gestation (Little, Snell, Gilstrap et al., 1990; Little and Snell, 1991; Little, Gilstrap et al., 1991; Little, Harstad et al., 1991; Little, Knoll et al., 1991; Van-Beveren et al., 2000), and the effects of gravity on reproduction and development (Little et al., 1987; Little and Duke, 1988).

I also collaborated with established faculty researchers on clinical trials (Hemsell et al., 1993, 1994, 1995), national impact assessments (Leveno et al., 1990), and birth certificate reliability of congenital anomaly reporting (Snell et al., 1992).

BEYOND FACULTY-RELATED RESEARCH

In my current position as Vice President for Academic Research at a university that is aggressively developing a research program, I continue to do research and publish. My interest in pharmacology in pregnancy (Little,

1999a, 1999b) has endured, and I also continue to work on SIDS (Little et al., in press), childhood obesity (Al-Haddad et al., 2000), and substance abuse during pregnancy. I am the PI on a multi-year USDA $18.6 million Data Warehouse and Data Mining research grant, on the biology faculty and I (an investigator) recently received NSF funding for a DNA sequencing laboratory. My specific use of the lab will occur after Dr. Malina and I return to the Valley of Oaxaca in 2002 to collect DNA from the Zapotec genetic isolate where I did my dissertation. A paperback handbook version of *Drugs and Pregnancy*, 2nd ed. (Gilstrap and Little, 1998) has been contracted by the publisher, and is currently underway. Another textbook co-authored with a psychiatrist, Dr. Kimberly Yonkers, professor of Psychiatry at Yale University Medical School, who counseled patients with me, *Treatment of Psychiatric Disorders during Pregnancy*, was published in January 2001 (Yonkers and Little, 2001).

In my present position, I make use of the research skills and the diversity of expertise by encouraging faculty research, grantsmanship, and publication. The variety of training in a physical anthropology program that included social, archeological, and linguistic anthropology is an asset. One is able to appreciate the research aspects of the humanities and social sciences, in addition to the physical sciences, and to work with faculty entertaining the "unique" appreciation for variety afforded as an anthropologist.

IMPLICATIONS FOR TRAINING IN PHYSICAL ANTHROPOLOGY

The first thing to remember about physical anthropology is that it can be a natural science discipline, or it can be what natural scientists call "soft science." If your goal is to do soft science, it was probably not important to read this chapter. The practice of a natural science discipline has certain demands, whether it is physical anthropology or chemistry or zoology. Some students take physical anthropology because it satisfies the natural science requirement, but frees them from taking the "hard stuff." At the outset of a physical anthropology training program, one should take the hard science. The undergraduate programs at a few universities offer degree programs called biological anthropology that require a science background, including two years of chemistry, mathematics through calculus, advanced biology courses, molecular biology, geology, physics, and statistics. For a physical anthropologist to possess such training means that he/she will be able to take relevant courses and training in nearly any field to complement the anthropology training. Some of the most interesting findings in physical anthropology today come from anthropologists whose scientific training included many courses outside the department, or "cross-training." Therefore, as in my career, a degree in anthropology with a strong base in natural science can foster employment in many varied disciplines related to physical anthropology.

REFERENCES

Aguila-Nelson, N., B. B. Little, R. Y. Ho, and A. Barnea. 1997. "Differential Potencies of Cocaine and Its Metabolites and Benzoylecgonine in Suppressing the Functional Expression of Somatostatin and Neuropeptide Y-Producing Neurons in Cultures of Fetal Cortical Cells." *Biochemical Pharmacology* (54): 491–500.

Al-Haddad, F., Y. Al-Nuami, B. B. Little, and M. Thabit. 2000. "The Prevalence of Obesity among School Children in the United Arab Emirates: Serious Public Health Implications." *American Journal of Human Biology* (12): 498–502.

Bawdon, R. E., L. L. Davis, and B. B. Little. 1989. "Rabbit Plasma Fibronectin Levels Associated with *Staphylococcus aureus* enterotoxin B: An Acute Phase Reaction." *Gynecologic and Obstetric Investigation* (28): 185–190.

Bawdon, R. E., A. M. Fiskin, B. B. Little, L. L. Davis, and G. Vergarra. 1989. "Fibronectin and Postpartum Infection in Rabbits: An Animal Model." *Gynecologic and Obstetric Investigation* (28):191–194.

Bohman, V. R., L. C. Gilstrap, K. J. Leveno, B. B. Little, S. M. Ramin, K. G. Goldaber, R. Santos-Ramos, and Jody Dax. 1995. "Cesarean Delivery: Subcuticular Suture versus Staples for Skin Closure." *Journal of Maternal-Fetal Medicine* (3): 212–215.

Bohman, V. R., L. C. Gilstrap, S. M. Ramin, B. B. Little, R. Santos, K. G. Goldaber, J. Dax, and K. J. Leveno. 1994. "Subcutaneous Tissue: To Suture or Not to Suture at Cesarean Section." *Infectious Diseases in Obstetrics and Gynecology* (1): 259–264.

Bohman, V., R. W. Stettler, B. B. Little, G. D. Wendel, L. J. Sutor, and F. G. Cunningham. 1992. "Seroprevalence and Risk Factors for Hepatitis C Virus Antibody in Pregnant Women." *Obstetrics and Gynecology* (80): 609–613.

Buschang, P. H., R. M. Malina, and B. B. Little. 1986. "Growth of Leg Length and Sitting Height for Mild-to-Moderately Undernourished Zapotec School Children Living in the Valley of Oaxaca, Mexico." *Annals of Human Biology* (13): 225–233.

Christmas, J. T., B. B. Little, W. L. Johnston, C.E.L. Brown, R. Santos, and S. K. Theriot. 1990. "Nomograms for Rapid Estimation of Intravascular Intrauterine Transfusion Volume." *Obstetrics and Gynecology* (75): 887–891.

Christmas, J. T., B. B. Little, K. A. Knoll, R. A. Bawdon, and L. C. Gilstrap. 1995. "Teratogenic and Embryocidal Effects of Zidovudine in Sprague-Dawley Rats." *Journal of Infectious Diseases in Obstetrics and Gynecology* (2): 223–227.

Christmas, J. T., G. D. Wendel, R. E. Bawdon, R. Farris, G. Cartwright, and B. B. Little. 1989. "Concomitant Infection with *Neisseria gonorrhoea* and *Chlamydia trachomatis* in Pregnancy." *Obstetrics and Gynecology* (73): 295–298.

Dobson, A., B. B. Little, L. L. Scott. 1998. "Prevention of Herpes Simplex Virus Infection and Latency by Prophylactic Treatment with Acyclovir in a Weanling Mouse Model." *American Journal of Obstetrics and Gynecology* (179): 527–532.

Fischer, M. D. 1980. "A General Simulation of Production and Consumption in the Valley of Oaxaca, Mexico." M.A. thesis, University of Austin-Texas.

Friedman, J. M., B. B. Little, R. O. Bost, S. G. Mize, and W. L. Singleton. 1986. "The Teratogen Information System." In R. Solomon, B. Blum, and M.

Jorgenson, eds. *MEDINFO: Proceedings of the Fifth Conference on Medical Informatics,* Vol. 15, IFID World Conference Series on Medical Informatics, Washington, DC, October 26–30, pp. 462–464.

Friedman, J. M., B. B. Little, R. L. Brent, J. F. Cordero, J. W. Hanson, and T. H. Shepard. 1990. "Potential Human Teratogenicity of Frequently Prescribed Drugs." *Obstetrics and Gynecology* (75): 594–599.

Gilstrap, L. C., and B. B. Little. 1992. *Drugs and Pregnancy.* New York: Elsevier Press.

———. 1994. "Medication during Pregnancy: Maternal and Embryofetal Considerations." In D. K. James, P. J. Steer, C. P. Weiner, and B. Gonik, eds. *High Risk Pregnancy: Management Options.* London: W.B. Saunders, pp. 229–252.

———. 1998, 1999. *Drugs and Pregnancy,* 2nd ed. New York: Chapman and Hall, Cambridge: Oxford University Press, and London: Arnold Publishers (Hodder Headline Company).

Gilstrap, L. C., B. B. Little, and F. G. Cunningham. 1991. "Medications in Pregnancy: Part II. Special Considerations." Supplement 11, *Williams Obstetrics,* 18th ed. Norwalk, CT: Appleton and Lange.

Harstad, T. H., P. H. Buschang, B. B. Little, R. Santos, D. M. Twickler, and C.E.L. Brown. 1994. "Ultrasound Anthropometric Reliability." *Journal of Clinical Ultrasound* (22): 531–534.

Harstad, T. H., B. B. Little, R. E. Bawdon, S. Sobhi, D. A. Roe, and K. A. Knoll. 1990. "Embryocidal and Teratogenic Effects of Pentamidine Isethionate Administered to Pregnant Sprague-Dawley Rats." *American Journal of Obstetrics and Gynecology* (163): 912–916.

Hemsell, D. H., P. G. Hemsell, B. J. Nobles, E. R. Johnson, and B. B. Little. 1993. "Abdominal Wound Problems after Hysterectomy with Electrocautery vs. Scalpel Subcutaneous Incision." *Infectious Diseases in Obstetrics and Gynecology* (1): 27–31.

———. 1995. "Cefazolin Inferior for Single-Dose Prophylaxis in Women Elective Total Abdominal Hysterectomy." *Clinical Infectious Diseases* (20): 677–684.

Hemsell, D. L., B. B. Little, J. Faro, R. L. Sweet, W. J. Ledger, A. S. Berkley, D. A. Eschenbach, P. Wolner-Hanssen, and G. Pastorek. 1994. "Comparison of Three Regimens Recommended by the Centers for Disease Control and Prevention for the Treatment of Women Hospitalized with Acute Pelvic Inflammatory Disease." *Clinical Infectious Disease* (19): 720–727.

Hernandez, C., B. B. Little, J. Dax, L. C. Gilstrap, and C. Rosenfeld. 1993. "Meconium Aspiration Syndrome (MAS): Prediction of Need for Neonatal Ventilation (NV)." *American Journal of Obstetrics and Gynecology* (169): 61–70.

Hewitt, J. D., and B. B. Little. 1981. "Examining the Empirical Basis of Sentencing Guidelines: The Partial Replication of a Reform Effort." *Journal of Criminal Justice* (9): 5206–5244.

Kemp, P. M., B. B. Little, R. O. Bost, and D. B. Dawson. 1996. "Whole Blood Levels of Dodecanoic Acid, a Routinely Detectable Forensic Marker for a Genetic Disease Often Misdiagnosed as Sudden Infant Death Syndrome (SIDS)-MCAD Deficiency." *American Journal of Forensic Medicine & Pathology* 17(1): 79–82.

Kessler, L. G., B. B. Little, M. W. Redrow, and N. R. Schneider. 1988. "Temporal Variation in Nucleolar Organizing Region Expression in Bone Marrow Cells of Individuals with Leukemia." *Cancer Genetics and Cytogenetics* (35):109–117.

King, T. A., J. M. Perlman, A. R. Laptook, N. Rollins, G. Jackson, and B. B. Little. 1995. "Neurologic Manifestations of In Utero Cocaine Exposure in Near Term and Term Infants." *Pediatrics* (96): 259–264.

Leveno, K. L., B. B. Little, and F. G. Cunningham. 1990. "National Impact of Tocolytic Therapy on Low Birth Weight." *Obstetrics and Gynecology* (76): 12–15.

Little, B. 1982a. "Prison Lingo: A Style of American English Slang." *Anthropological Linguistics* (Summer) 82: 206–244.

Little, B. B. 1982b. "A Numerical Taxonomy of the Primates." M.A. thesis, Ball State University, Muncie, Indiana.

———. 1983. "Sibling Similarity in Growth Status and Rate among School Children in a Rural Zapotec Community in the Valley of Oaxaca, Mexico." Doctoral dissertation, The University of Texas-Austin. University Microfilms, Ann Arbor.

———. 1989. "Gestation Length, Metabolic Rate, Body and Brain Weights among Primates: Epigenetic Relationships." *American Journal of Physical Anthropology* (80): 213–218.

———. 1991. "The Effect of Maternal Cocaine Use during Pregnancy on Intrauterine Development." *Mothers, Infants and Substance Abuse,* American Psychological Association Monograph, Georgetown University Child Development Center, Georgetown University Medical School, Washington, DC, pp. 6–33.

———. 1994. "Teratogenic Agents. *Precis V Antepartum Care.*" L. C. Gilstrap et al., eds. American College of Obstetricians and Gynecologists. An Update in Obstetrics and Gynecology. Washington, DC, (3): 138–143.

———. 1997. "Teratogenic Agents. *Precis VI Antepartum Care.*" L. C. Gilstrap et al., eds.. American College of Obstetricians and Gynecologists. An Update in Obstetrics and Gynecology. Washington, DC, (4): 1–34.

———. 1999a. "Medication during Pregnancy." In D. K. James, P. J. Steer, C. P. Weiner, and B. Gonik, eds. *High Risk Pregnancy: Management Options,* 2nd ed. London: W.B. Saunders, pp. 617–638.

———. 1999b. "Pharmacokinetics during Pregnancy: Evidence-Based Maternal Dose Formulation." *Obstetrics and Gynecology* 93(51001): 858–868.

Little, B. B., and R. E. Bawdon. 2000. "Antiviral Medication Use in Pregnancy." In L. Scott, L. Gilstrap, and S. Faro, eds. *Viral Infections in Pregnancy.* New York: Chapman and Hall.

Little, B. B., R. E. Bawdon, J. T. Christmas, S. Sobhi, and L. C. Gilstrap. 1989. "Pharmacokinetics of Zidovudine (AZT) during Late Pregnancy in Long Evans Rats." *American Journal of Obstetrics and Gynecology* (161): 732–734.

Little, B. B., P. H. Buschang, and R. M. Malina. 1988. "Socioeconomic Variation and Estimated Growth Velocities in a Subsistence Agricultural Community in the Valley of Oaxaca, Southern Mexico." *American Journal of Physical Anthropology* (76): 443–448.

———. 1991. "Heterozygosity and Craniofacial Dimensions of School Children from a Subsistence Community in the Valley of Oaxaca, Southern Mexico." *Journal of Craniofacial Genetics and Developmental Biology* (11): 18–23.

Little, B. B., and P. J. Duke. 1988. "Effects of Gravitational Forces on Reproduction and Development." *Comprehensive Therapy* (14): 3–5.

Little, B. B., F. E. Ghali, L. M. Snell, K. A. Knoll, W. L. Johnston, and L. C. Gilstrap. 1991. "Is Hyperthermia Teratogenic in the Human?" *American Journal of Perinatology* (8): 185–189.

Little, B. B., L. C. Gilstrap, and F. G. Cunningham. 1990. "Social and Illicit Substance Use during Pregnancy." Supplement 7, *Williams Obstetrics,* 18th ed. Norwalk, CT: Appleton and Lange.

———. 1991. "Medications in Pregnancy: Part I. Concepts of Human Teratology." Supplement 10, *Williams Obstetrics,* 18th ed. Norwalk, CT: Appleton and Lange.

Little, B. B., D. S. Guzick, R. M. Malina, and M. B. Ferreira-Rocha. 1989. "Environmental Influences Cause Menstrual Synchrony in University Coeds, Not Pheromones." *American Journal of Human Biology* (1): 53–57.

Little, B. B., T. H. Harstad, R. E. Bawdon, S. Sobhi, D. A. Roe, K. A. Knoll, and F. E. Ghali. 1991. "Pharmacokinetics of Pentamidine in Late Pregnant Sprague-Dawley Rats." *American Journal of Obstetrics and Gynecology* (164): 927–930.

Little, B. B., G. Jackson, and G. N. Wilson. 1996. "Is There a Cocaine Syndrome?" *Teratology* (54): 145–149.

Little, B. B., P. M. Kemp, R. O. Bost, L. M. Snell, and M. A. Peterman. In press. "Abnormal Allometric Size of Vital Organs Among Sudden Infant Death Syndrome Victims." *American Journal of Human Biology.*

Little, B. B., K. A. Knoll, F. E. Ghali, L. M. Snell, C. R. Rosenfeld, and N. F. Gant. 1991. "Heroin Abuse during Pregnancy: Effects on Perinatal Outcome and Early Childhood Growth." *American Journal Human Biology* (3): 463–468.

Little, B. B., and R. M. Malina. 1986. "Gene Flow and Variation in Stature and Cranio-facial Dimensions among Indigenous Populations of Southern Mexico, Guatemala, and Honduras." *American Journal of Physical Anthropology* (70): 505–512.

———. 1989. "Genetic Drift and Natural Selection in an Isolated Zapotec-Speaking Community in the Valley of Oaxaca, Southern Mexico." *Human Heredity* (39): 99–106.

Little, B. B., R. M. Malina, and P. H. Buschang. 1988. "Increased Heterozygosity and Child Growth in an Isolated Subsistence Agricultural Community in the Valley of Oaxaca, Mexico." *American Journal of Physical Anthropology* (77): 85–90.

Little, B. B., R. M. Malina, P. H. Buschang, and J. H. DeMoss. 1986. "Genetic and Environmental Influences on the Growth Status of School Children from a Rural Subsistence Agricultural Community in Southern Mexico." *American Journal of Physical Anthropology* (71): 81–88.

———. 1987. "Sibling Correlations for Growth Status in a Rural Community in Southern Mexico." *Annals of Human Biology* (14): 11–21.

———. 1990. "Sibling Similarity in Annual Growth Increments in School Children from Southern Mexico." *Annals of Human Biology* (17): 41–47.

Little, B. B., R. M. Malina, P. H. Buschang, and L. R. Little. 1989. "Natural Selection Is Not Related to Reduced Body Size in a Subsistence Agricultural Community in the Valley of Oaxaca, Southern Mexico. *Human Biology* (61): 287–296.

Little, B. B., S. M. Ramin, B. S. Cambridge, N. R. Schneider, D. S. Cohen, L. M. Snell, M.J.E. Harrod, and W. L. Johnston. 1995. "Risk of Chromosomal Abnormalities, with Emphasis on Live-Born Offspring of Young Mothers." *American Journal of Human Genetics* (57): 1178–1185.

Little, B. B., D. A. Roe, R. W. Stettler, V. R. Bohman, K. L. Westfall, and S. Sobhi. 1995. "A New Placental Enzyme in the Metabolism of Cocaine: An In Vitro Animal Model." *American Journal of Obstetrics and Gynecology* (172): 1441–1445.

Little, B. B., and L. M. Snell. 1991. "Brain Growth among Fetuses Exposed to Cocaine *In Utero:* Asymmetric Growth Retardation." *Obstetrics and Gynecology* (77): 361–364.

Little, B. B., L. M. Snell, and L. C. Gilstrap. 1988. "Methamphetamine Abuse during Pregnancy: Outcome and Infant Effects." *Obstetrics and Gynecology* (72): 541–544.

Little, B. B., L. M. Snell, L. C. Gilstrap, J. D. Breckenridge, and K. A. Knoll. 1990. "Effects of T's and Blues Abuse during Pregnancy on Maternal and Infant Health Status." *American Journal of Perinatology* (7): 359–362.

Little, B. B., L. M. Snell, L. C. Gilstrap, and W. L. Johnston. 1990. "Patterns of Substance Abuse during Pregnancy: Implications for the Mother and Fetus." *Southern Medical Journal* (83): 507–509, 518.

Little, B. B., L. M. Snell, L. C. Gilstrap, C. R. Rosenfeld, and N. F. Gant. 1990. "Failure to Recognize Fetal Alcohol Syndrome in Newborn Infants." *American Journal of Diseases in Children* (144): 1142–1146.

Little, B. B., L. M. Snell, W. L. Johnston, K. A. Knoll, and P. H. Buschang. 1990. "Blood Lead Levels and Growth Status of Children." *American Journal of Human Biology* (2): 265–269.

Little, B. B., L. M. Snell, V. R. Klein, and L. C. Gilstrap. 1989. "Cocaine Abuse during Pregnancy: Maternal and Fetal Implications." *Obstetrics and Gynecology* (73): 157–160.

Little, B. B., L. M. Snell, V. R. Klein, L. C. Gilstrap, K. A. Knoll, and J. D. Breckenridge. 1990. "Maternal and Fetal Effects of Heroin Addiction during Pregnancy." *Journal of Reproductive Medicine* (35): 159–162.

Little, B. B., L. M. Snell, M. K. Palmore, and L. C. Gilstrap. 1988. "Cocaine Use in Pregnant Women in a Large Public Hospital." *American Journal of Perinatology* (5): 206–207.

Little, B. B., L. M. Snell, T. T. Van Beveren, R. B. Crowell, S. Trayler, D. White, and W. L. Johnston (In review.) "Treatment of Substance Abuse during Pregnancy and Infant Outcome." *American Journal of Perinatology.*

Little, B. B., L. M. Snell, G. D. Wendel, L. C. Gilstrap, W. L. Johnston, and K. L. Gluck. 1991. "Prevalence of HIV in Pregnant Intravenous Drug Users in Dallas, Texas." *Texas Medicine* (87): 81–83.

Maberry, M. C., L. C. Gilstrap, R. E. Bawdon, B. B. Little, and J. Dax. 1991. "Anaerobic Coverage for Intraamniotic Infection: Maternal and Perinatal Impact." *American Journal of Perinatology* (8): 338–341.

Malina, R. M., and B. B. Little. 1981. "Comparison of TW1 and TW2 Skeletal Age

Differences in American Black and White and in Mexican Children 6–13 Years of Age." *Annals of Human Biology* (8): 543–548.

———. 1985. "Body Composition, Strength, and Motor Performance in Undernourished Boys." In Binkhorst, R.A., H.C.G. Kemper, and W.H.M Saris, eds. *Proceedings of Pediatric Work Physiology XI*. Champaign, IL: Human Kinetic Publishers, pp. 293–300.

———. In press. "Estimated Body Composition of Boys 9–16 Years of Age from a Rural Zapotec-Speaking Community in the Valley of Oaxaca." In L. L. Tapias, ed. *Homage to Santiago Genoves*. Mexico, D.F.: Universidad Nacional Autonama de Mexico.

Malina, R. M., B. B. Little, C. Bouchard, J.E.L. Carter, P.C.R. Hughes, and D. Kunze. 1984. "Growth Status of Olympic Athletes Less Than 18 Years of Age: Young Athletes at the Mexico City, Munich, and Montreal Olympic Games." In J.E.L. Carter, ed. *Physical Structure of Olympic Athletes, Part II. Kinanthropometry of Olympic Athletes*. Basel, Switzerland: S. Karger, pp. 183–201.

Malina, R. M., B. B. Little, and P. H. Buschang. 1986. "Sibling Similarities in the Strength and Motor Performance of Undernourished Children of School Age." *Human Biology* (58): 945–954.

———. 1991. "Estimated Body Composition and Strength of Chronically Mild-to-Moderately Undernourished Rural Boys in Southern Mexico." In R. J. Shepard and J. Parizkova, eds. *Human Growth, Physical Fitness and Nutrition: Medicine and Sport Science, Vol. 31*. Basel, Switzerland: S. Karger, pp. 119–132.

Malina, R. M., B. B. Little, P. H. Buschang, J. H. DeMoss, and H. A. Selby. 1985. "Socioeconomic Variation in the Growth Status of Children from a Subsistence Agricultural Community in Southern Mexico." *American Journal of Physical Anthropology* (68): 385–391.

Malina, R. M., B. B. Little, M. P. Stern, S. P. Gaskill, and H. P. Hazuda. 1983. "Ethnic and Social Class Differences in Selected Anthropometric Characteristics of Mexican-American and Anglo Adults: The San Antonio Heart Study." *Human Biology* (55): 867–883.

Malina, R. M., H. A. Selby, P. H. Buschang, W. L. Aronson, and B. B. Little. 1983. "Assortative Mating for Phenotypic Characteristics in a Zapotec Community in Oaxaca, Mexico." *Journal of Biosocial Science* (15): 273–280.

Malina, R. M., R. F. Shoup, and P. H. Buschang. 1987. "The Adaptive Significance of Small Body Size: Strength and Motor Performance of Children in Mexico and Papua, New Guinea." *American Journal of Physical Anthropology* (73): 489–499.

Malina, R. M., M. F. Skrabanek, and B. B. Little. 1989. "Growth and Maturity Status of Black and White Children Classified as Obese by Different Criteria." *American Journal of Human Biology* (1): 193–200.

Malina, R. M., A. N. Zavaleta, and B. B. Little. 1986. "Estimated Overweight and Obesity in Mexican American School Children." *International Journal of Obesity* (10): 483–491.

———. 1987a. "Body Size, Fatness, and Leanness of Mexican-American Children from Brownsville, Texas: Changes between 1972 and 1983." *American Journal of Public Health* (77): 573–577.

————. 1987b. "Secular Changes in Brownsville, Texas, Children in 1929, 1972 and 1983." *Human Biology* (59): 509–522.

Pena-Reyes, M., R. M. Malina, B. B. Little, and P. H. Buschang. 1995. "Consumo de Alimentos en Una Comunidad Rural Zapoteca en el Valle de Oaxaca." In R. M. Ramos-Rodriguez and S. Lopez-Alonso, eds., *Estudios de Antropologia Biologica: V. Coloquio de Antropologia Fisica "Juan Comos."* Mexico, D.F.: Universidad Nacional Autonoma de Mexico y Instituto Nacional Antropologia e Historia, pp. 407–414.

Ramin, S. M., L. C. Gilstrap, K. J. Leveno, J. Burris, and B. B. Little. 1989. "Umbilical Artery Acid-Base Status in the Preterm Infant." *Obstetrics and Gynecology* (74): 256–258.

Ramin, S. M., L. C. Gilstrap, K. J. Leveno, J. S. Dax, and B. B. Little. 1993. "The Acid-Base Significance of Meconium Discovered Prior to Labor." *American Journal of Perinatology* (10): 141–143.

Ramin, S. M., B. B. Little, and L. C. Gilstrap. 1993. "Survey of Operative Vaginal Delivery in North America in 1990." *American Journal of Obstetrics and Gynecology* (81): 307–311.

Ramin, S. M., B. B. Little, K. J. Trimmer, D. I. Standard, L. M. Snell, C. A. Blakely, and A. Garrett. 1994. "Methamphetamine Use during Pregnancy in a Large Urban Population." *Journal of Maternal-Fetal Medicine* (3): 101–103.

Ramus, R. M., S. M. Ramin, B. B. Little, and L. C. Gilstrap. 1992. "Early Repair of Episiotomy Dehiscence Associated with Infection." *American Journal of Obstetrics and Gynecology* (167): 1104–1107.

Roe, D. A., B. B. Little, R. E. Bawdon, and L. C. Gilstrap. 1990. "Metabolism of Cocaine by Human Placentae: Implications for Fetal Exposure." *American Journal of Obstetrics and Gynecology* (163): 713–718.

Snell, L. M., B. B. Little, K. A. Knoll, W. L. Johnston, C. R. Rosenfeld, and N. F. Gant. 1992. "Reliability of Birth Certificate Reporting of Congenital Anomalies." *American Journal of Perinatology* (9): 219–222.

Stettler, R. W., V. R. Bohman, B. B. Little, K. L. Westfall, and S. Sobhi. 1995. "Metabolism of Cocaine by Cholinesterase during Pregnancy: Maternal and Fetal Activity." *Journal of Maternal-Fetal Medicine* (4): 135–138.

Twickler, D. M., B. B. Little, A. J. Satin, and C.E.L. Brown. 1991. "Renal Pelvic-alyceal Dilation in Antepartum Pyelonephritis: Ultrasound Findings." *American Journal of Obstetrics and Gynecology* (165): 1116–1119.

VanBeveren, T. T., B. B. Little, and M. J. Spence. 2000. "An Adoption Cohort Study of Children Exposed to Cocaine Prenatally." *American Journal of Human Biology* (12): 417–428.

Wilson, E. E., B. B. Little, W. Byrd, E. McGee, and B. R. Carr. 1993. "The Effect of GnRH Agonists on Adrenocorticotropin and Cortisol Secretion in Adult Premenopausal Women." *Journal of Clinical Endocrinology and Metabolism* (76): 162–164.

Yonkers, K. A., and B. B. Little. 2001. *Treatment of Psychiatric Disorders during Pregnancy*. Cambridge: Oxford University Press and London: Arnold Publishers (Hodder Headline Company).

Chapter 12

Opportunities in Public Health and International Nutrition

Reynaldo Martorell

INTRODUCTION

I was born in Honduras. As a child, I collected polychrome pottery shards, clay figurines, whistles and flutes, and obsidian points. These were easy to find, but I particularly remember increasing my collection dramatically one day when a tractor was digging up an area to construct houses for workers in the banana plantations. I filled several shoe boxes with my best pieces and kept these under my bed. My mother threw them away when I left to go to high school in La Ceiba, a seaport in the Atlantic. She apologized for not valuing them and encouraged me to find some more. I did get a few more, which I still have.

When I was thirteen, I won a scholarship given by the Standard Fruit Company to children of its workers. This took me to a Jesuit high school in Belize, then a British colony, where I learned English. I do not know when I became aware of anthropology, but I do recall reading books about it in the library. Also, I wrote my senior paper on the peopling of the Americas.

The Jesuits encouraged me to go to college and offered me a scholarship to St. Louis University. My advisor in Belize suggested I study chemistry, a more "practical" subject for someone from a poor country, rather than anthropology. I agreed reluctantly, but in my sophomore year, I changed majors and graduated from St. Louis University with a degree in anthropology. Two months later, I enrolled in the University of Washington where I obtained a Ph.D. in biological anthropology.

I have never worked in an anthropology department, and many people who do not know me well assume I am a nutritionist. Currently, I am a professor of international nutrition at the Rollins School of Public Health of Emory University. This chapter is about opportunities in public health in general and in international nutrition in particular. My primary audience is biological anthropologists, either currently in graduate school or already trained, who may wish to seek career opportunities in a school of public health or a similar setting. The editor instructed me to describe opportunities primarily by telling my stories. Thus, the chapter does not provide a systematic review of opportunities in public health; rather, it is about what I have done in this field.

THE PUBLIC HEALTH PERSPECTIVE

Anthropology and public health have different perspectives. The mission of my institution, the Rollins School of Public Health of Emory University, is "to improve health and prevent disease in human populations around the world by acquiring, disseminating and applying knowledge" (Emory, 1999:6). We seek this goal through teaching, the conduct of research, and by improving the practice and profession of public health. The research we value most, whether basic or applied, is that which is relevant to the identification, characterization, and resolution of health problems in human populations.

Public health, therefore, is about improving health, understood in a broad sense, from the prevention of acute infectious diseases to the promotion of mental health. Having evolved out of medicine, public health is interventionist in approach. If a problem is uncovered, after careful study of its nature, the next step is a program of amelioration or prevention. We expect research in public health to contribute to the chain of events leading to solutions, implementation of these, and eventual prevention of the target problem.

There are several important differences between the public health perspective and that of anthropology, including biological or physical anthropology. Although both fields of study measure human variability and try to understand what makes us differ from each other, anthropology claims the entire range of diversity as its interest and incorporates the entire range of human experience, past and present. Commonly, anthropology considers the past, even the distant past, in order to understand human variation and function today. Public health, on the other hand, deals with problems that cause significant morbidity and/or mortality in contemporary societies. Public health is more entrenched in the present, and interest in the past is limited mostly to risk factor assessment and may involve collecting familial histories of disease, inquiring about ethnicity, and registering events and conditions over the life span. Anthropology is not about preventing disease or promoting health. In fact, anthropologists tend to be rather nonjudgmental about human conditions and are more likely to see the status quo as an adaptive solution to local conditions, despite functional costs. Anthropologists have been less likely than public health professionals to be motivated to change or improve the lot of those they study, but this may be changing. The Web page of the anthropology department at Emory notes, "The discipline is increasingly mindful of the inequities that people have been heir to and how these are perpetuated or reestablished in the present." Public health professionals are less timid and ardently profess their mission to be the dismantling of social and other inequities that lead to poor health.

There are some similarities. Public health and biological anthropology are concerned with populations and not with the individual. Both study complex problems, and both use an eclectic mix of disciplinary perspectives, from natural to social sciences, as well as varied methods, both qualitative and quantitative. Ethnographic and other anthropological techniques (e.g., focus groups) have become popular in public health research and are seen as complementary to survey research in representative samples. But there is a difference regarding the way the input of various disciplines is incorporated. The anthropologist is more likely to attempt to learn about these relevant fields and to integrate newly acquired expertise within the anthropological tradition, thereby creating subdisciplines of anthropology. Departments of anthropology may thus refer to having representation among their faculty in, say, economic anthropology, molecular anthropology, or physiological anthropology. Schools of public health are more likely to bring different types of professionals under one roof to work on problems of common interest. Research projects in public health tend to be staffed by teams, whereas it is not unusual for an anthropologist to work alone.

Faculty at schools of public health are very diverse. For example, my institution is organized around six departments and several centers. The departments are behavioral sciences and health education, biostatistics, environmental and occupational health, epidemiology, health policy and management, and my own department, international health. The faculty and research staff of each department come from a variety of disciplines. My department, for example, has faculty trained in epidemiology, a variety of fields of medicine, infectious diseases, nutrition, demography and reproductive health, policy and management, health economics, history, sociology, cultural anthropology, and biological anthropology (two of us). We are a diverse lot but we share a common mission, the improvement of human health.

In short, the academic culture of public health differs from that of anthropology. Public health research is focused on human health but can be broad in approach and methods. Some work is applied and deals with the functioning of programs, delivery of services, and evaluation of impact. Other research is more basic and oriented to fundamental questions. This second type of work tends to be hypothesis driven, often but not always uses experimental designs, and requires significant resources to undertake.

The pace in public health is fast, and there is less time for contemplation and scholarly work than in a school of humanities and sciences. Researchers are typically under tremendous pressure to crank out research proposals; in my own school, faculty members are expected to bring in 70 percent of their salary from grants. This is difficult for some, particularly at the early stages of a career. Although we provide full funding for two to three years for beginning assistant professors, this is not a lot of time. Also, we expect faculty to teach, and in my department this is two semester courses a year. My colleagues in anthropology at Emory are amused by the effervescence of our environment.

MY CAREER IN PUBLIC HEALTH

I am the Robert W. Woodruff professor of international nutrition at Emory's Rollins School of Public Health. I also chair the department of international health. I arrived here in 1993, after two years as leading professor, Division of Nutritional Sciences, at Cornell University and fourteen years at Stanford University, first as associate professor and later as professor in the Food Research Institute and the human biology program. My very first job was at the Institute of Nutrition of Central America and Panama (INCAP) in Guatemala. INCAP was for many years the premier center in developing countries for research and teaching about nutrition. It is much smaller today but still continues to be affiliated with the Pan American Health Organization.

My graduate training was at the University of Washington in Seattle. My program, under the direction of Professor Marshall T. Newman, combined biological anthropology with biomedical courses. Because it was not required of students in biological anthropology, I took no cultural anthropology or archaeology courses in graduate school. I identified child growth and development as my area of interest from the beginning and was able to constitute a committee that included faculty from biological anthropology (Marshall T. Newman and Daris Swindler) and from the medical school (Stanley Gartler, a geneticist, and Irwin Emanuel, a physician with graduate training in anthropology who directed the Child Growth and Mental Retardation Center). The courses I took included several in biological anthropology, population and human genetics, child growth and development, epidemiology, and nutrition. Although I never felt very knowledgeable in any of these areas, I later came to value the mix of perspectives I encountered. I found Professor Newman's views on the power of the environment in shaping human variation very compelling, and since then, I have been biased toward "nurture" rather than "nature" when assessing the relative importance of causes of human variation. One of Professor Newman's great interests was nutrition about which he wrote, "Human biologists have been slow to recognize the tremendous importance of nutrition as a key environmental factor affecting man's evolution and variability" (Newman, 1975:210). On reflection, many of the questions that have guided my research were also his concern.

While in graduate school, I was fortunate enough to hear of an opening at INCAP, in its Division of Human Development, through a visiting professor, Leonardo Mata, a microbiologist who had come to write "The Children of Santa María Cauqué," a classic account of the natural history of infection and malnutrition as uncovered through a longitudinal study of Guatemalan Mayan children (Mata, 1978). I applied and was accepted. At INCAP, I was able to use data from INCAP's Oriente Study to write a thesis on "Diarrheal Diseases and Incremental Growth in Young Guatemalan Children" (Martorell, 1973). Although I stayed at INCAP for just five years, the experience transformed me. I became deeply interested in public health and specifically in maternal and child nutrition. Also, I became more proficient in statistics and in data analysis, learned much about grantmanship, and was able to write and publish many papers with an internationally diverse and gifted team of researchers who were at INCAP at that time. This was in many ways a postdoctoral experience that gave me the basis for an academic career.

From Guatemala, I went to Stanford, the place where I developed the lines of research that occupy me today. I picked up much of what I know about the field of nutrition through teaching about the nutritional problems of women and children in developing nations. I was also able to maintain a broad interdisciplinary perspective through involvement in several programs, particularly the human biology program. There were many influential thinkers such as Paul Ehrlich, Luca Cavalli-Sforza, William Durham, and Partha Dasgupta, which made Stanford an intellectually stimulating environment. My own home, the Food Research Institute, was less interesting because it was mostly staffed by agricultural economists, a discipline that does not generally take human health into account. It was the lack of a school of public health and of colleagues in the area of nutrition at the Food Research Institute that led me away from Stanford to accept a position at Cornell's Division of Nutritional Sciences, perhaps the largest academic unit in this field. The move seemed logical because I had a fruitful working relationship and funded projects with colleagues such as Jean Pierre Habicht and Jere Haas, the latter a biological anthropologist and current director of nutritional sciences at Cornell. However, my family did not like the harsh winters of Ithaca, and I soon began to look for positions elsewhere. Two years later, an opportunity at the newly founded Rollins School of Public Health led me to Emory University, where I have been ever since. At first, I was engaged in establishing a program in nutrition; later, this was broadened into building the department of international health through my role as chair. From its beginning ten years ago, the school and its programs have grown explosively in size and reputation, with the end of growth still some years in the future. The university as a whole has also expanded rapidly, including its department of anthropology, with a strong program in biological anthropology. The setting at Emory is unusual because recently many institutions have had to contract rather than expand. The time at Emory has solidified my interests and commitments to nutrition and to public health. I rarely attend anthropology meetings now, mostly because of lack of time but to some extent because I find a certain cognitive dissonance with my former field. Although I still enjoy reading broad syntheses about human history and evolution, such as *Guns, Germs, and Steel: The Fates of Human Societies* by the physiologist Jared Diamond (1999), I find that few papers given at physical anthropology meetings hold my interest. This is not the case with the human biology meetings, but a crowded travel schedule keeps me from attending regularly. My major identification is first with nutrition and second with public health, although it is difficult to separate these two interests.

RESEARCH

Most of my research has focused on the causes and consequences of malnutrition in developing countries. My early work centered on the importance of infections, particularly diarrheal diseases, as causes of malnutrition (Martorell, 1973). Infections depress the appetite of children and also lead directly to energy and nutrient losses. Poor dietary intakes, both in terms of quantity and quality, and frequent infections are the twin, adverse forces through which poverty and its correlates cause malnutrition.

Malnutrition is technically inclusive of problems of excess (i.e., overnutrition), but in much of my work I have used this term as a synonym for undernutrition. Although there are clinical and biochemical indicators of poor nutrition, these are useful only at the extremes of severity. On the other hand, anthropometric variables are sensitive along the entire range of nutritional deficiency and are thus valued as indices of malnutrition (Martorell, 1995). An example is stunting, which is defined as lengths or heights two or more standard deviations below the age-sex specific reference median. In most papers published today, the reference population used in defining stunting is the World Health Organization/National Center for Health Statistics or WHO/NCHS reference curves, based on data from the Fels Research Institute and NCHS (Dibley et al., 1987). But is it appropriate to use reference data from the United States to judge the adequacy of the growth of children in places like Guatemala? This question preoccupied some of us at INCAP. We were able to establish that ethnic differences in growth appeared to be minor when one compared the size of well-to-do children from around the world. On the other hand, differences between high and low socioeconomic groups within countries were many times greater than any which could be ascribed to ethnicity and were easily demonstrable. We argued that the growth potential of preschool children from around the world was surprisingly similar across ethnic groups and that the use of reference data such as the WHO/NCHS curves was appropriate (Habicht et al., 1974). This conclusion has been born out by research over the last twenty-five years. Currently, I serve as chair of the advisory group to the World Health Organization's Multicentre Growth Reference study, which is an effort to derive reference data from healthy, breastfed children from California, Norway, India, Brazil, Oman, and Ghana. We expect differences among samples to be trivial. This "rainbow" reference is expected to be politically more palatable than the one currently in use, which is based on bottle-fed children from the United States.

In 1989, I published a paper entitled "Body Size, Adaptation and Function" (Martorell, 1989) as part of the proceedings of a symposium entitled "Small but Healthy? Perspectives on the Concept of Adaptation at the 86th annual meeting of the American Anthropological Association. A group of us attempted to debunk the notion that "small is healthy," that children who are small are not handicapped in any way, and that only those children who are clinically malnourished are unhealthy. I argued the contrary. In the abstract, I summarized my objections as follows.

> First, adults in developing countries have small body sizes largely as a result of poor diets and infection during childhood. Therefore, to acclaim small body sizes as a desirable attribute for populations is also to affirm that it is causes are desirable. Second, monitoring the growth of children is widely recognized as an excellent tool for detecting health problems. Growth retardation, rather than an innocuous response to environmental stimuli, is a warning signal of increased risk of morbidity and mortality. Third, the conditions which give rise to stunted children also affect other aspects such as cognitive development. Finally, stunted girls who survive to be short women are at greater risk of delivering growth retarded infants with a greater probability of dying in infancy. For all these reasons, small is not healthy.

The study of the functional consequences of malnutrition, including growth failure, has been the cornerstone of my research. Most of this work has been done in Guatemala, in collaboration with INCAP. From 1969 to 1977, INCAP carried out an ambitious food supplementation experiment, which has come to be known as the Oriente study (Martorell et al., 1995). The study was designed to test the hypothesis that malnutrition was a major cause of poor mental development through the conduct of a nutrition intervention. Two villages were randomized to receive a highly nutritious supplement called "Atole," made up of Incaparina, a vegetable protein mixture developed at INCAP, dried skim milk, and some sugar. One cup (180 ml) of Atole provided 162 calories and 11.2 g of high quality protein. Two other carefully matched villages received a low calorie drink, called "Fresco," which provided sixty-two calories but no protein per cup. These two beverages were offered twice daily at supplementation centers; consumption was *ad libitum* but was carefully recorded in the case of pregnant and breast-feeding mothers and for all children up to seven years of age. The design reflected the views of the time that protein was the key limiting nutrient in the diets of poor people in developing countries. Calories were not considered important at the time, and the reason that the Fresco was provided was to control for the social interaction associated with attending a`supplementation center. This was deemed extremely important because the mental development of children was the key outcome. Vitamins and minerals were added to Fresco, in equal concentration as the Atole, to further sharpen the contrast in terms of protein. Changes in physical growth were evaluated to confirm that the Atole was nutritionally effective.

Longitudinal data were collected in women throughout pregnancy and in children using the best possible methods. A battery of tests measuring motor development and a wide range of skills, such as memory, perception, vocabulary, and reasoning, was administered. Numerous anthropometric measures were taken at frequent intervals. Information about home dietary intakes, illnesses, household structure and composition, socioeconomic status, and many other aspects was also collected. This longitudinal study is one of the richest sources of longitudinal information about nutrition, growth, and development of children from developing countries. Hundreds of publications that use these data have appeared, as well as dozens of doctoral dissertations, including my own.

Space does not allow for a full account of the findings. Readers are encouraged to review a special issue of the *Journal of Nutrition,* which summarizes the Oriente study and subsequent follow-up studies (Martorell and Scrimshaw, 1995). Briefly, the rate of low birth weight was cut in half, but this occurred among women receiving Atole as well as Fresco. This was because energy, rather than protein, was limiting in the diets of women during pregnancy. Even though the Fresco had only a third of the energy concentration, women really liked it such that net calories from Fresco and Atole were nearly the same. In children, patterns of consumption were such that subjects in Atole villages received significant amounts of protein and calories whereas those in Fresco received only minor amounts of calories. Therefore, any benefit in children due to Atole relative to Fresco consumption cannot be ascribed to protein alone because calories were increased as well. The Atole but not the Fresco was found to significantly improve the growth of children, specifically linear dimensions and head circumference, but only up to three years of age. This may reflect the fact that children younger than three years of age have higher rates of diarrheal and other infections, greater relative nutritional requirements (i.e., per kilogram of body weight), and poorer growth than older children. Older preschool children from Guatemala and in most developing countries, although small because of past growth failure, grow as well as well-nourished children. A major disappointment for the psychologists involved with the study was the fact that the effects on mental development were very modest. Despite having a biologically effective nutritional treatment and a large and eclectic mixture of carefully conducted tests, there was little excitement in the final report to the National Institute of Child Health and Development (NICHD), which funded the study.

I left INCAP in 1977 just as the study was being completed. As the years passed, I began to wonder what had happened to the former participants of the study. Were the improvements in physical growth maintained? Did these result in better work performance? Might there have been effects on intellectual functioning? At Stanford, I had gotten weary of being asked by skeptical economists for evidence that nutrition programs contribute to building human capital. Measures of improvement in young children, such as better growth or even reduced case fatality rates, were not convincing, but it occurred to me that effects measured in young adults might, as this age group is the productive workforce. I thus formed a team, which in the end included Jere Haas and Jean-Pierre Habicht at Cornell; the psychologists Ernesto Pollitt at UC Davis and Patrice Engle at Cal Poly; John Himes, a biological anthropologist at Minnesota, and Juan Rivera, a Cornell-trained Mexican nutritionist at INCAP. With funding from NIH but later complemented by grants from The Pew Charitable Trusts and UNICEF for special substudies, we undertook the INCAP Follow-up Study in 1988–1999, when the former subjects of study were eleven to twenty-six years old. The basic hypothesis tested was that improved nutrition in early childhood led to young adults with a greater potential for leading healthy productive lives. We hired many of the field supervisors of the original study and located and measured former subjects in their villages of origin as well as migrants. The findings of the follow-up have proven very valuable and have been used to support the notion that nutrition interventions aimed at mothers and young children improve human capital and are thus long-term economic investments. Among the long-term effects we found are greater adult body size, improved work capacity, and enhanced intellectual performance. Contrasting with the lackluster results in childhood, we found the exposure to the Atole resulted in important improvement in intellectual performance as measured by tests of reading, numeracy, and general knowledge. Improved nutrition, we uncovered, was particularly effective in improving intellectual functioning among those of poorer socioeconomic status; also, the better performance of subjects in Atole over those in Fresco increased as the number of years of schooling increased. We have emphasized that these effects have been achieved through a well documented but small improvement in diet equivalent to a daily increase in Atole compared with Fresco villages of about 100 calories and nine grams of protein per day in two-year-old children.

The findings of the follow-up led us to future studies in the same population. Does the greater maternal stature and increased lean body mass in women with better childhood nutrition lead to improved birth weights? Are mothers who had better nutrition in early childhood and greater intellectual performance as adults better able to meet the needs of their children? Are they more nurturing, more likely to feed them better, more likely to vaccinate them on time and better at taking care of them when ill? Do the children of mothers with better nutrition in early childhood show better growth and development? My colleagues and I at Emory and INCAP approached the Thrasher Research Fund and NIH with these ideas about generational effects, and, with their assistance, we have just completed a longitudinal study of the children of the children of the Oriente Study. At the time of writing, we are about to undertake the analyses of these data. We are excited at the prospect of answering questions not previously possible.

We have also pursued other questions. With the assistance of the Nestle Research Foundation, we have just collected data on body composition, blood pressure, fasting glucose levels, and lipid levels in the former subjects of the Oriente study. We want to relate the nutritional history in early childhood to risk factors of cardiovascular disease in the adult. Barker (1992) has proposed that poor nutrition in utero and in infancy increases risk of chronic diseases of dietary origin. It has been suggested that if true, an epidemic of such diseases may result as developing countries improve economically, dietary patterns become "westernized," and sedentarism increases. Countries with a high proportion of individuals who were malnourished in early life would have a magnified response to these changes.

Mexico, specifically the National Institute of Public Health of Mexico, located in Cuernavaca, has become another site where I conduct research. This is due to the presence there of Juan Rivera, who moved from INCAP. We are undertaking a large, randomized controlled trial of micronutrient supplementation during pregnancy and birth outcomes with funding from the Thrasher Research Fund and UNICEF. We are also carrying out a companion trial of micronutrients and child growth and development from birth to two years with funding from the Micronutrient Initiative, UNICEF, and the Mexican Council of Science and Technology (CONACYT). The interest in micronutrients, for example, in iron, zinc, vitamin A, and folate, reflects the growing body of evidence that these and other nutrients are limiting in the diets of pregnant women and young children. This is because the diets of the poor are of low quality, with limited amounts of animal products and few fruits and vegetables. Although different in nature from the INCAP studies, the studies about Mexico are also about the functional consequences of nutritional deficiencies.

I have left out other current and past studies, but those discussed are illustrative of what I have done. In general, the studies I have undertaken have been complex and have involved many colleagues, too numerous to mention by name. Large field teams, of twenty to forty people, have been required in many cases. The data sets generated are enormous and have also required the hiring of data managers and statisticians. The cost of these studies consequently has been high; in total, I have obtained over $1.5 million in research funds since I left INCAP, and about half of this amount has come from NIH in the form of R01 grants. I am really grateful to the investigator-initiated grant process of NIH and a number of foundations. Grantmanship in the United States is extremely competitive. Not all of my ideas have received funding, and few of my proposals have been funded in the first try. In fact, one of the NIH proposals was funded on the third submission. Robert Klein, a psychologist and former director of the Division of Human Development of INCAP, once told me that a good proposal takes a lot of effort to write, but that the level of effort is nearly the same for one with a small as one with a large budget. In that case, he reasoned, why not write "big ones." I found this to be good advice. However, bigger budgets draw more attention from reviewers, and many foundations have funding ceilings. Also I have found small grants to be useful for conducting small pilot studies in support of larger proposals.

I would like to think that my work has led to new scientific insights about human function and that it also has had an impact on programs and policies. However, I recall one conversation late one night with a janitor at INCAP that makes me wonder. Don Eustaquio, or Don Taco as he was affectionately known, once asked me to explain to him what the INCAP Oriente Study was all about. After he heard me explain our effort to show that improved nutrition makes children grow better and be smarter, he paused for a minute or so and said, "But everybody knows this!"

PUBLISHING

I believe that researchers have an ethical obligation to publish their findings. Funds are scarce. Subjects of study also suffer inconveniences. These investments are only justified if the research is completed, the data properly analyzed, and the findings published. Publications in refereed journals are the most effective means of informing others about the findings. However, other means are also useful, particularly in international research. Participation in national and regional meetings is a good way of reaching the local research community. Publications in the language of the country, and for me this has meant Spanish for the most part, is another option. Even summaries or translations of articles are useful. Finally, it is important to reach policy makers when the research has program and policy implications. In my case this has been done through the auspices of the institutions with which I collaborate, such as INCAP, and through bilateral and international organizations.

In most instances, the field research I have been associated with has yielded large and complex data sets. This means that there are always opportunities for first-author publications for all members of a research team. Invariably, the limiting factor is people with good ideas and skills and not the availability of data. I have also always followed the rule that whomever writes the article gets first authorship. Another operating rule I have followed is that all participating institutions have rights and claims to the entire data set and to publications. Having been born in a developing country, I am very aware of reports of U.S. researchers exploiting foreign institutions, using them as mere data collectors, and not involving them as equal participants in research. I would not want to be accused of doing this. I really have not had the problems about authorship that sometimes others have had.

I have enjoyed attending professional meetings, both large and small. Until recently I always made it a point to present a paper that would later become an article for publication in refereed journals. Today I try to encourage my younger colleagues to adopt this custom. For me, professional meetings have been important for making contacts and for discussing potential collaborations. Professional meetings are also sources of ideas and new information and an opportunity for getting feedback about one's own work.

SERVICE

A considerable proportion of my time and energy has gone into assisting national, bilateral, and international organizations, as well as governments, to formulate policies and to design, implement, and evaluate programs. This has brought enormous satisfaction to me but also tangible rewards. These activities, like professional meetings, have been a source of ideas and contacts that have led to research opportunities for colleagues, students, or myself. These experiences have provided a broad context in which to place my research and have encouraged me to identify the policy and program implications of my research. Service appointments have taken me all over the world, and this has exposed me to contrasting levels of economic development, to a variety of cultures, and to many different types of public health and nutrition programs. These experiences have been useful in teaching in terms of breaching the gap between theory and practice, particularly now that I am in a school of public health.

National Academy of Sciences/Institute of Medicine

I would like to mention some examples of service activities, both national and international. The Food and Nutrition Board of the Institute of Medicine is an important institution for guiding policies and programs in food and nutrition in the United States and, to a limited extent, in developing countries. I served for six years on the Board; I was also vice chairman of its

Committee on International Nutrition and chaired a committee on Vitamin A Prevention and Control.

There was a lot of glamour to affairs of the Food and Nutrition Board. We often met in the stately Board Room in the marble building of the National Academy of Sciences on 2101 Constitution Avenue in Washington, DC and had summer meetings at the Academy's patrician facilities in Wood Hole, Mass. There were cocktails in the rotunda at 2101 Constitution Avenue and dinners at the finest restaurants. I met many influential men and women in government, industry, and academia and testified before Congress on behalf of initiatives of the Food and Nutrition Board.

But there was substance behind the glamour. Important topics were addressed, including the RDAs, the safety of meat and poultry in the United States, federal food regulations, nutrition labeling, diet and cancer, and many others. Remarkably busy people gave freely of their time to committee work. The evidence was reviewed dispassionately, and great care went into preparing reports.

The work we did on international nutrition was important to the U.S. Agency for International Development (USAID). For example, the committee on Vitamin A focused on the remarkable finding of Al Sommer and colleagues at the Johns Hopkins School of Public Health. They published the results of studies in Indonesia in which a single dose of vitamin A given every four months to preschool children reduced child mortality rates by a third. This finding seemed too good to be true because known approaches to mortality reduction beyond child vaccination, such as introduction of water and the improvement of personal hygiene and sanitation, were costly and difficult to implement. My committee was charged with the task of identifying the best methods and approaches for several studies that USAID was planning to fund to confirm the Indonesian findings. I remember Al Sommer was not happy with the many faults we identified in his previous work. The committee recognized the great merits of his research but felt it needed to identify all its possible shortcomings in order to design research of even better quality. I also ran into problems in the area of ethics. Two members of the committee would not go along with the recommendation that the design be a randomized controlled trial. The committee reasoned that the results were potentially so important that they needed to be unequivocal. A minority felt that denying vitamin A to some, that is, providing a placebo, was unethical because vitamin A is an essential nutrient. Lincoln Chen, with the Ford Foundation in India at that time, felt that other types of design should be used. The final report was signed by the majority and included two minority reports (National Research Council, 1987).

National Institutes of Health

The peer review system of NIH is not perfect, and I hope that ongoing reforms strengthen even more the emphasis on investigator driven research.

The system, as is well known, is highly competitive. To write a good proposal takes weeks, much more than the few days NIH claims it should take in its instructions to authors.

I was on the epidemiology and disease control study section in the late 1980s. We stayed in Bethesda in cheap motels, and government per diems meant dinner at modest restaurants. Interestingly, the NIH administrator of my study section was a biological anthropologist, Dr. Phyllis Eveleth. Study-section work was extremely hard. When I began, page limits had not been mandated, and some proposals were the size of telephone books. Later, page limits made the review process easier, but it was still the most arduous committee type work I have ever undertaken. We had twenty-five or so proposals to review three times a year, and primary reviewers wrote detailed critiques of about eight proposals. The meetings lasted two to three days, leaving little time per proposal. When my four-year term expired, I politely declined further involvement.

The experience benefited me in two ways. It exposed me to a broad range of research in epidemiology and to the remarkable creativity in design and study execution of some of the best scientists in the United States. It also taught me the subtleties of writing a good proposal. Although the content had to be good, the proposals that were being funded were those that excelled in substance as well as form. Crystal clear, compelling arguments about the scientific significance of the research and its potential implications for public health often made the difference in choosing among otherwise technically equivalent proposals. Resubmitted proposals that had angry rebuttals to reviewers' comments did not fare as well as those that also disagreed with the study section but that did so through carefully crafted reasons.

Other activities at NIH have provided me with the opportunity to influence policy. This has included membership in a five-year planning committee for NICHD and participation in meetings to outline policy in international research. Last week, while I was in Chile, I turned down an invitation to attend a workshop to be held at the National Nutrition Institute in Hyderabad, India, to begin discussing an Indo-U.S. program of research with sponsorship from NICHD. Normally a meeting such as this interests me because it might lead to future research collaborations, but there is a limit to what one can do. Learning how and when to say no remains a problem for me, although I do turn down many invitations. Fortunately, a young colleague from my group, Dr. Usha Ramakrishnan, herself a native of India, will represent Emory in this meeting, but I will have to teach her classes.

United Nations

My experiences with the United Nations agencies, principally the World Bank, UNICEF, the World Health Organization (including the Pan American Health Organization), the Food and Agriculture Organization and the

World Food Program have been varied and extensive. Through the World Bank, I have worked in India for over fifteen years. As part of World Bank missions, I helped state and union authorities design and evaluate nutrition programs and traveled to many cities and remote villages of this vast country. The most well known of the programs I came to be involved with was the Tamil Nadu Integrated Nutrition Project (TINP), perhaps the most successful, large-scale nutrition program aimed at women and children (Balachander, 1993). The success of this program was due to both design and managerial advances. The program was aimed at women during pregnancy and lactation and at children less than three years of age, including nutritional supplementation and counseling for children who were failing to grow. This contrasted with other projects in India, which were aimed at children less than five years of age but served mostly children older than three years. TINP was successful because it prevented malnutrition by focusing on the very young. The management of the project was the best I have seen. There was effective training and supervision, an efficient information system that identified bottlenecks at all levels, and a culture of experimentation with service delivery. Through operation research, options for improvement were tested, and the best approaches were adopted. This experience convinced me that it is possible to implement effective programs. However, corruption in the 1990s did great damage to the program, from which it never quite recovered. Also, we found it very difficult to replicate the success of this program in other parts of India, in part because this meant changing existing programs, which managers and workers resisted. Another problem with TINP is that it was identified too much with the World Bank and obviously with the State of Tamil Nadu. Had this been a central government initiative, its ideas might have been more readily accepted. Thus, the experience in India also taught me lessons about the role of politics in public health programs. I have worked with the World Bank in other parts of Asia and Africa, but the experiences in India have been the most rewarding.

Recently, I traveled to Jakarta on behalf of UNICEF to work with the government of Indonesia to define policies and programs in nutrition for the next five years. Indonesia's achievements in economic development and health have been remarkable. From being as poor as Bangladesh upon achieving independence from the Dutch, it had by the late 1990s reduced poverty significantly, eliminated famines, and improved dramatically in life expectancy, health, and nutrition. In fact, many Indonesian planners had begun to argue that attention had to be paid to the emergence of chronic diseases of dietary origin, the so-called diseases of affluence which include obesity, hyperlipidemias, hypertension, cardiovascular disease, and cancer. Then, almost overnight, the economy collapsed, and Indonesia was plunged to chaos. I was probably in one of the last delegations that Suharto received before resigning. Suddenly, attention had to be given to food shortages and the possibility of the reemergence of clinical nutritional deficiencies. How quickly the situation can change!

A recent trip, also with UNICEF, was to China, and its goal was to assist with strategies for improving the diets of infants and toddlers. It was my first trip to China, and it made a strong impression on me. I was well informed about China's economic development and knew that it will soon be the world's largest economy. But, despite the fact that I was in only three provinces and only in cities, the notable achievements of the Chinese, and the contrast with India, which also has 1 billion people, were strikingly evident. On the other hand, in Tianamen Square I witnessed police in a van quickly hauling a few Fulan Gong to jail. This underscores the intolerance of the Chinese government to dissent, and therefore, its fragility. Last week I was in Chile, and it was remarkable how Lagos, a Socialist, the first since Allende, narrowly defeated Lavin, a young conservative and former associate of Pinochet, in peaceful elections.

Nutrition is not the responsibility of any single UN agency. In order to coordinate activities among the various organizations, an entity called the Sub-Committee on Nutrition, or SCN, was created. For most of its history, WHO has hosted the secretariat of the SCN in its Geneva headquarters. A body of advisers from various disciplines and with wide geographic representation, called the Advisory Group on Nutrition, or AGN, assisted the SCN. I was chair of the AGN for several years. The AGN, as the Food and Nutrition Board does, undertook studies to resolve issues of importance and to reach consensus on scientific and policy questions. One of many studies I was involved in was about vitamin A. It turned out that USAID and others did fund a number of studies about vitamin A supplementation and child mortality. As the individual reports emerged, there was a range from even greater mortality decreases than found in the original study in Indonesia to no effects at all and even small increases in mortality. I proposed to the SCN that the AGN undertake a meta-analysis of the information to come up with a definitive answer about the benefits of vitamin A supplementation in deficient populations. With funding from the Canadian International Development Agency, Professor Beaton, a nutritionist from the University of Toronto, and I chaired a multidisciplinary group which in about a year issued a report confirming Sommer's findings (Beaton et al., 1993). The available evidence indicated a reduction in child mortality of 23 percent, a little less than reported originally for Indonesia. This report was useful to USAID, UNICEF, and others in convincing governments to launch vitamin A programs. I have attended several meetings at which Al Sommer, now dean of the Johns Hopkins School of Public Health, was also present and I no longer sense any resentment about my having criticized his study.

There were many other studies but perhaps the most ambitious was one entitled "How Nutrition Improves," which was directed by the secretariat of the SCN, John Mason, a British nutritionist (Gillespie, et al., 1996). A network of colleagues produced case studies of country experiences; these documented nutrition changes, the rate and pattern of economic development, and public and private investments in the social sector, including health and nutrition programs. We then undertook a synthesis to identify how nutrition improves. The conclusions we reached may appear obvious. For example, we found that nutritional improvements depended on national economic growth, but more so if this actually led to poverty reduction and to direct investments in health and education.

The SCN met once a year in any of several UN "capitals" which headquartered any of the organizations. For example, I remember attending meetings in Paris (UNESCO), New York (UNICEF), Rome (FAO), Geneva (WHO), and Washington (PAHO). By and large, the meetings were productive, but toward the end of my tenure, turf battles, instigated for the most part by representatives of one agency, made the proceedings unpleasant. By the time I finished my second elected term in 1996, I was glad to move on to other tasks. Since then, the leadership and staff of the SCN have been replaced, and the AGN has been disbanded. Through my role as chair of the AGN, I was able to see the great potential of the UN in action but also witnessed some of its problems.

Professional Societies

Although I belong to societies of three types, biological anthropology/human biology, public health and nutrition, it is with the latter that I have had much more to do. The principal nutrition society in the United States is the American Association for Nutritional Sciences (ASNS), formerly known as the American Institute of Nutrition (AIN). ASNS normally meets with other societies in huge gatherings known as "Experimental Biology" meetings. The journal of the ASNS is the *Journal of Nutrition*.

Nutrition is an eclectic field, and members of ASNS include basic scientists who work at the cellular level or with animal models, as well as clinical nutritionists, nutritional epidemiologists and social scientists such as economists and cultural anthropologists. About ten years ago, a group of us became dissatisfied that international interests were not well represented in the activities of the society. We proceeded to form a division within the society called the Society for International Nutrition Research (SINR). We meet with ASNS, but we are assigned several slots in the program, including at least one symposium and two mini symposia, several poster sessions, and a reception. I was able to convince Luis Mejia of the Kellogg company to provide us funding for a prize in research and later for student prizes. I am currently past president of SINR and remain very involved in its affairs.

Another problem was that the *Journal of Nutrition* was publishing little of interest to anyone interested in human nutrition, nutritional epidemiology, or international nutrition. At one SINR meeting, I documented for the membership that there were many more papers about rats, rabbits, pigs, and other animals than about humans. As a result of all of this, new sections of the journal were opened up, including one entitled "Community and International Nutrition," and I became a section editor for the journal in the early 1990s. The *Journal of Nutrition* is broader now than what it used to be.

SINR should appeal to any anthropologist interested in nutrition. Members include human biologists such as Linda Adair, Jere Haas, and David Pelletier and cultural anthropologists such as Gretel Pelto, Harriet Kunhlein, and Peggy Bentley. Anthropologists who are not members should consider applying.

MY LIFE AS DEPARTMENT CHAIR

For many years I managed to avoid administrative positions because I felt that this would take away time from what I really like to do, research and public service. The dean of our school, Jim Curran, the former czar for AIDS at the Centers for Disease Control and Prevention (CDC) is very persuasive and talked me into becoming chair about two years ago. I have considerably less time for research and public service despite the priority I give to these activities. I write fewer grant proposals and articles now, and a casualty of my appointment as chair was my long-term association with the World Bank in India. I teach only one course now, a survey course about international health, and in this I am assisted by a young biological anthropologist interested in environmental health, Dr. Rachel Albalak. She joined us recently after graduate training at Michigan with Roberto Frisancho.

The responsibilities of chairing a department of international health have broadened my focus because we have several areas of research and teaching and not just nutrition, my former sole concern. With our faculty, I completed a review of the graduate curriculum and of gaps in our program. Recruiting is a major responsibility, and our department has managed to attract several associate and assistant professors in the past two years and more are expected in the future.

Along with other chairs and senior staff, I assist the dean in setting policy for the school and in its administration. Also, since even before being chair, I serve on the Emory president's advisory committee. We review all tenured level appointments at the university and also provide advice on any issue presented to us by the president. I am also a member of several committees dealing with international affairs at Emory and I have served on search committees for senior administrators.

These roles have much to do with institution building and occupy a major portion of my time now. I suspect that as much I may try to avert it, administration and institution building will become even more important. I find considerable satisfaction in such work, perhaps because Emory and particularly our School of Public Health are growing rapidly. It is fun to attract young, capable people and to build new programs.

CONCLUDING REMARKS

There is no doubt in my mind that there are many opportunities in public health and in international nutrition for those trained in biological anthropology. A good source of information about openings and other opportunities is *The American Journal of Public Health.*

Students potentially interested in public health should take as much epidemiology and biostatistics as possible. If available, I would recommend completing a joint Ph.D./M.P.H. program. Fluency in at least one foreign language is good advice for anyone but especially for those interested in international work.

In conclusion, I would like to encourage biological anthropologists to explore opportunities in public health. I hope that by describing some aspects of my career, I have convinced readers that a biological anthropologist can be content in the public health setting.

REFERENCES

Balachander, J. 1993. "Tamil Nadu's Successful Nutrition Effort." In J. Rohde, M. Chatterjee and D. Morley, eds. *Reaching Health for All Delhi.* London: Oxford University Press, pp. 158–184.

Barker, D.J.P., ed. 1992. "Fetal and Infant Origins of Adult Disease." London: British Medical Journal.

Beaton, G. H., R. Martorell, K. J. Aronson, B. Edmonston, B. McCabe, A. C. Rossand, and B. Harvey. 1993. "Effectiveness of Vitamin A Supplementation in the Control of Young Child Morbidity and Mortality in Developing Countries." *ACC/SCN State-of-the-Art Series Nutrition Policy Discussion Paper No. 13.* Toronto, Canada: Toronto University Press, pp. 120.

Diamond, J. 1999. *Guns, Germs, and Steel: The Fates of Human Societies.* New York: W. W. Norton & Company.

Dibley, M. J., J. B. Goldsby, N. Staehling, and F. L. Trowbridge. 1987. "Development of Normalized Curves for the International Growth Reference: Historical and Technical Considerations." *American Journal of Clinical Nutrition* (46): 736–748.

Emory University. 1999. Emory, Rollins School of Public Health. Office of University Publications, Public Affairs.

Gillespie, S., J. Mason, and R. Martorell. 1996. "How Nutrition Improves." *ACC/SCN State-of-the-Art Series Nutrition Policy Discussion Paper No. 15.* Geneva: ACC/SCN, pp. 1–99.

Habicht, J-P., R. Martorell, C. Yarbrough, R. M. Malina, and R. E. Klein. 1974. "Height and Weight Standards for Pre-school Children: How Relevant are Ethnic Differences in Growth Potential?" *Lancet* (1): 611–615.

Martorell, R. 1973. "Diarrheal Diseases and Incremental Growth in Young Guatemalan Children." Doctoral Diss. University of Washington, Seattle, Washington.

———. 1989. "Body Size, Adaptation, and Function." *Human Organization* 14(1): 15–20.

———. 1995. "Promoting Healthy Growth: Rationale and Benefits." In P. Pinstrup-Anderson, D. Pelletier, and H. Alderman, eds. *Child Growth and Nutrition in Developing Countries. Priorities for Action.* New York: Cornell University Press, pp. 15–31.

Martorell, R., J-P. Habicht, and J. A. Rivera. 1995. "History and Design of the INCAP Longitudinal Study (1969–77) and Its Follow-up (1988–89). *Journal of Nutrition* 125 (Suppl. 4S): 1027S–1041S.

Martorell, R. and N. S. Scrimshaw, eds. 1995. "The Effects of Improved Nutrition in Early Childhood: The Institute of Nutrition of Central America and Panama (INCAP) Follow-up Study." *Journal of Nutrition* 125 (Suppl. 4S): 1027S–1138S.

Mata, L. J. 1978. *The Children of Santa María Cauqué: A Prospective Field Study of Health and Growth.* Cambridge, Mass.: MIT Press.

National Research Council. 1987. *Vitamin A Supplementation: Methodologies for Field Trials.* Washington, DC: National Academy Press.

Newman, M. T. 1975. "Nutritional Adaptation in Man." In A. Damon, ed. *Physiological Anthropology.* New York: Oxford University Press, pp. 210–252.

Chapter 13

Having Fun—A Jock in Two Worlds: Kinesiology and Human Biology

Robert M. Malina

EDUCATIONAL AND CAREER PATHS

The roots of the physical activity sciences are deeply imbedded in the field of physical education. Historically, physical education emphasized physical activity and performance in the context of education and sport. The field rapidly evolved in the 1960s, and there was considerable discussion of physical education as a profession versus physical education as a scientific discipline. Perceptions of physical education by the public and by university communities were often not favorable which relegated many departments to second class status on many campuses. There was likewise a widening gap between physical education as taught in the schools and physical education as pursued in graduate studies. As a result, graduate programs became more specialized, and those in the field identified with their specialization, for example, motor learning, motor development, sport psychology, sport sociology, leisure studies, exercise physiology, biomechanics, and others.

A corresponding trend was the emergence of new names for the field of study. Between 1960 and 1973, about thirty new designations were offered in an attempt to distinguish the profession and the discipline of physical education (Bouchard, 1976). A driving force was the negative connotation of the term physical education: "Name changes are occurring to explain either what people think we are doing, should be doing, or how we can camouflage the 'unsavory' connotations of *physical education*. We are becoming either human kinetics, kinesiology, ergonomics, sport studies, kinanthropology, or what have you" (Ziegler, 1982).

The search for an appropriate designation for the field that focuses on human movement in its many contexts continues, although kinesiology is presently the most common label.

My academic background is rooted to a large extent in this turmoil. My roots are in physical education, with bachelor (B.S., Manhattan College, 1959) and doctoral (Ph.D., University of Wisconsin, 1963) degrees in the field. The undergraduate emphasis was teacher preparation with a major in physical education and minors in biological science and history. The graduate emphasis, under the direction of Dr. G. Lawrence Rarick, eventually narrowed to motor development and physical performance during childhood and adolescence. During the course of study, I was exposed to the rich tradition of the study of physical growth and maturation in the context of performance (e.g., McCloy, 1936, 1938; Espenschade, 1940; Jones, 1949; Rarick, 1961) and to the first edition of Tanner's *Growth at Adolescence* (1955). The program also included, though indirectly, exposure to physical anthropology. Required reading in a course labeled kinesiology (which at the time referred to the biomechanics of movement) was Morton and Fuller's (1952) *Human Locomotion and Body Form.*

Upon completion of my degree, I expressed interest in further study of growth. Dr. Rarick put me in contact with Dr. Wilton M. Krogman at the University of Pennsylvania. During the interview, Dr. Krogman encouraged me to pursue an additional degree in anthropology. His rationale was similar to that implied in the initial discussion of the field of physical education, that is, the field's limited academic credibility.

I enrolled in the anthropology doctoral program at the University of Pennsylvania in the fall of 1963. Dr. Krogman, Dr. Loren Eisely, and Dr. Francis E. Johnston formed the core of the physical anthropology program, and each had a significant impact on my education and thinking. Analogous to corresponding changes in the field of physical education, this was the era of the "new physical anthropology" (Washburn, 1951, 1953). Population genetics and variability and human biology were emerging specializations. These were to a large extent new concepts for me. The study of human adaptability, spurred primarily by the writings of Dr. Paul T. Baker (Baker and Weiner, 1966), added another dimension. With the exception of genetics and evolutionary theory, my background from physical education in basic biological sciences—zoology, anatomy, microbiology, physiology and exercise physiology—served me well in anthropology. In contrast, concepts of variability, biological and cultural, were generally lacking in physical education. These perspectives developed in a variety of anthropology courses literally opened my eyes and broadened my horizons. The relevance of these concepts and others related to nutrition, for the study of growth, motor development, performance, and physical activity was immediately apparent (although some professors in cultural anthropology seemed reluctant to accept physical activity and sport as a legitimate area of study in the context of culture).

In addition to the program of study in anthropology, my time at the University of Pennsylvania offered the opportunity for direct involvement in study and research in growth and maturation at the Philadelphia Center for Research in Child Growth (now the Wilton M. Krogman Center). The environment of the center encouraged research on the normative and clinical aspects of growth and maturation. The mixed-longitudinal records of the center were readily available, and potential clinical applications in collaboration with colleagues at the Children's Hospital of Philadelphia were encouraged. As a result, I had the opportunity to study the growth of children with Thalassemia major both in Philadelphia and Ferrara, Italy, under the guidance of Dr. Irving Wolman, a pediatric hematologist.

At the conclusion of studies at the University of Pennsylvania, I accepted a position in the Department of Anthropology at the University of Texas at Austin in 1967 (the Ph.D. in anthropology was awarded in 1968). During my first year at Texas, Dr. Henry A. Selby encouraged me to accompany him for research in a Zapotec-speaking community in the Valley of Oaxaca, in southern Mexico. This was my first exposure to Latin America and marked the beginning of a series of studies in Oaxaca, which continue at present in the form of a follow-up of two communities that were initially studied in 1968 and 1971. Three central questions, among others, were the effects of marginal nutritional status on the growth of school age children, functional consequences of small body size, and secular change. The studies in Oaxaca and several periods of research at the Institute of Nutrition of Central America and Panama (INCAP) with Dr. Jean-Pierre Habicht nurtured developing interests in health and nutrition in Latin America. I eventually became involved at the Institute of Latin American Studies at the University of Texas, and regularly cotaught a seminar on health and nutrition in Latin America with Dr. Antonio Ugalde of the department of sociology.

After several years at the University of Texas, I was jointly appointed in the departments of anthropology and physical education (now the department of kinesiology and health education). My courses in anthropology—growth and maturation, motor development, youth sports—were cross-listed with kinesiology. Eventually, I worked to transfer my faculty line from anthropology to kinesiology due to tensions within anthropology. This took almost two years—moving across campus is more difficult than moving to another university! However, my courses were still cross-listed, and many anthropology students enrolled in two new courses—health and human variability, and human biology across the life span—that I taught in the kinesiology program, which featured a concentration in health and human development.

My career at the University of Texas thus followed a route from anthropology back to kinesiology, in a sense returning to my roots. However, my roots in physical education were broadly expanded as a result of concepts, ideas, and field research within anthropology, something that I do not believe would have occurred had I been affiliated exclusively with a department of kinesiology.

After twenty-eight years at the University of Texas, I accepted a position in the department of kinesiology at Michigan State University in 1995. This was an opportunity to focus some of my efforts on the study of youth sports, one of my primary areas of teaching and research interest. At Michigan State University, I am also affiliated with the department of anthropology as an adjunct professor and with the Center for Latin American and Caribbean Studies. Thus, the focus may be a bit different, but the expanded framework is still there.

AN EVOLVING BIOCULTURAL FRAMEWORK

The educational and career path, which combined physical education and anthropology, nurtured a primary focus on the growth and motor performance of children and adolescents in a biocultural context. The human species cannot be considered in an exclusively biological or in an exclusively cultural manner. The biological and cultural must be integrated for a more complete appreciation of the human condition.

Universal Tasks of Childhood and Adolescence— Growth, Maturation, and Development

All children and adolescents have three primary tasks: to *grow*—increase in the size of the body as a whole and of its parts from infancy to adulthood; to *mature*—progress toward the biologically mature state, which is an operational concept because the mature state varies with the body system; and to *develop*—acquisition of cognitive, affective, and behavioral competence or the learning of appropriate behaviors expected by society (Table 13.1). Growth and maturation are biological concepts, whereas development is a behavioral concept and is specific to the culture in which children and adolescents are reared. Culture, of course, refers to the amalgam of symbols, values, and behaviors that characterize the population.

The three terms are often treated as the same, yet they are distinct but interrelated tasks in the daily lives of children and adolescents for approximately the first two decades of life. The three processes occur simultaneously. They also interact to influence the child's body image, self-concept, self-esteem, and perceived competence, of course, within the specific cultural context.

Table 13.1
The Child as a Biocultural Individual—Components of Growth, Maturation and Development, and Their Potential Interactions

Growth	Maturation	Development
Size	Skeletal	Cognitive
Proportions	Sexual	Emotional
Physique	Somatic	Social
Composition	Dental	Moral
Systemic	Neuromuscular	Motor
	Neuroendocrine	

SELF-CONCEPT
SELF-ESTEEM
PERCEIVED COMPETENCE

Foci of the Physical Activity Sciences

Major foci in the physical activity sciences are physical activity per se, proficiency in motor skills, and physical fitness. Others areas of emphasis include physiological aspects of high performance, psychological and social aspects of physical activity, neuromuscular bases of motor learning, and so on. At present, the physical activity sciences are increasingly focused on issues related to public health, specifically obesity and degenerative diseases.

Physical activity is a behavior. It is viewed most often in the context of gross bodily movements associated with a significant increase in energy expenditure above resting levels, labeled as moderate-to-vigorous physical activity in the context of cardiovascular fitness and health. Physical activity is, however, more complex. It involves at least five major components related to energetics, biomechanics, muscular strength, motor skill, and context. The energetic component focuses on the balance between energy intake and energy output, the role of habitual activity in the development and maintenance of aerobic capacities, and the energy and fitness needs of activities of daily living. The biomechanical component is related to the effects of weight bearing and ground reaction forces generated in physical activities on connective tissues and joints, and especially on the accretion of bone mineral. The strength component deals with movement against a resistance, and refers to the activity needed to maintain muscular strength and power, specifically to carry out daily activities. The motor component deals with proficiency in a variety of movements. Movement, of course, is the substrate of physical activity. The context is the setting, broadly defined, within which physical activities take place. The context is determined by the culture within which the individual lives, and includes such things as what activities are acceptable, when they can be performed, and the value attached to the activity.

Discussions of physical activity usually refer to the estimated level of habitual physical activity, that is, the level of activity that characterizes the lifestyle of the individual, and patterns of participation in activities. Physical activity is usually quantified in terms of amount of time in activity (hour/week), an activity score, or energy expended in light or moderate-to-vigorous activities. Estimates are ordinarily derived from questionnaires, interviews, diaries, and heart rate integrators, or a combination of methods. Allowing for the limitations of techniques, presently available data suggest that estimated activity levels increase during childhood into early adolescence, and then decline as youth pass through adolescence. These trends are reasonably consistent across samples of North American and European youth (Malina, 1995; Armstrong and Van Mechelen, 1998).

The processes through which a child acquires proficiency in a series of basic movement skills, both gross and fine, comprise the domain of motor development. Independent walking is the fundamental human locomotor skill. Other basic skills include running, jumping, throwing, climbing, catching, striking, in addition to a host of manipulative skills, which are often labeled as fine motor. All individuals, excluding of course those with some central nervous system disorders, can perform basic motor skills, but levels of proficiency, that is, accuracy, precision, and economy of performance, vary considerably.

The development of proficiency in motor skills is a process of modification based upon the interaction of neuromuscular maturation, the individual physical and behavioral characteristics, the tempo of growth and maturation, residual effects of prior motor experiences, and the new motor experiences per se. Motor development also proceeds in the context of the environments in which the child is reared.

Movement is the substrate of physical activities, be it the subsistence, leisure, or high-level performance. Proficiency in motor skills may facilitate a wide range of activities; conversely, lack of proficiency may constrain opportunities for physical activity. In many developing areas, physical activity is the basis of subsistence.

Physical fitness is an adaptive state, which varies with growth, maturation, and aging, lifestyle, and level of habitual physical activity. Fitness has historically been viewed as having three basic components: muscular strength and endurance, cardiorespiratory endurance, and motor ability that are essential to carry out daily activities without undue fatigue and with sufficient reserve to enjoy active leisure (Clarke, 1971). For many years, assessment of physical fitness of children and adolescents focused on performance, for example, running speed (dashes), explosive power (standing long jump or vertical jump), agility (shuttle run), power and coordination (ball throw for distance), upper body functional strength (pull-ups), and abdominal strength and endurance (sit-ups).

The concept of physical fitness has since evolved from this primary focus on its motor and strength components (performance-related physical fitness) to more emphasis on health. Thus, the concept of health-related physical fitness emerged in the 1970s. It is defined by three components—cardiovascular endurance measured in a distance run, musculoskeletal function of the lower trunk measured by sit-ups for abdominal strength and sit and reach for lower back flexibility, and body composition estimated as the sum of the triceps and subscapular skinfolds (AAHPERD, 1984). Driving forces behind the move to health-related physical fitness was primary concern for several adult health issues—cardiovascular disease, low back problems, and obesity, and an underlying assumption that physical fitness during childhood and adolescence may help reduce the burden of these conditions in adulthood (Malina, 1991a).

The concept of physical fitness continues to evolve. More recent definitions address physical and physiological fitness in terms of morphological, muscular, motor, cardiovascular, and metabolic components (Bouchard and Shephard, 1994). Morphological fitness includes measures of subcutaneous fatness, fat distribution, and the body mass index. Metabolic fitness includes measures of serum lipids, blood pressures, blood glucose, and other risk factors for cardiovascular disease.

Childhood through Adolescence to Adulthood

The report of the surgeon general, *Physical Activity and Health* (U.S. Department of Health and Human Services, 1996) highlights the benefits of a physically active lifestyle for the health of individuals and the nation. At the same time, the report notes that the majority of Americans are not regularly active: almost one-half of youth age twelve to twenty-one years are not regularly active, 60 percent of American adults are not regularly active, and 25 percent of adults are not active at all. Given this state of affairs, calls for increasing daily physical activity in all segments of the population from early childhood through old age are common in discussions of public health policy. A lifestyle of regular physical activity presumably contributes to more efficient function of various systems, weight maintenance, reduced risk of several degenerative diseases, reduced risk of mortality, and overall improvement of quality of life.

Contemporary thinking in public health posits that childhood activity habits may influence health during childhood, as well as throughout life. A model illustrating potential relationships between physical activity in childhood and adolescence, and health during childhood, adolescence and adulthood is illustrated in Figure 13.1. Although evidence dealing with the

Figure 13.1
Potential Relationships between Physical Activity in Childhood and Adolescence, and Health, Including Health-related Fitness During Childhood, Adolescence, and Adulthood. Modified after Blair et al., 1989.

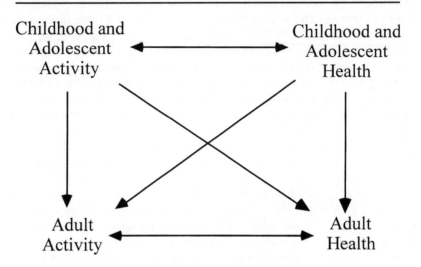

potential associations in the six pathways is suggestive, more data are necessary (Malina, 1996a, 2001).

RESEARCH ACTIVITIES

The research directions and topics that have predominated in my academic career have two common threads: first, a primary focus on children and adolescents, and second, collaboration with graduate students working under my supervision and colleagues at other universities. The subsequent discussion highlights several of these topical areas and important collaborators. Pertinent references are also indicated.

Studies of Philadelphia School Children

Initial studies of growth and maturation were set largely in the context of human biology and performance. My dissertation considered the growth, skeletal maturation, and motor fitness of American black and white children in Philadelphia. A number of comparative papers resulted from these initial efforts in growth research (Malina, 1966, 1969a, 1969b, 1970, 1971, 1972). This data set proved valuable from another perspective. As new questions arise in science and more appropriate methods of analysis are developed, an available data set is a potentially valuable resource. To this end, my dissertation data set for Philadelphia school children in 1965–1966 provided several opportunities. Early examples include parent-child correlations in height and sibling similarities in growth and performance (Malina et al., 1970, 1976; Malina and Mueller, 1981; Mueller and Malina, 1976, 1980); comparison of estimates of skeletal maturity with a change in the Tanner-Whitehouse method (Malina and Little, 1981); growth and skeletal maturity characteristics of children classified as obese by different criteria (Malina et al., 1989); and multivariate analysis of growth and motor fitness using principal components analysis (Malina and Moriyama, 1991). More recent examples include relationships between birth weight and growth and maturity status at school age (Malina et al., 1996; Malina, Koziel, et al., 1999), the contribution of biological maturity to individual differences in strength and motor fitness (Katzmarzyk et al., 1997), and genetic and environmental sources of variation in the body mass index in children (Katzmarzyk, Mahaney et al., 1999).

Studies in Oaxaca, Mexico

My research activities in the Valley of Oaxaca began in 1968 and continued through 1979. They focused primarily on school children and to a lesser extent on adults. Results of these studies suggest several trends for school children in this region of southern Mexico. The combined sample of school children from six communities in the Valley of Oaxaca—two rural Zapotec-speaking and two Ladino communities, and two urban *colonias*—have mean statures and weights that are smaller compared with middle-class children of Mexico City. Relative to Mexico City boys from low economic circumstances with an average per capita caloric intake of 1,564 kcal, Oaxaca boys compare favorably until ten years of age and then are consistently smaller. These general comparisons suggest that Oaxaca school children are, by Mexican standards, smaller than average but similar to Mexican children from the poorest economic conditions (Malina et al., 1972; Malina, 1983b). Menarche (probit estimate) occurs at 14.4±0.23 years, which is later by more than 1.5 to 2.0 years compared with better-off girls in Mexico, and is comparable to median ages for poor and/or not well-off girls in various parts of the world (Malina et al., 1977; Malina, Selby et al., 1980).

Within this composite sample, rural-urban comparisons give variable results. Children from the rural Zapotec communities are consistently shorter and lighter, and have smaller estimated midarm muscle circumferences than rural Ladino and urban *colonia* children. Differences between rural Ladino and urban *colonia* children are not significant (Malina, Himes et al., 1980). The results suggest that children in rural, indigenous communities in the Valley of Oaxaca probably experienced a history of more severe undernutrition compared with children in Ladino and urban communities, and that rural-to-urban migration did not result in improved growth status.

More detailed studies of school children from a single Zapotec-speaking community provide additional insights to the dynamics of growth and performance. Estimated growth velocities for body mass and stature of the Zapotec children indicate moderate growth deficits that accumulated throughout childhood compared with adequately nourished children, and especially diminished growth rates in estimated leg length (Buschang and Malina, 1983; Buschang et al., 1986). Estimated growth velocities show negligible differences between children in high and low socioeconomic status households within the community, suggesting that the growth deficits evident at school age occurred earlier in infancy or early childhood (Little et al., 1988a). Comparison of the growth status of children by origin of their parents indicates greater absolute and relative leg length and larger cranio-facial dimensions in offspring of native-immigrant matings relative to offspring native pairings, which suggests an influence of increased heterozygosity on growth (Little et al., 1988b, 1991).

Boys and girls from this rural Zapotec community have absolutely lower levels of strength and motor fitness compared with well-nourished children. Grip strength is appropriate for their body size, whereas running and jumping performances are less than expected. In contrast, throwing performance per unit body size is better than expected for the small body size (Malina and Buschang, 1985; Malina et al., 1987). The results are not consistent with the postulate of superior efficiency in association with reduced body size in undernourished populations (e.g., Stini, 1975; Martorell et al., 1978). Rather, they suggest variation with performance task. In addition, when age, stature and body mass are statistically controlled, other anthropometric dimensions add little to explaining the variance in strength and motor fitness in Zapotec children (Malina and Buschang, 1985). More recent analyses indicate that the body mass index (BMI) impacts the strength and motor fitness of boys and girls with poor nutritional histories currently living under inadequate nutritional circumstances differently than it impacts the strength and motor fitness of adequately nourished children (Malina et al., 1998).

Finally, surveys of school children in a rural Zapotec community in 1968 and 1978 indicated no differences in stature, weight, arm and estimated midarm muscle circumferences, triceps skinfold, and grip strength over the ten-year period (Malina, Selby et al., 1980). Data for adult stature, based largely on males, show no evidence of secular change between the 1890s and the 1970s (Himes and Malina, 1975; Malina et al., 1983). The results thus indicate no short- or long-term secular change in body size of children and adults.

It is appropriate to place these observations on children in the Valley of Oaxaca in the context of the summary of the report on the results of our ten-year follow-up, 1968–1978 (Malina and Selby, 1982:31–32):

The conditions of living of the villagers have not improved very much over the past decade, if taken household by household. . . . Public health measures over the past decade, however, improved the health conditions of the village quite remarkably. As a result of improved water treatment and health care, infant and child mortality has declined . . . (but) improvements in public health conditions have not existed long enough for their effects to be seen in the growth status of children. . . . [E]conomic conditions of the individual households which today are preventing the villagers from enjoying a decent life, will have to pick-up, in our view, if the advances of this decade are to be continued.

Studies of Belgian Youth

While a visiting professor at the Katholieke Universiteit Leuven in 1980, a collaborative relationship in the study of the growth and performance of Belgian youth was begun. Among many colleagues at Leuven, Dr. Gaston Beunen of the faculty of physical education and physiotherapy is the primary collaborator. Among these efforts, the longitudinal analysis of the growth and performance of Belgian adolescent boys is primary (Beunen et al., 1988). The results indicate growth spurts in several performance items that vary relative to peak height velocity (PHV). Speed, agility, and flexibility measure reach peak velocities, on average, before PHV, whereas strength and power tasks reach peak velocities after PHV. A follow-up study of a subsample of this longitudinal series indicates maturity-associated variation in fatness and relative fat distribution that persists into adulthood, at least to age thirty (Beunen et al., 1994).

Other collaborative efforts focus on the relationships among physical activity, fatness, skeletal maturation, and physical fitness. Among boys followed longitudinally from thirteen to eighteen years, those classified as active performed better than those classified as inactive only in pulse rate recovery after a step test (cardiorespiratory function) and the flexed arm hang (upper body muscular strength and endurance). On the other hand, active and inactive boys did not differ in leg lifts (abdominal strength and endurance), sit and reach (flexibility), static arm pull strength, the vertical jump (explosive power), a shuttle run (speed and agility), and speed of upper limb movement (Beunen et al., 1992). Boys and girls with excessive fatness do not perform as well as lean youth, and differences are especially apparent in items that require the support and projection of body mass (Beunen et al., 1983; Malina et al., 1995). The contribution of biological maturation to physical fitness operates largely through interactions with height and weight, and differs between boys and girls (Beunen et al., 1997).

Studies of Quebec Youth

The Quebec Family Study is an ongoing study of familial relationships in size, physique, body composition, physical fitness, risk factors for cardiovascular disease, and several indicators of lifestyle, including physical activity. The study was developed by Dr. Claude Bouchard, who completed his dissertation in anthropology under my supervision at the University of Texas as Austin. Collaborative activities with Dr. Bouchard, others at the Laval University, and Dr. Peter T. Katzmarzyk, a recent graduate from Michigan State University, have resulted in several insights into the study of somatotype and relationships between physical activity, physical fitness, and risk factors. Study of twin and familial similarities on Heath-Carter anthropometric somatotypes (Carter and Heath, 1990) indicate a significant genotypic contribution (Song et al., 1993, 1994). Related studies indicate significant associations between somatotype components and risk factors for cardiovascular disease in both children (Katzmarzyk et al., 1998a) and adults (Malina, Katzmarzyk, Song et al., 1997; Katzmarzyk, Malina, Song et al., 1999).

Among Quebec youth age nine to eighteen years, only 11 percent to 21 percent of the variance in health-related fitness items (sit-ups, static leg strength, PWC_{150}, skinfolds) is explained by energy expenditure in moderate-to-vigorous activity (Katzmarzyk et al., 1998b). Although there are significant associations between indicators of physical activity and fitness, a large fraction of the variability in fitness, about 80 percent to 90 percent, is not accounted for by physical activity, age, and sex, suggesting that other factors are involved and need to be considered.

Total cholesterol (TC), high-density lipoprotein cholesterol (HDL-C), low-density lipoprotein cholesterol (LDL-C), triglycerides (TG), and blood pressures (BP) are indicators of metabolic fitness. Correlations between indicators of metabolic fitness and physical activity (largely self-reported physical activity and sports participation) are often significant but consistently low (<0.3) in children and adolescents; some correlations, particularly for HDL-C reach ~0.4 (Despres et al., 1990; Malina, 1990; Armstrong and Simons-Morton, 1994; Riddoch, 1998). Correlations between TC, TG, and BP and measures of aerobic fitness (peak VO_2, step test) are also low, whereas those between fitness and HDL are more variable (Malina, 1990).

Studies of physical activity, fitness, and risk factors for coronary heart disease have generally relied on univariate statistical methods. Given that physical activity, physical fitness, and indicators of CHD risk are not easily quantifiable by a single measurement, a multivariate approach is preferable. Results of a canonical correlation analysis in Quebec youth indicate that 5 percent to 20 percent of the variation in the CHD risk factor variate is explained by the physical activity variate, whereas 11 percent to 30 percent of the variance in the CHD variate is explained by the physical fitness variate (Katzmarzyk, Malina, and Bouchard, 1999). An activity profile characterized by greater amounts of energy expenditure and energy expenditure in moderate-to-vigorous physical activity and lower amounts of time being inactive and watching television is associated with a more favorable metabolic risk profile—lower BP, serum TG, LDL-C and plasma glucose, and higher HDL-C. Similarly, a fitness profile characterized by low skinfold thicknesses and leg muscle strength (static strength of the quadriceps), and high PWC_{150} is associated with a more favorable metabolic risk profile. The canonical projections for abdominal muscular strength and endurance (sit-ups) are variable. The contributions of the two measures of muscular strength and endurance—quadriceps strength and sit-ups—may be influenced by strength-body mass relationships and heterogeneity of biological maturation. More mature youth are larger and stronger than less mature youth, but may have a poorer metabolic profile (Malina, 1990). Unfortunately, an indicator of biological maturation is not available for the Quebec youth. Nevertheless, the results highlight the relationships among risk factors for CHD, physical activity, and physical fitness in childhood and adolescence, and also illustrate the need to consider other factors that may influence the relationships.

Studies of Polish Youth

Collaborative studies with colleagues in Poland have concerned three longitudinal data sets in collaboration with Professor Tadeusz Bielicki, department of anthropology, Polish Academy of Sciences in Wroclaw and Dr. Barbara Woynarowska, department of school medicine, Institute of Mother and Child in Warsaw. A first effort considered interrelationships among indicators of skeletal, sexual, somatic, and dental maturity in boys followed longitudinally from eight to eighteen years in the Wroclaw Growth Study (Bielicki et al., 1984). A retrospective analysis of the longitudinal records of participants in sport from the Wroclaw Growth Study indicates different trends for males and females. Boys active in sport have a growth and maturation pattern characteristic of early maturers, whereas girls active in sport are taller and heavier compared with local reference values, but have a pattern of maturation characteristic of average maturing individuals. The pubertal progress of boys and girls active in sport during childhood and adolescence does not differ from nonathletic boys and girls (Malina and Bielicki, 1996). More recent analyses of this longitudinal sample considered changes in individual skinfold thicknesses and subcutaneous fat distribution relative to the timing of PHV (Malina, Koziel et al., 1999).

The other two series of studies of Polish youth in Warsaw focus on the growth, maturation, and aerobic capacity of children eleven to fourteen years of age in sports schools and considers adolescent growth and submaximal physical working capacity defined as power out put at a heart rate of 170 beats per minute (PWC_{170}) in active and nonactive youth eleven to eighteen years of age. Maturity-associated variation in maximal aerobic power (VO_2 peak) and ontogenetic scaling of VO_2 peak between eleven and fourteen years have been reported (Malina, Beunen et al., 1997; Beunen et al., 1997). The results suggest that scaling VO_2 for body mass varies with maturity status in boys but not in girls. In the other data set, active and nonactive boys and girls do not differ in the mean age at maximum growth in PWC_{170}, but youth active in sport have a greater maximal grain in submaximal power output (Malina, Beunen et al., 1997). Among girls, the interval between PHV and menarche, PHV (cm/year), ages at attaining stages three, four, and five of pubic hair and breast development (Tanner, 1962), and the estimated intervals between stages do not differ between girls active in sport and nonactive girls (Geithner et al., 1998). The results thus suggest that training for sport during puberty and the growth spurt does not apparently influence the timing and progress of somatic and sexual maturation in girls.

Studies of Female Athletes

Evidence suggests that successful female athletes in a variety of sports tend to be late maturing. Athletes in many, but not all, sports have a later mean age at menarche than nonathletes (Malina, 1983a). Although the later menarche is often attributed to the effects of regular training for sport during childhood, the evidence is not conclusive, and related factors are not considered. Prospective data for young athletes in a variety of sports are limited to small samples and selected sports; status quo data are also limited (Malina, 1998a). In contrast, the majority of data for athletes are retrospective, and it is not possible to establish causal relationships from such data. Correlations with years of training before menarche are often used to infer that training prior to menarche "delays" this maturational event. This is misleading. Assume that two girls begin training at six years of age; one is an early maturer who will attain menarche at eleven years, whereas the other is a late maturer who will reach menarche at sixteen years. A priori there will be a correlation between the two events; the early maturer will have five years of training before menarche, whereas the late maturer will have ten years of training before menarche. Training frequency and intensity are not quantified in such studies, and distinction is not made between initial participation in a sport and intensive training in sport. In some of the analyses, those who take up regular training after menarche, for example, some early maturers, are excluded in discussions of an assumed training effect. It is also important to note that not all athletes experience menarche late. The range of reported ages at menarche in 370 elite university athletes in seven sports (swimming, diving, tennis, golf, track and field, basketball, and volleyball) is 9.2 to 17.7 years, and early and late maturers are found in all seven sports (Malina, Katzmarzyk, Bonci et al., 1997). The range of ages in athletes completely overlaps that in 314 nonathlete students attending the same university, 9.1 to 17.4 years (Malina, 1998b).

How can the later mean ages at menarche in athletes be interpreted without exclusive reliance on training as the etiological factor? Menarche is a biological event. In adequately nourished individuals, age at menarche is a highly heritable characteristic (Tanner, 1962). Several of our studies considered factors related to menarche in a sample of elite university athletes. There is a familial tendency for later maturation in athletes. Mother-daughter and sister-sister correlations in families of athletes are similar to those in the general population (Malina et al., 1994).

Age at menarche is also influenced by several socially or bioculturally mediated variables, for example, socioeconomic differentials in some countries and positive secular changes in age at menarche in association with improved health and nutritional circumstances over time (Malina, 1979a, 1979b; Tanner, 1962). Sport specific selective factors must be considered as a part of this biocultural matrix in athletes. Number of children in the family is another consideration. Girls, nonathletes and athletes from larger families, tend to attain menarche, on average, at a later age than peers from smaller families. Moreover, the estimated sibling number effect, controlling for birth order, in athletes and nonathletes overlaps, 0.15 to 0.22 years per additional sibling in athletes and 0.08 to 0.19 years per additional sibling in nonathletes (Malina, Katzmarzyk, Bonci et al., 1997). Although data are not extensive, athletes tend to be from larger families than nonathletes (Malina et al., 1982; Malina, Katzmarzyk, Bonci et al., 1997). Given the active lifestyle of athletes in contrast to the general population, the significance of later menarche among athletes for later health and reproductive function needs attention (Malina, 1991b, 1998b).

Studies of swimmers provide additional insights to evaluating age at menarche in athletes. Data for young, Olympic, and national level swimmers from several countries in the 1950s to 1970s indicate mean ages at menarche that are similar age to nonathletes (about thirteen years), and there is no difference between younger and older swimmers (Malina, 1983a). However, university level swimmers from elite programs in the United States in the mid-1980s through the mid-1990s have mean ages at menarche of 14.3 and 14.4 years (Malina, 1996b). This trend probably reflects increased opportunities for girls in swimming. It was common for swimmers to retire by sixteen to seventeen years of age in the 1950s to 1970s. With the advent of Title IX legislation in the United States, many universities added and/or improved swim programs so that more opportunities were available. Also, later maturing age group swimmers, who catch up to peers in size and strength in late adolescence, may experience more success in swimming and persist in the sport. Another factor may be changes in the size and physique of female swimmers associated with the demands of the sport. A comparison of university level female swimmers in the late-1980s with those in the mid-1970s indicated that the former were taller and more linear, a physique characteristic of later maturers; the more recent swimmers were also significantly more androgynous in physique (Malina and Merrett, 1995).

Studies of Young Athletes

The study of the growth and maturity characteristics of successful young athletes has a long tradition. Rowe (1933), for example, raised the issue of training and growth of adolescent boys involved in sport, but did not take individual differences in biological maturation into account. Krogman (1959) reported accelerated skeletal maturity in successful little league baseball players and commented that the size and strength advantage associated with advanced biological maturation gives them an advantage in sport. More recently, concern has shifted primarily to young female athletes with the suggestion that intensive training for sport during childhood and adolescence may stunt the growth and delay maturation (American Medical Association/American Dietetic Association, 1991; Tofler et al., 1996). Thus, an issue of current interest is the critical appraisal of intensive training for sport as a factor that may negatively influence growth and maturation.

There is, however, confusion about the specific role of training for sport as a factor that may significantly influence indicators of growth status and rate, and especially sexual maturation. The confusion derives in part from a loose or imprecise use of the term training; lack of adequate longitudinal data for young athletes that span the growth spurt and pubertal maturation; a tendency to make inferences from highly select athletes to the general population; erroneous statistical inference, especially causal statements based on correlation; and failure to consider other factors that are known to influence indicators of growth and maturation.

Gymnastics is the only sport that consistently presents a profile of short stature in both sexes. Figure skaters of both sexes also present shorter statures, on average, though data are not extensive. Female ballet dancers tend to have shorter statures during childhood and early adolescence, but catch-up to nondancers in late adolescence. Athletes of both sexes in others sports have, on average, statures that equal or exceed reference medians (Malina, 1994, 1998a).

Body mass presents a similar pattern. Gymnasts, figure skaters, and ballet dancers of both sexes consistently show lighter body mass. But, weight-for-height in gymnasts and figure skaters is appropriate, whereas weight-for-height in ballet dancers and distance runners is low. In contrast, young athletes in other sports tend to have body masses that, on average, equal or exceed the reference medians, and that are appropriate for their heights (Malina, 1994, 1998a).

Similar trends are apparent in indicators of biological maturity status. With few exceptions, male athletes in a variety of sports tend to be average ("on time") or advanced in maturity compared with their age peers, whereas female athletes in several sports tend to be average or late in maturity. Gymnasts of both sexes are late in maturity during adolescence. In contrast, there is a relative lack of late maturing boys and of early maturing girls who are successful in sport during adolescence. In some sports, however, catch-up growth in late adolescence reduces the significance of maturity-associated variation in body size in the performances of boys in late adolescence (Malina, 1998a).

In the context of presently available data for young athletes, it is extremely difficult to establish causality for an influence, either positive or negative, of training for sport on growth in height and biological maturation. The data do not meet epidemiological criteria for causality (Susser, 1991; Gordis, 1996):

1. Strength of association—the stronger the association, the less likely it is due to other factors that influence the relationship. The many factors associated with variation in growth and maturation should be noted.

2. Specificity—there is a greater chance of causality if the outcome variable is related to few rather than many factors. And, many factors are known to influence commonly used indicators of growth and maturation.

3. Temporal sequence—exposure or postulated cause must be known to occur before the outcome. A temporal sequence is difficult to establish, particularly in cross-sectional studies. The vast majority of studies of athletes are cross-sectional. Female gymnasts are already shorter than average long before systematic training has begun, and some athletes do in fact take-up sport after menarche. The same applies to skeletal maturation. In some sports, for example, ice hockey and soccer, a broad spectrum of skeletal maturity is evident in late childhood and early adolescence. However, advanced skeletal maturity is characteristic of athletes in these sports in late adolescence. Sport-specific selection criteria associated with late maturation in some sports and early maturation in other sports clearly are also confounding factors.

   A related problem in evaluating the potential effects of training on growth and maturation is difficulty in separating training effects from those associated with normal growth and maturation. Many changes in physique and body composition attributed to regular physical activity are in the same direction as those that accompany normal growth and maturation. Further, physique is an important selective factor in some sports, and young athletes in a given sport tend to have physiques similar to those of adult athletes in the sport (Carter and Heath, 1990).

4. Consistency of observations—all studies dealing with the association should yield the same results. Variability in mean ages at menarche among athletes in different sports, among athletes within the same sport, and between adolescent and adult athletes in the same sport indicates inconsistencies. All female gymnasts are not late maturers; some in fact are early or average maturers with short parents.

5. Biological coherence—there should be a strong biological basis for the postulated cause-effect relationship, that is, consistent with current understanding of the physiology of growth and maturation. Sex differences in the growth and maturation of young athletes are not consistent with a hypothesized effect of intensive training. Early and average ("on time") maturity are characteristic of many young male athletes, in contrast to average and late maturity

which are characteristic of many young female athletes. Why would one expect boys and girls to respond differently to intensive training when the hormonal processes underlying growth and maturation are similar in both sexes? It has been proposed that males are "better prepared physically (than females) for metabolic demands during the development of reproductive maturity" (Warren 1983:370). This proposition presumably includes the demands associated with rigorous physical activity and training. When potentially confounding factors are controlled (e.g., early sport-specific selection for physical characteristics, parental size, variation in training intensity among sports, etc.), the few available longitudinal studies indicate no effect of regular training for sport on the timing and tempo of growth and maturation.

In the context of Warren's (1983) suggestion, it has also been proposed that "the significant gains in strength and muscle mass which are possible in prepubertal boys undergoing resistance training could accelerate pubertal onset" (Cumming et al., 1994:56–57). However, resistance training in prepubertal boys results in gains in muscular strength without muscular hypertrophy; pubertal boys, on the other hand, increase in both strength and muscle mass in response to resistance training (Sale, 1989). Presently available data are thus not consistent with the criterion of biological coherence.

When variation in methodology and sampling among studies of young athletes in a variety of sports is considered, it is clear that regular training for sport during childhood and adolescence does not influence attained height, rate of growth, and the timing and tempo of somatic, sexual, and skeletal maturation. The data emphasize a primary role for constitutional factors in the selection and sorting processes of competitive sport. If intensive training is a factor of any consequence in the size attained and maturation of young athletes, its effects must be partitioned from constitutional factors, social and environmental factors, and components of the overall sport environment.

Youth Sports

Sport is a highly visible form of physical activity, and is the primary source of activity for many children and adolescents. Mass participation in community sports is a major feature of daily living for American children. In an early survey of Michigan youth, more than one-half of children have their first experiences in organized sport by eight to nine years of age (Institute for the Study of Youth Sports, 1978). Given current interest in youth sports, it is likely that the age when the majority of youth have their first organized sport experiences has declined. Participation in organized sport increases during childhood, but then declines during the transition into adolescence, after about twelve to thirteen years of age (Institute for the Study of Youth Sports, 1976). The distribution of participants has the shape of a broad-based pyramid, with numbers of participants decreasing as sport becomes more demanding and specialized, and as interests of children and early adolescents change. The decline in youth sports participation after twelve to thirteen years parallels declining rates of participation in physical activities in general across adolescence (Malina, 1995).

Organized sport implies the presence of a coach, who is quite often a volunteer, and regular practices and competitions during the course of a season. Estimates of the number of participants in the United States for the mid-1990s suggest that approximately 22 million youth five to seventeen years of age participate in sport programs sponsored by community organizations. About 2.4 million youth participate in club sports which are generally fee-based as in gymnastics, figure skating, swimming, and, more increasingly, in soccer. An additional 14.5 million youth are involved in municipal recreational sports programs, which emphasize participation for everyone. Expressed as percentages of the U.S. population five to seventeen years of age in 1995 (about 48.4 million), 45 percent, 5 percent, and 30 percent participate in agency, club, and recreational sports, respectively (Ewing et al., 1996). Within the more restricted age range of high school students, about 5.8 million youth (40 percent of the high school age population) participate in interscholastic high school sports (Ewing et al., 1996).

The contribution of organized sport in the daily physical activity of children and adolescents is important because time devoted to physical education in American schools has declined. For many children and adolescents, sport is becoming a major venue for regular physical activity. And organized youth sports participants twelve to fourteen years of age have a greater estimated total daily energy expenditure and greater estimated energy expenditure in moderate-to-vigorous physical activity, and spent less time watching television than those who do not participate in sport (Katzmarzyk and Malina, 1998).

A related issue is the role of youth sports in different cultural settings. Most studies of youth sports have concentrated on North American and to a lesser extent on European youth. Nevertheless, participation in sport is a major activity in the lives of children and adolescents throughout the world. In this context, patterns of participation in sport and physical activity were addressed in urban Mexican youth nine to eighteen years of age (Siegel, 1999). Highlights of the results suggest the following: Motivation for participation and discontinuing participation in sport are quite similar in Mexican and U.S. youth. However, among reasons for dropping out of sport, Mexican youth appear to be more concerned about their studies than American youth, and this is apparent more so for females than for males. Further, task and ego orientation appears to vary within the Mexican culture compared with the United States. The pattern of participation in physical activity is also generally similar to American youth, but indicates several differences that are culturally based. Sport participants are also more habitually active than nonparticipants. Although the sociodemographic and biological variables included in the study accounted for less than 15 percent of the variance in sport participation and physical activity, they note an important role for the perceived physical activity status of the youngsters' parents as a determinant of participation in physical activity and sport.

IMPLICATIONS FOR YOUNG PHYSICAL ANTHROPOLOGISTS

My career in physical anthropology and the physical activity sciences has evolved with a focus on children and adolescents in a variety of contexts. My research and teaching activities have also straddled both fields, and hopefully will continue to do so. This has resulted in a healthy schizophrenia.

Departments of kinesiology tend to be compartmentalized and are often divided along social science-biological science lines. The biocultural approach or biobehavioral interactions are either not generally recognized or are given lip service. Some social scientists of physical activity and sport have what appears to be a biophobia. This is surprising because the essence of physical activity is the movement of the body in a variety of contexts. It is imperative that physical activity sciences recognize that biology can influence behavior and that behavior can influence biology. This is changing among many in the physical activity sciences, especially exercise physiologists, in light of the major influence of a sedentary lifestyle—a culturally mediated pattern—on the health of the nation. Clearly, physical activity is a behavior that has important biological and health implications. On the other hand, biological characteristics of individuals also influence their physical activity pursuits. This is especially evident in selection, by self or the sport system, for specific physical and physiological characteristics in many sports.

Departments of anthropology are also often divided among disciplinary lines, and biological anthropologists often have second-class status in many departments. Further, many anthropologists frown upon those with primary interests in physical activity and sport (unless, of course, they generate research funds and overhead for a department), and often do not recognize them as valid topics for "anthropological" study. With such a narrow view, they overlook the importance of physical activity and sport in cultures throughout the world, as well as the potential important of activity-related behaviors in reconstructing the lifestyle and health status of earlier populations. Years ago a colleague criticized the offering of a course on youth sports in the department of anthropology. My comment was straightforward—there are more people interested in sport throughout the world than are interested in the native languages of Brazil! This also applies to the population of Brazil!

Within physical anthropology and human biology, physical activity is often viewed in the context of subsistence activities and not very often in terms of the motor skills comprising the activities. Similarly, the motor activities of children, who are the next generation of adult producers in a community, are not often considered. The functional consequences of small body size for productivity is usually emphasized, but the consequences of small body size for activities that children do and other activities of adults are not generally considered.

In a career that has straddled both fields and included active membership in departments in both fields, I have lived a more or less schizophrenic academic life. Personally, I have enjoyed it for I was able to pursue interests that are important to me.

What suggestions can I offer to a young physical anthropologist with interests in the physical activity sciences? There is considerable overlap between physical anthropology and the physical activity sciences—the focus of study is the human species. The two fields differ in theoretical backgrounds and basic approaches. It is important, therefore, to recognize and appreciate the basic sciences involved in the study of physical activity, motor development, performance, and related domains. Also, recognize that physical activity and its many dimensions is a valid field of study. Historically, many departments in the arts and sciences looked down upon the physical activity sciences.

Collaboration and willingness to work with others are key ingredients to a successful career in any field. This involves nurturing academic and research relationships with students and colleagues who have similar interests. As a faculty member, you will work with students and in particular graduate students. As the supervisor of their academic progress through a program, it is essential that you treat and interact with graduate students as colleagues and collaborators. In addition to mentoring them directly (e.g., involving them in your research) and indirectly (e.g., by example, work ethic, etc.), you must be willing to work with them.

As your career develops, you will undoubtedly have opportunities to work with others in your field who have similar interests. In my own career, this occurred, to some extent, by helping those for whom English is not a first language. English is presently the language of science (for better or worse), and many colleagues throughout the world would like to have their work published in English. It is, however, a very productive activity. It not only helps them to get their work before a larger audience, it also helps you in your own writing. In addition, this type of assistance has contributed to the development of several collaborative research activities that persist to this day.

Another important ingredient is focus. Maintain focus on your primary academic interests. There will be many opportunities to jump to different areas, especially as pressure mounts to seek "hot" research topics that are fundable. It is quite difficult, for example, to obtain funding for projects dealing with healthy, adequately nourished, normal children and adolescents. Given this situation, many individuals with developmental interests jumped to studies of aging and the elderly, largely because of the more ready availability of research funds. And, given current concern for the epidemic of obesity among American youth, it is likely some of these individuals will move back into the developmental sphere!

Reading and integrating are important aspects of maintaining focus. Try to read widely in your area of interest and attempt to integrate the data into your teaching, research, and writing interests. An active research program should feed into your teaching interests. In this manner, your courses will be regularly updated by your research per se and related reading in the area. I have heard many colleagues both in kinesiology and anthropology comment that they are too involved in teaching to do research. I find this argument quite shallow. I would suggest that active involvement in research is an essential component for effective teaching.

Finally, be willing to work for your profession. When the opportunity or call comes, be willing to serve on committees, assist with programs, chair sessions at local and national meetings, and related activities. As your career develops, you will also be asked to review manuscripts for journals in your field. This is an important responsibility to your profession. In doing so, you have direct input into the quality of research that is published. Also in doing so, be sensitive to those for whom English is not a first language. There is nothing more frustrating for a non-English speaker than to receive reviewer comments to the effect that the language of the paper is poor. Respect their science and their willingness to try to publish in another language. How many of us in the United States will try to publish a paper in another language?

In summary, the potential for biological anthropology or human biology in the physical activity sciences is tremendous. Each field brings a somewhat different view of the world to the table. Nevertheless, the fields are complementary and can make significant contributions to each other and to issues related to human biology and public health both in developed and developing countries. More human biologists should venture into the area, and I suggest that they will find it very rewarding.

REFERENCES

AAHPERD. 1984. *Technical Manual, Health Related Physical Fitness.* Reston, VA: American Association for Health, Physical Education, Recreation and Dance.

American Medical Association/American Dietetic Association. 1991. *Targets for Adolescent Health: Nutrition and Physical Fitness.* Chicago: American Medical Association.

Armstrong, N., and B. Simons-Morton. 1994. "Physical Activity and Blood Lipids in Adolescents." *Pediatric Exercise Science* (6): 381–405.

Armstrong, N., and W. Van Mechelen. 1998. "Are Young People Fit and Active?" In S. Biddle, J. Sallis, and N. Cavill, eds. *Young and Active? Young People and Health-Enhancing Physical Activity—Evidence and Implications.* London: Health Education Authority, pp. 69–97.

Baker, P. T., and J. S. Weiner, eds. 1966. *The Biology of Human Adaptability.* Oxford: Clarendon Press.

Beunen, G. P., R. M. Malina, J. A. Lefevre, A. L. Claessens, R. Renson, J. Simons, H. Maes, B. Vanreusel, and R. Lysens. 1994. "Size, Fatness and Relative Fat Distribution of Males of Contrasting Maturity Status during Adolescence and as Adults." *International Journal of Obesity* (18): 670–678.

Beunen, G. P., R. M. Malina, J. Lefevre, A. L. Claessens, R. Renson, B. Vanden Eynde, B. Vanreusel, and J. Simons. 1997. "Skeletal Maturation, Somatic Growth and Physical Fitness in Girls 6–16 Years of Age." *International Journal of Sports Medicine* (18): 413–419.

Beunen, G., R. M. Malina, M. Ostyn, R. Renson, J. Simons, and D. Van Gerven. 1983. "Fatness, Growth and Motor Fitness of Belgian Boys 12 through 20 Years of Age." *Human Biology* (55): 599–613.

Beunen, G. P., R. M. Malina, R. Renson, J. Simons, M. Ostyn, and J. Lefevre. 1992. "Physical Activity and Growth, Maturation and Performance: A Longitudinal Study." *Medicine and Science in Sports and Exercise* (24): 576–585.

Beunen, G. P., R. M. Malina, M. A. Van't Hof, J. Simons, M. Ostyn, R. Renson, and D. Van Gerven. 1988. *Adolescent Growth and Motor Performance: A Longitudinal Study of Belgian Boys.* Champaign, IL: Human Kinetics.

Beunen, G. P., D. M. Rogers, B. Woynarowska, and R. M. Malina. 1997. "Longitudinal Study of Ontogenetic Allometry of Oxygen Uptake in Boys and Girls Grouped by Maturity Status." *Annals of Human Biology* (24): 33–43.

Bielicki, T., J. Koniarek, and R. M. Malina. 1984. "Interrelationships among Certain Measures of Growth and Maturation Rate in Boys during Adolescence." *Annals of Human Biology* (11): 201–210.

Blair, S. N., D. G. Clark, K. J. Cureton, and K. E. Powell. 1989. "Exercise and Fitness in Childhood: Implications for a Lifetime of Health." In C. V. Gisolfi and D. R. Lamb, eds. *Youth, Exercise, and Sport.* Indianapolis, IN: Benchmark Press, pp. 401–430.

Bouchard, C. 1976. "The Physical Activity Sciences: A Basic Concept for the Organization of the Disciplines and the Profession." *International Journal of Physical Education* (13): 9–15.

Bouchard, C., R. M. Malina, and L. Perusse. 1997. *Genetics of Fitness and Physical Performance.* Champaign, IL: Human Kinetics.

Bouchard, C., and R. J. Shephard. 1994. "Physical Activity, Fitness, and Health: The Model and Key Concepts." In C. Health, C. Bouchard, R. J. Shephard, and T. Stephens, eds. *Physical Activity, Fitness, and Health.* Champaign, IL: Human Kinetics, pp. 77–88.

Buschang, P. H., and R. M. Malina. 1983. "Growth in Height and Weight of Mild-to-Moderately Undernourished Zapotec School Children." *Human Biology* (55): 587–597.

Buschang, P. H., R. M. Malina, and B. B. Little. 1986. "Linear Growth of Zapotec Schoolchildren: Growth Status and Yearly Velocity for Leg Length and Sitting Height." *Annals of Human Biology* (13): 225–234.

Carter, J.E.L., and B. H. Heath. 1990. *Somatotyping—Development and Applications.* Cambridge: Cambridge University Press.

Clarke, H. H. 1971. "Basic Understanding of Physical Fitness." *Physical Fitness Research Digest,* Series 1, no. 1.

Cumming, D. C., G. D. Wheeler, and V. J. Harber. 1994. "Physical Activity, Nutrition, and Reproduction." *Annals of the New York Academy of Sciences* (709): 55–74.

Despres, J.-P., C. Bouchard, and R. M. Malina. 1990. "Physical Activity and Coronary Risk Factors during Childhood and Adolescence." *Exercise and Sport Sciences Reviews* (18): 243–261.

Espenschade, A. 1940. "Motor Performance in Adolescence." *Monographs of the Society for Research in Child Development,* Serial no. 24.

Ewing, M. E., V. D. Seefeldt, and T. P. Brown. 1996. *Role of Organized Sport in the Education and Health of American Children and Youth.* New York: Carnegie Corporation, Carnegie Meeting Papers.

Geithner, C. A., B. Woynarowska, and R. M. Malina. 1998. "The Adolescent Spurt and Sexual Maturation in Girls Active and Not Active in Sport." *Annals of Human Biology* (25): 415–423.

Gordis, L. 1996. *Epidemiology.* Philadelphia: Saunders.

Himes, J. H., and R. M. Malina. 1975. "Age and Secular Factors in the Stature of Adult Zapotec Males." *American Journal of Physical Anthropology* (43): 367–369.

Institute for the Study of Youth Sports. 1976. *Joint Legislative Study on Youth Sports Programs: Agency Sponsored Sports, Phase I.* East Lansing: Michigan State University, Institute for the Study of Youth Sports.

———. 1978. *Joint Legislative Study on Youth Sports Programs: Agency Sponsored Sports, Phase II.* East Lansing: Michigan State University, Institute for the Study of Youth Sports.

Jones, H. E. 1949. *Motor Performance and Growth.* Berkeley: University of California Press.

Katzmarzyk, P. T., M. C. Mahaney, J. Blangero, J. J. Quek, and R. M. Malina. 1999. "Potential Effects of Ethnicity in Genetic and Environmental Sources of Variability in the Stature, Mass, and Body Mass Index of Children." *Human Biology* (71): 977–987.

Katzmarzyk, P. T., and R. M. Malina. 1998. "Contribution of Organized Sports Participation to Estimated Daily Energy Expenditure in Youth." *Pediatric Exercise Science* (10): 378–386.

Katzmarzyk, P. T., R. M. Malina, and G. P. Beunen. 1997. "The Contribution of Biological Maturation to the Strength and Motor Fitness of Children." *Annals of Human Biology* (24): 493–505.

Katzmarzyk, P. T., R. M. Malina, and C. Bouchard. 1999. "Physical Activity, Physical Fitness, and Coronary Heart Disease Risk Factors in Youth: The Quebec Family Study." *Preventive Medicine* (29): 555–562.

Katzmarzyk, P. T., R. M. Malina, T.M.K. Song, and C. Bouchard. 1998a. "Somatotype and Indicators of Metabolic Fitness in Youth." *American Journal of Human Biology* (10): 341–350.

———. 1998b. "Physical Activity and Health-Related Fitness in Youth: A Multivariate Analysis." *Medicine and Science in Sports and Exercise* (30): 709–714.

———. 1999. "Physique, Subcutaneous Fat, Adipose Tissue Distribution, and Risk Factors in the Quebec Family Study." *International Journal of Obesity* (23): 476–484.

Krogman, W. M. 1959. "Maturation Age of 55 Boys in the Little League World Series, 1957." *Research Quarterly* (30): 54–56.

Little, B. B., P. H. Buschang, and R. M. Malina. 1991. "Heterozygosity and Craniofacial Dimensions of Zapotec School Children from a Subsistence Community in the Valley of Oaxaca, Southern Mexico." *Journal of Craniofacial Genetics and Developmental Biology* (11): 18–23.

Little, B. B., R. M. Malina, and P. H. Buschang. 1988a. "Socioeconomic Variation in Estimated Growth Velocity of Schoolchildren from a Rural, Subsistence Agricultural Community in Southern Mexico." *American Journal of Physical Anthropology* (76): 443–448.

———. 1988b. "Increased Heterozygosity and Child Growth in an Isolated Subsistence Agricultural Community in the Valley of Oaxaca, Mexico." *American Journal of Physical Anthropology* (77): 85–90.

Malina, R. M. 1966. "Patterns of Development in Skinfolds of Negro and White Children." *Human Biology* (38): 89–103.

———. 1969a. "Growth and Physical Performance of American Negro and White Children: A Comparative Survey of Differences in Body Size, Proportions and Composition, Skeletal Maturation, and Various Motor Performances." *Clinical Pediatrics* (8): 476–483.

———. 1969b. "Skeletal Maturation Rate in North American Negro and White Children." *Nature* (223): 1075.

———. 1970. "Skeletal Maturation Studied Longitudinally over One Year in American Whites and Negroes 6 through 13 Years of Age." *Human Biology* (42): 377–390.

———. 1971. "Skinfolds of American Negro and White Children." *Journal of the American Dietetic Association* (59): 34–40.

———. 1972. "Weight, Height and Limb Circumferences in American Negro and White Children: Longitudinal Observations over a One Year Period." *Journal of Tropical Pediatrics and Environmental Child Health* (18): 280–283.

———. 1979a. "Secular Changes in Growth, Maturation, and Physical Performance." *Exercise and Sport Sciences Reviews* (6): 203–255.

———. 1979b. "Secular Changes in Size and Maturity: Causes and Effects." *Monographs of the Society for Research in Child Development*, Serial no 179, 44 (3–4): 59–102.

———. 1983a. "Menarche in Athletes: A Synthesis and Hypothesis." *Annals of Human Biology* (10): 1–24.

———. 1983b. "Growth and Maturity Profile of Primary School Children in the Valley of Oaxaca, Mexico." Garcia de Orta Serie de Antropobiologia: Revista do Instituto de Investigacao Cientifica Tropical (Lisboa) 2 (1–2): 153–157.

———. 1990. "Growth, Exercise, Fitness, and Later Outcomes." In C. Bouchard, R. J. Shephard, T. Stephens, J. R. Sutton, and B. D. McPherson, eds. *Exercise, Fitness, and Health: A Consensus of Current Knowledge*. Champaign, IL: Human Kinetics, pp. 637–653.

———. 1991a. "Fitness and Performance: Adult Health and the Culture of Youth." In R. J. Park, and H. M. Eckert, eds. *New Possibilities, New Paradigms?* (American Academy of Physical Education Papers No. 24). Champaign, IL: Human Kinetics, pp. 30–38.

———. 1991b. "Darwinian Fitness, Physical Fitness and Physical Activity." In C.G.N. Mascie-Taylor, and G. L. Lasker, eds. *Applications of Anthropology to Human Affairs*. Cambridge: Cambridge University Press, pp. 143–184.

———. 1994. "Physical Growth and Biological Maturation of Young Athletes." *Exercise and Sport Sciences Reviews* (22): 389–433.

———. 1995. "Physical Activity and Fitness of Children and Youth: Questions and Implications." *Medicine, Exercise, Nutrition, and Health* (4): 123–135.

———. 1996a. "Tracking of Physical Activity and Physical Fitness Across the Lifespan." *Research Quarterly for Exercise and Sport* 67 (supplement): 48–57.

———. 1996b. "The Young Athlete: Biological Growth and Maturation in a Biocultural Context." In F. L. Smoll, and R. E. Smith, eds. *Children and Youth in Sport: A Biopsychological Perspective.* Dubuque, IA: Brown and Benchmark, pp. 161–186.

———. 1998a. "Growth and Maturation of Young Athletes—Is Training for Sport a Factor?" In K.-M. Chan, and L. J. Micheli, eds. *Sports and Children.* Hong Kong: Williams and Wilkins Asia-Pacific, pp. 133–161.

———. 1998b. "Physical Activity, Sport, Social Status, and Darwinian Fitness. In S. S. Strickland, and P. S. Shetty, eds. *Human Biology and Social Inequality.* Cambridge: Cambridge University Press, pp. 165–192.

———. 2001. "Physical Activity and Fitness: Pathways from Childhood to Adulthood." *American Journal of Human Biology* (13): 162–172.

Malina, R. M., G. P. Beunen, A. L. Claessens, J. A. Lefevre, B. V. Eynde, R. Renson, B. Vanreusel, and J. Simons. 1995. "Fatness and Physical Fitness of Girls 7 to 17 Years." *Obesity Research* (3): 221–232.

Malina, R. M., G. P. Beunen, J. Lefevre, and B. Woynarowska. 1997. "Maturity-Associated Variation in Peak Oxygen Uptake in Active Adolescent Boys and Girls." *Annals of Human Biology* (24): 19–31.

Malina, R. M., and T. Bielicki. 1996. "Retrospective Longitudinal Growth Study of Boys and Girls Active in Sport." *Acta Paediatica* (85): 570–576.

Malina, R. M., and C. Bouchard. 1991. *Growth, Maturation, and Physical Activity.* Champaign, IL: Human Kinetics.

Malina, R. M., C. Bouchard, R. F. Shoup, and G. Lariviere. 1982. "Age, Family Size and Birth order in Montreal Olympic Athletes." In J.E.L. Carter, ed. *Physical Structure of Olympic Athletes. Part I. The Montreal Olympic Games Anthropological Project.* Basel, Switzerland: S. Karger, pp. 13–24.

Malina, R. M., and P. H. Buschang. 1985. "Growth, Strength and Motor Performance of Zapotec Children, Oaxaca, Mexico." *Human Biology* (57): 163–181.

Malina, R. M., W. C. Chumlea, C. D. Stepick, and F. Gutierez Lopez. 1977. "Age at Menarche in Oaxaca, Mexico, Schoolgirls, with Comparative Data for Other Areas of Mexico." *Annals of Human Biology* (4): 551–558.

Malina, R. M., J. H. Himes, C. D. Stepick, F. Gutierez Lopez, and P. H. Buschang. 1980. "Growth of Rural and Urban Children in the Valley of Oaxaca, Mexico." *American Journal of Physical Anthropology* (55): 269–280.

Malina, R. M., J. D. Holman, and A. B. Harper. 1970. "Parent Size and Growth Status of Offspring." *Social Biology* (17): 120–123.

Malina, R. M., P. T. Katzmarzyk, and G. Beunen. 1996. "Birth Weight and Its Relationship to Size Attained and Relative Fat Distribution at 7–12 Years of Age." *Obesity Research* (4): 385–390.

———. 1999. "Relation between Birth Weight at Term and Growth Rate, Skeletal Age, and Cortical Bone at 6–11 Years." *American Journal of Human Biology* (11): 505–511.

Malina, R. M., P. T. Katzmarzyk, C. M. Bonci, R. C. Ryan, and R. Wellens. 1997. "Family Size and Age at Menarche in Athletes." *Medicine and Science in Sports and Exercise* (29): 99–106.

Malina, R. M., P. T. Katzmarzyk, and S. R. Siegel. 1998. "Overnutrition, Undernutrition and the Body Mass Index: Implications for Strength and Motor Fitness." In J. Parizkova and A. P. Hills, eds. *Physical Fitness and Nutrition During Growth.* Basel, Switzerland: S. Karger, pp. 13–26.

Malina, R. M., P. T. Katzmarzyk, T.M.K. Song, G. Theriault, and C. Bouchard. 1997. "Somatotype and Cardiovascular Risk Factors in Healthy Adults." *American Journal of Human Biology* (9): 11–19.

Malina, R. M., S. Koziel, and T. Bielicki. 1999. "Variation in Subcutaneous Adipose Tissue Distribution Associated with Age, Sex, and Maturation." *American Journal of Human Biology* (11): 189–200.

Malina, R. M., and B. B. Little. 1981. "Comparison of TW1 and TW2 Skeletal Age Differences in American Black and White and in Mexican Children, 6–13 Years." *Annals of Human Biology* (8): 543–548.

Malina, R. M., B. B. Little, R. F. Shoup, and P. H. Buschang. 1987. "Adaptive Significance of Small Body Size: Strength and Motor Performance of School Children in Mexico and Papua New Guinea." *American Journal of Physical Anthropology* (73): 489–499.

Malina, R. M., and D.M.S. Merrett. 1995. "Androgyny of Physique of Women Athletes: Comparisons by Sport and over Time." In R. Hauspie, G. Lindgren, and F. Falkner, eds. *Essays on Auxology.* Welwyn Garden City, Hertfordshire, UK: Castlemead Publications, pp. 355–363.

Malina, R. M., and M. Moriyama. 1991. "Growth and Motor Performance of Black and White Children 6–10 Years of Age: A Multivariate Analysis." *American Journal of Human Biology* (3): 599–611.

Malina, R. M., and W. H. Mueller. 1981. "Genetic and Environmental Influences on the Strength and Motor Performance of Philadelphia School Children." *Human Biology* (53): 163–179.

Malina, R. M., W. H. Mueller, and J. D. Holman. 1976. "Parent/Child Correlations and Heritability of Stature in Philadelphia Black and White Children 6 to 12 Years of Age." *Human Biology* (48): 475–486.

Malina, R. M., R. C. Ryan, and C. M. Bonci. 1994. "Age at Menarche in Athletes and Their Mothers and Sisters." *Annals of Human Biology* (21): 417–422.

Malina, R. M., and H. A. Selby. 1982. "Zapotec Restudy: Ten Year Follow-up of Zapotec Children. Report of Activities and Results of the Research Supported by National Science Foundation Grant BNS 78-10642" (July 1, 1982).

Malina, R. M., H. A. Selby, W. L. Aronson, P. H. Buschang, and W. C. Chumlea. 1980. "Re-examination of the Age at Menarche in Oaxaca, Mexico." *Annals of Human Biology* (7): 281–282.

Malina, R. M., H. A. Selby, P. H. Buschang, and W. L. Aronson. 1980. "Growth Status of School Children in a Rural Zapotec Community in the Valley of Oaxaca, Mexico, in 1968 and 1978." *Annals of Human Biology* (7): 367–374.

Malina, R. M., H. A. Selby, P. H. Buschang, W. L. Aronson, and R. G. Wilkinson. 1983. "Adult Stature and Age at Menarche in Zapotec-Speaking Communities in the Valley of Oaxaca, Mexico, in a Secular Perspective." *American Journal of Physical Anthropology* (60): 437–449.

Malina, R. M., H. A. Selby, and L. J. Swartz. 1972. "Estatura, peso y circunferencia del brazo en una muestra transversal de ninos Zapotecos de 6 a 14 anos." *Anales de Antropologia* (9): 143–155.

Malina, R. M., M. F. Skrabanek, and B. B. Little. 1989. "Growth and Maturity Status of Black and White Children Classified as Obese by Different Criteria." *American Journal of Human Biology* (1): 193–199.

Malina, R. M., B. Woynarowska, T. Bielicki, G. Beunen, D. Eweld, C. A. Geithner, Y. C. Huang, and D. M. Rogers. 1997. "Prospective and Retrospective Longitudinal Studies of the Growth, Maturation, and Fitness of Polish Youth Active in Sport." *International Journal of Sports Medicine* 18 (suppl. 3): S179–S185.

Martorell, R., A. Lechtig, C. Yarbrough, H. Delgado, and R. E. Klein. 1978. "Small Stature in Developing Nations: Its Causes and Implications." In S. Margen and R. A. Ogar, eds. *Progress in Human Nutrition*, Vol. 2. Westport, CT: Avi Publishing Co., pp. 142–156.

McCloy, C. H. 1936. "Appraising Physical Status: The Selection of Measurements." *University of Iowa Studies in Child Welfare* 12 (2): 1–126.

———. 1938. "Appraising Physical Status: Methods and Norms." *University of Iowa Studies in Child Welfare* 15 (2): 1–260.

Morton, D. J., and D. D. Fuller. 1952. *Human Locomotion and Body Form: A Study of Gravity and Man*. Baltimore, MD: Williams and Wilkins.

Mueller, W. H., and R. M. Malina. 1976. "Differential Contributions of Stature Phenotypes to Assortative Mating in Parents of Philadelphia Black and White School Children." *American Journal of Physical Anthropology* (45): 269–275.

———. 1980. "Genetic and Environmental Influences on Growth of Philadelphia Black and White School Children." *Annals of Human Biology* (7): 441–448.

Rarick, G. L. 1961. *Motor Development during Infancy and Childhood*, revised. Madison, WI: College Printing and Typing Co.

Riddoch, C. 1998. "Relationships between Physical Activity and Physical Health in Young People." In S. Biddle, J. Sallis, and N. Cavill, eds. *Young and Active? Young People and Health-Enhancing Physical Activity—Evidence and Implications*. London: Health Education Authority, pp. 17–48.

Rowe, F. A. 1933. "Growth Comparisons of Athletes and Non-athletes." *Research Quarterly* (4): 108–116.

Sale, D. G. 1989. "Strength Training in Children." In C. V. Gisolfi, and D. R. Lamb, eds. *Youth, Exercise, and Sport*. Carmel, IN: Benchmark Press, pp. 165–216.

Siegel, S. R. 1999. "Patterns of Sport Participation and Physical Activity in Urban Mexican Youth." Doctoral diss., Michigan State University, East Lansing, MI.

Song, T.M.K., R. M. Malina, and C. Bouchard. 1993. "Familial Resemblance in Somatotype." *American Journal of Human Biology* (5): 265–272.

Song, T.M.K., L. Perusse, R. M. Malina, and C. Bouchard. 1994. "Twin Resemblance in Somatotype and Comparisons with Other Twin Studies." *Human Biology* (66): 453–464.

Stini, W. A. 1975. "Adaptive Strategies of Human Populations under Nutritional Stress." In E. S. Watts, F. E. Johnston, and G. L. Lasker, eds. *Biosocial Interrelations in Population Adaptation*. The Hague: Mouton, pp. 19–41.

Susser, M. 1991. "What Is Cause and How Do We Know One? A Grammar for Pragmatic Epidemiology." *American Journal of Epidemiology* (133): 635–648.

Tanner, J. M. 1955. *Growth at Adolescence.* Oxford: Blackwell Scientific Publications.
———. 1962. *Growth at Adolescence,* 2nd ed. Oxford: Blackwell Scientific Publications.
Tofler, I. R., B. K. Stryer, L. J. Micheli, and L. R. Herman. 1996. "Physical and Emotional Problems of Elite Female Gymnasts." *New England Journal of Medicine* (335): 281–283.
U.S. Department of Health and Human Services. 1996. "Physical Activity and Health: A Report of the Surgeon General." Atlanta, GA: U.S. Department of Health and Human Services, Centers for Disease Control and Prevention, National Center for Chronic Disease Prevention and Health Promotion.
Warren, M. P. 1983. "Effects of Undernutrition on Reproductive Function in the Human." *Endocrinology Reviews* (4): 363–377.
Washburn, S. L. 1951. "The New Physical Anthropology." *Transactions of the New York Academy of Sciences* 13 (2nd series): 298–304.
———. 1953. "The Strategy of Physical Anthropology." In A. L. Kroeber, ed. *Anthropology Today: An Encyclopedic Inventory.* Chicago: University of Chicago Press, pp. 714–727.
Ziegler, E. G. 1982. "Physical Education—Dead, Quiescent, or Undergoing Modification?" *Journal of Physical Education, Recreation, and Dance,* January (53): 51–53.

Chapter 14

Government Research: Links to Biomedicine and Public Health

Ralph M. Garruto

SETTING THE CAREER STAGE

I never contemplated a career in biological anthropology. I am not sure many people do at a young age. Growing up in rural upstate New York played a major role in my interests in the life sciences, first in veterinary medicine, then in human medicine, and finally culminating in an interest in biological adaptation and the evolution of human populations. I had the good fortune to combine all these interests into a transdisciplinary career at the National Institutes of Health (NIH) at a time when an appreciation of broad-based thinking and approaches were still entertained in the rapidly developing life sciences and biomedicine. Today, reductionism in biology and medicine are in vogue, and theoretical constructs at the gene level are used to explain all levels of organization of biological systems, often in the total absence of epigenetic phenomena (Strohman, 1997). Yet, at the highest levels of organization (human population or species level), there remains an orchestration of events, both genetic and epigenetic, that determine biological outcome, ultimately with evolutionary consequences. Biological anthropology and my longtime interest in biomedicine have shaped my career path into what I call biomedical anthropology, which after almost three decades of first entering the field is now being considered as a formal degree program at the State University of New York at Binghamton. What follows is an intensely personal overview of my own career, and what I think are the important things to consider for a career path in biological anthropology in the area of biomedicine and public health.

Recommendations

As a biological anthropologist, entering a career in government research with links to biomedicine and public health, a student should consider the following:

- Training in the natural sciences as well as in anthropology and other social sciences
- Interests in biological, medical, or health-related areas
- Interests in population-based problems, methods, and solutions
- Interests in population adaptation and human evolutionary processes

EARLY TRAINING AND CAREER PATH: PREDOCTORAL

I received my B.S. degree in zoology and entered graduate school in anthropology under arguably the best biological anthropologist (human population biologist) of his time, Professor Paul T. Baker. Baker's Research Program, on human adaptation of Andeans to chronic hypoxic stress, was an identified part of the International Biological Programme (IBP), and the most productive and successful program within the human adaptability segment of the IBP.

As a graduate student, I went to the field twice, once soon after I completed my master's degree, which was on the relationship between body morphology and pulmonary function at high altitude, and, subsequently, for my dissertation research, which I actually started on my first trip to the Peruvian Altiplano. What was unique about Baker's program, and indeed the eclectic cadre of graduate students working under Baker, was the kind of undergraduate training they had, with few having had exposure to anthropology, and even fewer who were anthropology majors. Thus, graduate students in the program came from undergraduate backgrounds in geology, zoology, biology, premedicine, mathematics, physics, computer science, and forestry. We did not have pristine and polished backgrounds in anthropology; but what we did have were the natural science skills that, in addition to the coursework and training in anthropology, would prove critical to our development as transdisciplinary scientists in the years to come. This influence and exposure to the natural sciences cannot be understated, and today it has a major impact on how I choose and train my own graduate students.

Another aspect of predoctoral training was the close interpersonal and scientific relationship of the graduate students in biological anthropology at Penn State during the thirty-year Baker era. Certainly working on a large, defined research program was a big asset, and major training grants helped keep students together and focused. But there was something additional, a special chemistry among the graduate students that had great bearing on future collaborations, fieldwork, career options, and future student training, one generation removed. There was a camaraderie that does not go unnoticed, even to this day.

Annual scientific meetings were a very important part of our predoctoral training in biological anthropology. In my own case, I gave my first platform presentation at the Northeastern Anthropological Association meeting in Montreal six months after entering graduate school, and assisted older graduate students in their presentations at the American Association of Physical Anthropologists meetings in Chapel Hill, North Carolina, around the same time. Annual scientific meetings were and are critical to the development of a graduate student, and probably provide the major means of networking for internships, fieldwork, dissertation research, collaborations, and ultimately jobs, than any other single avenue I can recall. Communication and discourse on ideas orally, through poster presentations or through written publications, are the most important facet of a research career, whether in government, academia, or the private sector.

Coursework as a graduate student varied and was usually tailored to the student's individual needs. Thus, with a strong background in the natural sciences, I concentrated on courses in biological and general anthropology, while taking additional courses in physiology, genetics, and biostatistics. Baker's funded training program at the time encouraged cross-departmental training, and even cross-university training when students whose interests or course work we were not equipped to provide would be better served under the temporary direction of an outside mentor or program. Interestingly, there was no jealousy about sending one of our graduate students to another competitive program to train for three or six months, or even for a year. Nor did our program keep at bay students from other programs that wished to train with us. This maximized resources and increased collaborations, which had an overall positive affect on our career development.

Beyond this formal training, there were internships, although not called that at the time, that could be critical to a student's career development. It was so in my case. In my second year of graduate work, I went to the National Institutes of Health to work with Dr. D. Carleton Gajdusek, an experience that was to change my career path forever.

Fieldwork and/or wet or dry laboratory research take some getting used to, and they are often peculiar to the student's interest. In my own case, I combined, both in graduate school and beyond, something relatively unique at the time in biological anthropology, both fieldwork and wet laboratory research approaches. Today, the trend toward developing skills in both is gaining increasing acceptance and is providing new job opportunities for biological anthropologists, particularly at government research laboratories, in academia, and in professional schools of public health and medicine. One should remember, however, that one's dissertation project is primarily a training exercise and an important learning experience, and therefore, should be something that can be completed in a reasonable period of time.

Recommendations

Appropriate predoctoral training is critical for entry into the competitive federal arena of biomedicine and public health, particularly because the student trained in biological anthropology will be at a disadvantage in areas dominated by traditionally trained professionals from disciplines such as medicine, epidemiology and public health, and cellular and molecular biology. One will have to be in a position to "speak the language" of biomedicine and public health, and demonstrate early competence and knowledge well beyond traditional anthropology. In order to meet these challenges more easily, a student might consider the following:

- Choose your mentor/major professor wisely, selecting someone who is well known professionally and has a strong research record.
- Select course work carefully, particularly in the natural sciences, which enhance or fill gaps in your bioanthropological training.
- Consider supplemental, short-term, midcareer training options, such as special summer courses or courses or programs in other departments or at other universities.
- Attend scientific meetings very early in your graduate career, presenting scientific research in various formats, and begin the networking critical to career development.
- Develop an esprit de corps among your peers, which will pay dividends later in your professional career.
- During summers or on an off-semester, choose internship positions (paid or unpaid) and particularly at a government facility as a means of learning, networking, and providing you with future employment opportunities in biomedicine and public health.
- Develop wet laboratory as well as field research skills, a combination that is likely to provide you with opportunities not otherwise available to you in biomedicine.
- Keep your dissertation topic manageable and the time to degree within six years if possible.
- Seriously consider a one-, two-, or three-year post-doc position in one of the many government laboratories or field sites.

EARLY TRAINING AND CAREER PATH: POST-DOCTORAL

Three decades ago post-doctoral training was nearly unheard of in anthropology. Although it constitutes an important part of the career track in the natural sciences, in biological anthropology, it is still somewhat obscure. However, there is more precedence for post-doctoral training among those biological anthropologists interested in epidemiology, cellular biology, or molecular genetics. In my own case, I accepted a one-year position at the

NIH in an infectious disease laboratory where I worked on a noninfectious epidemiological problem, that of hyperendemic goiter and cretinism in a stone age culture in the central highlands of West New Guinea. I had started this project as a graduate student while an intern in the same laboratory at the NIH. This early research and publication of several articles from my doctoral work provided an important "jump-start" for my professional career in the highly competitive NIH environment.

Post-doctoral positions are extremely useful, and almost no one goes directly into a tenure track position in government or academia in the bio-medical sciences without three to seven years of post-doctoral experience. Yet, in my opinion, anything more than three years is much too long a time in a position that too often is not independent. Today, a biological anthropologist interested in working in a government biomedical or public health laboratory must have post-doctoral experience; and in fact, NIH is one of the premier institutions in the world that provides an extensive number of post-doctoral training positions.

An often-asked question is whether there is the potential for converting a post-doctoral position into a tenured or tenure-track position. In my own case, I went from a post-doctoral position to a tenure-track position and ultimately to a tenured position at the NIH, an event that is very unlikely to happen today. At the NIH, only a few young scientists are ever promoted to tenure from within. Today, it is a much better course to seek out the NIH for its post-doctoral training programs, then leave and establish a career else-where.

Recommendations

Increasingly, biological anthropologists are required to seek out and compete for post-doctoral positions as a reasonable way of achieving career training and jobs. It is recommended that biological anthropologists:

- Seek a post-doctoral position.
- Pick a high-profile laboratory or senior scientist to work with.
- Limit such positions to preferably two or three years at most (this is why one should keep the time to degree to six years).
- Plan to move to a tenure-track position in a government laboratory or else-where rather than linger on in the same laboratory where you had post-doctoral training.
- Consider returning to a federal institution after your career has taken off.

TRAINING ON THE JOB: A BIOLOGICAL ANTHROPOLOGIST AS AN NIH RESEARCH SCIENTIST

As mentioned earlier, I spent one year in post-doctoral status and was converted to a tenure-track position. During those earlier years, I relied on my dissertation research, early work on goiter and cretinism, and some work in population genetics to carry me through scientifically while I "geared up" my research program in the neurosciences; namely, taking over the then defunct project on Guamanian amyotrophic lateral sclerosis (ALS) and Parkinsonism dementia (PD). These two neurodegenerative disorders were found in extraordinarily high incidence in the Mariana Islands, together with two other foci in the Western Pacific: West New Guinea and the Kii Peninsula of Japan.

The project was (and remains) a fascinating one, especially because no one else in our world-class laboratory at that time had any immediate interest in it. Our laboratory took over the research program and field site on Guam by default, a program that had been in the hands of another NIH laboratory that was disbanded after its chief retired. The research program, data, and documentation were put in a dozen temporary file boxes, and no one knew what to do with the material. This provided an ideal scientific situation for an independent young professional to revitalize the program, one with significant bioanthropological overtones in a laboratory that spent a significant amount of its budget on biomedical problems in non-Western cultures. It took three years to "learn" the program and begin figuring out the next steps and research questions to ask, all of which culminated in my first trip to the western Pacific twenty-five years ago. I had a core project and one that for the next decade would take me many times to the western Pacific for extended fieldwork. I had found the right combination of long-time biomedical interests coupled with professional training as a biological anthropologist.

Opportunistic Research

In highly competitive scientific arenas, so-called opportunistic research is vital to the type of long-term, high-risk research I was conducting; that is, the search for unknown causes of neurodegenerative diseases and the elucidation of their cellular and molecular mechanisms of pathogenesis. Our laboratory was the first to report the discovery of a novel neurodegenerative disease called kuru among the Fore people living in the Eastern Highlands of Papua New Guinea (Gajdusek and Zigas, 1957). The laboratory had a long history of high-risk research projects that would last up to two decades or more before there were any results. It was critical, therefore, to develop what I call "spin-off" research while maintaining a core research program that might not pay dividends for years to come (see Table 14.1 for some examples). Thus, every field trip was geared toward the investigation of other problems of bioanthropological and biomedical interest, including the areas of population genetics, ecology, acute infectious diseases, seroepidemiology, bionutrition, and short-term laboratory-based research in combination with these opportunistic field studies. As a result, numerous collaborations were

Table 14.1
List of Core and "Spin-off" Research Areas and Research Field Sites

Core Research	"Spin-off" Research	Field Sites
Aging	Blood Physiology	China
Bionutrition	Growth and Development	Jamaica
Cellular and Molecular	Human Adaptation	Mariana Islands
Biology	Population Genetics	Philippines
Chronic Neurodegen-	Respiratory Physiology	New Guinea
erative Diseases	Seroepidemiology	Peru
Epidemiology		Siberia
Infectious Diseases		Western Caroline Islands
Natural Experiments		
Neurotoxicology		

established, which is the key to scientific productivity during the long "un-productive" phase of the high-risk core research.

The Evolution of a Research Program

In five years, the core program on Guamanian ALS and PD was in full swing and spin-off research projects and internal and external collaborations significantly developed. Unlike some of my colleagues who also left academic anthropology, I made it a point not to lose contact with the field and did my share of publishing in bioanthropological journals (Table 14.2). Too often, those who find themselves in a position where they are working outside of mainstream biological anthropology have a tendency to leave the field, rationalizing that they have to maintain an exclusionary allegiance to their "new" discipline and "have to publish" in their adopted discipline's mainstream journals for promotion purposes. However, because we are biological anthropologists and not epidemiologists, clinicians, cell and molecular biologists, and so on, cutting one's ties with biological anthropology in the long run can be professionally detrimental, let alone less rewarding.

What makes biological anthropologists working in biomedicine unique is their perspective and methods. If those are lost, then there is little difference between what we do and what others do in biomedicine; otherwise, it would be much more advantageous from the start to begin a traditional, biomedical-training program for your doctoral degree.

In time, the core research program on ALS and PD evolved to the point where new discoveries were made and secondary and tertiary level questions

Table 14.2
List of Journals Used for Publication of Core and "Spin-off" Research

Journal Names

Acta Neuropathologica

American Journal of Epidemiology

American Journal of Human Biology

American Journal of Medical Genetics

American Journal of Physical Anthropology

American Journal of Tropical Medicine and Hygiene

Annals of Human Biology

Annals of Neurology

Biological Trace Element Research

Biology International

Brain Research

Canadian Journal of Neurological Sciences

Collegium Anthropologicum

Dementia

Environmental Geochemistry and Health

Experimental Neurology

Human Biology

Human Heredity

In Vitro Cellular and Developmental Biology

Journal of Analytical Toxicology

Journal of General Virology

Journal of Infectious Disease

Journal of Medical Virology

Journal of Neurological Sciences

Journal of Neuropathology and Applied Neurobiology

Journal of Theoretical Biology

Laboratory Investigation

Lancet

Molecular and Cellular Neurosciences

Neurodegeneration

Neurology

Neuro-report

Neurotoxicology

Table 14.2   (continued)

New England Journal of Medicine
Nutrition
Proceedings of the National Academy of Sciences
Science
South East Asian Journal of Tropical Medicine
Trace Elements in Medicine
Trends in Neurosciences
Zeitschrift fur Morphologie und Anthropologie

became much more significant. The core research on ALS and PD evolved primarily from a field epidemiology and bioanthropology program to a laboratory-based research program with experimental modeling of these neurodegenerative Pacific diseases, both *in vivo* and *in vitro,* and eventually the evolution of the program was to include molecular biology, protein chemistry, neurotoxicology, and an understanding of their basic mechanisms of neurodegeneration. This entailed the learning of whole new sets of laboratory-based research skills. Short courses in cellular and molecular biology, electron microscopy, and virology were taken to supplement the on-the-job training experiences. Eventually, the field phase for this core program would end, only to be reactivated in the late 1990s because of further scientific needs and opportunities.

Exciting Science

Although NIH is certainly not what it used to be, it is still a very exciting place. As an intramural scientist, there is relative independence, which is often dependent on the laboratory chief. In my case, D. Carleton Gajdusek, who was an outside member of my doctoral committee, and who was the chief of our laboratory, provided the genius and the independence for young professionals to flourish. In 1976, recognition of his world-acclaimed science culminated in the awarding of the Nobel Prize to him for discoveries concerning new mechanisms for the origin and dissemination of infectious diseases. Having received a very hard-to-get invitation from the Nobel Committee, I attended the Nobel ceremonies in December 1976, a once-in-a-lifetime event. During those early years, I can imagine no better place for a young scientist to have been than at the NIH in Gajdusek's laboratory.

Many discoveries were made in the laboratory of which many of us were a part. We had the chance to tackle major scientific questions without regard for disciplinary boundaries. Anthropology never took an academic backseat in our laboratory during all the years Gajdusek was chief. Thus, it was common to have people from all over the world come to the laboratory, including well-known anthropologists, linguists, missionaries, chemists, physicists, biologists, biomedical scientists, and physicians, among others. In addition to the laboratory, Washington, DC, as a federal city with three branches of government, and the numerous federal agencies in and around the area, was a magnet for bringing people from all over the world. NIH was considered a "jewel in the federal crown."

What is most exciting about what I do is the way I do it. I have the opportunity to use a theoretical construct that marries the social, behavioral, and biomedical sciences in both field and wet laboratory settings. Thus, the ability to transcend disciplines, not just in theory, but also in practice, makes this the most rewarding job possible. It allows me to be who I really am, a biological anthropologist working in the federal biomedical sector on high-profile, high-risk, unique scientific problems with global as well as local and regional relevance.

Federal Biomedical Research: Advantages

Some advantages to working in the government biomedical research sector have already been mentioned. First and foremost is the fact that it represents one of the few opportunities available to do full-time (basic or applied) biomedical research on a twelve-month institutionally supported salary. That may seem like no big deal to many students, except when they consider that such a situation does not exist in academia except perhaps for a small number of endowed chairs or professorships at a few institutions across the country. If your heart is in full-time research, it is the best opportunity out there, bar none. The salary is often not as competitive as that in academia, although during the past decade, some strides toward improvement have been made. If you are a physician, there is a "variable incentive pay scale," above and beyond the regular pay scale, that helps to retain medical doctors.

The question of independence often comes up. At an institution like the NIH, younger scientists have often been exploited on the one hand, yet given an extraordinary opportunity on the other. Independence was primarily based on how much freedom your laboratory chief would allow. It was clear that few laboratories tolerated a young scientist coming into a well-recognized laboratory with their own research agenda. Yet one could, with the right mentor, work on an existing program, often taking on a new research direction that rightly could be called your own. Your research expenses were covered by the laboratory chief, who either allocated you a yearly budget, or signed off on equipment and supplies as your work progressed. The idea of having your own technician or secretary was rather absurd for a young professional, but both were available for the laboratory as a whole, and "sweet talking" usually worked well. This situation is quite different from academia where each professional competes in the extramural arena for research dollars to support their work. In academia, one is more independent, but one has to find the resources to support one's work. It is really a partial exchange of independence for resources. Currently at the NIH, there have been policy changes to alleviate the independence problems for young investigators, but the new system has produced other kinds of problems.

Two other advantages exist. The first is institutional resources, beyond the laboratory's operating budget, such as the National Library of Medicine, unlimited telephone use for professional calls, and seventy-five to one hundred lectures weekly that are open to all. The second is access to large government biomedical databases and sometimes publicly restricted information from places like the Defense Documentation Center. If you need data or some in-house publications from another government institution, they are often available if you are a federal scientist. Thus, accessibility can be an important issue depending on your research.

Federal Biomedical Research: Disadvantages

As enticing as the federal biomedical service appears to be, there are a few drawbacks. Perhaps first and foremost is a bureaucracy that has grown well beyond its intended means, incurring enormous costs that could otherwise be put to good use on research at the bench or in the field. Along with an NIH bureaucracy, which developed slowly at first, there was a change in the bureaucratic approach from proactive administrative support of NIH scientists to a position of monitoring the increasing administrative tasks given to NIH scientists. This represented a shift from an administrative leadership role to an administrative managerial role, which significantly increased the administrative burden of the NIH scientist. Thus, each intramural scientist was still dependent on the bureaucratic hierarchy for things from space to operating budget, and purchase of supplies to personnel hiring, and increasingly were susceptible to micromanagement and administrative accountability. Actual research time, academic freedom, and independence were slipping away. What may have been a smart administrative decision was not necessarily a smart scientific decision. From the early 1970s onward, politics played an increasingly important role in such premier government institutions as the NIH that had been carefully protected from political meddling, to one that required NIH and its scientists to be publicly responsive and fully accountable for what they did. The NIH budget soared and is predicted to double from $14 to $28 billion by 2003, 90 percent of it going to extramural research programs. Thus, there is much more money, more control and accountability, and less percentage of time actually spent conducting biomedical research.

Another potential problem found throughout the biomedical research community is the extreme competition that has developed between laboratories. Although this is true everywhere, it seems to be particularly aggressive and widespread at federal research institutions such as the NIH and leading biomedical research universities. Thus, although intramural NIH scientists do not have to compete for grants, it comes at a cost, predatory collegial behavior. You quickly learn how to swim with sharks. Also, as mentioned earlier, there is a lack of full independence compared with academia. In particular, biological anthropologists working in federal biomedical science are often second-class citizens working in an environment where physicians traditionally dominate, and now, where biological reductionism has taken hold in a major research and policy way. Thus, each biological anthropologist who enters the federal work force in biomedical and health sciences research should expect not only to carve out a unique niche, but also to have the tools and the desire to speak the language of the biomedical sciences. Such individuals must perform in a way that is exemplary beyond others who are traditionally trained in biomedicine. Thus, biological anthropology begins to take on a new meaning and an identity crisis may begin to develop.

Recommendations

Obviously working in the federal service can have its ups and downs. Generally, however, one is considered fortunate these days to land a scientific position at a place like the NIH, so it is important to make the most of it in order to enhance your career. Where possible, one should:

- Select a versatile research laboratory and preferably one that is very well known.
- Select a laboratory that has a need you can fill or a niche you can carve out for yourself. Be prepared to demonstrate or justify what you can do up front.
- Select a high-profile mentor or laboratory chief, hopefully one who sees you as other than an extra set of hands.
- Select a research project that is high risk, yet one that may have a big payoff.
- Select a research project that the laboratory will support, but one in which no one else in the laboratory has a primary interest or investment.
- Learn the often-kept secret "ins and outs" of the administrative system. Knowledge is power and a "how-to" ticket to getting what you want.
- Be opportunistic.
- Choose both core and spin-off research.
- Collaborate extensively.
- Take advantage of all the facilities a federal institution has to offer, for example, photographic and graphic art services, training courses, free interlibrary loan, bibliographic searches, central and remote computer facilities and services, and

so on, with the notion that someday you may move to an institution with less formidable resources.

- Attend both national and regional scientific meetings, often held locally, and in a place like Washington, DC, they are numerous. Attempt to go to smaller, "invitation only," local meetings, using the power of your institution to get your foot in the door. Many may let you sit in as a federal scientist because you cost them nothing.
- Network, network, network.

ACCOMPLISHMENTS AND FAILURES

Discussing one's scientific accomplishment can be a bit embarrassing. Judging one's own accomplishments should largely be left to others. However, it is acceptable to discuss such things in more general terms. Heading the list of any scientist's accomplishments are research discoveries that can be categorized in three ways: major, modest, and seemingly irrelevant. Most scientists have plenty of the latter, some have a number of modest discoveries, and a few have made major discoveries. Accomplishments can often be measured by one's discoveries, status in the field, number of publications, and service to one's profession. Discovery is often the result of a unique combination of intelligence, serendipity, and skill, often in that order. In more than a quarter-century as a federal biomedical research scientist, what "discoveries" I have made are still being evaluated by the judgment of my peers. (Interested readers may refer to the references which describe the research in detail.)

Beyond discoveries, research collaborations are an important part of my accomplishments. As stated earlier, they provide a means to quickly get your career "jump-started." They provide resources through subcontracts, consulting fees, or travel offers that you may not be able to manage on your own. Moreover, research collaborations provide an important mechanism to learn, and an important means of sharing ideas and a vehicle for cross-training of students.

Research training can be listed as another area of accomplishment. In my own case, I took advantage of additional course work, specialized summer training programs, and one-, two-, or three-day training sessions. As a federal scientist, you may be eligible to take full or part-time course work leading to an academic degree, and paid for by your federal agency. Because biological anthropologists are often undertrained in the biomedical sciences, it is important to seriously consider as much additional training as is necessary and permissible, which will rack up large numbers of points in the plus column.

In my own case, a final accomplishment has been in the area of international consulting and lecturing. The invitations to consult accrue slowly, but once you are on "the list," you have access to global cutting-edge science venues paid for by others. It can be a significant part of one's scientific career, and it is nice to be able to travel without worrying about digging deep into one's own pockets.

Finally, in a career guide such as this, it is not too unreasonable to mention one's failure. Failure in many ways is the foundation of discovery, the process of elimination, the trial and error of science. We all share in failure to a very large degree. It cannot be otherwise, at least in the short run. As a federal scientist, this is more likely to be true than in academia. Most of what we do (or should do) in the federal sector is to work on long-term, high-risk research. It was in part what the NIH was designed to do, but the failure rate can be high. Yet, if done properly, the failure rate is irrelevant because unlike the private sector, or even in academia, the federal biomedical research mission is different and one big discovery is enough to make up for a career-long dry spell if you are willing to survive the hiatus.

Recommendations

- For promotion purposes, publish a certain portion of your research in highly visible journals.
- Methods papers are usually the most highly cited. If it is relevant to your work and you are successful, it will vastly increase your number of citations (citation index) and visibility.
- See your own continued training as a career-long process.
- Accept the fact that you will fail, but it is usually never fatal. I have seen absolutely amazing recoveries over the past quarter-century of NIH scientists who I thought had no chance for a comeback after a political or scientific disaster.
- Do not forget to pass on what you know. Train and mentor students through internships or by other means.

WHAT IS LEFT: NEW DIRECTIONS

After the establishment of a secure career in government or elsewhere, there often remains a yearning for new challenges. This is most certainly what drives a research scientist. There are new questions posed, new problems to solve, and perhaps some new beginnings to add to one's late career development. Although this is true for all scientists, it is especially true for those working as tenured federal scientists in several ways. First, as mentioned previously, a tenured scientist in the federal workforce can embark, with administrative approval and often with financial support, on initiating a career change or career enhancement by pursuing additional formal education. The government requires a payback that is usually one year of service for each year of sponsored educational support. Second, there are mechanisms by which a federal scientist can pursue a research program outside their current agency, either at another federal institution or in academia, through an institution-to-institution cooperative agreement while still remaining a federal scientist. Finally, for those already in academia and the private sector, they have an even better chance of working in the federal scientific sector through the same sort of institution-to-institution agreement. During the past ten years, this has happened extensively at the National Science Foundation where university professors have been recruited for one, two, or more years to serve as program directors for biological anthropology. Thus, you can remain a federal career scientist, but switch later in life to new challenges and interests without risking your position or accrued benefits. If one needs or wants it, a rejuvenation program does exist.

A Career Change

Career changes are often unplanned. Serendipity and opportunism certainly play a major role. Many scientists choose to evolve from hands-on science to the role of science administrator within the same federal institution. Others are spurred on by wanting to find another way to contribute scientifically, a way that may have eluded them in the federal service. For federal research scientists, short-term mentoring of undergraduate, graduate, and medical students is often the only means of contributing to the development of young scientists. Teaching formal courses on government time is certainly not an option. Yet, because the NIH in many ways is run like an academic institution compared with most government agencies, there is often an interest in the ability to contribute academically to the long-term development of undergraduate, graduate, and medical education. That may be why the NIH is currently interested in becoming a degree granting institution like any academic institution, by proposing the development of an NIH Graduate School.

In my own case, I have long wished to be able to seriously contribute my ideas to the formal training of graduate students, and was successful in negotiating an institution-to-institution agreement permitting me the opportunity to develop new biomedical research initiatives and new academic programs on a university campus. These three areas, program development, research, and graduate education, have led me in new directions to fill out the remainder of my professional career as a federal scientist.

Recommendations

Having had a successful career, options become increasingly important and an integral part of one's late career. The federal service does provide options for a biological anthropologist. One should consider:

- Searching for opportunities within and outside your federal institution that may not be obvious or well known.
- Consider doing something you never would or could have considered earlier in your career.

RELEVANCE TO BIOLOGICAL ANTHROPOLOGY

Biological anthropologists are increasingly filling positions outside of traditional departments of anthropology as this guide demonstrates. They certainly occupy positions at a number of federal institutions and national laboratories. Yet, many go through an identity crisis and see little relevance in what they do now as compared with what they were trained to do. This is particularly true in today's increasing trend toward ultraspecialization. Traditionally, anthropologists are broadly trained, and it is usually easy to incorporate all sorts of subspecialization within the broader framework of the field. Yet, when you accept a position outside an academic department of anthropology, you do need to be responsive to the professional field you are serving. What should not change, however, is your bioanthropological perspective, as it will almost assuredly improve whatever you do.

The biggest problem in working in a setting or discipline other than traditional anthropology is the identity crisis mentioned earlier. In my own case, I remained a biological anthropologist, even though I was perceived by others outside anthropology as a "card carrying" epidemiologist, neuroscientist, geneticist, cell biologist, or molecular biologist. I was none of these, yet I was all of these. I am a biological anthropologist, a disciplinary thread that links all others. One is, therefore, in a position to contribute in a schizophrenic sort of way to both biological anthropology and other disciplines. Certainly you can continue serving your profession by maintaining linkages with biological anthropologists worldwide. In the federal service, you are allowed to accept nonpaid positions in academia as an adjunct professor, often as part of your official duties. You can hold office in professional societies and serve on scientific and professional committees. You can act, with permission, as a consultant (paid or unpaid) to numerous institutions, or serve as a reviewer of grants or for tenure promotions of others, and join editorial boards, all serving the field of biological anthropology. Most importantly perhaps is what you bring to and from biological anthropology—a perspective, new knowledge, and expertise to be exercised in both disciplinary arenas. This new infusion of expertise and knowledge is the driving force for the evolution of our discipline. Thus, the relevance of the nonanthropological sciences to biological anthropology, and vice versa, is obvious and certainly not exclusionary. The error some biological anthropologists make is choosing between disciplines when it is not necessary to do so. Biological anthropology together with other disciplines can be synergistic and even potentiating.

Recommendations

With regard to the relevance of biological anthropology to your adopted discipline:

- Accept a position in the federal sector that is obviously relevant to biological anthropology.

- Alternately, allow field and laboratory based research collaborations with biological anthropologists to flourish while you contribute to your primary federal position.

- Do not allow your broad bioanthropological perspective to change.

- Continue to contribute in various ways to the discipline of biological anthropology even if your job does not relate to it.

- Allow the other disciplines to identify you in a way which is most comfortable for them.

- At all costs, continue to maintain your ties with biological anthropology and, thus, your sense of identity.

OVERVIEW: A CAREER IN GOVERNMENT BIOMEDICAL RESEARCH

This chapter has been an attempt to give the prospective student some idea of what a career path in biomedicine and public health might be like for a biological anthropologist at a federal research institution. An attempt has been made to provide general recommendations, but the account and experiences of working in federal biomedical research is intensely personal.

My overall view is that working in biomedicine or public health at a federal facility is largely an untapped resource in the future employment of biological anthropologists. Although no one will recognize your potential for biomedical research or public health based on your disciplinary area, you have a unique opportunity to carve out a niche for yourself, if you can get your foot in the door. The best way to do this is through internships at the institution or agency at which you wish to do your post-doctoral training or be employed.

The recommendations listed here can act as an important guide, and most will be valid for a number of years to come. Certainly, the list of recommendations under each heading is not all-inclusive, and is not intended to be. They do represent a reasonable cross-section of the kind of things one should consider in preparation for a position in biomedicine and public health at a federal institution such as the National Institutes of Health, Centers for Disease Control, Environmental Protection Agency, National Center for Health Statistics, U.S. Department of Agriculture, Occupational Safety and Health Administration, National Oceanographic and Atmospheric Administration, and Department of Defense, among others, and the many national research laboratories across the country.

There is a serious need for broad-based but highly trained and skilled young professionals who are versatile and creative enough to meet the needs of the next millennium. Who better than biological anthropologists who have long been a part of a discipline that has always thought of itself as integrative and transdisciplinary? On many occasions in the past, when we have stepped outside of the traditional area of biological anthropology, we sometimes have had problems of acceptance; but we have also made significant inroads into other disciplinary areas. Today, with the use of new technology combined with a farsighted scientific philosophy, I see a great potential for biological anthropologists to go beyond our own traditional borders and contribute in significant ways to biomedicine and public health. This can only be met by the attraction of creative, versatile students willing to take the risk.

REFERENCES

Bailey-Wilson, J. E., C. C. Plato, R. C. Elston, and R. M. Garruto. 1993. "Potential Role of an Additive Genetic Component in the Etiology of Amyotrophic Lateral Sclerosis and Parkinsonism-Dementia in the Western Pacific." *American Journal of Medical Genetics* (45): 68–76.

Ballew, C., R. M. Garruto, and J. Haas. 1989. "High Altitude Hematology: Paradigm or Enigma?" In M. A. Little, and J. D. Haas, eds. *Human Population Biology: A Transdisciplinary Science*. New York: Oxford University Press, pp. 239–262.

Crews, D., and R. M. Garruto, eds. 1994. *Biological Anthropology and Aging: Perspectives on Human Variations Over the Life Span*. New York: Oxford University Press.

Duffield, P., D. Bourne, K. Tan, R. M. Garruto, and M. W. Duncan. 1994. "Analysis of the Neurotoxic Plasticizer N-butylbenzenesulfonamide by Gas Chromatography Combined with Accurate Mass Selected Ion Monitoring." *Journal of Analytical Toxicology* (18): 361–368.

Figlewicz, D. A., R. M. Garruto, A. Krizus, R. Yanagihara, and G. Rouleau. 1994. "Absence of Mutations in the Cu/Zn Superoxide Dismutase Gene in Amyotrophic Lateral Sclerosis and Parkinsonism-Dementia of Guam." *Neuroreport* (5): 557–560.

Flaten, T. P., and R. M. Garruto. 1992. "Polynuclear Ions in Aluminum Toxicity." *Journal of Theoretical Biology* (156): 129–132.

Gajdusek, D. C., and R. M. Garruto. 1975. "The Focus of Hyperendemic Goiter, Cretinism and Associated Deaf Mutism in Western New Guinea." In E. S. Watts, F. E. Johnson, and G. W. Lasker, eds. *Biosocial Interrelations in Population Adaptation*, pp. 267–285. 9th International Congress of Anthropological and Ethnological Sciences: Research Session, Detroit, Michigan, August 28–31, 1973. Mouton, The Hague.

Gajdusek, D. C., and V. Zigas. 1957. "Degenerative Disease of the Central Nervous System in New Guinea: The Endemic Occurrence of 'Kuru' in the Native Population." *New England Journal of Medicine* (257): 974–981.

Garruto, R. M. 1981. "Disease Patterns of Isolated Groups." In H. Rothschild, ed. *Biocultural Aspects of Disease*. New York: Academic Press, pp. 557–597.

———. 1991. "Pacific Paradigms of Environmentally Induced Neurological Disease: Clinical, Epidemiological and Molecular Perspectives." *Neurotoxicology* (12): 347–378.

———. 1994. "Influence of Human Populations on Microbial Biodiversity: Proliferation, Distribution, Evolution and Emergence of Human Diseases." In "Man, Culture, and Biodiversity." *Biology International* 32(Special Issue): 42–53.

———. 1995. "Biological Adaptability, Plasticity and Disease: Patterns in Modernizing Societies." In C.G.N. Mascie-Taylor, and B. Bogin, eds. *Human Variability and Plasticity*. Cambridge: Cambridge University Press, pp. 190–212.

———. 1996. "Early Environment, Long Latency and Slow Progression of Late Onset Neurodegenerative Disorders." In S. J. Ulijaszek, and C.J.K. Henry, eds. *Long-Term Consequences of Early Environment*. Cambridge: Cambridge University Press, pp. 219–249.

Garruto, R. M., and P. Brown. 1994. "Tau Protein, Aluminum and Alzheimer's Disease." *Lancet* (343): 989.

Garruto, R. M., and J. S. Dutt. 1983. "Lack of a Prominent Compensatory Polycythemia in Traditional Native Andeans Living at 4200 m." *American Journal of Physical Anthropology* (61): 355–366.

Garruto, R. M., T. P. Flaten, and I. Wakayama. 1997. "Effects of Acid Rain: A Natural Model of Aluminum Toxicity in Fish." In M. Yasui, K. Ota, and M. Strong, eds. *Mineral and Metal Neurotoxicology*. Boca Raton, FL: CRC Press, pp. 27–34.

Garruto, R. M., R. Fukatsu, R. Yanagihara, D. C. Gajdusek, G. Hook, and C. E. Firoi. 1984. "Imaging of Calcium and Aluminum in Neurofibrillary Tangle-Bearing Neurons in Parkinsonism-Dementia of Guam." *Proceedings of the National Academy of Sciences* (81): 1875–1879.

Garruto, R. M., D. C. Gajdusek, and K. Chen. 1980. "Amyotrophic Lateral Sclerosis among Chamorro Migrants from Guam." *Annals of Neurology* (8): 612–619.

———. 1981. "Amyotrophic Lateral Sclerosis and Parkinsonism-Dementia among Filipino Migrants to Guam." *Annals of Neurology* (10): 341–350.

Garruto, R. M., M. A. Little, J. D. James, and D. E. Brown. 1999. "Natural Experimental Models: The Global Search for Biomedical Paradigms among Traditional, Modernizing and Modern Populations." *Proceedings of the National Academy of Sciences USA* (96): 10536–10543.

Garruto, R. M., S. K. Shankar, R. Yanagihara, A. M. Salazar, H. L. Amyx, and D. C. Gajdusek. 1989. "Low Calcium, High Aluminum Diet-Induced Motor Neuron Pathology in Cynomolgus Monkeys." *Acta Neuropathologica* (78): 210–219.

Garruto, R. M., M. Slover, R. Yanagihara, C. Mora, S. S. Alexander, D. M. Asher, P. Rodgers-Johnson, and D. C. Gajdusek. 1990. "High Prevalence of Human T-lymphotropic Virus Type-I Infection in Isolated Populations of the Western Pacific Region Confirmed by Western Immunoblot." *American Journal of Human Biology* (2): 439–447.

Garruto, R. M., C. Swyt, C. E. Fiori, R. Yanagihara, and D. C. Gajdusek. 1985. "Intraneuronal Deposition of Calcium and Aluminum in Amyotrophic Lateral Sclerosis of Guam." *Lancet* (2): 1353.

Garruto, R. M., R. Yanagihara, and D. C. Gajdusek. 1985. "Disappearance of High Incidence Amyotrophic Lateral Sclerosis and Parkinsonism-Dementia of Guam." *Neurology* (35): 193–198.

———. 1988. "Cycads and Amyotropic Lateral Sclerosis/Parkinsonism Dementia." *Lancet* (2): 1079.

Lang, D. J., R. M. Garruto, and D. C. Gajdusek. 1977. "Early Acquisition of Cytomegalovirus and Epstein-Barr Virus Antibody in Several Isolated Melanesian Populations." *American Journal of Epidemiology* (105): 480–487.

Plato, C. C., R. M. Garruto, K. M. Fox, and D. C. Gajdusek. 1986. "Amyotrophic Lateral Sclerosis and Parkinsonism-Dementia of Guam: A 25-Year Prospective Case-Control Study." *American Journal of Epidemiology* (124): 643–656.

Plato, C. C., R. M. Garruto, and B. Schaumann, eds. 1991. *Dermatoglyphics: Science in Transition*. The National Foundation, March of Dimes. New York: Wiley-Liss.

Plato, C. C., R. M. Garruto, R. T. Yanagihara, K. Chen, J. L. Wood, D. C. Gajdusek, and A. H. Norris. 1982. "Cortical Bone Loss and Measurements of the Second Metacarpal Bone. I. Comparisons between Adult Guamanian Chamorros and American Caucasians." *American Journal of Physical Anthropology* (59): 461–465.

Plato, C. C., W. W. Greulich, R. M. Garruto, and R. Yanagihara. 1984. "Cortical Bone Loss and Measurements of the Second Metacarpal Bone. II. Hypodense Bone in Post War Guamanian Children." *American Journal of Physical Anthropology* (63): 57–63.

Rodgers-Johnson, P., R. M. Garruto, and D. C. Gajdusek. 1988. "Tropical Myeloneuropathies—A New Aetiology." *Trends in Neuroscience* (11): 526–532.

Strohman, R. C. 1997. "Epigenesis and Complexity: The Coming Kuhnian Revolution in Biology." *Nature Biotechnology* 15(March): 194–200.

Strong, M. J., and R. M. Garruto. 1991. "Neuron-Specific Thresholds of Aluminum Toxicity In Vitro: A Comparative Analysis of Dissociated Fetal Rabbit Hippocampal and Motor Neuron-Enriched Cultures." *Laboratory Investigation* (65): 243–249.

Strong, M. J., R. M. Garruto, J. G. Joshi, W. R. Mundy, and T. J. Shafer. 1996. "Can the Mechanisms of Aluminum Neurotoxicity Be Integrated into a Unified Scheme?" *Journal of Toxicology and Environmental Health* (48): 599–614.

Strong, M. J., R. M. Garruto, A. V. Wolff, S. M. Chou, S. D. Fox, and R. Yanagihara. 1991. "N-butylbenzenesulfonamide: A Neurotoxic Plasticizer Inducing a Spastic Myelopathy in Rabbits." *Acta Neuropathologica* (81): 235–241.

Strong, M. J., A. V. Wolff, I. Wakayama, and R. M. Garruto. 1991. "Aluminum-Induced Chronic Myelopathy in Rabbits." *Neurotoxicology* (12): 9–22.

Wakayama, I., V. R. Nerurkar, M. J. Strong, and R. M. Garruto. 1996. "Comparative Study of Chronic Aluminum-Induced Neurofilamentous Aggregates with Intracytoplasmic Inclusions of Amyotrophic Lateral Sclerosis." *Acta Neuropathologica* (92): 545–554.

Yanagihara, R. T., R. M. Garruto, and D. C. Gajdusek. 1983. "Epidemiological Surveillance of Amyotrophic Lateral Sclerosis and Parkinsonism-Dementia in the Commonwealth of the Northern Marianas Islands." *Annals of Neurology* (13): 79–86.

Yanagihara, R., R. M. Garruto, M. A. Miller, M. Leon-Monzon, P. P. Liberski, D. C. Gajdusek, C. L. Jenkins, R. C. Saunders, and M. P. Alpers. 1990. "Isolation of HTLV-I from Members of a Remote Tribe in New Guinea." *New England Journal of Medicine* (323): 994.

Yanagihara, R., C. L. Jenkins, S. S. Alexandar, C. Mora, and R. M. Garruto. 1990. "Human T-lymphotropic Virus Type I Infection in Papua New Guinea: High Prevalence among the Hagahai Confirmed by Western Analysis." *Journal of Infectious Disease* (162): 649–654.

Chapter 15

Private Industry: Research for Profit

Alan S. Ryan

When I entered graduate school in 1975, I had no idea that soon after earning my Ph.D. in anthropology I would spend the next twenty years of my professional life working in private industry. The thought of a nine-to-five job was not appealing, a destiny that most anthropology graduate students would reject outright. Most new anthropology Ph.D.s aspired to become a college or university faculty member in an anthropology department. Many anthropology faculty members reinforce this view by emphasizing that a job in academia is the ideal or only desirable career path. However, by the time I graduated in 1980, the number of Ph.D. physical anthropologists in the United States far exceeded the number of new faculty members hired in academia. In fact, only one-third of the Ph.D.s in physical anthropology that graduated in the 1980s found employment opportunities in U.S. anthropology departments (Wienker, 1991). Fortunately, from 1977 to 1991, the percentage of Ph.D. behavioral scientists (including physical anthropologists) employed in private industry more than doubled (National Academy of Sciences, 1995). Now more than ever, careers in private industry are becoming viable alternatives to a job in the academy. In several industries, physical anthropologists offer skills and talents that are critical for product development, clinical testing, marketing, professional services, scientific writing, sales analysis, and many other aspects of applied research.

For me, there were numerous opportunities in the health care industry. The thought of conducting scientific research in a health care/pharmaceutical company seemed appealing, especially in light of the shrinking academic job market that surfaced in the 1980s and continues to the present day.

Having celebrated my twentieth anniversary as a research scientist at the Ross Products Division of Abbott Laboratories, I can honestly say that my decision to work in private industry was not a mistake. I would choose the same career path if given the choice. Ross Products Division of Abbott Laboratories is a leading manufacturer of nutritional products that serve many pediatric dietary needs. Ross is also a world leader of adult nutritional products and has a long tradition of developing new and better drugs to treat medical conditions in children and adults. Scientists trained in physical anthropology can offer their expertise at each stage of product development, from product conception to its release to the marketplace.

This chapter describes the multiple roles that I, as a physical anthropologist, have had in the health care industry. Specifically, I will focus on how my studies of human growth and development and nutrition—integral components of physical anthropology—were critical to decisions for pediatric nutrition product research and development, marketing, and professional services. The skills that I believe make one competitive for employment in private industry are also described. As with any job, there are advantages and disadvantages. Working in private industry is not free of problems. To be fair, I describe not only the strengths but also the weaknesses of the job, keeping in mind that jobs in private industry vary considerably as they do in other settings, including the academy.

MY BACKGROUND

My undergraduate and graduate degrees are in anthropology with a focus on physical anthropology. I earned my undergraduate degree from S.U.N.Y at Binghamton, but most of my courses in physical anthropology were completed at Queens College in New York City. I was fortunate to be a student of the late Dr. Paul Mahler who taught me the fundamentals of physical anthropology and persuaded me to apply to graduate school. My initial interests were in human paleontology and dental anthropology. Paul was a student of Dr. C. Loring Brace from the University of Michigan. Following in Paul's footsteps, my graduate work was at the University of Michigan where I studied with Dr. Brace, who encouraged me to pursue my interests in fossil man and dental anthropology.

The anthropology department at Michigan provided exceptional training within the traditional four-field approach. Each of the physical anthropologists, including Milford Wolpoff, Frank Livingstone, Stanley Garn, and Roberto Frisancho, played an instrumental and important role in shaping my career. In addition to the required course work, there was an emphasis on research, publishing, and presentations. It was expected that graduate students present original data at professional meetings (e.g., the meetings of the American Association of Physical Anthropologists [AAPA] and the American Anthropological Association [AAA]), publish their findings in peer-reviewed journals, and submit grant proposals to support their dissertation research. Students were encouraged to complete courses offered by other departments such as statistics, computer programming, genetics, nutrition, physiology, public health, geology, cell biology, and anatomy. These courses provided students with a well-rounded education that allowed for research flexibility after graduation.

Because of my interest in human fossils and teeth, I began to explore the ways that new techniques can shed light on tooth use and diet in human evolution. In the 1970s and 1980s, archaeologists were examining microscopic wear patterns on stone tools to determine their use. Paleontologists also were considering wear striation orientation on teeth to describe movements of the jaw during mastication. I used a variety of experimental techniques to produce scratches or striations on teeth, first by hand and then using a machine initially designed to produce wear on stone tools. The experiments were designed to measure the forces that were necessary to produce wear on teeth using different abrasive materials. Wear striations were also measured and described (Ryan, 1979a, 1979b, 1979c). A scanning electron microscope was used to examine and document microscopic features of wear on artificially worn teeth. Comparisons were made with microwear found on modern and fossil teeth. Casts of teeth that preserved fine details of microscopic tooth wear were used instead of real teeth. Fossil teeth were too valuable to subject them to scanning electron microscopic analyses. The results were used as a foundation for publications, grant proposals, and for my dissertation research that considered anterior tooth use during the course of human evolution. I was interested in shedding light on the competing hypothesis, first developed by Brace (1964) and further described by Brace et al. (1981), regarding Neanderthal anterior tooth use and the selective forces responsible for their large anterior teeth.

One of the highlights of my graduate career was the opportunity to work with Dr. Donald C. Johanson who discovered "Lucy" (*Australopithecus afarensis*). Dr. Tim White, who at the time was finishing his doctoral dissertation at the University of Michigan, introduced me to Donald after he returned from a field season in Ethiopia. Donald invited me to study and evaluate the anterior dental microwear of *A. afarensis*. It was thrilling! I joined the team that presented the initial analyses of the *A. afarensis* material at the 1979 meetings of the American Association of Physical Anthropologists (Ryan, 1979d). Later, Donald and I described in detail the anterior dental microwear in *A. afarensis* (Ryan and Johanson, 1989).

The National Science Foundation (NSF) and the L.S.B. Leakey Foundation funded my dissertation research. I studied the majority of the Neanderthal and early hominid materials (*Australopithecus* and *Homo erectus*) housed in various museums around the world—a trip that I will never forget.

I used several modern human and nonhuman primate samples for comparison. I was confident (perhaps, too confident!) that with my well-rounded training and experience it would be easy to compete for and obtain a tenure-track position as a faculty member. However, in the year that I earned my Ph.D. (1980) only two tenure-track positions in physical anthropology/ anatomy were available in the United States. Both were offered to candidates who held temporary positions in departments that advertised the positions. I was fortunate to secure a two-year position as research investigator at the University of Michigan's Center for Human Growth and Development, working with Dr. Stanley Garn.

At the Center for Human Growth and Development, I left the world of the dead (fossils) and entered the world of the living (contemporary human growth and development and nutrition). It was easy to make this transition because of my broad background. However, initially I still aspired to become a university faculty member. During my two-year appointment, I studied a variety of health issues, including origins and trends in obesity, iron-deficiency anemia, and patterns of adipose tissue distribution (Garn and Ryan, 1981; Garn, Hopkins et al., 1981; Garn, Ryan, and Abraham, 1981a, 1981b; Garn, Ryan, Abraham, and Owen, 1981; Garn, Ryan, Owen, and Abraham, 1981; Garn, Ryan, Owen, and Falkner, 1981; Garn and Ryan, 1982; Garn et al., 1982; Garn and Ryan, 1983). With Dr. Garn's help and guidance, I gained knowledge of computer programming and proper use of statistical analyses of large databases from several national health and nutrition examination surveys. I also had the opportunity to participate in consulting projects with the Centers for Disease Control (CDC) (analysis of weight gain during pregnancy) and General Mills (trends in childhood obesity).

Prior to working with General Mills I was unaware of the breadth of research that was conducted in private industry. Because of my naiveté, I also did not know how to apply for a job in this exciting new world of research. Techniques such as networking, preparing a simple business resume versus an extensive Curriculum Vitae, job interviewing skills, and developing a well-orchestrated job campaign were not taught in many anthropology departments in the United States. The anthropology department at the University of Michigan was no exception. As mentioned earlier, from my experience as a graduate student, many faculty members did not feel that a job outside the academy was desirable or career enhancing. For many, this view has not changed. In their defense, most anthropology faculty members never had a job outside the academy. Consequently, they may not know the nature of the potential job market in private industry and may not have experience to counsel students in their search for alternative careers.

A headhunter from an executive search firm suggested I attend a seminar on job hunting. The money I spent for the two-day seminar was the best investment I ever made. Although I still aspired to become a faculty member, my two-year position was terminating with no academic position in sight.

The selection process for hiring new faculty members seemed slow (e.g., applications due in September–December, on-site interviews and presentations conducted the following April, and hiring decisions made in June). Following the lessons I learned at the job-hunting seminar, I drafted a two-page business resume, networked with individuals that I met at General Mills and CDC, and identified companies that would be interested in my skills. Within two weeks of my job search, I was asked by three companies to interview for a job. I was offered and accepted a research position in the Marketing Research Department at Ross Products Division of Abbott Laboratories, Columbus, OH.

During my career at Ross Products Division, I was involved in several research projects that were directly related to field of physical anthropology. The skills that I acquired during my graduate education were applicable to many components of the company's research programs and objectives.

FOOD CONSUMPTION PATTERNS

Nutrient Intakes of Infants

Ross Products Division has focused its efforts on manufacturing products that help meet both the routine and special nutrient needs of infants. Pediatric products include formulas for healthy, full-term infants, special formulas for infants with unique nutrition needs (e.g., premature infants and infants with metabolic disorders such as phenylketonuria, a defect in phenylalanine [PHE] metabolism characterized by the inability to convert PHE to tyrosine), and nutrition supplements for older children.

Without exception, breastfeeding is recognized as the standard for feeding infants. Nevertheless, iron-fortified infant formula is an excellent source of nutrition, either as an alternative for mothers who choose not to breastfeed their infants or as a supplement for lactating mothers. Physicians and health professionals routinely encourage mothers to breastfeed throughout the first year of life. If for any reason breastfeeding is not possible, then iron-fortified infant formula is recommended.

When I joined Ross Products Division in 1982, the recommendation concerning infant feeding practices during the second six months of life changed. The American Academy of Pediatrics Committee on Nutrition (1983) revised their recommendation by stating that although breastfeeding is the preferred method of feeding throughout the first year of life, whole cow's milk may be introduced after six months of age if adequate supplementary feedings are given. Supplementary feedings should include a "balanced mixture of cereals, vegetables, fruits, and other foods (thereby assuring adequate sources of both iron and vitamin C)" (American Academy of Pediatrics Committee on Nutrition, 1983:255). This recommendation had far-reaching implications, not only from the standpoint of declining infant formula sales but also whether a diet that included whole cow's milk could meet the growth and nutritional requirements of the six-to-twelve-month-old infant.

The Committee on Nutrition (1983:254–255) recognized that there "are many unanswered questions concerning the use of whole cow's milk in the second six months of life." These included whether there is adequate iron in the total diet when whole cow's milk is substituted for an iron-fortified infant formula and whether other foods such as iron-fortified infant cereal can meet the infant's need for iron. The committee was also concerned about whether infants would consume adequate amounts of essential fatty acids and ascorbic acid, nutrients not present in whole cow's milk but found in human milk and infant formula. Last, the committee was concerned about high renal solute load of whole cow's milk and whether high renal solute could lead to dehydration under conditions of illness, fever, or high environmental temperature.

Because of my previous experience with national surveys, I was asked to design, implement, and manage a large national survey of infant nutrition to address the questions raised by the Committee on Nutrition. The survey was designed to determine patterns of food consumption, nutrient intakes, and growth of American infants ranging in age from six to thirteen months. I worked with Ross Products Division biostatisticians and those at The Ohio State University to design the survey and analyze results. A private research firm was hired to conduct the survey. Nutrient intakes and growth (weight, length, head circumference, skinfold thicknesses) were considered in 1,200 infants. Nutrient intakes were evaluated according to different foods (milk and milk products, iron-fortified formula, noniron-fortified formula, infant cereal, commercial baby foods, and home-prepared table foods). Infants who received any human milk were not considered because human milk intake was not measured.

The results of the survey indicated that a large proportion of infants who were fed a diet that included cow's milk received amounts of sodium, potassium, and chloride which exceeded the recommended safe and adequate ranges, and amounts of linoleic acid (an essential fatty acid) below the recommended minimum of 3 percent of dietary energy. The estimated dietary renal solute load of infants fed cow's milk was approximately twice the amount of that of infants fed standard proprietary formula. Infants fed either cow's milk or noniron-fortified formula had median intakes of iron below the 1980 RDA of 15 mg/day; a low percentage of these infants (< 23 percent) were given medicinal iron supplementation. In contrast, infants fed a diet that contained an iron-fortified formula attained a more balanced intake of nutrients; median intakes of all nutrients of these infants were at appropriate levels and within recommended safe and adequate ranges. There were no significant differences in growth between infants fed diets that included cow's milk or infant formula.

The results from this survey were published in several peer-reviewed journals (Martinez, Ryan et al., 1985; Ryan, 1988; Ryan, Martinez, Krieger et al., 1985; Ryan et al., 1986, 1987; Ryan and Martinez, 1987b) and presented at several scientific meetings (Martinez, Krieger et al., 1985; Ryan, 1985; Ryan, Krieger et al., 1985; Ryan and Martinez, 1984, 1985a, 1986a, 1986b). The survey findings also compared favorably with other surveys of infant nutrition (Martinez and Ryan, 1985; Ryan and Martinez, 1985b; Montalto et al., 1985). These findings, as well as those from other studies that demonstrated that iron status is significantly impaired when whole cow's milk is introduced into the diet of the six-month-old infant (Fomon et al., 1990; Ziegler, 1990), resulted in a reversal of the Committee on Nutrition's 1983 recommendation. In 1992, the Committee on Nutrition recommended that the only alternative to breast milk is iron-fortified infant formula during the first twelve months of life (American Academy of Pediatrics Committee on Nutrition, 1992). The American Academy of Pediatrics (1992) recommends that whole cow's milk and low-iron formulas not be used during the first year of life.

Nutrient Intakes of the Elderly

Americans over age sixty-five constitute one of the fastest growing segments of the U.S. population. As a result, more emphasis is being placed on geriatric health care, including nutrition. Underlying the effort to meet dietary requirements is to prevent diet-related chronic diseases and minimize unwanted food-drug interaction. For the elderly, Ross Products Division manufactures nutrition products that provide basic nutritional support and those that meet specific patient needs. Patient conditions such as diabetes, HIV/AIDS, impaired gastrointestinal function, malabsorption, and renal failure are examples of disease states for which specialized Ross products are available.

The food consumption patterns and nutritional status of older Americans have been evaluated in large-scale national surveys, including three National Health and Nutrition Examination Surveys (NHANES I, II, III) and the Nationwide Food Consumption Surveys. In general, food intake data from these surveys suggested that the elderly consumed less food than required to meet energy and nutrient recommendations. They also demonstrated that a substantial percentage of the elderly population had vitamin and mineral intakes less than two-thirds of the RDA (Zheng and Rosenberg, 1989). Before the release of the dietary data from NHANES III (released in 1998), I helped design and implement a nationwide food consumption survey of older Americans (Ryan et al., 1992). This survey considered dietary information for 474 individuals aged sixty-five to ninety-eight years interviewed in 355 households (twenty-four-hour dietary recall). Analyzed indicators of dietary quality were nutrient intake, food group intake and frequency, and the number of meals skipped.

Results indicated that substantial percentages of those surveyed had inadequate intakes of energy and nutrients. Over 40 percent of men had intakes of vitamins A and E, calcium, and zinc below two-thirds the RDA. For women, over 40 percent had intakes of vitamin E, calcium, and zinc that were below two-thirds the RDA. Additionally over 20 percent of older men and women skipped lunch.

We suggested that there is a need for nutrition educators to increase nutrition and food awareness among elderly persons. Many older persons do not make appropriate food choices. The potential impact that cultural and economic factors have on the dietary patterns of older Americans is becoming better understood. Social isolation may adversely affect dietary quality (Walker and Beauchene, 1991). Type of living arrangement (alone, with spouse, or with another relative or nonrelative) also influences the quality of nutrient intakes (Ryan et al., 1989). For example, we reported that more men living alone consumed a poor quality diet than did men living with a spouse (Ryan et al., 1989). For women, income level was more strongly associated with dietary patterns than living arrangement. More poor women than poor men had poor-quality diets. In a low-income household, women were willing to sacrifice their dietary intake, and ultimately their health, to ensure that their spouses were better fed.

TRENDS IN BREASTFEEDING AND INFANT FORMULA USE

The Characteristics of Breastfeeding

Through large, national mail surveys, Ross Products Division has been monitoring trends in infant milk feeding since 1954. From an anthropological point of view, it is interesting to evaluate cultural and demographic factors that influence choices of infant feeding. From a business perspective, surveys serve as a marketing and forecasting tool by providing timely information on use of different formulas and milks in the marketplace. Breastfeeding information published and distributed by Ross Products Division represents a valuable and timely resource for health professionals and government agencies concerned with monitoring trends in maternal and child health.

It is noteworthy that the use of cow's milk as an infant feeding has declined markedly during the last twenty-five years. The reported decline in the prevalence of anemia in the United States from the 1960s to the present has been attributed to the generalized improvement of iron nutrition in infancy (Yip, Binkin et al., 1987; Yip, Walsh et al., 1987; Ryan, Martinez et al., 1990). Undoubtedly, the decline in the prevalence of anemia corresponds to recommendations made by the American Academy of Pediatrics Committee on Nutrition (see earlier). During this time period, there were substantial increases in breastfeeding (Ryan, 1997a) and use of iron-fortified formula; these increases have been at the expense of whole cow's milk, low-fat milk, and low-iron infant formula (Ryan, Martinez et al., 1990; Ryan, 1997b).

Anthropological insight into cultural and demographic factors that influence infant feeding has proven useful in determining why mothers choose to breastfeed their infants. Breastfeeding is most common among women who live in the western portion of the United States, and among women who are white or Asian, older in age, college educated, and not employed outside the home. Recent increases in breastfeeding were greater in groups that have been historically less likely to breastfeed. These include women who are black, younger in age, employed outside the home, no more than grade school educated, and living in the southern region of the United States. The recent increases in breastfeeding among groups that were historically less likely to breastfeed is encouraging and may be related to national and regional intervention programs designed to educate economically disadvantaged women about the benefits of breastfeeding.

It is clear that attitudes about breastfeeding vary considerably in different populations and regions of the United States (Martinez, Krieger et al., 1985; Ryan, 1997a; Ryan and Martinez, 1987a, 1989; Ryan and Gussler, 1986; Ryan, Martinez et al., 1985; Ryan, Wysong et al., 1990; Ryan et al., 1991). Regardless of socioeconomic status, mothers living in the western states are more likely to breastfeed their infants than those residing elsewhere. The western portion of the country provides a cultural environment that fosters the breastfeeding experience. Anthropological training provides the background needed to study this cultural phenomenon to help identify the cultural conditions that affect maternal decisions to breastfeed.

PROFESSIONAL SERVICES

Mexican-American Growth and Development

Companies typically serve their customers by providing current information about their products. Ross Products Division is no exception. However, because Ross's customers are health professionals (e.g., physicians, nurses, and dietitians), new scientific developments are highlighted, as well as the relative health and nutritional status of different populations who many benefit from Ross's products.

Mexican-Americans constitute one of the fastest growing populations in the United States. In 1982–1984, the National Centers for Health Statistics conducted a special survey, the Hispanic Health and Nutrition Examination Survey (HHANES), which considered the health and nutritional characteristics of three Hispanic subgroups (Mexican Americans, Puerto Ricans, and Cuban Americans) living in the continental United States.

Working with Dr. Alex Roche and his colleagues from the Division of Human Biology at Wright State University, and with scientists from the National Centers for Health Statistics, I analyzed the anthropometric measures of growth (weight, stature, head circumference, body mass index, skinfold thicknesses) and nutritional status of Mexican-American children. The results were presented at the 1989 meetings of the American Association of Physical Anthropologists, published in a special supplement of the *American Journal of Clinical Nutrition* (Ryan and Roche, Supplement to Volume 51, Number 5, 1990) and in other journals (Frisancho and Ryan, 1991; Ryan et al., 1994, 1996; Ryan, Roche et al., 1999; Wellens et al., 1995).

Our findings showed that Mexican-American children tended to be short and overweight, especially after twelve to fourteen years of age, even after poverty level was considered. In older Mexican-American children, there was a deficit in stature relative to data for non-Hispanic whites in the Second National Health and Nutrition Examination Survey (NHANES II). Compared with non-Hispanic whites, body mass index (BMI) tended to be larger in Mexican-Americans, at almost all ages in each sex. Data for triceps, subscapular, suprailiac, and medial calf skinfold thickness measurements indicated that Mexican-American children also tended to have thicker skinfold thicknesses than non-Hispanic white children or non-Hispanic black children. The findings suggested tendencies to greater amounts of total body fat for Mexican-American children than for non-Hispanic white children or non-Hispanic black children.

Initially, deficits in stature were thought be the result of a secular effect because the older children were born earlier when nutritional conditions could have been worse. However, analyses of weight, stature, and BMI data for Mexican-American children from the latest National Health and Nutrition Examination Survey (NHANES III, 1988–1994) revealed that for each gender, values for weight and BMI, but not for stature, from NHANES III were significantly larger than those from HHANES (Ryan, Roche et al., 1999). The similarity of findings for stature from NHANES III and HHANES indicated that shorter statures of Mexican-Americans were not cohort-specific but may be genetic or ethnic in origin. The findings also indicated that Mexican-American children were getting heavier and fatter over time.

BMI is used commonly to screen for obesity because of its high correlation with total body fat (Roche, 1984). The tendency to larger values for BMI in Mexican-American children is important in the context of public health because BMI tends to track well after childhood, and high BMIs in adulthood constitute an important risk factor for diabetes and cardiovascular disease.

Fundamental issues that are of interest to physical anthropologists, such as patterns of growth and development and body composition, are also of interest to those caring for patients and using nutritional products, especially those that are involved in implementing nutrition-based intervention programs. The goal is to reverse the trend toward increasing body weight and thereby decrease risk factors for adult diseases in Mexican Americans.

Lending a Helping Hand

Although I was trained in physical anthropology, during my career at Ross Products Division I have been required to analyze and publish studies that were unrelated to the field. One is expected to lend a hand to other colleagues, especially if one has experience publishing in peer-reviewed journals. Consequently, I studied the professional role and image of dietitians (Ryan et al., 1988a, 1988b; Finn et al., 1991; Foltz et al., 1993), the functions of dietitians who provide nutrition support to patients with inherited metabolic disorders (Acosta and Ryan, 1997), job opportunities for pediatricians (Martinez and Ryan, 1989), improvements in the behavior and physical manifestations in previously untreated adults with phenylketonuria using a phenylalanine-restricted diet (Yannicelli and Ryan, 1995), and formula tolerance in breastfed and exclusively formula-fed infants (Lloyd et al., 1999). I was also asked to write a review article describing infant formula and medical food research (Ryan et al., 2000).

CLINICAL STUDIES

Requirements for Evaluating Infant Growth and Development

In 1988, the American Academy of Pediatrics at the request of the Food and Drug Administration convened a task force on clinical testing of infant formula to recommend the types of clinical studies to be conducted to ensure the safety and suitability of infant formulas before they are marketed (American Academy of Pediatrics, 1988). Clinical infant formula trials are needed to supplement laboratory studies and studies with animal models. Laboratory analysis ensures that adequate quantities of all essential nutrients are present in the formula. Animal studies establish formula safety and may identify formula efficacy and the safety of novel ingredients. Clinical testing with infants is essential for determining whether a formula supports normal growth and development, whether it is tolerated or accepted by the infant, and whether nutrients are absorbed and physiologically available.

Determination of the rate of weight gain is considered to be the most valuable component of the clinical evaluation of the infant (American Academy of Pediatrics, 1988). The task force recommends that weight gain be measured over a period of three to four months starting soon after birth and no later than one month of age. When a new infant formula is tested, it is necessary to enroll a control group of subjects fed a commercially available formula. In the absence of a significant difference in weight gain, data for gain in recumbent length are not considered essential in the clinical testing of an infant formula. Similarly, data for head circumference are not critical. However, to ensure formula safety, many clinical studies conducted by industry consider data for both recumbent length and head circumference.

Regardless of whether an infant is enrolled in a clinical study, all pediatricians routinely measure growth of infants in their care. Gains in weight and length of young infants reflect long-term developmental and physiological processes that can only be achieved if the infant's nutrient requirements are met.

For the clinical testing of an infant formula, a randomized, controlled, blinded study using concurrent treatment and control groups is the most sensitive test for measuring nutritional adequacy. Thus, studies of early infant growth and development are the foundation for pediatric product research and development. Clinical studies must be completed prior to the release of a new formula into the marketplace.

Following the American Academy of Pediatrics task force recommendations, infants are typically enrolled into a clinical study shortly after birth and studied for at least four months. Early infancy is a period of rapid growth and development at a time when the infant allocates a higher percentage of nutrient intakes for growth than during later infancy. During this period, infant formula serves as the sole source of nutrition. Solid foods that can either hide or compensate for a deficiency in a formula are usually not consumed.

Clinical Studies of Infant Formula Composition

Physical anthropologists may play a variety of roles in designing, implementing, and monitoring growth studies. Because physical anthropologists have expertise in anthropometry and growth analyses, they can teach physicians and staff the proper anthropometric techniques used to measure infants. Anthropologists may also evaluate whether other measurements in addition to weight such as length, head circumference, skinfold thicknesses, and bone density should be included in a study.

Plotting each infant's measurements on the National Centers for Health Statistics (NCHS) reference curves (Hamill et al., 1977) makes quantitative evaluations of growth possible. These reference curves are used by many physical anthropologists to evaluate growth of infants and youth in the United States and elsewhere. The longitudinal analysis of weight identifies those infants whose growth is not following expected patterns. Comparisons of group measurements between infants fed either a clinical infant formula or a control formula can identify differences in growth as a result of differing formula compositions.

A good example of how altering the composition of an infant formula can produce subtle variation in growth is the addition of long-chain polyunsaturated (LCP) fatty acids to infant formula. Two LCP fatty acids, docosahexaenoic acid (DHA) and arachidonic acid (AA), are of particular interest. Presently in the United States, infant formulas do not contain the LCP fatty acids that are found in human milk. The reason is that infant formulas derive their fat from vegetable oils, which lack LCP fatty acids but contain precursor essential fatty acids linoleic and alpha-linolenic acid. DHA is one of the most abundant LCP fatty acids in the structural membranes of the central nervous system (O'Brien et al., 1964) and in the retina of the eye (Anderson, 1970). Metabolites of AA, on the other hand, mediate the secretion of several hormones associated with growth and basic metabolic functions (Root, 1992).

DHA is transferred across the placenta, particularly during the last trimester of pregnancy. Infants born prematurely may have a dietary requirement for DHA because they may not receive all of the last trimester's supply and may not adequately elongate alpha-linolenic acid, a precursor (Uauy et al., 1994). As an additive to infant formulas, DHA can be obtained from marine oil, fungal and algae extracts, and egg yolk phospholipids. However, these commercial ingredients are structurally different from triglycerides or phospholipids in human milk.

Using DHA from a marine source (fish oil), clinical studies have shown a transient increase in visual acuity at two or four months of age in preterm infants fed formulas with DHA (Birch et al., 1992; Carlson et al., 1996). However, compared with controls, infants fed formulas with DHA had significantly lower z-scores (a measurement that indicates the number of standard deviations away from the mean) for weight, recumbent length, and head circumference beginning at forty weeks of age (Carlson et al., 1996).

We conducted a randomized, blinded clinical infant feeding trial to evaluate measures of growth and body composition in sixty-three healthy, low-birth-weight infants who were randomly assigned to an infant formula with DHA from fish oil or to a control formula (Ryan, Montalto et al., 1999). Preterm infants were evaluated prior to and after hospital discharge. Growth (weight, recumbent length, head circumference), regional body fatness (triceps, subscapular, suprailiac skinfold thicknesses), circumferences (arm, abdominal, chest), and estimates of body composition determined by total body electrical conductivity (TOBEC) (fat-free mass [FFM]) were evaluated.

Although infants in both feeding groups were well within the age-appropriate NCHS references throughout the study, we found that growth was slower in males fed DHA formula than those fed control formula. They had significantly smaller gains in weight, length, and head circumference and had lower fat-free mass. Among females, there were no significant differences between the feeding groups in measures of growth or body composition.

Some scientists would argue that because LCP fatty acids are found in human milk they should be added to infant formula. However, DHA and AA, like most nutrients, are not presently available as pure ingredients. Thus, considering results of growth studies, the argument of adding DHA alone would be beneficial to infants remains unproven. Additional research is needed to shed light on the levels that DHA and AA can be added to infant formula to promote optimal growth and development.

The analyses of anthropometric data from an anthropological perspective provide an appreciation of the variation in human growth and an understanding of whether differences in growth have real biological meaning. Many physical anthropologists have extensive experience in body composition research; this knowledge can be applied directly to many fundamental studies conducted in the pharmaceutical and health care industry.

How we feed our infants appears to influence their long-term development and health. There is emerging evidence that hypertension, cardiovascular disease, respiratory disease, and diabetes are related to poor health and nutrition of the infant and mother. Barker (1994) and his colleagues argue that undernutrition during infancy permanently changes body's structure, physiology, and metabolism and leads to coronary heart disease and stroke later in life. Future changes in infant formula composition are likely to be designed to have a positive, long-lasting effect on physical growth and development; such issues are of great interest to physical anthropologists and to the field.

Iron Nutrition during Infancy

The human brain undergoes rapid growth throughout the first two years of life. Nutrient deficits at the time of brain growth spurt may lead to permanent alteration in learning abilities. Iron-deficiency anemia serves as an excellent example of a nutrient deficiency that may have long-term consequences (Ryan, 1997b). Although Barker (1994) has described the relationship between undernutrition in infants and adult diseases, Lucas (1991) has coined the term *nutritional programming* to describe the process by which the adequacy or deficiency of a nutrient at a critical period of infant development results in a permanent change in the older child. For example, Lozoff et al. (1991) and De Andraca et al. (1990) reported that children who were iron-deficient as infants and given iron therapy had significantly lower scores than nonanemic controls in intellectual, linguistic, motor, pyschoeducational, and visual-motor integrative abilities at five to six years of age.

These findings suggest that optimal nutrition in infants during the critical period of brain development may be linked to later developmental outcomes.

Because pediatric nutrition products are fed to millions of infants, caution needs to be taken before changes in formulation are introduced into the marketplace. Carefully controlled clinical studies are imperative to determine whether a research formula supports optimal physical growth of infants. The study of human growth has been an integral component of physical anthropology since the founding of the discipline. One of the earliest pioneers of anthropology, Franz Boas, is remembered for his consideration of factors that influence human growth. Physical anthropologists will continue to play a key role in the development of infant formulas as long as the study of human growth and development is essential to ensure product efficacy and safety.

REQUIRED TRAINING

Attitude and Latitude

The field of anthropology offers a refreshing way of looking at culture, human diversity, and our origins. For example, *National Geographic*'s pictorial description of a paleoanthropologist discovering an early hominid creates a romanticized impression that anthropologists spend most of their time in exotic places. However, harsh reality is that anthropologists typically spend more time in the office and classroom than in the field. Further, because of the changing job market, anthropologists are just as likely to be well-paid corporate employees as they are to be watching apes in the rain forest.

In general, anthropologists are trained to have a multicultural perspective and consider people and scientific information in a larger cultural context than do other scientists. This cultural sensitivity has become important, especially in light of a growing diverse workplace and global marketplace. When a new anthropology Ph.D. faces the dilemma of earning a living, the decision to explore alternative careers should not be made reluctantly. Rather, new anthropology Ph.D.s should follow their tradition of taking a holistic approach by reaching out to people, including those in the private sector.

From the start, graduate students should entertain the notion that there are rewarding careers outside the ivory tower. For preparation, it is worthwhile to complete advanced courses in statistics, computer programming, journalism, economics, geology, biology, nutrition, anatomy, and public health. These courses will provide a broad view of contemporary issues that may be relevant to private industry. They will also offer insight into how departments other than anthropology are training their students for positions within and outside of academia.

To gain firsthand experience of what it is like to work for a company, the first step is to become a summer intern. If an internship program/referral service does not exist in your department, it is time to establish one. Summer intern programs not only provide on-the-job experience, but they also help establish important ties to decision makers who may offer the intern employment after graduation. Many intern programs allow students to become part of a research team. Interns are expected to complete a project before they return to school.

Physical anthropologists have acquired quality skills that they can offer a company. However, finding employment in private industry sometimes depends more on how these skills are marketed than on one's training. There are various techniques that anthropology job seekers can use to market their skills; many are applicable to finding employment in the academy as well. Techniques such as how to develop a well-orchestrated job campaign, how to write an outstanding resume, the use of personal recommendations, when and how to answer advertisements, when to use an executive search firm, how to network, what to say during an interview, and how to negotiate for maximum starting salary have been described in detail elsewhere (Bolles, 1984). Personnel counseling professionals and agencies that help people find employment teach these techniques.

The objective of a job campaign is to generate interviews and job offers. To meet this objective, you need to determine your marketability (what talents you bring to the company) and identify those industries that may be interested in your skills. For physical anthropologists, the list of industries could include health care, dental products, food processing and distribution, medical/surgical equipment, international trade and economics, industrial distribution, and so on. As you identify the companies, keep in mind how your skills relate to their needs. For example, computer programming, foreign language, scientific writing, and communication skills, talents that anthropologists often take for granted, may represent important assets to a research and development department.

At the start of your job search, it is essential that quality written materials be developed. An outstanding résumé leads to job interviews. A résumé should be designed to sell your skills rather than your background so that the reader can understand how your skills can be applied effectively. You will need outstanding letters for a variety of opportunities, such as contacting friends, colleagues, executive search firms, and for answering advertisements. Personalizing your letters by describing yourself and your accomplishments in the first person may help increase reader interest.

Always be prepared before you interview for a position. Find out about the company's profile, including latest research and product development. The goal is to project an enthusiastic and confident personality. Do not underestimate the importance of a good appearance. I am often amazed at the clothes that anthropologists wear at professional meetings! In private industry, you should always look like a winner. Decision makers are well aware that the appearance of their personnel is a reflection of their firm.

THE ADVANTAGES AND DISADVANTAGES OF WORKING IN THE "REAL WORLD"

Meeting Basic Needs

From my personal experience (rather biased, perhaps), choosing a career in private industry (i.e., working for a large corporation or a small company that makes a profit) usually results in a higher starting salary than one can expect in academia. In addition to salary, companies generally offer generous promotion opportunities, attractive stock options, profit sharing, paid vacations, payment for travel to professional meetings, and comprehensive health benefits. Not all companies are alike, however. Some may offer high starting salaries and longer vacation time; others may offer lower starting salaries but better promotion opportunities. In any case, salary increases and promotions are typically based on performance. If you do a good job, you can expect decent salary increases and periodic promotions.

Research Opportunities

Research is centered on developing new products. Short- and long-term research programs are developed and managed with the primary purpose of increasing the "bottom line." Scientists provide input to decisions on product development and management. If you have a good idea for a research program and can sell it to your peers and upper management, there is a good chance that it will be funded. When a research program is chosen, scientists are asked to manage, supervise, and complete various assignments and projects. Often periodic and final reports, including presentations to other business units (e.g., marketing, quality assurance, manufacturing), are required. There are often opportunities to publish data in peer-reviewed journals, but this may not be a company priority. Sometimes, it may be necessary to work after business hours to prepare a manuscript for publication. This extra effort will be valuable if the objective is to continue publishing original data that are of interest to other physical anthropologists.

Some Pitfalls

In private industry, the tenure system does not exist. Job security in business is subject to many factors, some of which may be totally out of one's control and not directly related to performance. Downsizing is more common then ever. Sometimes a person can lose his job simply because of a lower seniority status or falling profit margins. However, the experience one gains in a position usually provides the background needed to obtain another job. Even though some companies are downsizing, their competitors are growing and often hire those that have been recently laid off.

Although anthropology faculty members can take a sabbatical to conduct fieldwork or write a book, for scientists working for a company free time away from the office is limited to vacation time earned each year. In business, it would be difficult to work on a project that would take years to complete, except if it was part of a major long-term research program that was designed to develop a new product. Typically, after one task is completed, another is put on your desk.

Although anthropology faculty members are afforded seemingly unlimited academic freedom, with the decline in government and private funding of research, they have become more flexible in their research pursuits, that is, they are willing to work on projects that can be funded rather than those they would like to do. Thus, physical anthropologists that previously studied high-altitude adaptation are now considering the nutritional status of the elderly because it is perceived as a priority for NIH funding. In private industry, academic freedom is not an option. Research is for profit. Presentations at scientific meetings and published manuscripts serve the interests of the company by highlighting its latest scientific discoveries and developments.

SOME FINAL THOUGHTS

The mismatch between the number of new physical anthropology Ph.D.s and traditional teaching/research-oriented jobs in academia has led to a changing job market. Today, physical anthropologists are playing a central role in industry and commercial life. Anthropologists contribute directly to the national and international goals of technologic, economic, and cultural development, not only as researchers but also in a wide variety of other professional roles. As demonstrated in this book, physical anthropology Ph.D.s who have taken alternative careers are doing applied research and development in industry, working in government or nonprofit organizations, consulting, or are self-employed.

Anthropology graduate education should prepare students for alternative positions in an increasingly interdisciplinary, collaborative, and global job market. Working in private industry should not be viewed negatively. Anthropology faculty members should offer better career information and guidance so that their students can make well-informed decisions in planning their professional careers. Additionally, faculty members should not see their sole mission as producing the next generation of academic physical anthropologists.

As the country responds to increased economic competition, urgent public health care needs, environmental problems, and other pressing issues, there will be an increased demand for scientists that can bridge the gap between people and industry. Physical anthropologists have the skills and talents that will allow them to play an even more important role in society than they have in the past.

REFERENCES

Acosta, P. B., and A. S. Ryan. 1997. "Functions of Dietitians Providing Nutrition Support to Patients with Inherited Metabolic Disorders." *Journal of the American Dietetic Association* (97): 783–786.

American Academy of Pediatrics, Committee on Nutrition. 1983. "The Use of Whole Cow's Milk in Infancy." *Pediatrics* (72): 253–255.

——. 1988. *Clinical Testing of Infant Formula with Respect to Nutritional Suitability for Term Infants.* Elk Grove Village, IL: American Academy of Pediatrics, Committee on Nutrition.

——. 1992. "The Use of Whole Cow's Milk in Infancy." *Pediatrics* (89): 1105–1109.

Anderson, R. E. 1970. "Lipids of Ocular Tissues. IV. A Comparison of the Phospholipids from the Retina of Six Mammalian Species." *Experimental Eye Research* (10): 339–344.

Barker, D.J.P. 1994. *Mothers, Babies, and Diseases in Later Life.* London: BMJ Publishing Group.

Birch, E. E., D. G. Birch, D. R. Hoffman, and R. D. Uauy. 1992. "Dietary Essential Fatty Acid Supply and Visual Acuity Development." *Investigations in Opthalmology and Visual Science* (33): 3242–3253.

Bolles, R. N. 2000. *What Color Is Your Parachute?: A Practical Manual for Job-Hunters and Career Changers.* Berkeley, CA: Ten Speed Press.

Brace, C. L. 1964. "The Fate of the 'Classic' Neanderthals: A Consideration of Hominid Catastrophism." *Current Anthropology* (4): 3–43.

Brace, C. L., A. S. Ryan, and B. H. Smith. 1981. "Dental Wear in La Ferrassie I: Comment." *Current Anthropology* (22): 426–430.

Carlson, S. E., S. H. Werkman, and E. A. Tolley. 1996. "Effect of Long-Chain n-3 Fatty Acid Supplementation on Visual Acuity and Growth of Preterm Infants with and without Bronchopulmonary Dysplasia." *American Journal of Clinical Nutrition* (63): 687–697.

De Andraca, I., T. Walter, M. Castillo, P. Pino, F. Rivera, and C. Cobo. 1990. "Iron Deficiency Anemia and Its Effects upon Psychological Development at Preschool Age: A Longitudinal Study." *Nestle Foundation Nutrition Annual Report*, pp. 53–62.

Finn, S. C., M. B. Foltz, and A. S. Ryan. 1991. "Image and Role of the Consultant Dietitian in Long Term Care: Results from a Survey of Three Midwestern States." *Journal of the American Dietetic Association* (91): 788–792.

Foltz, M. B., M. R. Schiller, and A. S. Ryan. 1993. "Nutrition Screening and Assessment: Current Practices and Dietitians' Leadership Roles." *Journal of the American Dietetic Association* (93): 1388–1395.

Fomon, S. J., K. D. Sanders, and E. E. Ziegler. 1990. "Formulas for Older Infants." *Journal of Pediatrics* (116): 690–696.

Frisancho, A. R., and A. S. Ryan. 1991. "Decreased Stature Associated with Moderate Blood Lead Concentrations in Mexican-American Children." *American Journal of Clinical Nutrition* (54): 516–519.

Garn, S. M., P. J. Hopkins, and A. S. Ryan. 1981. "Differential Fatness Gain of Low Income Boys and Girls." *American Journal of Clinical Nutrition* (34): 1465–1468.

Garn, S. M., and A. S. Ryan. 1981. "Replicating the Income Related Reversal of Fatness." *Ecology of Food and Nutrition* (10): 237–239.

——. 1982. "The Effect of Fatness on Hemoglobin Levels." *American Journal of Clinical Nutrition* (36): 189–191.

———. 1983. "Relationship between Fatness and Hemoglobin Levels in the National Health and Nutrition Examinations of the USA." *Ecology of Food and Nutrition* (12): 211–215.

Garn, S. M., A. S. Ryan, and S. Abraham. 1981a. "The Black-White Difference in Hemoglobin Levels after Age, Sex, and Income Matching." *Ecology of Food and Nutrition* (10): 69–70.

———. 1981b. "New Values Defining 'Low' and 'Deficient' Hemoglobin Levels for White Children and Adults." *Ecology of Food and Nutrition* (11): 71–74.

Garn, S. M., A. S. Ryan, S. Abraham, and G. Owen. 1981. "Suggested Sex and Age Appropriate Values for 'Low' and 'Deficient' Hemoglobin Levels." *American Journal of Clinical Nutrition* (34): 1648–1651.

Garn, S. M., A. S. Ryan, G. Owen, and S. Abraham. 1981. "Income Matched Black-White Hemoglobin Differences after Correction for Low Transferrins." *American Journal of Clinical Nutrition* (34): 1645–1647.

Garn, S. M., A. S. Ryan, G. Owen, and F. Falkner. 1981. "Developmental Differences in the Triceps and Subscapular Fatfolds during Adolescence in Boys and Girls." *Ecology of Food and Nutrition* (11): 49–51.

Garn, S. M., A. S. Ryan, and J.R.K. Robson. 1982. "Fatness-Dependency and Utility of the Subscapular/Triceps Ratio." *Ecology of Food and Nutrition* (12): 173–177.

Hamill, P.V.V., T. A. Drizd, C. L. Johnson, R. B. Reed, and A. F. Roche. 1977. "NCHS Growth Curves for Children. Birth–18 Years, United States." Washington, DC: U.S. Government Printing Office. *Vital and Health Statistics Series 11, no. 165* (DHHS publication PHS 78-1650).

Lloyd, B., R. J. Halter, M. J. Kuchan, G. E. Baggs, A. S. Ryan, and M. L. Masor. 1999. "Formula Tolerance in Postbreastfed and Exclusively Formula-Fed Infants." *Pediatrics Electronic Pages* (103): e7, 1–6.

Lozoff, B., E. Jimenez, and A. W. Wolf. 1991. "Long-Term Developmental Outcome of Infants with Iron Deficiency." *New England Journal of Medicine* (325): 667–694.

Lucas, A. 1991. "Programming by Early Nutrition in Man." In G. R. Bock, and J. Whalen, eds. *The Childhood Environment and Adult Disease.* New York: John Wiley & Sons, pp. 38–55.

Martinez, G. A., F. W. Krieger, and A. S. Ryan. 1985. "Factors Affecting Mothers' Decision to Breast Feed or Bottle Feed." *1985 Program and Abstracts—Joint Statistical Meetings,* Las Vegas, 223.

Martinez, G. A., and A. S. Ryan. 1985. "Nutrient Intakes in the United States during the First 12 Months of Life." *Journal of the American Dietetic Association* (85): 826–830.

———. 1989. "The Pediatric Marketplace." *American Journal of Diseases of Children* (143): 924–928.

Martinez, G. A., A. S. Ryan, and D. J. Malec. 1985. "Nutrient Intakes of American Infants and Children Fed Cow's Milk or Infant Formula." *American Journal of Diseases of Children* (139): 1010–1018.

Montalto, M. B., J. D. Benson, and G. A. Martinez. 1985. "Nutrient Intakes of Formula-Fed and Cow's Milk-Fed Infants." *Pediatrics* (75): 343–351.

National Academy of Sciences. 1995. *Reshaping the Graduate Education of Scientists and Engineers.* Washington, DC: National Academy Press.

O'Brien, J. S., D. L. Filerup, and J. F. Mean. 1964. "Quantification of Fatty Acid and Fatty Aldehyde Composition of Ethanolamine Choline and Serine Phosphoglycerides in Human Cerebral Gray and White Matter." *Journal of Lipid Research* (5): 29–330.

Roche, A. F. 1984. "Anthropometric Methods: New and Old. What They Really Tell Us." *International Journal of Obesity* (8): 509–524.

Root, A. W. 1992. "Mechanisms of Hormone Action: General Principles." In W. Hung, ed. *Clinical Pediatric Endocrinology*. St. Louis, MO: Mosby-Year Book, Inc., pp. 1–12.

Ryan, A. S. 1979a. "A Preliminary Scanning Electron Microscope Examination of Wear Striation Direction on Primate Teeth." *Journal of Dental Research* (58): 525–529.

———. 1979b. "Wear Striation Direction on Primate Teeth: A Scanning Electron Microscope Examination." *American Journal of Physical Anthropology* (50): 155–168.

———. 1979c. "Tooth Sharpening in Primates." *Current Anthropology* (20): 121–122.

———. 1979d. "Scanning Electron Microscopy of Tooth Wear on the Anterior Teeth of *Australopithecus afarensis*." *American Journal of Physical Anthropology* (50): 468.

———. 1985. "Anthropological Research in the Health Care Field." *American Anthropological Association Meeting Abstracts* 134.

———. 1988. "The Role of Bioanthropology in the Infant Formula Industry: Dietary Iron Status of American Infants." *Central Issues in Anthropology* (7): 39–56.

———. 1997a. "The Resurgence of Breast-feeding in the United States." *Pediatrics Electronic Pages* 99: e12.

———. 1997b. "Iron-Deficiency Anemia in Infant Development: Implications for Growth, Cognitive Development, Resistance to Infection, and Iron Supplementation." *Yearbook of Physical Anthropology* (40): 25–62.

Ryan, A. S., J. D. Benson, and A. M. Flammang. 2000. "Infant Formulas and Medical Foods." In M. K. Schmidl and T. P. Labuza, eds. *Essentials of Functional Foods*. Gaithersburg, MD: Aspen Publishers, pp. 137–163.

Ryan, A. S., L. D. Craig, and S. C. Finn. 1992. "Nutrient Intakes and Dietary Patterns of Older Americans: A National Study." *Journal of Gerontology: Medical Sciences* (47): M145–M150.

Ryan, A. S., M. B. Foltz, and S. C. Finn. 1988a. "The Role of the Clinical Dietitian: I. Present Professional Image and Recent Image Changes." *Journal of the American Dietetic Association* (88): 671–676.

———. 1988b. "The Role of the Clinical Dietitian: II. Staffing Patterns and Job Functions." *Journal of the American Dietetic Association* (88): 679–683.

Ryan, A. S., and J. D. Gussler, eds. 1986. *The International Breast-Feeding Compendium: Updated Appendix to Volumes 1 and 2, Third Edition, 1984*. Columbus, OH: Ross Laboratories.

Ryan, A. S., and D. C. Johanson. 1989. "Anterior Dental Microwear in *Australopithecus afarensis:* Comparisons with Human and Nonhuman Primates." *Journal of Human Evolution* (18): 235–268.

Ryan, A. S., F. W. Krieger, and G. A. Martinez. 1985. "Factors Affecting Mothers'

Decision to Breast Feed or Bottle Feed." *American Statistical Association Proceedings of the Social Statistics Section,* pp. 387–391.

Ryan, A. S., and G. A. Martinez. 1984. "Iron Intake in Infancy by Demographic Characteristics." *American Anthropological Association Meeting Abstracts* 186.

———. 1985a. "Nutrient Intakes of Infants in the United States: Results from Two National Nutrition Surveys." *American Journal of Physical Anthropology* (66): 224.

———. 1985b. "Iron Intake in the United States during the First Year of Life According to Demographic Characteristics." *Ecology of Food and Nutrition* (16): 21–32.

———. 1986a. "Defatted Milk Use during Infancy." *American Journal of Physical Anthropology* (46): 260.

———. 1986b. "Nutrient Intakes of Infants in the WIC Program: Results from a National Survey." *American Public Health Association Program and Abstracts,* 23.

———. 1987a. "Incidencia de la lactancia materna en la poblacion Hispanoamericana de Los Estados Unidos, 1986." *Medico Interamericano* (6): 52–53, 57.

———. 1987b. "Physical Growth of Infants 7 to 13 Months of Age: Results from a National Survey." *American Journal of Physical Anthropology* (73): 449–457.

———. 1989. "Breastfeeding and the Working Mother: A Profile." *Pediatrics* (83): 524–531.

Ryan, A. S., G. A. Martinez, and F. W. Krieger. 1987. "Feeding Low-Fat Milk during Infancy." *American Journal of Physical Anthropology* (73): 539–548.

Ryan, A. S., G. A. Martinez, and D. J. Malec. 1985. "The Effect of the WIC Program on Nutrient Intakes of Infants." *Medical Anthropology* (9): 153–172.

———. 1986. "More on Nutrient Intakes of Infants Fed Cow's Milk or Formula." *American Journal of Diseases of Children* (140): 407–408.

Ryan, A. S., G. A. Martinez, J. L. Wysong, and M. A. Davis. 1989. "Dietary Patterns of Older Adults in the United States: NHANES II 1976–1980." *American Journal of Human Biology* (1): 321–330.

Ryan, A. S., G. A. Martinez, and R. Yip. 1990. "Changing Patterns of Infant Feeding in the United States: Evidence to Support Improved Iron Nutritional Status in Childhood." In S. Hercberg, P. Galan, and H. Dupin, eds. *Recent Knowledge on Iron and Folate Deficiencies in the World.* Colloque INSERM, Vol. 197, pp. 631–639.

Ryan, A. S., M. B. Montalto, S. Groh-Wargo, F. Mimouni, J. Sentipal-Walerius, J. Doyle, J. S. Siegman, and A. J. Thomas. 1999. "Effect of DHA-Containing Formula on Growth of Preterm Infants to 59 Weeks Postmenstrual Age." *American Journal of Human Biology* (11): 457–467.

Ryan, A. S., and A. F. Roche. 1990. "Growth of Mexican-American Children: Data from the Hispanic Health and Nutrition Examination Survey (1982–1984)." *The American Journal of Clinical Nutrition,* Supplement to Volume 51, Number 5.

Ryan, A. S., A. F. Roche, and R. J. Kuczmarski. 1999. "Weight, Stature and Body Mass Index Data for Mexican Americans from the Third National Health and Nutrition Examination Survey (NHANES III, 1988–1994)." *American Journal of Human Biology* (11): 673–686.

Ryan, A. S., A. F. Roche, R. Wellens, and S. Guo. 1994. "Relationship of Blood Pressure to Fatness and Fat Patterning in Mexican American Adults from the Hispanic Health and Nutrition Examination Survey (HHANES, 1982–1984)." *Collegium Antropologicum* (18): 89–99.

Ryan, A. S., D. Rush, F. W. Krieger, and G. Lewandowski. 1991. "Recent Declines in Breast-feeding in the United States, 1984 through 1989." *Pediatrics* (88): 719–727.

Ryan, A. S., R. Wellens, A. F. Roche, and R. J. Kuczmarski. 1996. "Reference Data for Arm Muscle and Arm Adipose Tissue Areas in Mexican Americans from the Hispanic Health and Nutrition Examination Survey (HHANES 1982–1984): Comparisons with Whites and Blacks from NHANES II (1976–1980)." *American Journal of Human Biology* (8): 389–403.

Ryan, A. S., J. L. Wysong, G. A. Martinez, and S. D. Simon. 1990. "Duration of Breastfeeding Patterns Established in the Hospital, Influencing Factors: Results from a National Survey." *Clinical Pediatrics* (29): 99–107.

Uauy, R. D., D. R. Hoffman, E. E. Birch, D. G. Birch, D. M. Jameson, and J. Tyson. 1994. "Safety and Efficacy of Omega-3 Fatty Acids in the Nutrition of Very Low Birth Weight Infants: Soy Oil and Marine Oil Supplementation of Formula." *Journal of Pediatrics* (124): 612–620.

Walker, D., and R. E. Beauchene. 1991. "The Relationship of Loneliness, Social Isolation, and Physical Health to Dietary Adequacy of Independently Living Elderly." *Journal of the American Dietetic Association* (91): 300–306.

Wellens, R., A. F. Roche, A. S. Ryan, S. Guo, and R. J. Kuczmarski. 1995. "Head Circumference Reference Data for Mexican American Infants and Young Children from the Hispanic Health and Nutrition Examination Survey (HHANES 1982–1984): Comparisons with Whites and Blacks from NHANES II (1976–1980)." *American Journal of Human Biology* (7): 255–263.

Wienker, C. W. 1991. "Career Alternatives for Physical Anthropologists." *Practicing Anthropology* (13): 27–30.

Yannicelli, S., and A. S. Ryan. 1995. "Improvements in Behavior and Physical Manifestations in Previously Untreated Adults with Phenylketonuria Using a Phenylalanine-Restricted Diet: A National Study." *Journal of Inherited Metabolic Disorders* (18): 131–134.

Yip, R., N. J. Binkin, L. Fleshood, and F. L. Trowbridge. 1987. "Declining Prevalence of Anemia among Low-Income Children in the United States." *Journal of the American Medical Association* (258): 1619–1623.

Yip, R., K. M. Walsh, M. G. Goldfarb, and N. J. Binkin. 1987. "Declining Prevalence of Anemia in Childhood in a Middle Class Setting: A Pediatric Success Story." *Pediatrics* (80): 330–334.

Zheng, J. J., and I. H. Rosenberg. 1989. "What Is the Nutritional Status of the Elderly?" *Geriatrics* (44): 57–64.

Ziegler, E. E. "Milk and Formulas for Older Infants." 1990. *Journal of Pediatrics* (117): 576–579.

Chapter 16

Independent Consulting: Making Your Own Rules

Marilyn R. London

In 1997–1998, more than 11,000 students received degrees in anthropology from the institutions indexed in the American Anthropological Association's Guide to Programs. In 1998–1999, the number was over 12,000. The majority of these degrees were undergraduate (9,229 in 1997–1998, 10,079 in 1998–1999), but 12 to 13 percent received degrees at the master's level, and about 5 percent were awarded doctorates (AAA, 1998, 1999). These individuals are now entering graduate programs or, having completed the desired degree, seeking employment. It goes without saying that 23,000 new anthropology jobs did not open up over the past two years, and it is unlikely that there will be significantly fewer graduates this year—or the next. The competition is stiff for anthropology positions at every level, both in and outside of academia, but this is nothing new. In 1986, at the annual meeting of the American Association of Physical Anthropologists (AAPA), the Career Development Committee presented the results of research they had done on the membership. The committee had sent out questionnaires to individuals who had received the Ph.D. within the previous twenty years, and had also collected data from all departments offering degrees in physical anthropology. Although it was not the object of the original research, they learned that in 1985 there were 495 active physical anthropologists at the Ph.D. level, and 499 Ph.D. candidates. These were attention-getting numbers, but few people noticed. The truth then, as now, is that some graduates are simply not going to find the positions they desire, at least not immediately. There are, however, alternatives to taking a job outside of anthropology.

Employers are starting to recognize anthropologists as an important part of the workforce, especially in areas where an understanding of cultural and linguistic differences may be important. Education departments, health care administrators, and court systems are all finding that employees with an anthropological background can make the difference between failure and success in a program. It is less obvious how physical or biological anthropologists can contribute to the workplace outside of the field. If employers know anything about anthropology, it is usually something about the cultural approach; if they know about physical anthropology, they can't conceive of a way to put fossil-hunters to work on their projects. Some of the other chapters in this book illustrate where biological anthropologists can look for employment outside of the traditional universities and museums. This chapter addresses doing anthropology as an independent contractor or consultant. It will also discuss using anthropological skills in nontraditional jobs.

According to Working Today, a nonprofit organization in New York City for people who work on their own, independent workers now make up 30 percent of the labor force in the United States (Working Today, 1999). This percentage is probably representative of anthropologists today. I was asked to write this chapter because I am presently working as an independent contractor, using my anthropological skills. I am actually contracted to several organizations, and I anticipate that this multitasking approach will continue. My current projects include teaching an introductory biological anthropology course at the University of Maryland (as a lecturer); documenting a research collection of human skeletal material at the Smithsonian Institution; analyzing human remains which were recovered during construction in a municipal park in New York City; writing a children's book on bones; working as part of the medicolegal investigation team for the Rhode Island Office of the Medical Examiner (London et al., 1997); and evaluating applicants for positions on an advisory board for the National Cancer Institute. In the recent past, I have also edited manuscripts for biomedical journals, coedited a book on anthropology (Selig and London, 1998), and cowritten an anatomy book for children (London and Owsley, 1998). None of these projects is full time; some are short term. Over the past two years, I have discovered that overlapping projects seems to work for my lifestyle; others may prefer to take on one thing at a time.

How did I reach this point in my career, where I am working on many endeavors at once? Why do these institutions feel justified in contracting me to work on such a variety of efforts? My training is fairly standard in the field; I took primatology, human evolution, and population genetics courses like most students do. I received a bachelor's degree in anthropology from the George Washington University and earned a master's degree in biological anthropology at the University of New Mexico. In undergraduate and graduate schools, I participated in research projects and seminars on epidemiology, population biology, clinal variation, skeletal aging, and forensic anthropol-

ogy. I attended training courses in forensic science. These are fairly specialized areas, not much in demand in the general workplace, but the skills I
developed during my training have definite applications outside of anthropology.

I have been employed in a variety of positions that might not seem to be
anthropological at first blush, but often required an anthropological perspective or a specialized skill I had. I worked for several years in a dialysis unit
of a large hospital, documenting patient admissions, complications, and outcomes, including survival. I spent a year documenting historical changes in
U.S. county lines for an educational software development group. I interviewed cardiac patients for a nursing intervention study in a community
health program at Brown University. All these jobs required attention to
detail, an appreciation of cultural and temporal changes in communities, and
familiarity with the scientific method. And from each of these positions I have
learned new skills to add to my Curriculum Vitae. Recognizing, developing,
and marketing your anthropological skills will improve your chances for
fulfilling employment, especially if you choose to become an independent
consultant.

ASSESS YOUR SKILLS

Although readers of this book have specialized in physical anthropology
to one degree or another, most of us have taken courses in the four sub-
fields of anthropology. Class projects and research in these (and other)
courses have developed skills that we usually identify as "anthropological."
However, each of these areas of competence—none particularly exclusive to
anthropology—is marketable, and the suite of skills that we acquire in our
field is unique. Students in education, business, political science, sociology,
and other fields do not usually have the chance to acquire or develop the
range of qualifications which are all (or most) necessary for our studies.
Consider the following list of proficiencies. I have indicated how I have used
my training in these areas in past and current projects; make your own list
of experiences for each category.

Interviewing

Biological anthropologists frequently collect data from living humans, and
our ethnology coursework teaches us to be sensitive to cultural differences.
We have already developed the interpersonal skills necessary to reassure our
subjects, ask difficult questions, and obtain the desired information. I used
this background to conduct a series of interviews with each of 125 female
heart patients enrolled in a community health research project in New England. Everyone else on this project had a nursing degree, but the principal
investigator wanted one team member who was trained as an anthropologist.

Writing

Class project reports, term papers, grant proposals, requests for information, theses, and dissertations are all ways that we learn writing skills. Nearly every professional position will require the ability to write quickly and well. I have written book chapters and articles with the same approach I developed as a student for research papers—collect data, organize it, outline and write each section, review, edit, and rewrite. I was asked to write an article for the Virginia Museum of Natural History magazine (London, 1998b), and this led to a second article (London, 1998a), a presentation at an exhibit opening, and an appointment as a research associate at the Museum.

Editing

Departmental newsletters and journals, data verification, reference checking, and library skills provide the general background you need to edit. (You must also have an understanding of the subject area.) Using my knowledge and liberal access to reference materials, I have edited many biomedical (mostly molecular biology) manuscripts for publication, and coedited a museum periodical and a book of collected articles on anthropology. I have also worked on copyediting projects for professional meeting abstracts and for book chapters.

Computer Skills

Programming, statistical packages, spreadsheet software, word processing, and Internet familiarity are necessary for almost any job. Even if you don't know the specific software being used on a project, once you have used one it is not difficult to learn another. Although job advertisements may specify particular software packages, employers are frequently willing to talk to applicants who have a background in similar software. I have had to learn to use new software at virtually every job I've taken over the past twelve years.

Statistics

Understanding probability and statistical methods is extremely important, not only for the analysis of your own data, but also to help you present the data in an understandable form to the audience. Whether you are testifying in court, publishing the results of your analysis, or presenting someone else's theories in the classroom, you must be able to defend your statistics.

Language(s)

Possession of reading, writing, and listening comprehension in more than one language can expand your opportunities. Even a couple of years of high school Latin gives you an advantage in writing and editing, especially in bio-medical areas. An understanding of other languages, at the very least, gives a writer or editor the ability to recognize misspelled or misused words.

Data Collection

Understanding the concept of standardized variables and scoring tech-niques, development of questionnaires and data collection forms, anticipa-tion of intra- and interobserver errors, and skills in training a team of data collectors are all skills. If you can set up a rigid data collection program and develop a data verification procedure from the beginning, you will be a valu-able team member. Many professionals who might consult you or hire you onto a special project have not had a scientific research background, and they are looking for collaborators who do.

Data Analysis

Meaningful interpretation of data and recognition of problem areas are essential to biological anthropology. We are familiar with large data sets, and we know what the hazards can be. When I took over an epidemiology project on diabetic versus nondiabetic patients several years ago, I discovered that the "control" population had been drawn from a computer database, and that no one had checked to see if these control patients were still alive. In fact, some were not, but the fact that they had no hospitalizations during the study period was counted in their favor! Because I asked to look at the raw data, I was able to catch this problem before the results were submit-ted for publication.

Photography

Black and white photography for publications, slide photography for pre-sentations, videotaping, and darkroom skills can be listed on the CV or brought up in the interview. Your familiarity with photographic equipment and procedures may make you an attractive candidate for a project.

Lab Skills

Technical skills in biology and chemistry are increasingly important in biological anthropology. As with some of these other skills, a knowledge and appreciation of the techniques, the time frame for completing them, and anticipation of associated problems will allow you to discuss laboratory pro-cedures intelligently. Specialized skills in this category might also include scanning electron microscopy and radiography, and even casting techniques.

Teaching

Your teaching assistantships and guest lectures have provided you with organizational and audience experience that can be applied to running workshops and training sessions, as well as to teaching jobs. I have been on the faculty of several weeklong training seminars, and I am currently developing a continuing education course in forensic anthropology for a local police department, through the University of Maryland. I have also taught two-day courses on bones and diseases of aging to senior citizens, and an eight-week continuing education course on the human skeleton to homicide detectives and the general public.

Public Speaking

Presentations given at professional meetings and to your local anthropology organizations, demonstrations given at high schools, and interaction with the media about your field and research projects all increase your level of comfort in front of an audience. Most of us collect photographic slides to use in lectures and professional talks. Always be prepared to give an impromptu talk on your research to an interested organization, from a family member's community service association to a local professional group looking for a dinner speaker. As the public learns more about physical anthropology, more opportunities will open up for us all.

Curation and Museum Skills

Most of us have spent a great deal of time in museums, and the concepts of storage, labeling, documentation, conservation, and administration of collections are familiar to us. I have taken several short-term contracts in museum settings, from inventorying artifacts from Chaco Canyon to documenting skeletal material scheduled for repatriation.

Research Design

Many of the previously mentioned proficiencies are part of research design. The ability to ask relevant questions, to anticipate problems, and to see the overall picture in a research project will assist you in writing research proposals and summaries.

Administrative Skills

Offices held in student and professional organizations indicate that you have organizational and leadership talents, and they also imply that others are willing to trust you with decision making and fiscal responsibilities.

Art/Graphics

If you have done your own field drawings and/or provided graphics for projects, these skills may be useful almost anywhere. I'm not trained as an artist, but I was able to provide some of the drawings needed for the children's anatomy book mentioned earlier. Also, the ability to translate raw data into viewer-friendly graphs (and graphics) is highly valued. If you can use a computer graphics program to produce elegant signs, enhance field drawings, or illustrate a research result, you will be even more in demand.

Don't simply list your abilities and talents on a résumé; present them within the context of your previous work and research and demonstrate how they can be applied to new situations.

DEVELOPING YOUR SKILLS

The previous section discusses the application of biological anthropology skills and knowledge. However, we are not born with our expertise; it has to be developed. Keep in mind that virtually all successful anthropologists started their professional lives with an introductory course in the field. You just have to decide what to do after that first step.

While you are in school or working at your first job, take advantage of every activity that you can fit into your schedule. Get involved in writing, editing, and interviewing for the department newsletter. Serve as an officer in a student or professional group to gain administrative experience. Join committees where your talents and connections can be put to use. While I was an undergraduate, I worked at the university library and sat on the Exhibits Committee; we had access to wonderful artifacts from the anthropology department for the library display cases.

Improve your public speaking abilities by giving lectures to schools, clubs, or senior citizens groups. Teachers and program planners are always interested in guest speakers, especially if they bring slides, hand-outs, and demonstration materials. A box of human and nonhuman bones, slides of fieldwork in another part of the world, or a demonstration of early tool making will keep the attention of almost any class for an hour or so.

Offer to give a lecture in a colleague's class if you are not teaching. Students' questions give new perspectives to your research, and writing out and articulating your thoughts for the lecture illustrate any need for reorganization.

Sponsor or plan special programs within your department or as part of a professional organization. You will expand your administrative and organizational capabilities, and it is also a terrific way to network with other professionals.

Research, write, and submit papers at local and national meetings. Find out which organizations are holding meetings near you, and attend or even give a presentation. Most professional societies have themes for their annual meetings that may be related to your research.

Take courses in other departments to learn new theories and laboratory techniques. Most anthropology departments don't have their own molecular biology or scanning electron microscopy laboratories, but these facilities can usually be found somewhere on campus.

ASSESS YOUR KNOWLEDGE—
HOW CAN IT BE APPLIED?

It is often difficult for anthropologists to determine where their specialized knowledge can be used in the workplace. Sometimes it requires a little brainstorming. Here are a few examples of applications of a biological anthropology background to the needs of employers.

Anatomy

Knowledge of human anatomy and physiology, along with medical terminology, can be important to an organization that is collecting medical data from patients or hospitals. These groups often have employment advertisements under "research" or "biostatistics." Hospitals, clinics, and sometimes individual doctors look for employees and consultants who are already familiar with medical jargon.

Biomechanics

Engineering, architecture, and design firms have to take body shape, size, and motion into account when planning work and living spaces. Orthopedic and sports medicine clinics may have projects that require knowledge in this area.

Growth and Development

Pediatric clinics and hospital units, dental research groups, and food manufacturers need staff who understand normal growth and development, variability within and between populations, and factors that affect changes in individuals and groups.

Epidemiology

State departments of health, medical examiner systems, and health research centers recognize the anthropologist's role in data collection and interpretation. The Centers for Disease Control in Atlanta has nearly twenty physical anthropologists on the staff—more than most university departments.

Genetics and Molecular Biology

Biotechnology firms and government agencies are struggling to train enough people to advance these fields at a competitive pace. Look at the literature on the Human Genome Project and other major programs, and market your skills where you see a niche that meets your interests.

General Anthropology and Scientific Method

Editing, science writing, and product development are all possibilities for this background. Many communities have natural history museums or science centers, and schools are always looking for teaching materials. Museum shops and product development departments need specialists to advise them on educational toys and literature.

Think about your own interests and areas of expertise, and look at the newspaper to see which jobs require those proficiencies. Don't look under "anthropologist" because most employers don't realize that they need us; look in every section for a couple of weeks to see how your local newspaper advertises. The hospital epidemiology job I held for five years was advertised as a "Biopsychosocial Research Assistant"—and that's how I was identified on my hospital employee badge. But I was doing anthropology.

USING THE ANTHROPOLOGICAL PERSPECTIVE

When you decide to get involved in a project, sell yourself by marketing not only your specific abilities, but the whole substructure of anthropology. A school system where the students come from thirty different cultures will appreciate having someone on the administration who understands how culture can affect behavior. Integrating the anthropological perspective into a medical research program may encourage participation by patients who might not otherwise get involved. You may also discover research possibilities related to your own interests while you are analyzing data on a project. This happened to me when I worked in the dialysis unit; I learned that people with kidney failure develop pathological conditions of the bones (renal osteodystrophy), and published several papers on the subject with the medical research team (Chazan et al., 1991; Libbey et al., 1993; London et al., 1994).

NETWORKING

If you decide that you want to try contracting or consulting, tell everyone that you intend to do so. When I quit my last full-time job, I told several people in person, by telephone, and by e-mail that I was seeking contracts and short-term work. Within days I had a writing project that has led to two others, and a short-term project I took with a local consulting group has developed into a long-term consulting agreement for writing, editing, and special projects when I am available.

Meet the other anthropologists in your region. Don't focus on other biological anthropologists; you probably already know each other. But archaeologists and anthropology teachers in your region may know about projects in which you can get involved.

Join organizations and participate. The more professionals you know, the better your chances are for getting contracts. Keep in touch with colleagues from undergraduate and graduate school. Write to faculty members and let them know you are interested in consulting.

RESEARCH

In recent workshops presented by the Career Development Committee of the American Association of Physical Anthropologists, the committee stressed the importance of assembling a teaching portfolio before interviewing for teaching positions. This portfolio should contain a summary of courses you have previously taught, syllabi for courses you would like to teach, and a statement of your teaching philosophy. If you want to consult as a researcher, you should collect similar information for a research portfolio—summaries of completed research projects, proposals for research you want to do, and a statement about your research goals. This will force you to document your accomplishments and objectives, and it will establish a legitimate researcher background to prospective employers.

POSSIBLE EMPLOYERS

By now, you should be brainstorming about the kinds of organizations in your area where a biological anthropologist could find contract or consulting work. Here is a short list of organizations and the kinds of projects you might participate in.

Community colleges—courses; special programs

Continuing education programs—short courses for special interest groups

Museums and museum publications—articles on your area of expertise; special projects; research affiliations; product development

Hospitals—medical research

Department of health—epidemiology projects

Engineering firms—cultural resource management at construction sites

Universities—research projects; courses

Contracting firms that work with large research organizations—conference planning; editing; special projects

Parks departments—nature center administration and programs

Contract archaeology firms—cultural resource management

High schools—speakers series; science fair administration; courses

Government agencies—short term projects; contracting to fill a temporary vacancy; training programs

You should also consult publications that are targeted to anthropology careers to get ideas about applying your background to a job (Omohundro, 1998).

WORKING INDEPENDENTLY

The subtitle of this chapter is "Making Your Own Rules," but it might be more aptly called "Making Your Own Schedule." When you sign a contract with an organization, you are really playing by their rules, and you must know what those rules are. It is often difficult to anticipate problems that may arise during a contract, but you should definitely ask questions about travel, extensions, report formats, and financial limits before you sign.

It is important to remember that we do not need to reinvent the wheel when it comes to being independent workers. There are lots of part-time, consulting, contracting, and temporary employees in the world, and they are being studied by economists, sociologists, and political scientists to evaluate their needs and their impact on society. Monographs, journals, and popular magazines on working can be found in libraries and bookstores, and there is more and more information on the World Wide Web every time you check. Get advice and help when you are first testing the waters. Talk with your colleagues and your professors. Consult with other contractors, the Small Business Administration, an accountant, and the Department of Labor, if necessary. Visit the Working Today Web site (http://www.workingtoday.org) to learn about the advantages and disadvantages of working on your own.

A big benefit of working as a consultant or contractor is the control you have over your time. You can choose not to take on a project if you are too busy or just not interested. Of course, this control is not absolute; often, contracts will run longer than anticipated. Sometimes funding does not come through. You may need to juggle several contracts at once, and you will definitely need some flexibility in your schedule. For instance, at the beginning of 1999 I started an eight-week cultural resource management project 250 miles away; more than six months later I came home, bringing another year's worth of work with me. During part of the time I was out of town, I had to return one night a week for a course I had agreed to teach. So "control" may be a relative term in contracting.

There are some aspects of contracting and consulting that may not appeal to you; taxes become much more complicated, for instance. When you are not a "real" employee, no organization withholds taxes from your pay, and you must file and pay your taxes quarterly. When you have an employer, that person or organization must pay one-half of your FICA taxes, but when you are self-employed, you contribute both halves (with some modifications). If you employ any help, you are responsible for half of each employee's FICA, plus insurance and other costs; you may also be responsible for workers' compensation for employees. Some of the rules regulating taxes and benefits are controlled by the federal government, and some are regulated at the state level. You may be able to deduct a lot of your expenses from your taxable income; be sure to check with an accountant and read all of the available Internal Revenue Service literature on self-employment. Keep records of everything: receipts, cash flow, projects completed and dates, future commitments, and so on. If you get involved in several projects at once, it is easy to lose track of these things.

If you desire health insurance, you will have to pay for it yourself. However, you may be eligible for group rates if you are a member of a professional organization, such as the American Anthropological Association. The contract may not protect you in case of injury or job-related illness. Retirement planning is your responsibility, as well. Most advisors will tell you to start early and think big. You will have to consider investment options and other financial plans. Having some financial assets will make it easier to borrow money when you need it, as well.

When you are negotiating a contract, keep all of these financial obligations in mind, and be sure to charge enough to live on after you have paid for everything you need. If you are unsure what to charge, ask the organization how much they pay other consultants with your background and experience. Most companies and agencies will give you a range of hourly wages or per-project fees. Be honest with yourself and with the contracting organization when deciding on your compensation.

Even if you are organized and good at juggling projects, there may be times, such as during a family emergency, when you need a back-up system. When you are negotiating a contract, make sure that you are permitted to subcontract at least some percentage of the job, if needed. Sometimes the organization itself will contract a colleague directly. Then develop a network of colleagues who are interested in the same kind of work, and keep in touch with them in case you need some help.

SUMMARY

When I was working full time in a nonanthropology job (and I have to admit it is hard to put an anthropological spin on some jobs), I found that I was spending every evening and weekend working on anthropological projects. I was using up all of my vacation time going to anthropology meetings and giving presentations to high schools and professional groups. Even though I was earning a good salary and had great benefits, I felt that the job was an intrusion into my life as an anthropologist. When I turned in my resignation, I felt relief and exhilaration, even though I suddenly had no income. I did have the advantage of being married to someone who was also making a good salary (and who supported my decision), and I might not have resigned if I hadn't had that safety net. However, as I mentioned previously, I had two contracts within days, and both of those have engendered more consulting projects. For the first year, my income was irregular and low, but if it had been necessary, I could have lived on it. Right now I have several concurrent contracts, and I get one or two calls a month about future projects. I have turned down a few proposals in the past year, recommending colleagues for them. Although I get overwhelmed at times, I am learning to budget my time and resources so that I don't get consumed by the work. If this level of demand continues, I may have to consider forming a consulting group, but it hasn't come to that yet. And if the contract work disappears over the next few years—well, I can always get a job.

ACKNOWLEDGMENTS

For information on anthropology jobs, I would like to thank Kathleen Terry-Sharp and other staff members at the American Anthropological Association. For letting me pick their brains, I thank Diane France, Marcella Sorg, and M. Cassandra Hill.

REFERENCES

American Anthropological Association. 1998. *Guide: A Guide to Programs; A Directory of Members, 1998–1999.* Arlington, VA: American Anthropological Association.
———. 1999. *Guide: A Guide to Programs; A Directory of Members, 1999–2000.* Arlington, VA: American Anthropological Association.
Chazan, J. A., N. P. Libbey, M. R. London, L. Pono, and J. G. Abuelo. 1991. "The Clinical Spectrum of Renal Osteodystrophy in 57 Chronic Hemodialysis Patients: A Correlation between Biochemical Parameters and Bone Pathology Findings." *Clinical Nephrology* 35(2): 78–85.
Libbey, N. P., J. A. Chazan, M. R. London, L. Pono, and J. G. Abuelo. 1993. "The Relevance of Mineralization Lag Time in the Evaluation of Histological Changes in Renal Osteodystrophy." *Clinical Nephrology* 39(4): 214–223.
London, M. R. 1998a. "Man and the Ice Age." *Virginia Explorer* (Fall 1998). Martinsville, VA: Virginia Museum of Natural History.
———. 1998b. "Ice Age Settlers of North America." *Virginia Explorer* (Fall 1998). Martinsville, VA: Virginia Museum of Natural History.
London, M. R., F. J. Krolikowski, and J. H. Davis. 1997. "Burials at Sea." In W. D. Haglund and M. H. Sorg, eds. *Forensic Taphonomy: The Post-Mortem Fate of Human Remains.* Boca Raton, FL: CRC Press, pp. 615–622.

London, M. R., and D. W. Owsley. 1998. *Human Anatomy;* Manual to accompany the Smithsonian *Anatomy Lab*™ (ages 8 and up), produced by the Natural Sciences Industries, Ltd., West Hampstead, NY.

London, M. R., N. P. Libbey, D. G. Shemin, and J. A. Chazan. 1994. "Renal Osteo-dystrophy and Dialysis Artifacts as Indicators of Identification." *Forensic Science International* (65): 81–96.

Omohundro, J. T. 1998. *Careers in Anthropology.* Mountain View, CA: Mayfield Publishing Company.

Selig, R. O., and M. R. London, eds. 1998. *Anthropology Explored: The Best of Smithsonian AnthroNotes.* Washington, DC: Smithsonian Institution Press.

Working Today. 1999. Web site (http://www.workingtoday.org/).

Chapter 17

Journalism: Bringing Science to the Public

Kate Wong

If you are studying physical anthropology and enjoy writing, you might consider a career in publishing. Science journalism is a wonderful way to stay involved with your field and science in general if you don't want to be a research scientist. Science writers and editors generally have science backgrounds, and although they may cover a variety of scientific topics, they usually have a specialty. With a degree in physical anthropology, you may have enough experience in biology and anthropology to qualify for a position with a publication looking for someone with that kind of expertise.

In my case, a B.S. in physical anthropology and zoology led to a job with a science magazine where I research, write, and edit articles geared toward the educated layperson. I use my basic science background everyday, whether it's verifying the mathematical calculations in an article, or editing a piece on how CD players work. With regard to physical anthropology, my training in this area and specific interest in paleoanthropology has made me the staff "expert" on such matters. Because the magazine I work for presents feature articles authored mostly by scientists, I put forth proposals suggesting topics for articles and the scientists whom I think should write them based on what I've learned from following the journal reports and talking with researchers. Similarly, when relevant manuscripts or article proposals from outside come in, I am often asked to evaluate them from a content perspective. But it is writing in particular that really allows me to explore my interests—both in physical anthropology and other areas—and share those interests with the public.

A CLOSER LOOK

In a typical month (the magazine I work for is published monthly), I research a few feature articles, edit the letters to the editors or a column on how things work, and report and write a news story. Research entails proofreading and fact-checking articles on a wide variety of topics—from astrophysics to animal behavior—to ensure their accuracy. Editing requires that I shape a piece—whether it's a letter from a reader regarding an article we ran on *T. rex*, or a scientist-authored article describing the mechanisms of the polymerase chain reaction—so that it's clear and concise, while preserving the author's "voice." Depending on the nature of the article, I may have to work closely with an art director in order to develop an informative and attractive accompanying illustration. In researching and editing, I draw heavily on the scientific foundation upon which my degree in physical anthropology was built. All those prerequisite courses I took in college such as calculus, physics, and chemistry are quite helpful. I still sometimes have to consult a textbook, or pick the brain of a neighboring editor with a different area of expertise, but I generally find that my basic training has prepared me well for the tasks at hand.

Writing is perhaps the most challenging—and for me the most rewarding—part of my job. First I have to find something newsworthy (which can be difficult at a monthly publication, where we put an issue together two months before it hits the newsstands). Sometimes the idea comes out of a presentation given at a conference, sometimes it comes from advance press releases from journals, sometimes it's a tip from a scientist, and sometimes it's just a new angle on previously reported research. With my scientific training, I can spot a potential news item through the veil of jargon—especially with regard to physical anthropology, whose jargon I am most familiar with. As a writer it's my job to transform those tedious technical reports into sparkling stories for lay people. Of course I can't write a piece from journal reports alone—I need to interview people, which is much easier and more productive if you are familiar with the topic.

Clearly plenty of journalists who do not have degrees in physical anthropology (or any other science) still write about it, but you have a better chance of getting the facts straight and writing something more insightful than someone who hasn't ever studied this subject. As an insider, you should be able to find the most relevant researchers for comments, and they'll probably give you more to go on because they'll be at ease conversing with someone who understands what they're saying.

And you'll probably find that you're comfortable writing about topics outside of physical anthropology. For example, through writing about human evolution, I became interested in the evolutionary history of other creatures. So I now also follow research in the field of vertebrate paleontology and have written about topics such as whale evolution and the first mammals.

In order to keep up with what's going on in the field, I try to read the scientific journals regularly. I also go to a few conferences every year to make new contacts, renew old ones, and observe research trends. If someone is working on a particularly interesting project, I may suggest to the board of editors that we invite that person to write an article for us, and I always come back from a conference with an idea for a news story that I can write up for the next issue. These meetings provide great opportunities to travel and talk with researchers in person about what they're doing. And if you can get an assignment in the field, you can really do some interesting things. For example, as I write this chapter I'm preparing a "field notes" account of my visit to a cave once inhabited by Neanderthals in Croatia, where I was on assignment for a conference on Neanderthals and human evolution in central Europe.

Writing for the public about physical anthropology is rewarding because there's a tremendous amount of public interest in all of the areas this field comprises, and the public needs science writers to make the information digestible. People also like to get a sense of whom the researchers are, something that doesn't usually come across in a formal scientific report. I have found that in covering human evolution the big personalities and heated debates make for especially captivating stories. Of course, you're bound to ruffle some feathers when you write about contentious subject matter—and I've received my share of hate mail—but researchers are generally pleased to see their field in the news and will help you in whatever way they can.

GETTING THERE

Course distribution requirements for a degree in physical anthropology span many areas, and if you take advantage of that you can immerse yourself in subjects ranging from genetics to archaeology. Taking some graduate-level courses as an undergrad made me more competitive when I applied for jobs. (They also gave me a better sense of what physical anthropology is all about.) Of course strong research skills are required for reporting and fact-checking, so making yourself Internet savvy and familiarizing yourself with database research will stand you in good stead. Typing and word processing skills are also critical, and proficiency in a foreign language (in my case, French) is a plus.

You probably won't, however, figure out what you want to do with your life just by going to class. Whether it's working with a professor on an outside research project or writing for the school paper, the average college or university campus affords numerous extracurricular opportunities to develop one's potential career interests. From an early age, I had always been fascinated with natural history museums. So when I was a student, I found a part-time job as a docent at my university's natural history museum. That helped me get a similar job at the American Museum of Natural History in New

York City after I graduated, which in turn led to my job at the magazine. Although I didn't anticipate pursuing publishing while I was a student, it was, in retrospect, a fairly logical path: science museums and science magazines are quite similar in that both aim to educate the public in an accessible, engaging way.

I was hired in an entry-level position as a researcher for the magazine's copy and photo departments. This stimulated my general interests in science and art, but about a month into the job I found myself missing physical anthropology. So I took a couple of days off to attend the annual meeting of the American Association of Physical Anthropologists (AAPA). Although I didn't set out to do any reporting, a story fell into my lap and I pitched it to the news editor when I returned. He bravely accepted my proposal and I set about writing the piece, with no idea of how to approach such a task. Eventually I turned in something I was fairly satisfied with, but the edited version that came back to me was virtually unrecognizable.

Students who major in a science often don't get enough training in writing—an invaluable skill whatever your career choice. My own coursework included a variety of literature and art courses, which set me apart from other science majors when I applied for jobs. Yet despite having more writing experience than most science majors, I still had a long way to go, as evidenced by my heavily edited first attempt at journalism.

Luckily, I've had the opportunity to learn how to write and edit on the job. This, however, is unusual. Indeed, almost all science writers and editors have studied journalism at some point, and the unfortunate reality is that if you're not hired to write, you're probably not going to be given a chance to write. If you think you might be interested in science writing, take a journalism course, or get involved with the school newspaper. And if that further piques your interest, consider pursuing another degree in journalism. In fact, several universities (including the University of California at Santa Cruz and New York University) offer master's programs specifically in science writing. The vast majority of students who choose and are accepted into these programs have science—not journalism—degrees. This can be the perfect way to make the transition from science to science writing.

Regardless of whether you decide to go to journalism school or wing it based on your scientific merits, most employers will want to see your clips. These can be tricky to acquire in the fledgling stage of your career because few employers are willing to take a chance on someone who doesn't have any experience. But bear in mind that the clips don't have to come from print publications—they can be from the Web. And because of the high turnover rate for electronic material, Web-based publications are often less particular about their writers' credentials. So if you make a strong pitch, you might be able to write a Web feature without submitting any clips. Another place to look for writing opportunities if you're trying to get your foot in the door is your university's press office.

Many science writers start out freelancing. Freelance writing and editing generally pays well, but as with all freelance work, it takes a while to establish yourself to the point where you have a reliable source of income. It also takes a certain amount of self-discipline, but many people prefer freelancing to full-time work because of the flexibility it permits. Others combine a full-time job with freelancing on the side to supplement their income.

THE LOWDOWN

In publishing you really have to be a team player. When you write you have to work with an editor. And when you edit you have to work with authors and art directors. Manuscripts go through various stages of editing and illustration prior to publication and you have to be prepared to make changes, even if you don't always agree with them.

Journalism is also very much deadline-oriented, so if you have trouble meeting deadlines, this probably isn't the career for you. Depending on the frequency of publication and the length of your article, you may have anywhere from a few months to a few hours to report and write, or edit an article. And there are tight deadlines for each stage of preparation, not just that first draft. All these deadlines can make for long hours. Reporters, especially, do not have nine-to-five jobs, particularly when they're just starting out. I know some young reporters working for daily or weekly publications who regularly put in eleven-hour days. If you thrive under pressure this is fine, but if you can't handle stress well you may want to look to other job possibilities. My own schedule varies: we have a "hell week" every month as the issue nears completion, and if I'm working on a complicated story, I often have to burn the midnight oil.

Competition can be fierce in journalism, especially among news-focused publications. Because the magazine I work for is a monthly publication centered on expert authors talking about their own research, there isn't so much pressure to break the news. But there's always the underlying concern that someone is going to scoop you on an investigative piece, and it can be challenging to find an angle that will still be fresh when the issue finally hits the newsstand a couple of months down the road.

You also have to be prepared to deal with people who are suspicious of reporters, either because they have been burned themselves by reporters in the past, or because reporters have an unfortunate reputation for misquoting people or getting the story wrong. But if you demonstrate that you can handle the material and are determined to make your story as accurate as possible, this should reassure your sources. (This is a fairly minor concern anyway because, by and large, researchers like to talk about their work—especially if it means that they're going to get some publicity out of it.)

One last thing to be aware of, especially if you have an advanced degree, is that when you're writing for a lay audience about your own area of expertise you can't necessarily write about it at the level at which you would like to read about it. Even the news sections in journals such as *Science* and *Nature* have a "popular" feel, though the scientific reports do not. You have to keep the layperson's interests in mind, and this often means glossing over a lot of details that you would otherwise include. This has definitely been a source of frustration for me, although it is getting easier. But I still tend to get so intensely interested in the science that I way overreport stories, after which I have to agonize over what information to include and what to leave out. Even when I think I've achieved the right level of explanation, my editor will come back to me and say that a favorite paragraph is not working, too complicated. Sometimes I can reword it, but sometimes it just has to be cut. Perhaps the number one rule in this business is that you can't be wedded to your words.

FINAL THOUGHTS

When I decided to put graduate school on the back burner, I was nervous about leaving the academic environment. But working for a science magazine has been an exciting way to maintain my ties to physical anthropology and science in general. And if you enjoy learning, writing and editing are great ways to get your mind around complex subjects. As they say, the true test of whether you understand something is whether you can explain it to someone else—the added challenge in journalism is that you have only a very limited space for your explanation. I still haven't decided whether I'll go back to school, but in the meantime I've developed a whole new set of skills, and I have a creative outlet for sharing what I learn with the public.

Chapter 18

Forensic Science as a New Arena for a Human Biologist

Moses S. Schanfield

On May 8, 1990, nine-year-old Rebecca O'Connell went to a Seven-Eleven near her home in Sioux Falls, South Dakota, but she did not return home. A massive search was organized of the area, to no avail. Her naked body was found in a field in Lincoln County, south of Sioux Falls, the next day. Her throat had been cut, and she had been sexually assaulted, anally. Her body had been out in a heavy rainstorm all night, with over an inch of rain falling, and it was approximately forty hours between the estimated time of death and the collection of physical evidence from the body.

A sexual assault kit was collected at autopsy and sent to the State Crime Laboratory in Pierre. The kit consisted of swabbings of the vaginal vault, anal/rectal region, and oral cavity, reference blood, hair specimens, and pubic hair combings. The results of testing the submitted evidence and known reference material at the State Crime Laboratory were not promising. Evidence of sexual assault in the form of sperm was only found in the anal/rectal swabs, and one exterior skin swabbing was too small for analysis. No significant amounts of seminal plasma were detected. The seminal plasma contains most of the genetic markers routinely used to profile semen evidence, including the ABH blood groups (if the semen donor is a secretor of blood group substance), the enzyme PGM1, and the immunoglobulin allotypes GM and KM markers. The sperm contain DNA, which can also be used to produce genetic profiles, but more on this later. No ABH antigens were detected, and the enzyme profiles matched the victim. Unfortunately, these results did not provide any information about the assailant.

In the meantime, the police were developing a list of possible suspects, as well as those that could be excluded. Unfortunately, with the information available, none of the suspects could be excluded. On or about May 20, 1990, law enforcement agents from South Dakota contacted me to see if we could confirm some of the work done, as well as test for the GM and KM allotypes (inherited variation on antibody molecules, that have marked variation in frequencies within and between human populations; these are very useful forensically and anthropologically). On May 22, 1990, evidence was received at Analytical Genetic Testing Center, Inc. (AGTC) for analysis.

Analysis of the submitted evidence confirmed the results of the South Dakota laboratory, and extended the results to indicate that, with the exception of sperm, there were no soluble markers left to test. It was determined that a small amount of degraded DNA could be extracted from the sperm fraction. There was not enough DNA to do restriction fragment length polymorphism (RFLP) or what is know as "DNA Fingerprinting" in the popular press, but there was probably enough DNA for testing using DNA amplification via the polymerase chain reaction (PCR). PCR is a form of biological photocopying, which amplifies small sequences of DNA. At the time, AGTC was still validating the PCR system to test for the genetic marker DQA1, which is part of the HLA (major histocompatibility) region, so the evidence could not be tested in Denver. It was suggested that the evidence go to a laboratory in California.

The evidence was sent to California and tested, and results were obtained. In conjunction with other investigative material, all of the suspects, except one, Donald Moeller, and 8 percent of the Caucasian population were eliminated. These results may not be the one in a million, billion, or trillion that the newspapers like to publish for DNA cases, but with the other evidence generated by law enforcement investigators in South Dakota, a good case was built against Donald Moeller. However, it would not be until the spring of 1992 that pretrial hearings and motions on the admissibility of the DNA evidence would begin. I participated in the hearings involving the admissibility of evidence in Canton, South Dakota, on June 12, 1992.

In the period of time between the original analysis of evidence in the Rebecca O'Connell case in May 1990, and the evidentiary hearings in South Dakota in June 1992, AGTC had not only started doing PCR cases with the system DQA1, but we also had started testing evidence for the amplified fragment length polymorphism (AFLP) APOB (apolipoprotein B). The latter PCR system has over twenty alleles and produces band patterns that look like the "DNA Fingerprints" produced by single locus RFLPs. During the hearings in June, it was decided to try to do APOB on the extracted DNA, to see if better individualization of the evidence could be obtained.

The trial was scheduled to begin the week of August 10, 1992; APOB results were actually obtained on Thursday August 13. The results obtained from testing DNA from the rectal/anal swabs did not exclude Donald

Moeller. In fact, the combination of the APOB and DQA1 data indicated that only approximately one in 1,400 Caucasians could have contributed the DNA found in the sperm fraction. Reports were prepared and sent to the prosecutor and, in turn, the defense attorneys. However, the judge decided not to allow the APOB data as evidence. (The photo on the following page contains a photograph of the APOB results that include those of Donald Moeller.) This would have been the first time APOB would have been used in a U.S. court; however, the trial judge felt there was enough evidence to convict the defendant, without potentially setting up an issue for an appeal. The judge was correct, Donald Moeller was convicted, and given the death penalty as punishment, for the murder and sexual assault of Rebecca O'Connell.

The case was appealed to the appellate court, and the conviction was overturned due to judicial misconduct. However, the appellate court supported the PCR testing. This permitted additional testing. A second trial was conducted during which the APOB was used with other markers. The inclusion probability rose to over one in a million. Donald Moeller was convicted for a second time and given the death penalty. I just received an e-mail message from the second district attorney indicating that there is a new appeal challenging the APOB testing. So the story continues.

Now that the reader has been lured into the intellectually titillating world of forensic science, or more appropriately, forensic biology, one might ask, "How did a human biologist/population geneticist find a job conducting forensic biology?" After all, the traditional association between physical anthropology and the medical/legal professions has been primarily skeletal identification. A brief biography is provided below.

POST-DOCTORAL TRAINING AND EMPLOYMENT HISTORY

My post-doctoral training was at the University of California Medical Center in San Francisco. My primary assignment was with the department of medicine, working in the laboratory of Hugh Fudenberg in the area of immunogenetics. Specifically, I was looking at the role that genetic markers had on antibody molecules in the immune response to infectious agents, as well as other properties of antibody molecules. This work was an extension of my dissertation research at the University of Michigan for my Ph.D. in human genetics that applied principles from population genetics, immunogenetics, and anthropology. Because of the nature of my research on genetic markers on antibodies, and the method of detecting these markers using antibody coated red blood cells, most of my work was done at the Irwin Memorial Blood Bank. This was an important attribute of my training when I was looking for job opportunities.

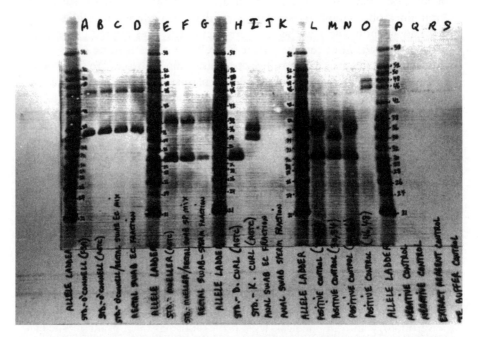

A photograph of the transparency prepared for court, including the evidence from the Rebecca O'Connell case. Lanes labeled A through S contain evidence and controls; the other lanes are allele ladders used to size the results. Lanes A and B are amplified DNA originating from Rebecca O'Connell. Lane D is the epithelial cell fraction from the rectal swab that should match Rebecca O'Connell. Lane C is a mixture of Rebecca O'Connell and the epithelial cell fraction. All of these items match. Lane E is the DNA amplified from the known blood standard of Donald Moeller. Lane G is the DNA amplified from the sperm fraction of the rectal swab. Lane F is the mixture of Donald Moeller's amplified DNA and the evidence. Again the bands all match. Lanes H and I are two other suspects in the case. Lanes J and K represent the anal swab extracts that did not amplify. Lanes L through O are positive controls. These were known DNA samples that were amplified with the evidence. Lanes P through S are negative controls. These lanes should show no amplification product. They are used to verify that there was no contamination of the reagents used or the test procedure.

Historically, I had long ties to blood banking and antibody molecules. After my senior year at the University of Minnesota and before I left for Harvard University, I worked at the War Memorial Blood Bank in Minneapolis. There I first started doing laboratory testing on the immunoglobulin allotypes, as well as other genetic markers to try to understand the cause for nonhemolytic transfusion reactions. At that time, in the early 1960s, little was known about the cause of reactions that did not destroy red blood cells after transfusion, but rather caused fever, hives and, in some cases, life-threatening reactions called anaphylactic transfusion reactions. We were looking at the possibility that incompatibility in plasma proteins could be causing these reactions. That did not turn out to be the case, but it provided the opportunity to learn about testing for different genetic markers, including immunoglobulin allotypes and other electrophoretic procedures. I also became more involved with research on blood groups and antibodies to blood groups.

Subsequent to my post-doctoral training, I spent a year as a research geneticist in San Francisco. With my laboratory experience at the Irwin Memorial Blood Bank, I became involved with the blood banking community and gave talks at their meetings, including one that was held at Asilomar, near Monterrey, California. I applied for academic positions in 1974 and 1975 but could not obtain one. However, during the blood bank meetings and job searching, I was made aware of a position at the Milwaukee Blood Center as head of the Blood Bank and Blood Group Reference Section. I was offered and accepted the position. I worked there for three years and completed tasks that I was initially employed to do, which was move the laboratory to a new facility, and switch to a fee for service cost recovery plan for the blood group reference laboratory and blood bank. I also reinstituted the paternity testing program.

With the completion of the projects I was hired to do, I started looking for academic positions. Again, I was unsuccessful. However, while attending blood bank meetings and conferences, I was offered a position at the Headquarters Laboratory of the American Red Cross (ARC) to do similar projects. In this case, it was to move the laboratory out of the downtown headquarters, make several laboratories cost recovery, and improve the services of the blood group reference laboratory. Ultimately, I also acquired the responsibility of managing the HLA laboratory that included the production of reagents for the ARC system of regional laboratories. After five years at the ARC, I had completed my original assignments and decided to find another position. Again, my first choice was an academic position; however, none came my way.

My training had been on the hands-on side of laboratory testing for genetic markers, either serologically (using antibodies to detect inherited variation) in the form of blood typing or GM and KM testing, or electrophoresis (using electrophoresis to separate inherited variation). I did not have the opportunity to do fieldwork, as many anthropologists do, but rather samples were sent to me for testing. My first contact with forensic sciences was in 1974, when I was asked if GM and KM testing could be done on bloodstains. At that time, I trained a forensic scientist in Oakland involving GM and KM typing. From time to time after that, forensic scientists would send me interesting cases to do GM and KM testing. In 1980, a forensic scientist in Oakland sent me a muscle extracted from a torso found floating in the San Francisco Bay with the question, "What was the race of the individual?" An anthropologist at UC Berkeley had said it was a Filipino. The GM markers, which have significantly different distributions in different racial groups, indicated that in all likelihood the individual was African American.

In 1983, I left the American Red Cross to help set up a private paternity testing laboratory in Atlanta, GA. When that laboratory changed hands at the end of 1984, we set up our own laboratory in 1985, conducting paternity testing and forensics. The markers used in parentage or paternity testing are the same ones used traditionally in anthropological studies; some of them are also used in forensics, though some of the testing procedures differ from those used routinely in the parentage testing laboratory, but not from those used in a blood bank reference laboratory.

Forensic biology should not be confused with traditional forensic anthropology, which typically tries to determine the age, sex, and race of skeletal remains. Skeletal remains are not frequently involved in criminal investigations. In contrast, forensic biology or forensic genetics is a frequent aspect of modern criminal investigations. The skills needed to be a forensic biologist are not that different from those needed to be a biologist or a human biologist. All of my training in chemistry, biology, genetics, and genetic marker testing that I have done since my undergraduate training has been of use. The major difference between doing genetic marker testing on human populations from, say, Siberia, and crime scene evidence, is that you must determine what you are testing, before it can be tested for genetic markers.

When samples are collected in the field from aboriginal populations or in cases of disputed paternity, the origin of the specimens and their nature are known. However, when materials are collected at a crime scene, the first question asked is, "What is it?"

The most common crime scene evidence encountered are mixtures of seminal plasma/sperm and vaginal secretions, semen stains, neat vaginal secretions, bloodstains, and mixtures containing one or more of the following: blood, semen, saliva, and urine. The first thing that has to be done is to identify what material you are working with. Not all red stains on a pair of pants are blood. Potential evidentiary material is screened with presumptive tests, and then confirmed. Presumptive tests are usually chemical tests that, in the presence of the material of interest, cause color change reactions. However, such tests do not always indicate whether the material is human in origin.

Sexual assault cases make up between 65 and 75 percent of the evidence submitted to crime laboratories. Therefore, identifying semen is one of the most important tests that are performed in a crime laboratory. One of the most common screening tests for semen (seminal plasma) involves the detection of the enzyme acid phosphatase (hereafter referred to as AP). Though AP is found in low levels in most tissues and body fluids, it is only found in high levels in seminal plasma. In most laboratories, after a sample is found to be positive for AP, a sperm search is conducted to confirm the presence of sperm. This serves two functions. The first is the confirmation of semen, the second is detecting the presence of sperm, because, if DNA testing is to be performed, this is the required component. If no sperm are detected, then it is likely that DNA testing will be unsuccessful. It should be noted that the detection of sperm does not guarantee the success of DNA testing. If no sperm are detected, then detecting another protein such as P30 is important to determining the presence of semen.

Studies indicate that the liquid component of semen, the seminal plasma, is washed out more quickly than the sperm components. You can think of this as flowing water washing down a streambed. The water washes out the silt and lighter components, but the rocks take longer to remove. Thus, if the victim is alive, in the first twenty-four hours, sperm wash out more slowly, such that individual sperm can be found for days after sexual intercourse, whereas the liquid components disappear rather quickly. If the victim is not alive, other external factors take over, including the position of the body, weather conditions, decomposition, and so on.

In the Rebecca O'Connell case, there was weak AP activity on the rectal/anal swabs, but P30 was not detectable, indicating that the seminal plasma had largely drained due to gravity (her body was facing uphill), or had been washed away, as she was naked in a heavy rain. However, sperm were observed, confirming the fact that sexual intercourse had occurred, and ultimately allowing for the detection of DNA from the probable perpetrator.

The tests for blood typing known samples such as blood in stains, and stains of mixed semen, represent standard blood banking procedures used by any experienced technologist working in a good blood bank. This is probably one of the reasons that medical technologists from the field of blood banking are now seeking careers in forensic biology. The electrophoresis procedures used to identify enzyme variation, and the new isoelectric focusing procedures, are the same genetic systems used in the laboratory for paternity testing. The primary difference is that when typing evidence, there is a much higher likelihood of not getting results.

In the Rebecca O'Connell case, though the victim was a secretor or partial secretor of blood group substance, no blood group substance was found in the rectal/anal swabs. We confirmed these results for the crime laboratory in South Dakota. Also, the genetic patterns of the enzymes that were detected, primarily the enzyme PGM1 (phosphoglucomutase 1) which is

A picture of Dr. Schanfield, in the laboratory, with the PGM1 gel generated in the Rebecca O'Connell case. The tip of the mechanical pencil is next to the PGM bands from the rectal swab in this case. It is obvious from the photograph that the bands are much darker than the surrounding bands, indicating increased PGM1 activity.

routinely tested in semen stains, and ESD (esterase D) and GLO1 (glyoxalase 1), which are rarely tested in semen stains, were identical to Rebecca O'Connell. Further, the reaction pattern of PGM1 was consistent with having originated from a deceased body with post mortem changes (see photo above). The origin of the PGM1 was the other testing that the South Dakota crime laboratory wanted confirmed. Our results were in agreement with theirs, even though we used a different method to identify PGM1. These results, with the overall lack of sperm and seminal plasma, suggested that the enzymes detected had all originated with the victim, and could provide no information about the semen donor. This was a major issue at trial, because if the enzymes had come from the semen, they would have excluded the suspect, Donald Moeller, which would have contradicted the DNA evidence generated.

THE ROLE OF THE HUMAN BIOLOGIST
IN FORENSIC BIOLOGY

Historically, the individuals involved in testing biological evidence were the same individuals that tested explosives, gunshot residue, identified drugs, and performed a myriad of other tasks in a crime laboratory. Years ago, they were called "forensic chemists." Most tests that were conducted were basic chemical tests, involving crystallography and microscopic techniques. As serological tests developed, primarily involving ABO blood group serology, the same people did the testing. Most of these individuals had chemistry degrees. In the late 1970s and early 1980s, electrophoresis and more sophisticated serological tests were introduced. By then, forensic scientists testing biological evidence were being called "forensic serologists," and it was becoming obvious that chemists were not the best individuals to do the job. A new group of individuals started coming into the field, people with biology or medical technology degrees. Now, serological testing is becoming less and less important. The present focus is on electrophoresis and DNA technology whether RFLP or PCR. Crime laboratory directors are looking for molecular biologists or human biologists to act as forensic scientists. There is a need for individuals who like to do laboratory work at both the molecular (DNA) and protein level and who have knowledge of human biological/population biology.

An area of training directly relevant to forensic biology is population genetics and population structure. The calculations used in forensic biology are similar to those used for genetic and population analyses. The difference between human biology and forensic biology is not large; in the former, the observed frequencies are compared to expected frequencies, while in the latter, the estimated phenotype frequencies are used to determine the likelihood that evidence and a suspect could match by chance. Another area of DNA technology that has become popular is the issue of population substructuring. This area is not foreign to human biologists interested in population biology.

Individuals interested in forensic biology must accept the reality that they will be taking the results that they generate to court; they will become part of the criminal justice system. Ultimately, this means that the individual will testify on the stand and must face the rigors of cross-examination. Not all individuals are capable or interested in putting up with that type of intellectual challenge.

TRAINING REQUIREMENTS FOR FORENSIC BIOLOGY

Forensic biologists are also called examiners, analysts, or any number of different names. They are hired by city, county, state, federal, military, and private laboratories conducting tests on crime scene material or forensic database samples. So how does a biological anthropologist find a position in forensic biology? There are two primary determinants. The first is course-work. A background in basic chemistry, biology, molecular biology, genetics and population genetics as well as anthropology is essential. If there are any forensic science courses available at your university, take them. The second, which is much more important, is contact with a crime laboratory. I cannot emphasize this enough. If you are interested in working in a laboratory set-ting, do an internship in a laboratory. Crime laboratories do not like to hire untrained individuals. The cost of training is prohibitive, so crime laborato-ries or companies like people with experience. Once you have been trained, it is much easier to get a position. At the present time, with the expansion of forensic DNA testing, there is an overall shortage of individuals trained to do DNA testing. This is especially true at the masters and Ph.D. level. If you think you might be interested in a career in forensic biology, contact your local crime laboratories, meet with them, find out about the jobs, and what you would be doing, and if you think you would like to do it, see if you can volunteer. This will increase the likelihood of getting a job in this fascinating line of work.

DAILY REQUIREMENTS OF A FORENSIC SCIENTIST

My daily tasks include reviewing the paternity and forensic cases that we receive, and generating reports that may have profound effects on peoples' lives. In the extreme case, the evidence generated could lead to someone being convicted of a heinous crime and given the ultimate penalty, death. In other cases, a man is either reassured or unhappily informed that he is the father of a child that he will have to support for the next eighteen years. It is rarely dull work, and thus far, most individuals, including myself, have had a challenging professional career. I have learned a great deal about the distribution of genetic markers in populations, and have also had the oppor-tunity to develop new polymorphic systems that can be used, not only in forensic analysis, but also to characterize more exotic human populations. I have also traveled all over the United States to testify in court. It should be pointed out that most crime laboratories only provide services for local areas, so the opportunity for travel is often limited.

What is the size of the job market in forensic science? There are approxi-mately 300 crime laboratories in the United States, employing approximately 1,000 forensic serologists. With the increase in violent crime, it is likely that there will be more jobs in the future, especially if the economy improves. There are jobs routinely advertised for people with training in DNA tech-nology. Further, the number of child support cases increases on a regular basis indicating that this sector of laboratory testing will not decrease in the near future. Physical anthropologists with appropriate graduate training and experience, particularly in lab techniques and human genetic variation, should be able to compete effectively for such professional careers.

ACKNOWLEDGMENTS

The author would like to thank Thomas A. Wahl, Senior Forensic Geneticist, Analytical Genetic Testing Center, Inc., for reviewing the manuscript and correcting any errors in facts or procedure. The author would also like to thank the Lincoln County Prosecutor's Office, Canton, South Dakota, and Rex Riis of the South Dakota State Crime Laboratory, Pierre, South Dakota, for the opportunity to work on the Rebecca O'Connell case.

DISCLAIMER

Any errors of fact or procedure in this article are the sole responsibility of the author and do not reflect on Analytical Genetic Testing Center, Inc., the Lincoln County Prosecutor's Office, or the South Dakota State Crime Laboratory.

Index

About the Editor and Contributors

ALAN S. RYAN received his Ph.D. in anthropology from the University of Michigan, Ann Arbor in 1980. For almost twenty years he has been employed by Ross Products Division, Abbott Laboratories in Columbus, Ohio. He started as a marketing research analyst and is now a senior research scientist in the Pharmaceutical Research and Development Department. He has published extensively on infant feeding practices, breastfeeding trends, infant and childhood growth and development, body composition, and iron-deficiency anemia. He has expertise in the analysis of nutrition, body composition, and growth data from large national surveys (e.g., the Second and Third National Health and Nutrition Examination Surveys [NHANES II and III] and Hispanic HANES). He still maintains an active interest in paleoanthropology and dental anthropology. In addition to his responsibility at Ross Laboratories, Dr. Ryan serves on the Career Development Committee of the American Association of Physical Anthropologists. After twenty years of service in the United States Navy Reserves Intelligence Division, he retired at the rank of Commander.

EVELYN J. BOWERS-BIENKOWSKI is an associate professor in the Anthropology Department of Ball State University in Muncie, Indiana. She received her Ph.D. in anthropology from the University of Pennsylvania. Her research interests include genetic variation and selection on human ontogeny and its relationships to population variation and growth. She has published on variation in longevity and causes of death in the Orkney Islands and on growth variation in children, in particular those with clefts of the lip, palate, or both. For this work she received favorable comment in the Moet-Hennessy-Louis Vuitton "Science pour l'Art" Prize Competition in 1996. In addition to research and teaching, she serves on the Task Force on the Status of Women of the College of Sciences and Humanities of Ball State University, and on the Committee on Professional Advancement of the American Association of Physical Anthropologists.

RALPH M. GARRUTO is Research Professor of Anthropology and Neuro-sciences at the State University of New York at Binghamton, and Senior Research Biologist at the National Institutes of Health in Bethesda, Maryland. He received his Ph.D. from Pennsylvania State University (human biology program) in 1973. As a human population biologist, his research focus has been on natural experimental models of disease using both a field and laboratory approach. He has conducted fieldwork among remote and modernizing populations in the Pacific Islands, China, Siberia, and South America. He has published extensively in human population biology, epidemiology and genetics, and in cell and molecular biology. He is a member of the U.S. National Academy of Sciences and the Third World Academy of Sciences.

KEVIN D. HUNT was educated at the University of Tennessee (B.A., 1980) and the University of Michigan (M.A., 1982; Ph.D., 1989). He was a postdoctoral fellow at Harvard University from 1989 to 1991 working under Richard W. Wrangham, with whom he has collaborated in the study of primate feeding behavior at the Kibale Forest Reserve, Uganda. His doctoral dissertation research was on the locomotion and posture (positional behavior) of chimpanzees and baboons. He has studied chimpanzees and baboons at Gombe in Tanzania, chimpanzees at Mahale, Tanzania, and chimpanzees, mangabeys, redtail monkeys, and blue monkeys at the Kibale Forest in Uganda. Currently, he studies the ecology of chimpanzee bipedalism at the Semliki Valley Wildlife Reserve, Uganda. His principal research interests are functional morphology, the evolution of human bipedalism, australopithecine and ape ecology, and the evolution of the hominid face. He is an associate professor of anthropology at Indiana University and an adjunct professor in the animal behavior program.

GARY D. JAMES is a research professor in the Decker School of Nursing, an adjunct professor of anthropology, and Director of the Institute for Primary and Preventative Health Care at Binghamton University. He received his Ph.D. in anthropology (human biology program) from Pennsylvania State University in 1984. He has published extensively on the health effects of modernization, the biological stress response to behavioral and social environmental stressors, circadian blood pressure variation and cardiovascular disease risk, and women's cardiovascular health. He is an elected fellow of the Society of Behavioral Medicine and a member of the Harvey Society.

ANDREW KRAMER is an associate professor and Head of the Department of Anthropology at the University of Tennessee. Educated at Berkeley (B.A.) and Michigan (M.A., Ph.D.), he is a paleoanthropologist whose research focuses on reconstructing human evolution. His work has taken him around the world: from Southeast Asia to Africa and from Europe to the Middle East. His ongoing field project in Java, Indonesia, has received external grant support from the National Science Foundation, the Wenner-Gren Foundation for Anthropological Research and the L.S.B. Leakey Foundation. He is the author of over twenty articles, chapters, and reviews in the top domestic and international journals in his discipline. Since joining the University of Tennessee faculty, he has received awards from the College of Arts and Sciences for his teaching and advising and has been recognized for his research by the university's chapter of Phi Beta Kappa.

BERT B. LITTLE is Associate Vice President for Academic Research at Tarleton State University in Stephenville, Texas, Adjunct Professor in the Graduate School of Human Development at the University of Texas at Dallas, and Research Scientist in the Division of Clinical Pharmacology at the V.A. Medical Center, Dallas, Texas. He received his Ph.D. in physical anthropology from the University of Texas at Austin. His research interests include human genetic isolates, human growth and development, human teratology, childhood obesity, substance abuse during pregnancy, and pharmacology. He has published books on medical therapy for pregnant women, drug abuse in pregnancy, and psychiatric disorders during pregnancy. He is on the editorial board of more than a dozen medical and scientific peer-reviewed journals.

MARILYN R. LONDON earned her M.A. in biological anthropology at the University of New Mexico after receiving her B.A. in anthropology from the George Washington University. She is a research collaborator in the Department of Anthropology at the Smithsonian Institution, the forensic anthropology consultant to the Office of the Medical Examiners, State of Rhode Island, and a lecturer in the department of anthropology at the University of Maryland. She is a fellow of the Washington Academy of Sciences and currently serves as the president-elect of that organization. She is also a fellow of the American Academy of Forensic Sciences and an active member of the American Association of Physical Anthropologists, serving on its Career Development Committee. In 1998 she co-edited the book *Anthropology Explored* with Ruth Osterweis Selig. Ms. London is a research associate of the Virginia Museum of Natural History, Interim President of the Anthropological Society of Washington, and a member of the U.S. Department of

Health and Human Services D-MORT Team, which responds to mass disasters.

ROBERT M. MALINA is Professor of Kinesiology and Adjunct Professor of Anthropology at Michigan State University. He taught at the University of Texas at Austin for twenty-eight years and moved to Michigan State University in 1995. He has earned Ph.D. degrees in physical education (University of Wisconsin, Madison, 1963) and anthropology (University of Pennsylvania, Philadelphia, 1968), and an honorary doctorate from the Catholic University of Leuven (1989). His primary area of interest is the biological growth and maturation of children and adolescents with a focus on performance, youth sports and young athletes, and the potential influence(s) of physical activity and training for sport. Related areas of interest are the role of physical activity in the well-being of children and youth and the influence of chronic undernutrition on the growth, performance, and physical activity of Latin American youth, with a primary emphasis on Mexico. The research in Mexico continues at present in the form of a follow-up study of two communities initially studied in 1968 and 1971, and this research also extends to the study of the motivations of urban Mexican youth for participation in sport and physical activity. Dr. Malina is presently editor-in-chief of the *American Journal of Human Biology,* past editor of the *Yearbook of Physical Anthropology,* and serves on the editorial boards of eleven journals in the sport sciences and biological anthropology. He was section editor for growth and development for the *Exercise and Sport Sciences Reviews* from 1981 to 1999.

REYNALDO MARTORELL, a native of Honduras, is Robert W. Woodruff Professor of International Nutrition and Chair of the Department of International Health of the Rollins School of Public Health of Emory University. He received a Ph.D. in biological anthropology from the University of Washington in 1973 and began his career as a scientist in the Division of Human Development of the Institute of Nutrition of Central America and Panama (INCAP). He was a faculty member at Stanford and Cornell prior to coming to Emory. His major research interest is the relationship between nutrition and growth and development, particularly in the context of poverty in developing countries. He is an advisor to national and international organizations (including the Pan American Health Organization, WHO, UNICEF and the World Bank) on food and nutrition policy and on the design and evaluation of nutrition programs.

STEPHEN T. McGARVEY is an associate professor of community health and Director of the International Health Institute at Brown University. He received his Ph.D. in anthropology from Pennsylvania State University and an M.P.H. degree in epidemiology from Yale University. His research interests and publications include the impact of modernization on cardiovascular disease risk factors, gene and environment interactions on obesity and Type 2 diabetes, and the ecology, morbidity, and immunology of *Schistosomiasis japonica.*

MOSES S. SCHANFIELD was Laboratory Director of Analytical Genetic Testing Center, Inc. in Denver, Colorado at the time the article was written. He is currently the Laboratory Director of the Monroe County Public Safety Laboratory, a regional crime laboratory serving eight counties in western New York. He received his Ph.D. in human genetics from the University of Michigan, after receiving his master's degree in anthropology from Harvard University. His research areas include: applied genetics, forensic genetics, paternity testing, anthropological genetics, evolutionary biology of immunoglobulin allotypes, human evolution and adaptation, the genetics of the immune response, and the genetic analysis of autoimmune diseases. He has published over 100 articles in these areas. In addition to his research interests, he serves on the editorial board of *Human Biology.*

PHILIP L. STEIN received his B.A. in zoology and M.A. in anthropology at UCLA. He began his community college teaching career at Los Angeles Pierce College in 1965. He has held several teaching and administrative positions at the college, and is currently Professor of Anthropology and Department Chair. Mr. Stein is a fellow of the American Anthropological Association and a long-time member of the American Association of Physical Anthropologists. He is active in the Society for Anthropology in Community Colleges, serving as president in 1995–96. He and his colleague Bruce Rowe are the authors of the widely used text *Physical Anthropology* and are currently writing the eighth edition to be published in 2003.

ANNE C. STONE (Ph.D. Pennsylvania State University, 1996) is presently an assistant professor in the department of anthropology at the University of New Mexico. Her research focuses on human and chimpanzee population genetics and evolution. Dr. Stone is a member of the American Association of Physical Anthropologists, the Society of Molecular Biology and Evolution, the American Association of Anthropological Genetics, and the American Anthropological Association.

MARK F. TEAFORD is a professor of anatomy at Johns Hopkins University. He did his undergraduate work at the University of Pennsylvania and received his Ph.D. in anthropology from the University of Illinois. His research interests focus on primate diet and evolution, particularly studies of tooth wear, dental morphology, and the evolution of human diet. He has served on the editorial boards for *The American Journal of Physical Anthropology, The Journal of Human Evolution,* and *The American Journal of*

Primatology and has served as the vice president of the American Association of Physical Anthropologists.

DOUGLAS H. UBELAKER is a curator of physical anthropology at the Smithsonian Institution's National Museum of Natural History and a professorial lecturer in the departments of anatomy and anthropology at the George Washington University. He received his Ph.D. from the University of Kansas in 1973. His research interests include human skeletal biology and its forensic applications. Since about 1977 he has served as the primary consultant in forensic anthropology for FBI Headquarters and has reported on over 700 cases.

CURTIS W. WIENKER is a professor of anthropology at the University of South Florida, Tampa. He received his Ph.D. degree from the University of Arizona, and his research interests include forensic anthropology, biomedical anthropology, cultural influences on human biology, and the population biology of African-Americans, Cuban-Americans, and Cubans. He has also published on applied physical anthropology and non-traditional careers for physical anthropologists. He currently chairs the Career Development Committee of the American Association of Physical Anthropologists.

KATE WONG is Senior Online Editor at *Scientific American* magazine. She received her bachelor of science degree in anthropology-zoology from the University of Michigan. Though she covers topics ranging from particle physics to conservation biology, she takes an especially keen interest in developments relating to paleoanthropology.